SHIRLEY RENDER

FOREWORD BY MAX WARD

DOUBLE CROSS

THE INSIDE STORY OF
JAMES A. RICHARDSON AND
CANADIAN AIRWAYS

D0912963

DOUGLAS & McINTYRE

VANCOUVER/TORONTO

Dedicated to my children, Kelly and Matthew

"Hold Fast to Your Dreams"

Douglas & McIntyre Ltd.
2323 Quebec Street, Suite 201
Vancouver, British Columbia
V5T 4S7

Canadian Cataloguing in Publication Data

Render, Shirley, 1943-
  Double cross

  Includes bibliographical references and index.
  ISBN 1-55054-722-4

  1. Richardson, James A. (James Armstrong), 1885-1939.   2.
Canadian Airways Limited—History.   3. Airlines—Canada—History.
4. Canadian Airways Limited—Biography.   I. Title.
HE9815.C34R46   1999   387.7′06′571   C99-910679-1

Editing by John Eerkes
Design by Peter Cocking
Typesetting by Brenda and Neil West, BN Typographics West
Printed and bound in Canada by Friesens
Printed on acid-free paper ∞

The publisher gratefully acknowledges the support of the Canada Council for the Arts and of the British Columbia Ministry of Tourism, Small Business and Culture. The publisher also acknowledges the financial support of the Government of Canada through the Book Publishing Industry Development Program for its publishing activities.

Canada

Contents

Foreword

TIME EXPOSES THE SUCCESSES and failures of us all, but one wonders why the political leaders of James A. Richardson's time would purposely block a well-respected, creative citizen from shaping and expanding an industry then in its infancy. Beginning with one aircraft and a vision, Richardson built a national company that showed every sign of making Canada a world leader in airway development. Why did his company not achieve its grand objective? The answer probably lies in people's capabilities to handle power, rather than in some higher order of political foresight.

Shirley Render's book is timely. There have always been questions about the fate of Canada's first major airline, Canadian Airways Limited. Although the government's role in creating Trans-Canada Air Lines is no secret, no book so far has told the story of the role played by the military, especially the chief of the general staff, in civil aviation in Canada. *Double Cross* uncovers the events of the 1930s that ultimately changed Canadian aviation history. How many Canadians know that their country could have been a world leader in airway development if the Canadian government had made different decisions? In this book we discover who made the decisions and gain an insight into why they acted as they did.

As an aviation entrepreneur, I can only marvel at James Richardson's courage in championing civil aviation in Canada as early as the 1920s. In Richardson, Canada had a man who was prepared to use his personal fortune to underwrite the cost of developing a national company, one that would carry the nation's flag around the world. More than once, he was misled, and Canadian Airways paid the price. In the result, Canadians received a government-owned company, and taxpayers paid the cost.

James Richardson was the right man at the right time to pull the aviation industry together, set it on a sound economic basis and send it on its way. Shirley Render has made an important contribution to Canadian aviation history by showing how Richardson struggled to provide the best possible service in an often hostile political climate. The government of Canada could have ensured his success. But then it would not have been able to squander huge sums of taxpayers' money dragging a government airline into commercial reality.

James Richardson's struggle was not entirely in vain. Today, his dream of flying "over the top of the world" is alive in the form of Canadian Airlines, which has also adapted Canadian Airways' famous Canada goose logo for its own use.

MAX WARD
MAY 6, 1999

Acknowledgements

Double Cross was written in two stages at two different periods of my life. The initial research and writing was done in 1980–82 for my master's thesis on Canadian Airways Limited. I planned to expand it into a book. As it happened, my life became exceptionally full. I became president of the Western Canada Aviation Museum and editor of its 32-page magazine, was elected to Manitoba's legislature as the MLA for St. Vital in 1990, and wrote *No Place for a Lady: The Story of Canadian Women Pilots, 1928–1992* (1992). I put the book on hold.

However, always at the back of my mind hovered my intention to write the full story of James A. Richardson and his airways companies. Ken Molson's *Pioneering in Canadian Air Transport* is a very useful book, but Molson's focus was different from mine. My interest was in the national and international aviation picture and the role that Richardson expected his company to perform. I wanted to know what motivated the actions of the key players. I needed to examine both sides: James Richardson's and the government's.

As an idealistic university student in the early 1980s, I believed government's written records. When I began working on the manuscript for *Double Cross* in October 1997, I had been in government for seven years. I was no longer naïve. Thus when I returned to the original research material, I looked at it with new eyes and a brain that knew full well that the written record often says what it wants history to record. I learned to read between the lines. Even so, the written word did not begin to tell it all.

These acknowledgements are my attempt to thank some of the people who filled in the gaps and others who encouraged and supported me in what turned out to be a far greater task than I had anticipated.

I owe deep gratitude to many people. At the top of my list is my family: my parents, Harold and Mary Hurst, my brothers and sister, husband and children. In particular, my children, Kelly (and Darryl Lazarenko) and Matthew, who were always there for me and told me that I could indeed write this book.

I owe a special debt to the Richardson family, who from the start encouraged me to explore the history of their father's airways companies.

George T. Richardson, son of James A. and current chairman of James Richardson & Sons, Limited, took time out from his busy schedule in the early 1980s to talk with me when I was doing my master's thesis on Canadian Airways. His remembrances, then and now, helped to give me an understanding of his father and the times. That this story could be written at all is due to George Richardson, who saved the files from being fed to the furnace at the former Canadian Airways head office building. By chance he walked into the building shortly after the CPR bought Canadian Airways and discovered the caretaker dumping these records into the furnace. How many boxes of records were lost is not known, but George Richardson immediately had the remaining material sent over to the Richardson firm for safekeeping. The Western Canada Airways–Canadian Airways Limited files now fill sixty-nine boxes, a comprehensive record of the dream of James A. Richardson.

The Honourable James Richardson, son of James A., would not let me forget that I had said that I was going to write a book, and he prodded me into gear in 1996. Agnes Richardson Benidickson and Kathleen Margaret Richardson, daughters of James A., helped to flesh out the personalities of their parents.

I had the honour of meeting "Punch" Dickins in the late 1970s and maintained my contact with him until he died. Each time I saw him, either at a World War I Flyers Reunion or when I was doing the research for *No Place for a Lady* (for which Punch wrote the foreword), Punch would tell me a story. Others, such as the irrepressible "Babe" Woollett, filled out what the written record does not tell. I was lucky indeed to catch these marvellous old-timers before they flew their last flight. Their remembrances added the human factor to the story.

Thanks to my publisher, Scott McIntyre, whose enthusiasm convinced me that I could turn an academic thesis into a good story. A grateful thank-you to my editor, John Eerkes, who soothed my insecurities about my manuscript with his first words to me. It was a privilege to work with someone like John, who was always so willing to be a sounding board and always prepared to give a helping hand as deadlines loomed and niggling details were not yet completed.

Special thanks to friends, such as Lee Anderson, Mary Dixon, Cheryl McDougall, Keith Olson and Brenda Trevenen, who believed in me and told me that I could do a book of this magnitude as well as carry on being a member of the legislative assembly and not collapse in the midst of it all.

I must acknowledge Gordon Emberley, a founding member of the Western Canada Aviation Museum, who sparked a passion in me for preserving Canada's remarkable aviation history.

A special thank-you to Max Ward, an aviation entrepreneur who, like Richardson, created a first-class airline, for writing the foreword to *Double Cross*.

My grateful thanks to Provincial Archives of Manitoba staff Peter Bower, Barry Hyman, Elizabeth Blight, Lynn Champagne and Chris Kotecki, and to Leslie Castling of the Legislative Library, who were always obliging. Staff at the National Archives of Canada were equally helpful; I must single out Glenn Wright, for his help in the early 1980s, and Timothy Dubé for helping me meet my latest deadlines. I am grateful to Christine Way, crown copyright officer, Public Works and Government Services Canada, for granting permission to reproduce excerpts from federal crown copyrighted publications, and to Danielle P. Hawwa, Legal Services, House of Commons, and Mark Audcent, Office of the Law Clerk and Parliamentary Counsel, to reproduce parliamentary materials. I would also like to thank John Teskey and Linda Baier of the Harriet Irving Library, University of New Brunswick, for granting permission to use material from the R.B. Bennett Papers from the library's Archives and Special Collections. Ellinor Swettenham graciously granted permission to quote from John Swettenham's biography of General McNaughton.

I am also grateful to the following individuals for granting permission to reproduce extracts from newspaper stories: Crosbie Cotton, editor in chief, *Calgary Herald*; Theresa Butcher, librarian, *The Financial Post*; Barb Gustafson, managing editor, *Prince Albert Daily Herald*; John Sullivan, assistant managing editor, *Winnipeg Free Press*; and Stella Holt, permissions editor, *Vancouver Sun*.

Particular thanks to archivist Doug Panting of James Richardson & Sons, Limited, for helping me find some very special photographs, Bev Tallon of the Western Canada Aviation Museum and John Bradley of the Canadian Forces Photo Archives, who came to my rescue when I needed photos in a hurry. Thora Cooke, Benson Wincure and Joyce Goodhand of the Western Canada Pictorial Index and Stephen Lyons of Canadian Pacific Archives, Andrew Geider of Canadian Airlines Archives and Peter Pigott also assisted.

A thank-you to Professors Gerald Friesen, John Kendle, Ian Kerr and Ed Rea of the University of Manitoba, who encouraged me in my thesis, and to Renée Fossett, who prepared the index.

Financial help from the University of Manitoba and the J.S. Ewart Memorial Fund made it possible for me to spend time at the National Archives of Canada in Ottawa.

The Sources and Bibliography identify all those who helped me. In addition to those mentioned above, I also want to acknowledge Group Captain A.J. Bauer (Ret'd); Jim Bell, aviation enthusiast; Bill Dodge, grandson of C.D. Howe; Dr. Alec Douglas, author of the second volume of the official RCAF history; Mary Fletcher Lizette, personal secretary to Muriel Richardson (Mrs. James A.); Don Pearsons, #1 Canadian Air Division; Wayne Ralph, author of *Barker VC;* Claude Taylor, former president, Air Canada; Rex Terpening, Canadian Airways air engineer; Don Watson, former president, Pacific Western Airlines; Chris Terry, director general of the National Aviation Museum; and the Western Canada Aviation Museum volunteers, especially former Canadian Airways employees who shared their memories with me.

Introduction

I N 1930, JAMES ARMSTRONG RICHARDSON, president of James
Richardson & Sons, Limited, was the moving spirit behind the formation of the largest flying organization in Canada. His vision of
aviation as a tool for developing the natural resources of the North and
for tying the country together economically, as well as his belief that its
control must remain in Canadian hands, prompted his formation of
Western Canada Airways in 1926 and Canadian Airways Limited in
1930. Richardson's efforts might have placed Canadian Airways and
Canada in the lead in global airways development if Prime Minister
R.B. Bennett had not clipped Canadian Airways' wings.

What began as a goal to use aircraft to open up and develop the
North quickly turned to something even more far-ranging—airways
across the Atlantic and the Pacific Oceans, overland to Asia and
"around the world and over the top." The mass of Canadian Airways
Limited's records reveal James Richardson's dream and plans for his
companies. His son George reminisced, "We had a big globe of the
world in our library and I can recall, long before the age of the jet aircraft, Father tracing air routes over northern Canada to Europe, Japan

and Asia, and hoping that someday Winnipeg would become the centre in North America for routes over the Pole."

The Richardson family had long been interested in communication and transportation and, at one time, ran a fleet of sailing ships on Lake Ontario. James A. Richardson continued the family tradition and, with James Playfair, formed the Great Lakes Transportation Company, with Playfair as president and Richardson as vice-president. When they sold the company to Canada Steamship Lines in 1926, Richardson was already turning his mind to the latest innovation in transportation: aviation. It was to be the most daring, exciting and emotionally draining of all his ventures. George Richardson recalled, "My father was involved and engaged in a variety of different types of business during his career, but even as a small boy I had a very definite impression that his involvement with what my father called 'the Airways' was very different than any other business activity."

Transportation has always been an important part of Canada's national and economic development and a factor in Canadian politics. Indeed, it is doubtful if the growth of any modern nation has been so predicated on the progressive growth of transport technology. Surprisingly, though, air transport received scant attention and assistance from the Canadian government, whose officials were oblivious to the importance of aviation, and as a result its development was left largely to private enterprise. In Canada, aviation flew by itself. Great Britain and the United States used commercial aviation to advance their national interests, but the Canadian government did not integrate its handling of aviation with its wider national needs. Canada stood alone among the major western nations in its lack of a national air service.

The great airway systems of the world were built up in the late 1920s and early 1930s by national companies that had the support of their governments. Here, too, the Canadian government fumbled. It ignored the fact that all of the most direct routes from North America to Europe and Asia passed over its territory. With this advantage, Canada could have taken the lead in international airway development; at the very least, the Canadian government should have been at the forefront in establishing the trans-Canada, trans-Atlantic and trans-Pacific airway systems.

The government also erred in its dealings with the Americans. It granted what appeared to be innocuous concessions that gave the Americans firm holds on valuable routes. Ottawa turned a blind eye to this "peaceful penetration" of American companies. Richardson established Canadian Airways to help resolve Canada's airways problems and did so on the understanding that his company would become Canada's "chosen instrument." However, the fall of the Mackenzie King government in 1930 and the Great Depression changed the course of events.

The aviation question involved decisions that were pertinent to Canada's development at both the national and international levels. Unfortunately, the new Bennett government had no policy regarding the development of the trans-Canada airway in particular or commercial aviation in general. Policy development was left in the hands of civil servants who had no special knowledge or understanding of the potential value of commercial aviation.

The disposition of civil aviation under military control was another mistake that took the government seventeen years to correct. As Manitoba lawyer James Coyne acidly remarked, "Civil oil and military water don't mix." Canadian Airways' problems with the military were compounded by having to work with a government committee dominated by representatives from the Department of National Defence, hampered by internal departmental rivalry and chaired by a chief of the general staff who lacked any useful knowledge of commercial aviation and was more interested in protecting the air force.

In 1932, Prime Minister Bennett cancelled Canadian Airways' air mail contracts, wiping out its financial underpinnings. Believing himself betrayed, morally and legally, by the government, Richardson saw Bennett as the culprit. Although Bennett must bear the ultimate responsibility, General Andrew McNaughton, chief of the general staff and Bennett's key air adviser, must also bear much of the blame.

Not surprisingly, Canadian Airways and the other pre–World War II aviation companies in Canada consistently lost money, and their growth was haphazard and plagued with problems. Their major hurdle was an unsympathetic and unrealistic government that, for a variety of reasons, provided little practicable support. This resulted in the air transport industry being pioneered, financed and developed largely by private enterprise. The ultimate success of the industry grew out of the efforts of a few bold men who were determined to keep Canada apace with other countries. The key figure during the formative years was James A. Richardson.

In fact, the development of commercial aviation in Canada and the circumstances leading to the creation of Trans-Canada Air Lines in 1937 and Canadian Pacific Airlines in 1942 are largely the story of Richardson and his airways companies. C.D. Howe, federal minister of transport in 1936, has long been touted as the saviour of Canadian aviation because of his creation of Trans-Canada Air Lines. But in-depth research reveals another story behind the official version. The myth of Howe and his airline needs to be re-examined. From James Richardson's viewpoint, government had betrayed him again.

Little credit has been given to Richardson, who was uniquely aware of the potential role of commercial aviation in Canada's economic and national growth. To those who did not know him, Richardson seemed an unlikely candidate to establish an airways company. He was better known as the president of Winnipeg's James Richardson & Sons, Limited, the largest privately owned grain and investment business in Canada. A quick look at his background will help to explain why a grain man got into the flying business.

James Richardson & Sons, Limited, was established in 1857 in Kingston, Ontario. It became one of Canada's oldest, most influential and wealthiest institutions. Over the years its associated companies were engaged in grain merchandising, grain elevator and terminal operations, the investment securities industry, real estate and many other business enterprises. The Richardson family became one of Canada's foremost business families. It remains one of Canada's most private families.

James Armstrong Richardson, grandson of the founder, was born in 1885 in Kingston and educated at Queen's University. While still a young man, he headed one of the largest grain businesses in the world and became one of Canada's top-ranking directors. He held directorships in numerous companies allied to the grain trade, communications, transportation and finance. The Canadian Bank of Commerce, the Canadian Pacific Railway and the Canadian Committee of the Hudson's Bay Company were just three of the directorships that Richardson held. Regarded as the modern founder of the firm, he was president from 1918 until his death in 1939. It was he who determined the firm's western orientation and moved the head office from Kingston to Winnipeg in 1924. James Richardson & Sons' main business was the grain trade, but Richardson, an enterprising and visionary individual, added other ventures and steadily moved the firm into a variety of areas. In many ways, he helped to shape Canada's development in the twentieth century.

Richardson was a progressive and successful businessman who had an uncanny ability to know what move to make next. In the 1920s he guided the firm into the field of investment securities and, in 1926, bought memberships in the Montreal Stock Exchange. Soon the firm acquired memberships in all Canadian stock and commodity exchanges, and offices were opened throughout Canada as the business developed. He ensured that the company always used the most advanced equipment. Typical was the firm's "enlarged private wire system," which after 1928 was operated by teletype machines. The company was the first in the Canadian grain and brokerage business to use teletype machines for the transmission of orders and information between all its offices and their markets. In 1929, in a dramatic reminder that Canada had an inland seaport in Manitoba, Richardson sent the first shipment of wheat via the port of Churchill, on Hudson Bay, to England. Significantly it was Western Canada Airways, his company, that secured the railway terminal at Churchill.

Communications were another interest of James Richardson. Although radio was still in the pioneer stage in the 1920s and its enormous possibilities for education, entertainment and commercial advertising were as yet undreamed, that did not deter him from having the firm do some experimental work in radio broadcasting in 1925. A pioneering spirit who most enjoyed building something new, Richardson established a 500-watt transmitter (CJRM) at Moose Jaw, Saskatchewan. A year later it began broadcasting news about the weather, crops and grain prices for prairie farmers (and a little music for the lonely farm wives). CJRM was followed in 1928 by CJRW, a 1,000-watt transmitter, and a short-wave transmitter, CJRX, the first in Canada to inaugurate a regular daily service of programs by short-wave. In 1933, a licence was taken out to operate CJRC from Winnipeg, and the firm enlarged the CJRC studios at the Royal Alexandra Hotel. The station still operates in

Winnipeg, as CKRC. In 1940, CJRM, CJRC and the two short-wave stations were sold to the Sifton family. James Richardson & Sons operated CJRL in Kenora, Ontario, from 1943 to 1951.

The above record gives only a glimpse of a man whose prodigious energy flowed in a dozen directions. He was one of the best-informed men in Canada on every branch of the grain trade. He was also a shrewd businessman. He was a man of vision, quickly grasping the potential of radio broadcasting. Visionary, too, is the only word to describe a man who would sink more than $3 million of his personal money in the untried field of aviation.

What manner of man was he? What was most revealing in my research was the fact that nowhere, in magazine or newspaper articles from around the country, in personal interviews with former colleagues or employees and in the Canadian Airways records, did I find a dissenting note on the character of James A. Richardson. Obviously the man was not perfect, but his imperfections seemed to err on the side of being "too trusting" and "too much the gentleman" rather than being a slick businessman, ready to take advantage of anyone. The following excerpt, from an editorial in the *Winnipeg Free Press* written the day after his death, perhaps best illustrates what Winnipeggers and, indeed, Canadians thought of him.

> There was a transparent honesty about him as rare as it was fine and simple; and it was reinforced by candor, by kindness and by courage ...
>
> Mr. Richardson belonged to the ranks of what is known as Big Business. He was a Millionaire, a Grain Baron, one of the men whom Mr. Aberhart would call a "Big Shot," a "Tycoon." He was also, however, a Westerner and he never forgot it for a moment ... This member of an old and wealthy eastern family, this director of many companies, who spent his business life with bankers and in corporation board rooms, fought the battle of Western Canada from one end of this continent to the other. He never stopped ...
>
> His faith and his conviction about what was good for Canada was identical with that of a quarter-section farmer in north-western Saskatchewan ... He wanted to see the Prairies prosperous not because that would mean prosperity for his own companies and money in his

pocket. He believed that plenty on the Prairies meant plenty for Canada as well. He wanted to see his country prosper and grow great, and he worked at the job night and day. He was a very great Westerner and a great Canadian as well.

As a good Canadian, Richardson believed that Canada also must control its destiny in the air, and he was prepared to use his personal fortune to ensure that Canadian aviation remained in Canadian hands. His single-mindedness and devotion to this cause were exceptional, but he paid the ultimate price for his all-out effort. Muriel Richardson, his wife, believed that the worry, the energy and, above all, the disappointment in what he believed was an ultimate betrayal by men whom he trusted caused his premature death at the age of fifty-four. Fittingly, on his gravestone, poised for flight, is the symbol of his dream, his first plane, the Fokker Standard Universal, G-CAFU, *The City of Winnipeg.*

Although his energies were directed toward the commercial side of aviation, Richardson also made a point of assisting the RCAF, which in December 1935 thought highly enough of him to appoint him as Honorary Wing Commander of 12 Squadron (now 402 City of Winnipeg Squadron). L.W. Brockington, a former rector of Queen's University, remembered Richardson as "the only big businessman I have ever known in many parts of the world who was absolutely without guile. He was really, quite simply, a good man. I don't think there was any price in money or in power that could have made him do a thing which he knew to be wrong."

How does one write about a man like this without gushing? I wanted to write an accurate and objective history of James A. Richardson and his airways companies. To begin, I read the documents in the Canadian Airways archives. Richardson's letters and memoranda were useful in revealing him through his own words and actions. Concerned that I present both sides, I also pored through the mass of letters and memoranda from key politicians and departmental officials in Ottawa, those who made policy and controlled the purse strings. They were revealing in what they said about Richardson and his company and just as revealing about their own character. The civil-servant mandarins wrote with a certain sense of history. Newspaper and magazine articles, biographies about the "Ottawa men" and personal interviews helped to flesh out the picture.

I have always felt that there was more to be said about C.D. Howe and the creation of Trans-Canada Air Lines, that the Richardson side needed to be told. What emerged was not a dry, dusty history of a businessman and his company, or a government and its civil service working always for the greater glory of Canada, but a story, filled with intrigue, political manoeuvrings, turf protection and double-dealings, that changed the course of the nation's history.

"Civil Oil and Military Water Don't Mix"

"THE AEROPLANE is an invention of the devil and will never play any part in such a serious business as the defence of a nation, my boy," retorted cavalryman General Sam Hughes, minister of militia and defence, to aviation inventor John McCurdy in August 1914, when McCurdy recommended the formation of a Canadian air service during World War I. His words carried weight; aviation would struggle to achieve an identity for the next forty years.

Although Canada's contribution to the "war in the air" was a notable one, the Canadian government had taken no direct part in it. Canadians had a brilliant record in the air services, but all active service units overseas and training bases in Canada were under the jurisdiction of the United Kingdom authorities. Canadian airmen fought as colonial recruits in British organizations. Not until the 1918 enemy submarine attacks on Canada's Atlantic coast and the torpedoeing of an oil tanker near Halifax did the government take steps to establish coastal air patrols and authorize a Royal Canadian Naval Air Service. This service was in the early stages of formation at the close of the war and was disbanded as a result of the Armistice, as were the Canadian aviation organizations at home and overseas.

There was no provision for a Canadian air force in peacetime. General Sam Hughes's earlier pronouncement still echoed strongly. Despite an all-star cast of decorated war heroes like Billy Bishop, Billy Barker and "Red" Mulock, who advocated for a Canadian air force, the Dominion government did not conceive the coming importance of aviation for military or commercial purposes and initially promoted neither. Soon, however, the military side would gain the upper hand and civil aviation would be forced to jostle for attention with the priorities of the all-powerful military authorities.

Prior to World War I, Canada had not reached the stage where control of aviation was necessary. It entered the postwar period without any air organizations or legislation on aviation matters. As many of Canada's returning airmen established flying operations, however, it soon became apparent that some form of legislation to control flying would be necessary. The government ignored the issue. In March 1919 the Canadian Pacific Railway (CPR) requested an extension of its charter to include the operation of aircraft, and the government was forced to respond. Canada was in an excellent position to deal with aviation intelligently, because its statutes contained no reference whatever to aeronautics, and the war organizations at home and overseas had been disbanded. The government's freedom of action was complete.

Its response was the Air Board Act of 1919, which established an air board that had broad powers over all forms of aeronautics. The act was based largely on the anticipated requirements and trend of aviation development, with understandably little recognition that flying would become as important in peace as it had been in war. Unfortunately, officials shifted from foot to foot in the certainty of a general election, and this too hindered straightforward planning. Thus the act did little but bring air transport under the control of the Canadian government and provide for licensing and safety regulations. It did not help that the first air board, appointed by an order in council, included not a single airman or any member who was "air-minded." The board's duties were to control civil aviation, conduct the flying operations for all government departments and organize a temporary air force. It enacted regulations and, in early 1920, created the Canadian Air Force. With its work completed, it resigned, and a new board was formed on April 20, 1920. The minister of militia was chairman.

Surprisingly, a naval member of the first board, John A. Wilson, secretary of naval service, was to become remarkably air-minded. In fact, he was one of the few civil servants in the early 1920s who had any inkling of just how important commercial aviation would become. The same cannot be said for his boss, Major General Andrew McNaughton, who would become chief of the general staff of the Department of National Defence (DND) in 1929. McNaughton and Wilson were the two most influential individuals in shaping policy on aviation matters. In the early 1920s they worked in relative harmony, but soon a divergence of direction became apparent. McNaughton, a tall, lean, intense and domineering soldier who came out of World War 1 a brigadier general, and Wilson, a long-time affable civil servant and a founding member of the Canadian Geographical Society, had little in common. McNaughton, with his forceful personality, did not practise the art of accommodation. There was a silent contest of wills between the two men, and civil aviation would be the loser.

John Wilson was born in 1879 in Scotland and trained as an engineer. He came to Canada in 1905, joining the newly formed Department of Naval Service in 1910. He became secretary of the Canadian Air Force and later controller of civil aviation within DND. It is difficult to get a handle on Wilson's personality. His photographs show a well-built, innocuous-looking, fair-haired man with a pleasant smile. He never dominated any group picture and he rarely looked into the camera, as if deliberately not drawing attention to himself. His many memos and letters, however, provide a glimpse of his character. Unassuming, Wilson never claimed any credit for himself and freely gave credit where credit was due. He comes across as the epitome of the faithful public servant: intelligent, somewhat visionary and not afraid to voice his opinion, as long as it was within bureaucratic confines.

Wilson was also a staunch supporter of the Canadian Air Force, but he did not want fighter pilots in the air force; he wanted administrators. Wilson believed that Canadians would not approve of a "fighting" air force. He saw an air force performing civil operations, rather than one being trained in "air power," as the route to go to receive government money. He was likely correct. However, as he discovered, once created, the Civil Government Air Operations (performed by air force pilots) were impossible to eliminate. A cancellation of this area would have destroyed the young air force. As a result, Canadian Air Force pilots would not be trained in fighting tactics until the late 1930s.

Andrew McNaughton, born in 1887 in Saskatchewan, was an engineer, a scientist and a commander of the Canadian Corps Heavy Artillery in World War I. He went on to become the youngest chief of the general staff in Canada's history and one of the most powerful public servants in the country. According to historian James Eayrs (whom McNaughton's biographer, John Swettenham, quotes), "McNaughton dominated his colleagues in the military establishment as a great oak dominates a scrub forest." While admitting that many considered McNaughton "inflexible," Swettenham explained that "his conclusion became his purpose, and his firmness in that often gave him the reputation of being inflexible." Swettenham wrote that McNaughton "didn't forgive easily those who crossed him on a matter of basic principle. His fights were never entered into for reasons of self-interest." McNaughton described himself as someone who would resort to whatever was necessary to achieve his goal if he believed in what he was after. "I am convinced in the rightness of what I have set out to do ... by whatever method is necessary." With these few words, a picture emerges of a man who so believed in his own judgment and his rightness in action (because it was for the good of Canada) that he would do whatever was necessary to obtain his way.

McNaughton was also a vain man. His letters and memos reveal that he was not above patting himself on the back. He wrote memos to himself, to tuck away in the filing cabinet, when he was in a particularly self-congratulatory mood. There is no question that McNaughton was a good soldier and scientist and loved his country. What must be questioned are the lengths to which he was prepared to go to get his way and his judgment on matters outside his expertise. McNaughton was a soldier, not an airman, and he was a public servant, not a businessman.

What was to be done with aviation? Government responded with its familiar first step: strike a committee. Air Board officials called an interdepartmental conference on air development in January 1920. And so began the first manoeuvres in rival departmental jealousies and political sleights of hand that characterized Canada's destiny in the air for another quarter of a century. With all the games going on behind the scenes, the military, the most organized and consistent of the players, would very shortly come out on top with its own department.

In 1920, the question of air mail was on the agenda. It was given short shrift because it would require heavy subsidies from the government and would compete with the railways, which were already overextended and in debt. Wilson disagreed with this view; he believed that government should promote airway development. He was, however, sufficiently concerned about civil aviation's fate to begin writing memos. Over the next decade he would write masses of them: to the deputy minister of militia, to General McNaughton and to the deputy minister of national defence. Unfortunately, the communication appears to have been one-way; only rarely did Wilson's memos prompt a response.

Wilson wrote eloquently and succinctly, but in fact he had little clout, as far as commercial operations went. This was most unfortunate, because he was one of the few who saw the potential of commercial aviation for the national and international advantage of Canada. That his recommendations were so often ignored is surprising, because he was a senior bureaucrat and his opinion was sought and respected. The most likely explanation is that he and McNaughton had different agendas, and McNaughton was both the stronger personality and Wilson's superior. "For the good of Canada," McNaughton could block what he wished.

Although departmental officials decided that developing intercity air mail and passenger services was out of the question, they had no qualms about using government aircraft to carry out government work for activities such as aerial photography and fishery patrol. This was the start of the ubiquitous Civil Government Air Operations. The intention at the time was that the government would withdraw from each field when the experimental period had passed, leaving further development to commercial operators. However, while its stated purpose was to demonstrate to the public the usefulness of aircraft in peacetime, its ultimate aim was to provide an outlet for the air force. To be fair, there was no precedent for the maintenance of a large standing air force in Canada, and thus the decision that "a widespread, self-sustaining and practical development of Civil Aviation in the Dominion must be the basis of [Canada's] Air Power" is understandable. However, between 1921 and 1925 the hours of civil flying done by the air force almost equalled (and sometimes exceeded) the total of commercial flying.

The Department of National Defence was created in 1922 (the act was proclaimed in 1923) by consolidating the militia, the navy, the Royal Canadian Mounted Police and Engineering Services into a single department. The Air Board ceased to exist. Unfortunately, the reorganization of air services under DND resulted in practically all civil positions being abolished and aviation being treated as if it were a wholly military concern. No recognition was given to the fact that a large part of the administration of air matters dealt with purely civil functions, which had little relation to the Canadian Air Force.

All air services were grouped into one directorate, civil government pilots were all commissioned as part of the air force, and the air force made civil government operations its principal objective. Most of the air force appropriation, the majority of officers and men, and the best equipment were devoted to them. Control of civil aviation was administered by Wilson, secretary of the Canadian Air Force. The director of the air force was responsible for the control of all civil and military activities and reported to the chief of the general staff, who was responsible to the minister of national defence.

Wilson foresaw trouble. To his friend Ellwood Wilson he wrote, "I am coming to see more and more that the real strength of Canada in the Air depends on the commercial development more than any other factor and that without it we can not really expect to have a sound foundation for aviation in this country." Government's only role, he felt, should be in experimental work, "in blazing a trail."

Convinced that the government was treading where it should not, Wilson wrote a damning seven-page memo to the deputy minister of national defence on November 2, 1922. He pointed out that the interests of the Canadian Air Force and the Civil Government Air Operations and the control of civil aviation were "distinct and separate in their purpose, requirements and aims and that the interests of one were often diametrically opposed to those of the other" and should not all be placed in one directorate. He argued against the air force carrying out the work of all three branches without regard to whether it was civil or military work. "The militarization of the staff has been extended even to those officers in charge of commercial aviation so that even this phase of work is entirely carried out by military personnel ... It is surely fundamental that the government relationship with commercial firms should be controlled by the Civil Head of the Department and not by military officers."

How accurate Wilson's predictions would be; a few years later, he wrote that from 1925 to 1930 "the tail of Civil Operations wagged the Air Force dog." This happened because of the overextension and over-elaboration of Civil Government Air Operations. "The obvious fact that these in the long run, must be on an economic basis, was forgotten." Risking McNaughton's wrath, Wilson accused the Canadian Air Force of exploiting every possible outlet for its purposes. "Operation after operation was proposed which involved the transportation of men and supplies to districts now served efficiently by commercial companies who have done all the pioneer work, without mention of the possibility of patronizing their services. This is defended on the ground that the Department does not wish to dismiss its personnel. Yes, but [it is] only because of the over-extension in past years of Civil Government Air Operations that this crisis has arisen."

Wilson tried to warn government officials by drawing an analogy to the railways, "where the company which pioneered railway development is now faced with government competition and the consequent duplication of services to the extent of bankruptcy to both. The commercial operator cannot live in competition with freely given service, without regard to expense, from this Department ... The commercial operator should be encouraged to expand his work and use should be made of the services he is now operating or is willing to finance, by every government service requiring air transport."

Blissfully ignorant of the potential of commercial aviation for Canada's national development, government officials disregarded Wilson's warning. They were more interested in protecting the air force. Seven months later, Wilson again pleaded for a policy for commercial aviation. In a May 21, 1923, letter to the deputy minister, Wilson again minced no words. "Though much has been written and spoken about it being the policy of the Air Force to encourage civil aviation, the fact remains that almost nothing material has been done for the past three years."

As it turned out, the growth of commercial aviation and the expansion of the civil government operations and their divergence from military duties soon necessitated another change in the control of aviation.

In yet another memo to the deputy minister, on April 20, 1927, Wilson sought another reorganization, but his pleas for recognition of the commercial aspect of aviation were again ignored.

In July 1927, a compromise solution was sought by dividing the administration of all air activities into four directorates: the Royal Canadian Air Force (RCAF), the Civil Government Air Operations, the Civil Aviation Branch and the Aeronautical Engineering Services. The resulting arrangement was so confusing, since the RCAF continued to provide the personnel for the Civil Government Air Operations, who were under civil administration, that another change was made in 1930.

Civil Government Air Operations and the Aeronautical Engineering Services were again united with the RCAF under the chief of the general staff, and the Civil Aviation Branch remained under the deputy minister. Although these changes lessened the military influence in commercial aviation matters, the Civil Aviation Branch was not an autonomous unit. It stayed under military influence and had no minister who was immediately responsible for its welfare. Why was there such confusion? More to the point, why was there no intercity airway development? Many factors can be cited.

First, there had been little guidance or vision from the top. Since 1919, none of the three prime ministers, Robert Borden, Arthur Meighen and Mackenzie King, had been particularly air-minded. They had, for the most part, left the management of air matters first to the Air Board and then to DND. By 1926, this attitude of leaving the commercial operators to fend for themselves had become firmly entrenched. Although General McNaughton advocated airways development and admitted that there was a great deal to be said in favour of direct subsidies, he would not recommend any change in the government's policy.

Except for John Wilson, few government officials realized that Canada's real strength in the air would depend on the nation's commercial development—without it, Canada would not have a solid foundation for future aviation enterprises. Nor did they stop to think that if government did not scale down its civil air operations, there would be little incentive for businessmen to invest private capital in aviation concerns. McNaughton was protecting the RCAF. To have cut back or cancelled the government air services at that time would have wiped it out. While McNaughton was chief of the general staff, commercial aviation took a back seat to the military. That the government made four changes in the administration of aviation within ten years and allowed the air force to perform civil government duties and to usurp business from the commercial companies demonstrates its ambivalence on aviation development.

Lack of an aviation policy contributed to this state of affairs. To say that the Canadian government was slow to realize the potential of commercial aviation for Canada's economic well-being would be an understatement. Officials were content to have civil aviation under the military umbrella, ignoring the fact that the interests of both were often diametrically opposed. As late as 1926, government officials would not admit that they were a mite tardy in establishing intercity services. The 1926 *Report on Civil Aviation* was smug and self-congratulatory *on what government had not done.* "The value of the development and experimental work done in many fields of civil aviation by the Dominion government is great ... [Civil Government Air Operations] blazed the trail for commercial flying ... private effort unassisted would have taken many years to establish," wrote good public servant John Wilson.

As for not establishing scheduled air routes, Wilson, spouting the government line, rationalized that they had "little prospect of substantial revenue for some years." This too was not altogether correct; air mail revenues would prove to be very lucrative to the government after the initial period. The government's decision to do nothing "was wise," Wilson concluded. Most of his memos for the next decade would continue to justify government inaction. Only rarely would Wilson rock the boat and speak his mind.

The scenario in Canada was that flying was carried out by three major groups: the RCAF (government), the Civil Government Air Operations (government) and the commercial companies. All were grouped under the Department of National Defence. It is doubtful that an analogous situation existed in any other country. Neither did other nations allow the military to usurp commercial operations, which was why there were large and viable commercial companies in England, the United States, Germany and France. This is not to say that civil aviation did not owe much to the air force; to deny this would be churlish. But the bottom line, as far as the commercial operators were concerned, was that as long as the Civil Government Air Operations had no definite policy, commercial companies would be at a huge disadvantage. The conflict between private enterprise and the use of public money to carry out national objectives, as well as the problem of how far government should interfere in economic affairs, only added to their insecurity.

Finally, the government also sent out confusing messages. Mackenzie King and McNaughton were not prepared to assist intercity airway development but spent approximately $1.8 million between 1927 and 1930 on the airship mooring mast at St. Hubert airfield as part of the British Empire airship venture. Undoubtedly King was captivated by the pomp surrounding the airship venture and the record-breaking flights of the day. However, the destruction of the R-101 airship in 1930 caused that whole program to be abandoned; the money had been wasted. Although Mackenzie King obviously responded to national and empire needs when he agreed to the airship venture, he and the rest of his government evidently never felt that national prestige warranted direct government financial assistance for other Canadian airway developments. The government's thinking regarding civil aviation was simple: no subsidies. This was the stage onto which Canada's would-be "entrepreneurs of the air" walked.

Air transport as a commercial enterprise was unknown until the end of World War I. At war's end, Canada found itself with thousands of enthusiastic and experienced pilots and mechanics who had nowhere to go. Nevertheless, war surplus planes were cheap and were eagerly bought up by those who hoped to make money by flying. For those who barnstormed and gave "passenger hops," interest initially was intense, rates were high and business flourished. However, by the end of 1920 public interest was waning, money was not so plentiful and most of the pilots were bankrupt. Those who tried to haul freight or carry passengers discovered that military aircraft were entirely unsuitable for commercial use.

The first real attempt to use aircraft for commercial transport was made in 1920. The airplane spurred a rediscovery of the Canadian northwest. The discovery of crude oil at Fort Norman in the Northwest Territories, late in the fall of 1920, led to the first large-scale attempt to establish long-range air transport in the Far North. Imperial Oil purchased two all-metal Junkers JL-6 aircraft to transport executives and speed up communications between Edmonton and the newly discovered oil field at Fort Norman on the Mackenzie River. Little was known about winter flying, however, and the venture failed. Lack of experience in dealing with the intense cold, blizzards, rough landings in unknown country, inadequate supplies and unsuitable equipment were some of the problems.

In 1922, a British Columbia syndicate purchased one of the Imperial Oil aircraft to open up placer deposits in northern British Columbia. This time, lack of financing caused the venture's demise. Failure aside, it was probably the first time an aircraft was used to open up mining properties, which until then were reached only by long, tedious trips by pack horse and canoe in summer and by dog team in winter. Of interest also was the fact that air services in Canada generally started from the railhead northward to outlying regions, rather than paralleling existing surface routes, as they did in most countries.

During the mid-1920s, prospecting fever was at its height, and prospecting and mining created new opportunities for commercial air services. Laurentide Air Service was one of the few success stories. Formed in Montreal in 1922, it made headlines when it established an air service from Haileybury, Ontario, to Rouyn, Quebec, where the Noranda Mine was being developed. By 1923, it had twelve aircraft and a large contract from the Ontario government for surveying and fire patrol, but the creation of the Ontario Provincial Air Service in 1924 would ultimately put Laurentide out of business. Also, beginning in 1923, Dominion Aerial Explorations performed forestry work for the Quebec government and Fairchild Aerial Surveys primarily did photographic work.

In 1925, the discovery of gold in Red Lake and other areas of northwestern Ontario marked a turning point in northern flying. It provided the lure for the creation of a number of one-man aviation outfits, some of which would last. Gold at Red Lake prompted Jack Hammell in 1925 to ask the Ontario Forestry Branch to fly in ten tons of supplies late in the fall to enable development to proceed without interruption during freeze-up, before ground transport could move. The operation was so successful that the mining industry immediately latched onto the possibilities of using aircraft not only to develop mining properties where other means of transport were lacking, but also to speed up development even when ground transport was available. Hammell (with backing from James Richardson) went on to form Northern Aerial Minerals Exploration Ltd. in 1928.

Even so, most of the commercial flying in the early 1920s was sporadic and unorganized, and little of it survived. The problems were many. The postwar slump, starting in 1922, damaged the already frail structure of these companies. Money was tight, risk capital was not available, and most companies were underfinanced and improperly organized. "It was hard to raise money for flying at that time," explained pilot H.A. "Doc" Oaks, formerly of Patricia Airways and Exploration, "so we traded our claims for sufficient money to buy one airplane." There were technical and management problems. The war-surplus planes were not made for commercial purposes and could not carry a sufficient payload to make a profit; nor were they sturdy enough to withstand either the cold of winter operations or the ruggedness of Canada's terrain. Most of the companies were run by men whose experience was limited to flying. They were pilots, not businessmen.

By 1925, barely half a dozen aviation companies remained. The scene was sombre. Civilian aviation was slowly suffocating in the grip of the military. It was into such a setting that James Richardson strode, with his enthusiasm, his firm's prestige and his vision of aviation's potential. Richardson established Western Canada Airways in December 1926 to provide transportation into the mining area of Red Lake, and the company prospered. In fact, in 1927 Laurentide Air Service and Western Canada Airways were operating the only two self-sustaining air routes in the British Empire: Laurentide's Haileybury–Rouyn run and Western Canada Airways' Sioux Lookout–Red Lake route.

Although Laurentide eventually went out of business, Western Canada Airways was successful beyond all expectations. In 1929, its Sioux Lookout base was the second-largest operating base for commercial aircraft in North America, second only to Chicago. A variety of circumstances would soon bring James Richardson and the federal government together, and Richardson would move onto the national stage.

Golden Days:
Western Canada Airways

ESTERN CANADA AIRWAYS operated in a blaze of publicity because in the 1920s there was no such thing as a routine flight. Its pilots, most with distinguished war records, went on to even more spectacular achievements in northern operations. Flying under primitive conditions over vast, difficult terrain in the most challenging weather conditions, they created new legends for themselves and their country. Pilot and plane did more to open up and reveal the undeveloped wealth of northern Canada than men on foot, in canoes or on dog sleds had done in the previous centuries. The North had remained almost a sealed book until the airmen explored it. This period was the most colourful, adventure-crammed and remarkable era of Canada's aviation history.

Canada's bush pilots were a uniquely Canadian breed who endured incredible hardships in a relentless environment. They represented the spirit of adventure and determination in trying to make a living out of flying. Fur-clad and courageous, with the glamour of movie stars, they flew north into the unmapped hinterlands of the last great frontier. With little if any radio communication, plane and pilot often disappeared for days on end. They were dependent upon fuel caches being left in remote areas, on compasses made unreliable by magnetic influences and on maps that had large chunks labelled "UNEXPLORED."

Pilots were vitally reliant on the toughness and ingenuity of their air engineers, whose capacity for improvisation was legendary. These men worked magic with their emergency repairs to failed engines and damaged aircraft. Dubbed "the black gang," they bore the brunt of the day's work. Often working in the open, under harsh conditions, air engineers spent long hours in sub-zero temperatures in winter or with blackflies in summer. Until Tommy Siers introduced the oil dilution system in the late 1930s, engine oil had to be drained every night to prevent it from freezing. Pilot Stan McMillan remembers taking the oil to bed with him to keep it warm.

When overnighting away from base, pilots placed poles under aircraft skis to prevent their freezing to the snow and threw a tarp over the engine. Before dawn, the air engineer would warm the engine oil on a makeshift stove and heat the engine with a blowpot. Before either cooled off, he would yank off the tarp and pour in the oil, while the pilot would start the airplane. If the engine didn't catch quickly the oil was again drained, and pilot and mechanic would start the whole numbing process over again. Heated workshops and sophisticated machinery to deal with crippled aircraft were unknown in the bush. If marooned in winter, the pilot or mechanic donned snowshoes and tramped out "HELP" on the snow to attract the attention of searchers. On at least one occasion, "Babe" Woollett spelled out "LAND HERE YOU BASTARDS."

The pioneer period had great romantic appeal. The harsh environment, the hazards of cold, snow, ice, unreliable engines, the isolation and inadequate maps all added to the usual obstacles of developing a new frontier. There was no doubt that the success of an operation depended upon the skill, courage and persistence of the pilots. They had to rely on their own sense of direction, have an exceptional memory for topographical features and generally fly "by the seat of their pants."

It was the precariousness of the flying that fascinated the public and the media alike. Newspaper reporters and radio announcers adored Canada's bush pilots and broadcast every achievement, often magnifying them. Among the pilots, "Punch" Dickins retained an almost legendary status. In fact, there were many great moments in Canada's aviation history and dozens of stories to tell: Dickins's pioneering flight over the uncharted Barren Lands, Walter Gilbert's historic flight over the magnetic north pole into "the purple twilight," Leigh Brintnell's flying the first prairie air mail. These men conquered a vast, difficult terrain in the most challenging weather conditions and established international reputations. This was the golden era of bush flying.

A chance encounter at Minaki, Ontario, in the summer of 1926, with Jack Modder Clarke, a World War I pilot, provided the catalyst for James Richardson's move into the world of aviation. Clarke told Richardson that he wanted to establish a company to serve the mining areas of northwestern Ontario and northern Manitoba but needed money. Always receptive to new ideas and eager to test their possibilities, Richardson agreed to be the financial backer. A deal was struck.

Richardson, a businessman first and foremost, had already done some homework. Knowing that war surplus planes were not suitable, he methodically made inquiries about aircraft, engines and repair facilities. He was impressed with the sturdy aircraft that Fokker was manufacturing and gave Clarke the go-ahead to buy two Fokker Universal Standard aircraft. When he discovered a few months later that Clarke had ordered Waco aircraft, which Richardson did not think were the best available, he wired Clarke at the Waldorf Hotel in New York, on September 11, 1926: "Do not want us start out with anything other than very best equipment in every particular. Would sooner delay little." Clarke ignored Richardson, and Richardson cancelled their agreement. Central Canada Airways was grounded before it flew a mile.

Although Clarke was out of the picture, it is doubtful that Richardson would have let the matter die. His interest in aviation had been piqued, and more importantly, he saw its potential for Canada's economic and national development. George Richardson recalled, "Father was interested in the development of Canada, particularly northern Canada, and he had a clear vision of what aviation could do to assist with the development. The frustrations, the hours of dedication and the financial costs were all secondary to the achievement of his vision. He spared neither time nor effort in the pursuit of his dream." More specifically, as James Richardson wrote to George Barr of Canadian Vickers, he wanted to help keep Canada "in the front line of progress in air transportation" and, of course, to assist in the development of Canada's natural resources.

Richardson's correspondence suggests that he was making numerous inquiries in central Canada and the United States about aircraft manufacturing and aviation companies, and he was already involved in a number of aviation concerns. He invested $30,000 in Fairchild Aviation in 1926 (formerly Fairchild Aerial Surveys) and was on its board of directors. In 1927, he worked with John E. Hammell to establish Northern Aerial Minerals Exploration, providing about 25 percent of the capital. Richardson was also a director and principal shareholder in Cyril Knight Prospecting and shortly would become involved in the Vickers Syndicate, the Aviation Corporation of Canada and MacDonald Brothers (later Bristol Aerospace) in Winnipeg.

In 1928, he became a director of North American Aviation (which owned Sperry Gyroscope of New York and Atlantic Seaboard Air Express); Eastern Air Transport; and Ford Instruments. In 1929, he bought five hundred shares in St. Louis Aviation. Richardson also contacted Anthony Fokker of Atlantic Aircraft with the idea of establishing a manufacturing link in Winnipeg. He evidently contacted DND at some point, for it was John Wilson of DND who recommended Richardson to "Doc" Oaks.

H.A. "Doc" Oaks was a World War I pilot and Distinguished Flying Cross recipient. He was also a Queen's University graduate in mining engineering and had worked as a geologist, prospector and pilot. His last job had been with Patricia Airways, which had been formed in March 1926 to provide transportation into the recently discovered gold fields at Red Lake. Oaks believed the company was poorly organized and left it in October. Nonetheless, his experience had made him aware of the potential benefit of air transport to the mining industry. Oaks approached Richardson with the proposal that he would provide the operating management and be chief pilot if Richardson would provide the money for an airways company. Impressed with Oaks's business sense, academic background and well-rounded practical experience, Richardson agreed.

Never one to waste time, Richardson asked Oaks to draft a plan of operations. Oaks moved quickly and on November 2, 1926, handed over a draft plan for a one-aircraft operation for the Hudson–Red Lake area. Richardson brought in John Hunter, his key executive at James Richardson & Sons, to evaluate the plan. Hunter approved it, and Richardson authorized Oaks to purchase the necessary equipment. On December 10, 1926, Western Canada Airways Limited was incorporated. Richardson's focus was on northwestern Ontario and central Manitoba. However, Western Canada Airways' charter showed that he was anticipating something far more sweeping than a company oriented only to the mining industry in Ontario and Manitoba. The charter, a federal one, allowed the company to expand into air services, aircraft manufacturing, research, speed and trial tests, flying clubs, photography, mapping and radio stations.

Western Canada Airways' president was James Richardson, the vice-president was Mrs. Muriel Sprague Richardson, the secretary was John Hunter, the treasurer was J.A. MacDougall, and the managing director and chief (and only) pilot was "Doc" Oaks. To keep a close watch on the company, Richardson based the head office and repair shops in Winnipeg. This was not an unusual decision, because Winnipeg was home to James Richardson, his wife and their four children: Agnes McCausland Richardson (Benidickson), James A. Richardson, George Taylor Richardson and Kathleen Richardson. The company's original capital stock of $200,000 was held by Richardson personally. The firm of James Richardson & Sons was not financially involved in any of his airways companies because Richardson did not want to risk the firm's money. From the start Western Canada Airways would be his "baby"; for Richardson, aviation would be a passionate affair.

Western Canada Airways was in business with the arrival of its first plane, an open-cockpit, 200-horsepower Fokker Universal Standard, bearing the Canadian registration G-CAFU and appropriately named *The City of Winnipeg*. It was capable of operating on wheels, skis or floats to utilize, for takeoffs and landings, the hundreds of lakes and rivers in northern Ontario and Manitoba. The company's advance advertising stated, "Captain Oaks explains that his plane carries five passengers comfortably, that flying togs are unnecessary and that passengers step inside and close the door and are whisked away at a speed of 100 miles per hour to the gold fields." The plane arrived on Christmas Day, a unique present for Richardson.

Western Canada Airways earned its first dollar on December 27,

1926, when it carried seven hundred pounds of miscellaneous freight and fifty pounds of dynamite from Pine Ridge to Narrow Lake in Ontario. Oaks was the pilot, and newly hired Al Cheesman was the mechanic. By the end of December the new company had transported three paying passengers and 850 pounds of freight to the Red Lake area, for a total revenue of $180.

From then on the little base at Hudson, Ontario, was continuously busy. Operating out of a tiny building, little more than a hut, half buried in the deep snow of an exceptionally severe winter, Oaks and Cheesman used it for everything from storing freight and spare parts to running the business. Despite the desolation of the little station, they were proud of the newly printed passenger tickets and the sign over the door that advertised "Western Canada Airways." Flying conditions were spartan. The pilots usually took the seats out, and passengers sat on the cargo. The aircraft carried anything the pilots could stuff through the cabin door, including smelly packs of husky dogs, horses and even bulls.

The company's breakthrough came in early 1927 when, in a desperate last-minute effort to obtain vital facts on the Churchill harbour, the Department of Railways and Canals issued a tender to ferry men and supplies from the last northern railhead in Manitoba to the port of Churchill by April 1, "before the ice breaks up the Churchill River." Western Canada Airways received the contract, probably because no one else would bid on it. The freight was to include one ton of dynamite, an amount never before carried by aircraft. As it turned out, the department woefully underestimated the loads. To carry out the job, Oaks purchased two more Fokker Universal aircraft from New York and hired two more pilots, Rod Ross and Fred Stevenson. This was the Stevenson of Stevenson's Field, the name by which Winnipeg's municipal airport was known until 1958, when it was renamed Winnipeg International Airport.

Stevenson, a well-decorated World War I pilot, had, after the war, flown delegates between London and Paris during the 1919 peace conference, taught White Russians in the Crimea how to fly (for this he received the Order of St. Stanislas), barnstormed throughout Manitoba and flown with the Ontario Provincial Air Service from 1924 to 1926, before joining Western Canada Airways. He made many trips with the company, but three were epic-making and earned him a reputation as Canada's leading commercial pilot and the prestigious Harmon Trophy. In winning the award for Canada, Stevenson was in most distinguished company: Charles A. Lindbergh won both the international and U.S. trophies. Stevenson was the only Canadian ever to win this trophy.

Fred Stevenson was a daredevil with little respect for rules. In 1919, much to the consternation of his passengers, two French diplomats, he "looped the loop" while transporting them between London and Paris during the peace talks. However, his easygoing, nonchalant attitude was ideal for an environment in which each flight was an experiment. Equally important, he was a risk-taker and an innovative thinker. On one of his early trips he tied toboggans to the wheels of his aircraft so that he could land on snow. He also had an irreverent sense of humour that eased many a tense situation.

Wanting to give his pilots more training on the Fokker aircraft, "Doc" Oaks arranged for the Fokker test pilot, Bernt Balchen, to be loaned temporarily to Western Canada Airways for the Churchill operation. Evidently the primitive conditions at the Hudson base and Stevenson in particular left a lasting impression on Balchen, for he mentioned them thirty years later when he wrote his autobiography, *Come North with Me.*

We follow the lantern down the railroad embankment along a narrow path and ahead of us I see the pink glow of a Yukon stove lighting the windows of a snow covered shack. It is little more than a lean-to but the lantern's rays reveal an impressive sign over the door, "Western Canada Airways." This is the administration building, ticket office, freight station and passenger terminal for the whole flying gold rush.

As we push open the door and stamp the snow from our feet a group of men around the pot-bellied stove peer at us curiously through the murk of spruce wood smoke and stale tobacco. The warmth is welcome and my three mechanics make for the stove at once. One of them, a youngster from Jersey City, lifts his coat tails and extends his rear end towards the heat, shaking himself gratefully ...

Stevenson is scrunched so far down in his chair that he is almost sitting on the back of his neck. His legs are propped on a high shelf, a pair of moose hide moccasins comfortably crossed and a curved pipe is hooked in his mouth, the bend of the stem following the line of his long angular jaw. He waves a hand languidly in greeting.

The young mechanic from Jersey is fidgeting beside the stove and his eyes move around the little room in embarrassment. He inquires in a low voice, "Which door is the men's room?" Captain Stevenson unlocks his moccasin feet from the shelf, clambers to his full height and rips a page from the Eaton's Mail Order Catalogue hanging on the wall. He opens the outside door and points to the darkness and swirling snow. "There's the whole wide world, Sonny Boy," he drawls, "and if you can't help yourself, you're no man for the north country."

In charge of the airlift was Rod Ross, with Stevenson and Balchen as the pilots and Cheesman as mechanic. The four men made an effective team. They made twenty-seven round trips of four hundred air miles each from the operations base at Cache Lake, at the end of steel, to Fort Churchill. These pioneering flights were made with no landing fields, no lighting, no navigation or radio aids, no facilities such as hangars in which to do repairs, and sketchy maps. Although Fokker had an excellent reputation, his aircraft, sturdy as they were, were not built to operate in extreme cold. They often broke down away from base when flying in sub-zero weather. To add to the hardship, the pilot sat in an open cockpit and the airlift was carried out in the dead of winter.

Certainly radio communication would have made the operation safer, and in one instance it would have made life easier and less exasperating for Stevenson. On April 8, 1927, a broken oil line forced him to make an emergency landing when he was returning to Cache Lake from Churchill. Landing CAFU some fifty miles from Cache Lake, Stevenson knew that Balchen's aircraft, CAGD, was temporarily out of commission, so he could expect no help from Balchen; besides, the weather had deteriorated so much that no one would be looking for him anyway. He put on his snowshoes and began walking. On April 12, Balchen and Cheesman set out in CAGD looking for Stevenson. They spotted the aircraft, landed for Cheesman to make the necessary repairs, and then Cheesman flew it back to Cache Lake. At 5 A.M. Stevenson, exhausted and frozen, staggered into the camp—to see his aircraft already there.

Despite the primitive conditions and the hazards of winter flying, all supplies were delivered within the contractual period. The operation was a magnificent achievement. Western Canada Airways successfully completed the first large airlift in Canada. In fact, at that time it was probably the largest airlift completed anywhere in the world in winter conditions away from settled areas. "The Churchill operation," as it became known, proved that aircraft could transport bulky and heavy freight into distant and otherwise inaccessible areas. It opened the eyes of government and mining officials to the potential of aircraft in the North. It took airlifting out of the unique and moved it a long step toward the commonplace. In doing so, these Western Canada Airways flights gave a tremendous impetus to the whole scope and concept of aviation.

Richardson proudly released a news brief of his company's successful movement of men and equipment "in unprecedented weather conditions, with the result that the survey work was accelerated by many months." The news of the airlift flashed around the world: "A new venture in the way of transporting supplies to the Hudson Bay district, when speed was essential and when dog teams would prove too slow, was the successful one undertaken by Western Canada Airways, who carried 16,000 pounds and twelve men in three weeks from Cache Lake to Fort Churchill," proclaimed the *Toronto Evening Telegram* on May 5, 1927.

It appears that Oaks intended to film the airlift. Whether it was Richardson or DND who requested this is not known. As it turned out, the movie camera did not work, but Oaks's letter to A.T. Cowley of DND, dated May 4, 1927, clearly described some of the difficulties. "The rubber shock absorbers were useless in the cold. The Churchill conditions were more strenuous, encountering hard step drifts up to two feet high which had a tendency to annihilate the Fokker ski pedestals." Oaks wrote that he had redesigned the pedestals and tail ski and made new engine cowlings while Cheesman rigged up a stovepipe arrangement for heating the engine. The sense of humour that bush pilots seemed to have in abundance was evident in his final paragraph. "Pilots of this Company have formed a Dog Mushers Society. Qualifications for entrance require that a pilot shall have mushed at least 100 miles. Membership in the Society entitles the pilot to let his whiskers grow."

In July 1928, Leigh Brintnell, Western Canada Airways' new general manager (Oaks left to fly for Jack Hammell's Northern Aerial Minerals Exploration in March 1928), took delivery of the first of fourteen Fokker Super Universals to be operated by Western Canada Airways and Canadian Airways. The main differences between it and the Fokker Universal were that the pilot sat inside an enclosed cockpit, the horsepower was doubled (400-horsepower Pratt & Whitney engine) and the cabin could carry six passengers, two more than the Universal. On August 16 "Punch" Dickins, another distinguished World War I pilot, took delivery of the second Super Universal, G-CASK, which was destined to become the most famous aircraft ever registered in Canada. Her very first trip, a flight across the Barrens, would help her pilot win the prestigious McKee Trophy, Canada's top aviation award.

Lieutenant Colonel C.D.H. MacAlpine, president of Dominion Aerial Explorations, needed another aircraft for his exploration work along the west coast of Hudson Bay and into the interior; specifically, he wanted to go to the Sherritt Gordon Mines at Cold Lake, to Chesterfield Inlet and possibly on to Lake Athabasca. The primary purpose of MacAlpine's trip was to study the possibilities of prospecting by air. He asked Western Canada Airways if he could charter one of its aircraft and pilots.

This would be no routine trip over well-travelled territory. It would be an epic-making journey in which pilot and mechanic would encounter, in one trip, almost all of the problems of pioneer Arctic flying. The constant worry about fuel when flying far from the source of supply was a major problem. Much of the area over which MacAlpine and the crew would be flying had no fuel caches. There was no room for any miscalculation in compass headings, although the likelihood of distorted compass readings was high. Adding to these navigation difficulties was the fact that most of the flying was over territory that had few landmarks to guide them and where much of the map was marked "UNEXPLORED." If forced down over the Barrens, they could expect to find little vegetation or animal life to help them survive. This vast tundra had driven other unfortunates to cannibalism and starvation. It was not a trip for the faint of heart.

The famous flight across the Barrens began on August 28, 1928, with Dickins at the controls and accompanied by air engineer Bill Nadin,

Colonel MacAlpine and Richard Pearce, editor of the *Northern Miner*. The flight covered four thousand miles over twelve days. More than fifty years later, his flight across the forbidding yet majestic vastness of the Barrens remained a vivid memory for Dickins. "This was all unmapped territory. The larger lakes were dotted in, but the area from Baker Lake to the east end of Lake Athabasca was marked UNEXPLORED. We stuffed the airplane full of gas from the Hudson Bay supplies, took on extra provisions, consulted an 80-year-old Eskimo and laid out a compass course to follow." Dickins counted on his skill at dead reckoning, "flying by the seat of your pants," to get him to his destination.

The personality of the pilot was very important in those days. He had to have good sales skills because he was often the company's public relations man. A sense of humour was a definite asset, but perhaps even more important was a manner that inspired the passengers' confidence. Although a pilot might admit that he was "temporarily misplaced," he rarely admitted that he might be lost. Dickins's passengers were concerned that most of his map was labelled UNEXPLORED. Though he tried not to show it, Dickins was also concerned, especially since he could not count on his magnetic compass settings to be reliable that far north. His gentle joking and landing "for a cup of tea" alleviated the anxieties of nervous passengers. Fifty years later, Dickins remarked that over the twelve days they had quite a few cups of tea. "The night before we left, Colonel MacAlpine asked how was I going to navigate over the UNEXPLORED territory. I said to him, 'I'll follow the letters UNEXPLORED. When you see them, tell me.'"

Fine weather and good visibility marked their first hour of flying. "I was able to identify quite a few places and that gave me confidence that the plot I had made was accurate . . . There was not much to go by. About four hours out we came to the height of land where water would flow down south and west into Lake Athabasca and the Mackenzie River basin. I knew we were on the right track."

Problems came when they approached the treeline again. Forest fires and haze greatly reduced visibility. "My passengers were nervous. To divert their fears, I said we would land and have a cup of tea. My mechanic was from England and had only been in Canada for three months. He was somewhat anxious because there was no one around [he was used to the built-up areas of England, not the vast, remote areas of northern Canada]. He was also hungry and said he 'could sure go for a ta'penny bun.' Because this trip included aerial mapping as well, they all decided to call the lake Ta'penny Lake."

The next day the haze had cleared enough to allow them to take off for Fort Smith, some 250 miles to the west. They reached the north shore of Lake Athabasca, and the next day they set course for Fort Smith. The night before, however, the temperature had dropped to about 20°F, and the next morning Dickins found ice on the floats and frost on the wings; he scraped it off and everything seemed all right. "I checked the gas gauge and we took off. We were over Slave River when all of a sudden, everything was quiet. 'Nothing is going on,' I thought to myself. We were gliding along beautifully. I was out of gas. I landed and got out the tea pail again."

This was no laughing matter. There were no villages nearby and no gas caches. Pondering the advisability of trying to paddle or float the airplane downstream, about thirty-five miles to Fort Smith, Dickins spotted a steamboat on the river. "I don't know who was most surprised; they or us. 'Are you fellows in trouble?' one of them called. 'You wouldn't have any aviation gas, would you?' I asked. 'Yes, I have 10 barrels for a fellow named Dickins. I think he's coming flying here next winter.' Colonel MacAlpine thought that it was pretty smart to get gas that fast."

That was the first and last time Dickins ever ran out of gas. What had happened was that the gas gauge had frozen the previous night; condensation in the bottom of the tank, where the gauge was located, had given a false reading. That, combined with strong headwinds, resulted in the plane running out of gas before they reached their destination. "I always used a dipstick after that," admitted a sheepish Dickins.

The Mackenzie River is Canada's greatest river system, second only to the Mississippi in North America. It is three hundred miles longer than the St. Lawrence and drains an area larger than Quebec. In early 1929, Dickins tackled the mighty Mackenzie. He successfully expanded Western Canada Airways' operations when he began a series of trips down its almost two-thousand-mile length to check on the possibility of starting an air service. Each trip out, he pushed a little farther along the Mackenzie, dropping fuel drums along the way. He made stops at every trading post to see the people, to show them the airplane and to advertise the flying service.

These trips were made in the worst weather possible, yet Dickins's official reports were written sparingly, almost casually, glossing over life-threatening occurrences. For instance, on January 23, Dickins, accompanied by air engineer Lew Parmenter and a postal inspector, set off in the Fokker Super Universal SN for a trip down the Mackenzie, then on to Fitzgerald and Fort Providence, with stops at Resolution and Hay River to pick up a load of furs. Here is part of his account for Western Canada Airways' records.

> Had temperatures down to 62[°F] below zero and 54 below with a 50 mile wind ... The rubber shock absorbers on the undercarriage are not much good at extreme temperatures, freezing solid, and makes landing just the same as if the tubes were solid in the legs ... At Resolution I landed in a heavy snowstorm and made a good landing but ran over a drift that I could not see and the right leg folded up and then the left. There was no jar of any kind and the passenger thought that it was the normal way for a machine to land.
>
> After the legs folded I switched off and pulled the nose up to save the engine but both blades of the prop bent and one blade was cracked about 6 inches from the tip. This blade broke off when we tried to straighten it so we cut the other off to it and set them at 18 degrees pitch. The legs we fixed by straightening them as much as possible and then cut off the cracked part and inserted water pipes inside and riveted them into place.

Dickins's first experience with bad surface conditions was the landing just described. Fifty years later, he provided a few more details. Even though he did not over-elaborate, it was clear that ingenuity, toughness and a sense of humour were definite prerequisites for being a bush pilot in the 1920s.

> The conditions did not look too bad from the air, but it was hard to tell where the ground was. The snow drifts were very hard and angled. About the fourth drop the plane's undercarriage broke, it went down on its belly and broke the propeller. There was no communications. The nearest radio station was 150 miles away at Fort Smith. I had to figure out how we were going to get out. So we sent

a dog team out (it took 5 days). Meanwhile we found some water pipes, levered the plane up on gas drums, took the prop off. This took 1½ days. Then sawing with hacksaws we took one foot off each end of the prop (took the bent parts off), so it was two feet shorter than it should have been. We took off and arrived at Fort Smith about 15 minutes after the dog team.

The irony of the dog team beating the airplane was not lost on Dickins.

On March 6, 1929, Dickins crossed the Arctic Circle about ten miles north of Good Hope. This was the first commercial flight in Canada to cross the circle. On July 1, he flew the complete length of the Mackenzie River to Aklavik on the Arctic Ocean in an attempt to get the business from the northern part of the river. His flights laid the basis for the most publicized air mail service in the world, from Fort McMurray, Alberta, to Aklavik, nearly three hundred miles beyond the Arctic Circle at the mouth of the Mackenzie. The service held the distinction of being the world's "farthest north" air mail service. Trips formerly made by dog team, taking some seventy days of travel, were now made by aircraft in approximately eleven hours' flying time over an elapsed period of forty-eight hours.

That trip too remained etched in Dickins's memory.

When I finally arrived at Aklavik it was midnight. The sun was still shining. There were about 40 to 50 Eskimos on the shore. I stood on the muddy bank and looked one way at the Arctic on one side and the other way up the river and could not help but think of the source and Mackenzie, who took 6 months by canoe 140 years previous and that I, Dickins, was doing some pioneering. I felt very humble. Maybe Mackenzie had stood on that same bank.

Dickins had brought fresh vegetables, eggs and newspapers with him. "I thought what a difference the airplane was going to make to these people and I knew the airplane was here to stay. The next summer we had five airplanes working in that district."

Western Canada Airways' aircraft penetrated deeper and deeper into the continent, gradually superseding the dog teams of former years. Supplies of fresh vegetables and fruit arrived with increasing regularity at remote points. Prospectors, traders, hunters and trappers shared with doctors, Mounties and missionaries the benefits of the airplane as the time of travel was reduced from weeks and days to hours.

The discovery of important minerals was directly attributable to flying. Horace Young, manager of the Howey Gold Mines in Hudson, wrote that "airplane service has been of incalculable benefit to operations and will continue to be a factor in holding down costs." Richardson authorized Western Canada Airways pilots to carry prospector Gilbert LaBine on his exploratory flights for uranium if they were going to be flying in the vicinity. LaBine travelled well over three thousand miles with pilots such as "Punch" Dickins and Leigh Brintnell and was billed for fewer than six hundred; the rest were on the house. "You never know where one of these little experiments may lead," Richardson said.

Dickins recalled that Brintnell had flown LaBine into the northeast corner of Great Bear Lake in the summer of 1929 and he had found some copper, but LaBine was not satisfied. In September 1929, Dickins was due for a flight in the area. He contacted LaBine and asked him if he wished to come along. "I was doing a little sketch mapping, saw a little island at the mouth of the bay. There was a great deal of discoloration; it was like the colours of the rainbow. Gilbert came up and hit me on the shoulder and shouted in my ear, 'Can you find this island again?' He wanted to come back. I said yes because it was a fantastic island in the sun." In April 1930, Dickins and Walter Gilbert flew LaBine and his crew to the island. LaBine discovered the source of pitchblende, and Eldorado became history.

The West was proud to count James Richardson as one of theirs. "For years the West has been neglected as a field of aeroplane travel ... We have to thank Mr. James Richardson of Winnipeg ... Western Canada Airways financed by Mr. Richardson is a true product of western optimism and courage. Its assistance to the mining fields of Red Lake, Woman Lake and Central Manitoba is a valuable feature in their development," proclaimed the editorial in the *Mining and Industrial News* on March 25, 1927.

From his office in Winnipeg, Richardson watched the rapid development of Western Canada Airways with great interest. In those early years, Richardson laid down the principles that were to guide him in his operation of Western Canada Airways and later in Canadian Airways Limited. He kept himself informed about aircraft, flying, manufacturing and the aviation industry in general. He bought the best equipment available and, above all, emphasized safety. He wrote to Oaks in March 1927, "I want to see every possible precaution taken to provide every safeguard for our work and no flying done except when our equipment is in absolutely perfect condition and no one put in charge of a plane who is not thoroughly competent and experienced." He surrounded himself with the top men in the field, encouraged them to develop the lines of operation and listened to their advice. He also knew his company and his people intimately and was concerned about their welfare.

Branson St. John, a former clerk, remembered James Richardson. "I was about 15 years old. I was the office boy at the time ... I remember Mr. Richardson coming in. He was a big sturdy man. He didn't announce himself. He just strode in." His daughter Kathleen remembered her father in much the same way. "He was a large gentleman; genial, affable. He didn't walk down the platform [at the train station], he strided down the platform. For a big man, he went quickly. He was light on his feet."

Eventually management and administration staff moved to a building at the foot of the Norwood Bridge, just off the Red River on St. Mary's Road, a mere fifteen-minute walk from Richardson's office in the Grain Exchange. It was not uncommon for Richardson to walk across the bridge to see how things were going or to visit the shops at the foot of Brandon Avenue, on the other side of the river. Mechanic Don Whellams recalled one such visit. "One day he came across and found most of us stretched outside on the grass ... We were doping the wings of one of the planes and were overcome with the fumes and had gone outside to recover." On hearing that, Richardson ordered a better system of ventilation.

The men enjoyed having the president of the company take the time to visit. "A person that stirred up a great deal of interest was Mr. James Richardson, a well-respected man and known to everyone as the Chief, and quite rightly so," recalled mechanic Reg Nichols. It was well known among pilots and mechanics that Richardson's office door was always open to them. His secretary had been instructed that whenever one of his pilots wanted to see Richardson, particularly if he was from out of town, Richardson could be interrupted and the pilot shown in. It is little wonder that Richardson commanded loyalty from his staff.

While encouraging individual effort in his people, Richardson also kept a close watch on the company, and when he intervened, he did so tactfully. He was also quick to praise. His letter to Oaks on February 26, 1927, shows how he combined a pat on the back to his chief pilot with a reminder about safety and a few suggestions about expanding services. "You have yourself established confidence in the minds of everyone you have taken out and in from the mining field . . . I am most anxious that the reputation you have established should be fully lived up to by the Company and that we should be very sure of the competency of any man to whom we entrust the plane. I am just passing along these thoughts while they are in my mind and would be glad to discuss them with you and any other thoughts and ideas you may have."

Understanding the value of keeping his people informed about company happenings, Richardson began a company magazine, *The Bulletin*, in July 1929. The editor throughout its lifetime was W.B. Burchall. Also about this time, Richardson introduced the company's logo. He wanted his aircraft to be easily identified and to send the message that his service was safe and reliable. He also wanted the logo to represent Western Canada Airways' mandate of opening up the North. One of the suggestions put forward was the beaver. Richardson snorted, "A beaver! Gosh, when did a beaver ever fly?" He chose the Canada goose, which Professor V.W. Jackson, a biologist at the agriculture college at the University of Manitoba, described as a "noble, game, intelligent, resourceful, organized bird which was recognized a mile high by its orderly formation and its steady progress and its northerly destiny . . . It represents nationality, long migratory flights, strength on the wing, regularity and organized flight. In short it is symbolic of all that is best in Canadian air travel." The logo became a familiar sight on all the company's aircraft, properties and publications. The grey goose, its wings in flight, breaking through a closed circle and bearing the name *Western Canada Airways* was seen all across western Canada and later, with the formation of Canadian Airways Limited, from sea to sea.

The airline's non-scheduled services were of utmost importance to the economic development of Canada and provided the only effective access to many of the vast, undeveloped areas of the North. By 1929, practically every district beyond the railhead was within flying range. Full of pride for his company, Richardson wrote to a friend, "Western Canada Airways are credited with being the only successful unsubsidized air service in the British Empire." He ended wryly, "We operated the first year without losing any money but that is about all that can be said."

Western Canada Airways' creation in 1926 represented the beginning of the air transport industry in Canada on a sound financial basis and with adequate organization. From the start, Richardson applied to the company the successful techniques of administration and organization that he used in his grain business. He meticulously chose an initial core of experts, delegated authority and relied upon their advice before making any major decisions. Certainly Richardson's choice of "Doc" Oaks as Western Canada Airways' first general manager and chief pilot was a fortuitous one. Undoubtedly, his combination of skills contributed to the company's initial success. It is more than mere coincidence that the airline's first pilots all had distinguished flying careers in World War I and that Western Canada Airways, and later Canadian Airways Limited, provided most of the winners of the annual McKee Trophy, Canada's most prestigious aviation award. "Doc" Oaks was the first McKee Trophy winner.

The growth of Western Canada Airways was phenomenal. From a one-machine operation at Sioux Lookout in December 1926, the operation had spread by 1930 to include northwestern Canada to the Pacific and Arctic coasts and an inventory of fifty-one single-engine aircraft, one tri-motor, eighty-seven engines, hangars, docks and quantities of skis, floats and other material. Its success virtually dictated that it follow a policy of extension and development of its territory and services. In 1929, Western Canada Airways was the second-largest air transport company in the British Empire, exceeded only by Britain's Imperial Airways. This growth, although it coincided with an era of great prosperity, was remarkable in that it was unassisted by government subsidy. In less than three years Western Canada Airways had put Canada in the front rank of air freighting, and the company led North America in tonnage carried. The company's success showed that commercial aviation, when run on sound business principles and with competent technical know-how, had a place in the Canadian economy.

The Chosen Instrument:
"One Good Show from Coast to Coast"

INETEEN TWENTY-SEVEN was a critical year for aviation in Canada; Canada was in the Dark Ages. There were few intercity services and no national east–west air mail and passenger link. The airports were primitive and the supply of pilots was running short. Even more alarming, Canadian businessmen were beginning to patronize American services and American companies were tapping Canadian east–west traffic. Canada had to take steps to form its own airway if it did not want to become a mere extension of the American airline system. It lagged dangerously behind most of the western world. The situation was even more serious on the international level.

By the late 1920s, aviation was passing out of its pioneer stage. The control and handling of international air routes were becoming important. Canada held the geographical advantage of having the most direct routes from North America to Europe and Asia pass over its territory. Although permission for airlines to fly into a country and to build bases there had to be obtained from the country concerned, air route development was open to anyone who took the initiative. Because the Maritime provinces and Newfoundland were considered the most suitable

39

takeoff sites for trans-Atlantic flights and the overland route to Asia passed over Canadian territory, Canada held the key to world airways development. It could take the lead in establishing the trans-Canada, the trans-Atlantic and trans-Pacific or overland routes to Asia. Instead, it allowed American companies to base themselves in Canada (to be ready for eventual trans-Atlantic flying) and to operate Canadian inter-city services. The international agreement between Canada and the United States allowed Americans to fly American-registered aircraft into Canada and to land, so long as it was not for commercial purposes. The Americans pushed the agreement beyond its limits while DND turned a blind eye.

Meanwhile, officials of Imperial Airways of Great Britain and Pan American Airways (Pan Am) of the United States were making secret agreements to cooperate in the development of the trans-Atlantic airways and were negotiating with Newfoundland, which was not yet a part of Canada. These negotiations were usually transacted by airline officials, because they had more flexibility than government officials. Imperial Airways was Britain's "chosen instrument," as was Pan Am in the United States, for international airways development.

"Chosen instrument" was an expression used to identify the company that had been chosen by its nation's government to operate its national or international air routes. The chosen instrument held a pre-ferred position in the airline business and received government assis-tance, either in the form of lucrative air mail contracts or direct cash contributions. Canada was at a definite disadvantage in not having a chosen instrument to work through and consequently found itself left out of these talks.

The Canadian government could no longer pretend that its policy of doing nothing "was wise," as Wilson had written in 1926. The obvi-ous answer was for Canada to establish its own chosen instrument that would operate the trans-Canada airway and cooperate with other national airlines in the development of international air routes. Air-lines in Britain, Europe and the United States were all subsidized by their governments; government also provided navigational aids, weather reporting facilities and training programs. All of these things remained to be done in Canada. But to implement any of it, a policy was needed. To its discredit, the federal government never officially framed a comprehensive policy until 1937, and by then Canada was out of the race for international airways development.

The importance of the trans-Canada airway was initially underestimated by officials, who saw it simply as a domestic line and not as an integral part of the trans-Atlantic and trans-Pacific systems. It did not help that there was no department solely responsible for the development of civil aviation. As a result, the "aviation question" was tackled in a piecemeal fashion. It was a comedy of errors.

For instance, while the Department of National Defence took care of air agreements between Canada and the United States, the Civil Aviation Branch of DND was nominally in charge of domestic air affairs. The introduction of air mail services in Canada brought in the Post Office department, but here too, the responsibility was shared between DND and the Post Office. DND advised the Post Office on the routes and the commercial operators to be chosen, but the ultimate responsibility for the selection of routes, the contractor and the determination of air mail rates lay with the Post Office. Although not initially involved in airways matters, the Department of Railways and Canals stepped into the picture in the early 1930s to protect its interests, and by 1933 the Department of External Affairs was also involved. With no overall government policy for the development of Canada's air services, with the conflicting interests that were bound to develop among the various departments and with no minister to promote its interests, the growth of commercial aviation in Canada was seriously hampered.

There was dissension from the start. The RCAF wanted to carry the mail, but the Post Office preferred commercial companies because it wanted the air mail to pay for itself. The postmaster general, P.J. Veniot, had issued a number of air mail contracts in 1927 and 1928 to companies in eastern Canada. Not only were these companies in financial difficulties in 1928, but having five different companies run the air mail service was not conducive to building an efficient transcontinental air mail service. Veniot believed that the only way to bring the Canadian air mail service up to par with the American service was to support one strong Canadian company. Mackenzie King, finally feeling the pull of national and empire needs, was ready to move. What really lit the fire under the government was the threat in 1928 of five major eastern aviation companies being sold to Americans.

A firm believer that Canadian aviation must remain in Canadian hands, James Richardson was prepared to step in. Although his interest in airways matters was primarily in the West, he had kept himself informed of events, not only in eastern Canada but also in the United States and Britain. One of his contacts was Colonel R.H. Mulock, a former Winnipegger and one of the most decorated fliers of World War I. "Red" Mulock was considered by many to be one of the top aviation authorities in Canada. Although instrumental in the formation of the Canadian Air Force, Mulock was unhappy with the way it had been organized, and he had become a director of Canadian Vickers of Montreal. His real desire was to be directly involved in the operating end of an aviation company, and he approached Richardson. There was no place for him with Western Canada Airways, but because of his knowledge of aviation affairs and political contacts in the East, Richardson had been using Mulock in a semi-official capacity to keep him advised of airways happenings.

When Richardson learned of the financial precariousness of the eastern companies and the encroachment of American interests, he began eyeing the eastern Canadian companies with the idea of putting together a trans-Canada operation. He entered into a "gentleman's agreement" with the Liberal government of Mackenzie King to establish a Canadian transcontinental company to provide mail and passenger services and to block the Americans from taking control of Canada's airways. The understanding between the government and him was that he would form a strong national company that would operate the trans-Canada service and become Canada's chosen instrument in national and international airways development. His company would receive the main air mail contracts, which would constitute the secure financial basis that Richardson required to establish a strong national company. The agreement happened in this way.

Since making its first flights, Western Canada Airways had carried mail into the Red Lake area but had been unable to charge for the service. Wishing to put the mail on a business basis, "Doc" Oaks asked Richardson to contact postal authorities in Ottawa about the possibility of Western Canada Airways charging for its mail delivery. On March 4, 1927, the company was given permission to issue its own air mail stamps at ten cents each and to carry mail into central Manitoba and northwestern Ontario. This was a semi-official air mail service authorized by the Post Office to carry mail at the risk of the sender, upon prepayment of a fee, usually twenty-five cents, in addition to regular postage. The fee, which went to the company, helped to reimburse it for its trouble and was covered by an adhesive label known as a "sticker" to differentiate it from the official postage stamp.

The Post Office had provided strict instructions. Western Canada Airways was, first, to write "By Aerial Mail" on the address side; second, to attach the special sticker on the reverse side; and, above all, to ensure that no expense was "to be borne by the Post Office." On June 1, 1927, Fred Stevenson flew the first air mail in Manitoba from Lac du Bonnet to Long Lac, completing in less than two hours a round trip that usually took four days.

Western Canada Airways' financially successful operations in the midwest encouraged Richardson to think of extending its services across the Prairies. To underwrite this new route, Richardson wanted the security of a Post Office contract because passenger and express air services in their initial stages were usually run at a loss. Mulock had told Richardson that "his friends" in the Post Office would "look favourably on a sound air mail system between Winnipeg, Calgary, and Edmonton." Mulock said that the government had let a contract to Canadian Transcontinental Airways of Quebec for carrying mail on the north shore of the St. Lawrence and from Moncton to the Magdalen Islands and that if the government gave out contracts in these sparsely populated districts with very little political pressure, it could do the same for Western Canada Airways.

With this advice, on March 28, 1928, Richardson applied for a contract to carry the mail between Winnipeg and Calgary, with the option of extending the service to other prairie cities. He also asked for a monopoly of the air mail in the area, a four-year contract and the assurance the government would provide weather advisory services and lighted beacons along the route. Well aware that Canada lagged behind other countries, the Post Office and DND were receptive to Richardson's overtures. However, matters moved at an aggravatingly slow pace.

P.T. Coolican, the assistant postmaster general, wrote company secretary John Hunter on April 3, stating that while the question of establishing air mail services in western Canada had been raised, there was no official response from government. He was prepared to discuss it with Richardson, but Richardson must realize that it was an expensive proposition for the government. Hunter tactfully responded on April 9, "The prairie route from Winnipeg to Calgary offers a splendid opportunity for experimentation in air mail services. We have a natural desire to have the West share with the East in carrying on such experimental services." Ottawa obviously did not agree. Mulock alerted Richardson on May 11 that the estimates of $250,000 before the Treasury Board were all earmarked for the eastern air mail.

Slow to anger, Richardson immediately but tactfully wired Charles Stewart, the minister of the interior, "It seems to me the West is entitled to as much consideration in the way of a fast mail service as is the East." Appealing to the government's vanity, Richardson pointed out that the most logical service would be the Winnipeg–Calgary one because twenty-four hours could be clipped off the delivery time and the government would receive much applause for its new, speedy service. To ensure that his message reached those with clout, Richardson also wrote to C.A. Dunning, the minister of railways and canals; Robert Forke, the minister of immigration and colonization; and James Robb, the minister of finance. Having been told that Veniot would fall into line behind the other ministers, Richardson did not write Veniot.

Stewart and Robb replied quickly and favourably. The reason for the holdup became clear in Dunning's reply, which indicated that Veniot wanted DND to do some survey flights in the summer, and therefore he would make no decision until after that. Now thoroughly annoyed with what he believed were unnecessary tests, Richardson fired off letters to a number of influential people, requesting them to put pressure on the government. To Duncan Cameron, president of the Winnipeg Board of Trade, on May 14, Richardson scathingly wrote that the postmaster general's explanation made no sense, since the West was the only area where experimental flights in both winter and summer had been carried out.

On May 19 he wrote to G.M. Bell, president of the *Calgary Albertan*, thanking him for a favourable editorial and adding: "It would appear though that political considerations are the only ones that have weight with the Postmaster General ... If the West does not speak for itself they can count on getting no consideration whatever. The intention seems to be to use all money for the air mail service in the East and then advise the West that the Government services will test out the western fields and find out if they are suitable."

Richardson's letters set off a barrage of newspaper headlines: "WEST NEEDS AIR MAIL SYSTEM" and "AIR MAIL FOR THE WEST." His strategy worked; on May 29, Mulock telegrammed with the information that $150,000 had been voted in the supplementary estimates for the air mail, and though it had not yet been tagged for any special run, likely it would be earmarked for the West.

All through the spring and summer, the uncertainty continued. Richardson decided not to wait any longer. Concerned by the decision to have DND make test flights, likely in aircraft unsuitable for commercial purposes, and annoyed that they would not be authorized until summer, Richardson bluntly told the Post Office that Western Canada Airways would run any necessary experimental flights. Veniot weakly responded that he did not think that the Post Office could "go by an experiment made by a private company." Richardson ignored Veniot and telegrammed Coolican on September 13, 1928, that the company was establishing regular passenger and express services between Winnipeg, Regina and Calgary and would carry the mail at a nominal cost to demonstrate its feasibility to the Post Office and the public.

Richardson then directed his treasurer, J.A. MacDougall, to write Coolican, confirming the telegram as well as advising that Western Canada Airways would be using a de Havilland 61 Moth, an eight-passenger biplane, and that it was the company's intention to begin a regular passenger and express air service two times a week each way. "We would be prepared for the present to carry mail on a nominal cost basis. We would appreciate your views," was the conciliatory final sentence.

Shrewdly, Richardson let it be known that he had invited Manitoba's premier, John Bracken, to be on the first flight, had alerted civic officials and reporters along the route, and was expecting plenty of publicity. His tactic worked. On November 22, 1928, Coolican authorized Western Canada Airways to carry out an experimental air mail service between Winnipeg and Regina, Regina and Calgary, and Regina and Edmonton from December 10 to December 29.

There was a downside to proceeding at this time, and that was the weather. Both Leigh Brintnell, the general manager, and John Wilson were worried. "It is a pretty severe test to choose the three weeks in the year when the light is shortest and the weather may be pretty uncertain, although if you can come through that period, we should be able to face all ordinary hazards," Wilson wrote to Brintnell on November 27. Wilson added that Coolican was "worried over the closeness of the schedule west-bound, it leaves no great margin, but I guess you have no choice because of the train schedules." Brintnell already realized that Coolican was going to be a difficult person to work with, because Coolican already had written him warning that Western Canada Airways "must not fail as that would detract from the air mail service."

Nevertheless, the company began its test flights in the uncertain weather conditions of December with Premier Bracken (who became known as "the flying premier") as its first passenger. The experimental service was a success, and Coolican said he was prepared to discuss a regular air mail service with Richardson. Although the Post Office verbally approved Western Canada Airways' operations and schedules for the service in December 1928, Coolican did not write Hunter until March 7, 1929. Although his letter was positive ("I am anxious to discuss with your company the question of regular air mail service between Winnipeg, Regina, Calgary and Edmonton"), the Post Office inexplicably delayed telling Western Canada Airways that it had the contract until June 25, 1929, and further postponed matters by refusing to sign the contract until October 18 of that year. For a Post Office that was in a hurry to catch up with the rest of the world and that wanted to stave off American companies who were busily applying for air mail contracts, the delay was inexcusable.

Politics and competing interests within the departments were causing the problem, and rate-setting was part of the holdup. The federal government treated the West differently. "In view of the rate paid by the Post Office for Montreal's air mail service, I do not feel the Post Office should take this stand with us. We are prepared to revise downward somewhat but in addition the government should recognize the cash duty we have paid on our equipment, amounting to about $200,000," John Hunter wrote on April 5, 1929, to Peter Heenan, MP for Kenora–Rainy River. Heenan's name often appeared on coded letters and telegrams to Western Canada Airways; likely Richardson knew him through his summer residence at Coney Island, on Lake of the Woods.

Political lobbying also contributed to the delay. In a July 1 letter to his friend Jack Hammell, Richardson wrote "that once it became known that Western Canada Airways was to receive the prairie air mail contract, people without experience or equipment endeavoured through political pressure to try and get in some place on the contract ... We [told] the Government that we would either take it all or not any of it ... Political objectors, though, succeeded in delaying the signing of the contract and this delayed Wilson from proceeding immediately with his plans ... for beacon lights." Mulock later added another dimension: "DND and Civil Government Aviation were opposed on principle to large combines and considered that the Western Lines of Canadian Airways Limited had more than its share of government contracts."

On April 10, 1929, Brintnell telegraphed Hunter from Ottawa, saying that sixty-five cents was the Post Office's top figure. Since this was nowhere near what the eastern companies were being paid, Richardson was convinced that the Post Office was deliberately turning the screws on the West because the Post Office would not allow Western Canada Airways' full operating expenses, landing fees or airport costs to be included in the rate. Since they seemed to be at an impasse, Hunter telegraphed him back the same day, recommending that Brintnell should accept the figure, "but the contract must definitely be for four years and not too many strings to it to operate against us in view of the low figure we are accepting." The feeling was that the Post Office attitude on the rate of pay was "take it or leave it."

To offset this dictatorial attitude, Richardson wanted the security of a four-year mail contract. Brintnell finally succeeded in negotiating for seventy-five cents a mile and wrote Hunter the details on April 18. "This price is very low but due to the fact they have only $800,000.00 voted for air mail, our contract takes about $725,000.00 of this. I went over every phase of the contract and had to fight them on every paragraph." The government took on the responsibility of surveying the route and installing beacons and emergency landing fields.

Just as officials were ready to sign the contract, Heenan sent a coded telegram to Hunter on April 23 warning that Great Western Airways of Calgary was strongly lobbying the minister for part of the contract.

"Come East and try to get the Order through," he wrote. A day later, another coded telegram arrived on Hunter's desk: "Coolican wants you in the East when the other company is giving their case for counter argument." On May 6, Richardson wrote to R.B. Bennett, leader of the Opposition and a political friend, asking him to "help push forward the signing of the contract." He then made a series of strongly worded phone calls that resulted in a flurry of letters being sent on May 28 from influential Manitobans to Prime Minister Mackenzie King, demanding the implementation of the prairie air mail, and that the contract be given "to one company, Western Canada Airways, without further delay."

Again the pressure tactics worked. On June 4, 1929, Veniot told Mulock, "Tell Richardson that the contract will be let within ten days and so no chance for anyone else." According to Mulock, four other groups were hovering around the political trough, all wanting the contract and all with powerful backing among the ministers. These groups owned no aircraft and had no experience in running an airways company. The battle was on for the lucrative prairie air mail contract. Mulock explained, "It is very difficult trying to keep the western mail in Western Canada Airways."

On June 25, Coolican telegrammed Western Canada Airways that it had received the contract for the entire service. The signing, however, was delayed until October 18; more politicking had delayed matters. Signing for the government were G.J. Desbarats, the deputy minister of national defence, and P.T. Coolican, the deputy postmaster general. Western Canada Airways was to provide a service between Winnipeg and Edmonton via Regina, Saskatoon and North Battleford, and also between Regina and Calgary by way of Moose Jaw and Medicine Hat.

The Post Office set December 2, 1929, as the starting date. Western Canada Airways hired extra pilots and bought special mail planes— only to discover that DND did not, after all, want the company to begin at that time. Richardson turned to the Post Office for permission to start at once, flying daylight hours only. The request was denied because the beacons were not all installed, and the company was forced to wait until March 1930. For Richardson the delay meant that all overhead costs, depreciation, insurance and salaries accumulated until the air mail was begun. Coolican was unsympathetic. "Expenses not understood," he telegrammed Brintnell on January 28, 1930. "Your contract does not specify any definite inauguration date. Lighting arrangements not under control of this Department."

The correspondence shows that Coolican was correct: no "day" was specified. This had been left blank, but the year "1929" was typed in. He too had been upset over the delay in lighting, which was DND's responsibility, and in exasperation he told Brintnell that Western Canada Airways could start anytime. Uneasy, Richardson had personally called Coolican to confirm this, but Coolican backed down and said no to a daylight service. He wired Richardson on November 11, 1929, "There is no benefit to the Post Office. Day service will be anticlimactic as the Postmaster General has gone on record on the night service and such a service would make it impossible to defend or even excuse the delays of the past six months."

The Post Office's vacillation had delayed John Wilson's authorization for the construction of the beacons. Political haggling and patronage bids for building the landing fields and providing the navigational aids that the federal government was to provide slowed down the process. The foot-dragging forced the West to wait two extra years for its air mail service.

Western Canada Airways was to provide "sober, steady and honest men as pilots, with a preference to be given to British subjects. Each pilot and air engineer will hold a certificate issued by the Minister of National Defence authorizing him to act as pilot or air engineer ... There will be a deduction in pay or fines by the Postmaster General if the mails become wet or are lost or are destroyed ... The company must defend the mail if there is a forced landing ... The company may also carry passengers and packages but preference must be given to the mail contract and mail must be kept safe from the passengers."

"Punch" Dickins and Leigh Brintnell, who had made the experimental flights, now turned the operation over to ten specially selected pilots: Milt Ashton, Roy Brown, Buck Buchanan, Neville Cumming, Con Farrel, Harold Farrington, Ken Hollick-Kenyon, A.E. Jarvis, Don MacLaren and Tommy Thompson. All were former bush pilots and, typical of this group of men, they soon came up with the following homily:

Air Mail may be lost but must not be delayed.
Passengers may be delayed but not lost.

"There will be no stunting or wing walking without approval from Head Office." With this directive (not entirely tongue in cheek) to its ten air mail pilots, Canadian Airways, still operating as Western Canada Airways in the West, began the prairie air mail service in March 1930. This was the first step toward building the transcontinental air mail route. Richardson's idea was to perfect the prairie and eastern Canada services while waiting for DND to build airfields across northern Ontario. The first service was established between Winnipeg and Calgary via Moose Jaw, Regina and Medicine Hat, with a northern link to Saskatoon, North Battleford and Edmonton. This was the first regular scheduled night air mail service in Canada.

The West was ecstatic. Winnipeg Mayor Ralph Webb sang Richardson's praises to the *Winnipeg Free Press* on March 3: "Mr. Richardson has brought the whole of the commercial world and the north country to the door of our city. Now with the air mail Winnipeg's business section is in close touch with every part of Canada and the world." On the same day, the *Calgary Daily Herald* outdid the *Free Press* in its description of the glories of air mail: "West Plains Spanned by Air Mail Service Monday in 9 Hours. A sturdy hornet of the heavens sped eastward this morning carrying the first night mail in the name of His Majesty The King. Like some satanic spectre . . . her wing tips, green and red, her landing lights like eyes that spotted fire, she screamed into the sky and . . . wheeled with a parting snarl to lose herself among the stars and add her moaning to the music of the spheres."

The flight east left Calgary at 2:15 A.M. and arrived in Winnipeg at noon. Air mail was five cents "from any point in Canada." The second day of service brought more accolades from the *Free Press* and Mayor Webb, who commended the Hudson's Bay Company for putting up a beacon on its Portage Avenue store. "It is the second largest of its type in the world. It is like a lighthouse. It can be seen for 100 miles."

Meanwhile, the eastern Canada air mail system began to unravel. As the prairie air mail drama was being played out, another scene was unfolding in the East. Again, James Richardson and the Canadian government were the main players. This time there was little foot-dragging, and for once, all seemed to be in agreement as to what to do.

By the late 1920s, there were five principal aviation companies in eastern Canada: International Airways, Canadian Transcontinental Airways, Fairchild Aviation, General Airways and Canadian Airways (the predecessor to Richardson's company, bearing the same name). International Airways had purchased Canadian Airways in the fall of 1928, and with it the Toronto–Montreal air mail contract. Canadian Airways continued to operate under its own name. Most of these companies were run at a loss, and their only valuable assets were their air mail contracts. Richardson was aware of the situation but had no wish to become involved. However, he had sent John Hunter, his number one man at James Richardson & Sons and Western Canada Airways, to the East on a number of scouting trips in late 1928 to look over the finances, management and operating practices of the companies.

Richardson's assessment of the companies and his strategy were spelled out in Hunter's letter to Mulock on October 17. "Mr. Richardson is prepared to ... start out with a new company ... and go right after business, or on the other hand let matters simmer along as they are now, probably getting worse, and take over the present amalgamated companies but of course eliminate a lot of deadwood." Richardson chose the latter course because starting an opposition company might mean an indefinite period of waiting to obtain any mail contracts.

Hunter asked Mulock to take charge of the situation and to keep them "constantly posted on developments with a view to our taking the proper step at just the right time ... We feel of course that Fairchild operating company should also be brought into this picture and in any scheme of course that we would undertake we would naturally wish for the support of the Post Office and the Canadian Pacific and include interests that would be of some use, and at the same time there would be direct cooperation and association with the Western Canada Airways Limited."

Richardson wired Hunter on November 24. "I think the present Eastern set-up and personnel leave much to be desired ... Some of these people including Drury are only interested from the point of view of promotion and I have no sympathy whatever with this point of view." Perhaps the most significant observation was his final sentence: "I do not think the present stage of development justifies any public participation."

On December 1, Richardson wrote to Sir Edward Beatty, president of the CPR. The participation of the railways was crucial. Richardson had no wish to create unnecessary duplication or destructive competition. There was a lesson to be learned from Canada's railway history: only one major airline should connect the major Canadian cities. Already Sir Henry Thornton, president of the CNR, was upset because Western Canada Airways was using CPR's express service; he wanted CNR to be considered also. Richardson wrote Beatty on October 13, 1928, "It has never been my intention to cooperate exclusively with CP. I felt this was only inviting trouble and would have the effect of putting the Government into the field, either directly or indirectly."

Richardson believed that Canada had neither the population nor the resources to warrant two national airlines. Over his private wire he told Hunter, "Canada cannot stand competitive lines at present. There is not the business in the country to warrant them nor the stock to handle them. England and Germany saw a situation such as this long ago and settled the matter for once and for all by subsidizing one company only."

Richardson too wanted the clout that both railway presidents would bring. Beatty, in particular, would be a coup for Richardson to capture. As president of the CPR from 1918 to 1942, Beatty was a transport giant. He dominated the world's largest privately owned railway system. He was also a man after Richardson's heart. He detested state ownership in industry and, like Richardson, was aware of his role as a great business leader and how he could use it to contribute to Canada's welfare. He was Richardson's soul-mate. Like Richardson, Beatty did not view his position as simply a way to make money but also as a way to contribute to Canada's development. Beatty would become one of Richardson's closest advisers on airways matters.

Richardson filled him in on the details of the eastern companies, explaining that they "lack management and direction and employ methods of securing business with which I do not wish to be associated. I would be glad, though, to see the Eastern companies properly set up and coordinated, and put under management which would give promise of developing along sound lines ... It was my intention, before giving any serious consideration to anything in the East, to consult with you and advise you fully in regard to any thoughts I had in regard to matters of aviation." He said that Hunter would be in Montreal and would be free to discuss the situation with Beatty.

"My dear Jim," Beatty enthusiastically responded on December 10. "I had the pleasure of a few minutes' interview with Mr. Hunter ... I explained to Mr. Hunter that we could not very well afford to overlook the possibilities of the rapid development in air services and that while we had the right to engage in them under an amendment to our charter, we would much prefer an alliance with a strong, exclusively air service company if that were found to be possible."

International Airways, in particular, was in financial difficulties, and its shareholders, a group of Hamilton businessmen, had just sold 51 percent of the stock to Victor Drury of Drury and Company, an investment company. Drury intended to sell his shares to Major General John F. O'Ryan, president of Colonial Air Transport, an American company. O'Ryan was also president of Canadian Colonial Airways, a subsidiary of Colonial Air Transport.

In a joint agreement between American and Canadian postal authorities in October 1928, Canadian Colonial had been awarded the air mail contract between Montreal and Albany. O'Ryan wanted more air mail contracts in order to gain more footholds in Canada, so that his company would be in a position to link up with whatever company established a trans-Atlantic air service. Long-range aircraft were still in the future, and the key to trans-Atlantic thinking was to use the two closest points of land in Europe and North America for takeoff and landing. Newfoundland and Halifax were geographically closer to Europe than any point on the U.S. coast.

Drury had already begun negotiations with O'Ryan when Mulock told Richardson of the possible sale of International Airways to O'Ryan. Richardson moved quickly to block this. His overriding concern was to prevent the Americans from gaining control of the Canadian airways system. Even when offered the chance of investing in Boeing Aircraft of Canada, he refused. "Aviation in Canada should be controlled by Canadians."

Richardson first obtained government approval for his proposed intervention. He did this by sending Hunter east to work with Mulock to obtain the support of the government, the CPR, the CNR and "other useful interests." Hunter reported that Mackenzie King "would be glad to cooperate with a private company by giving out government contract work." There were numerous coded telegrams in the October–December

1928 correspondence and telegrams to and from member of Parliament Heenan in Ottawa. In a coded telegram to Hunter on December 12, 1928, Heenan stated that Mulock saw the prime minister, Postmaster General P.J. Veniot, Defence Minister J.L. Ralston and "certain numbers of other departmental officials" and that "they are pleased to see the situation being handled."

Richardson next contacted the shareholders of International Airways and asked them to hold off selling to O'Ryan because he would raise the necessary Canadian money. To that end, the Vickers Syndicate was formed on January 19, 1929, with six shareholders: Richardson, Drury, Senator Donât Raymond, Frank Ross, Noah A. Timmins and the CPR. Richardson acted for the CPR, who preferred to remain anonymous in this venture. Why the secrecy was attempted is unknown, because soon the CPR's participation in the syndicate became public. The syndicate then began to negotiate with Canadian Transcontinental Airways. This company operated out of Quebec, and if the syndicate expected to acquire control of the area east of Montreal, it needed control of Transcontinental. O'Ryan obviously had the same idea, for he too was negotiating with Transcontinental, this time on behalf of American Airways. The race was on.

Whether Richardson and O'Ryan were aware of each other's presence is unknown. But it must have been a highly dramatic moment when Richardson, closeted with the men who controlled Canadian Transcontinental, was handed a crumpled note warning him that O'Ryan was upstairs in the same hotel and had just announced his intention of going $100,000 better than Richardson's offer for controlling interest. Absolutely adamant that Canadian aviation remain in Canadian hands and prepared to take heavy personal risks, Richardson took complete responsibility for the financing. The syndicate was successful and closed the deal with Transcontinental on June 19.

An operating committee, composed of Mulock, Ellwood Wilson of Fairchild Aviation and John Hunter, was in charge of the syndicate. Mulock was made managing director of Interprovincial Airways, the "old" Canadian Airways (the predecessor company) and Canadian Transcontinental. The companies continued to operate under their own names. On July 19, 1929, the syndicate formed the Aviation Corporation of Canada to act as a holding company for these recently acquired companies.

The idea of the Aviation Corporation likely came from Richardson; he had a stock interest in the Aviation Corporation of America, which had been incorporated on March 1. That corporation was one of four large holding companies formed in 1928–29 in the United States to exploit the willingness of the public to invest in anything to do with aviation. Richardson was offered two fully paid shares in the Aviation Corporation for each share he held in International Airways. He accepted and instructed John Hunter to represent his interests as one of the directors.

The Aviation Corporation of Canada now controlled all the companies that held air mail contracts in eastern Canada, the training schools of International Airways at Hamilton, Toronto, Montreal and Sherbrooke, and the main aerial survey company in Canada. General Airways, which had no air mail contract, was the only major company in the East not controlled by the corporation.

In the West, Western Canada Airways had been acquiring control of most of the principal companies there. It was on the verge of taking over "Wop" May's Commercial Airways, which had been operating in the Edmonton area. Western Canada Airways had already taken over, on May 1, 1928, Pacific Airways, of Vancouver, at Don MacLaren's request. When it appeared that matters were going to disintegrate again in the East, it made sense to pull Western Canada Airways and the Aviation Corporation together into one company, with Richardson at the head. He made his move.

As he explained in a letter to his friend James Playfair:

> I was dissatisfied with the way Aviation Corporation in the East was being conducted and there was a substantial amount of money owed to the Canadian Bank of Commerce in connection with the stock purchase of the Canadian Transcontinental Airways. I got busy on the picture myself, spent a lot of time on it and worked very hard to try and get the whole thing put in good shape and on a sound business basis. The set-up appealed to Sir Henry Thornton and to Mr. Beatty and they agreed on behalf of their respective railroads to subscribe $250,000 each to the company. All the other companies were sponged out and stock in the Canadian Airways issued.

With those pungent words, the new company was about to be born. But Richardson still needed the CNR to participate. On June 26,

1929, in a coded telegram to Richardson, Hunter wrote that Sir Henry Thornton had seen Drury the day before and "discussed the situation, agreeable to go 50–50 with Sir Edward Beatty ... Saw Sir Edward Beatty, told Drury." Thornton was well aware of Richardson and Beatty's close contact. In June he had complained to Mulock that he was being left out and that the CPR was doing business with Western Canada Airways. On July 17, Thornton wrote Richardson, "I would prefer to work with your company and the CPR, if it can be arranged." Replied Richardson on July 31, "I welcome the opportunity."

Both Richardson and Beatty wanted Thornton to join forces with them to prevent any "wasteful competition." Apparently they had difficulty in restraining him from setting up his own company. Richardson was adamant in his belief that Canada could not support two transcontinental aviation companies. "I told him [Thornton] that I thought it possible to maintain one good show from coast to coast, that our Air Mail contracts should enable us to function satisfactorily ... and while we would not be able to make any money in the strict sense of the word, we should be able to earn enough ... to replace old equipment with new ... [and] we would make a direct and valuable contribution to the railways and this appeared to be a matter in which the two railways might co-operate instead of compete."

Two men more different than Beatty and Thornton cannot be imagined. Beatty had nothing but admiration for the CNR's previous president, D.B. Hanna, who had had the nearly impossible job of welding together the sprawling miles of disconnected, badly planned, competitive railway systems that made up the CNR, but he had little use for Thornton. Needless to say, Beatty and Thornton clashed. They were opposites in personality and outlook. Thornton, appointed president in 1922, was a huge man and very sociable; Beatty was small and shy. Thornton was an expansionist and spent taxpayers' money easily, while Beatty was cautious and conservative in money matters.

Between 1926 and 1928 Beatty found himself competing with a man who spent public money lavishly. As the 1932 *Report of the Royal Commission on Railways* said, "Running through its [Canadian National's] administrative practices, however, has been the red thread of extravagance. The disciplinary check upon undue expenditure, inherent in private corporations because of their limited financial resources, has not been in evidence." Thornton would resign after the report. As it turned out, Thornton and Beatty worked in harmony with Richardson on the soon-to-be-born "new" Canadian Airways Limited.

Although discussions about the formation of the new company had begun late in 1929, the plans had been delayed by a number of factors. Beatty was in Europe, and Thornton could not commit until he had received approval from the governor general in council. There were also problems in settling on a board of directors that both Thornton and Beatty would approve. As a result, most of 1930 was spent untangling the confused bookwork and finances of the eastern companies, strengthening them and creating an effective board of directors.

The correspondence between Richardson and Beatty during this time shows how the two prominent Canadians mapped out the future of Canada's aviation development. In a candid letter to Beatty on February 10, 1930, Richardson revealed his goal. "It would be desirable to coordinate the whole of the aviation business right across the land, and if set up properly it seems to me it should be an unquestioned success. In the Western Canada Airways we have gathered together a remarkably fine personnel in the shape of pilots and mechanics and Brintnell has proved himself able as an Operations Manager." Beatty replied on April 17: "This company would take a moderate participation in the company or companies formed to make a strong airways corporation. Sir Henry Thornton ... stated that he would take a similar position and would explain the situation to Mr. Drury, who had approached him."

Correspondence next revolved around the board of directors. On May 24, Richardson wired Beatty the names of H. Robinson and T. Russell but said, "No one between Winnipeg and Vancouver unless Whitmore, might be useful." Beatty wired back the same day, "Excellent ... you should insist on being President." Two days later, Richardson wrote Beatty to say that he had seen Thornton and "he is agreeable to all names cabled you ... but insists Drury must be director and Vice President or he will not associate Canadian National ... Do you concur proceeding this basis?" Beatty replied the same day, "Would suggest ... that ... need not be added or Drury unless Thornton committed to latter ... Would also suggest for purpose of strengthening company with government with public that you suggest to Thornton names of Sir Charles Gordon and Sir Herbert Holt."

A day later, Beatty clarified his objection to Drury: "He would not add strength to organization in any way ... What are reasons given for his suggested inclusion ... In no circumstances could I accept him as Vice President or as an executive or as an administrative officer." Replying on the same day, Richardson wrote, "Drury claims representing Timmins/Raymond and himself or half of Eastern Syndicate ... and Thornton seems to regard Drury as his representative and friend. His demands were most emphatic. Wants to know if he can tell Drury and Thornton your objection." Beatty replied on the following day, "No objection. Tell Thornton, Drury to be only an ordinary director, not an officer." With relief, Richardson wrote Beatty on May 30, "Thornton said yes to Vice President with you. Drury to be an ordinary director." Beatty replied to Richardson the next day, "Quite agreeable."

It came to light later that Drury wanted to be president of the new company. In an undated letter to Richardson, tucked in the September 1929 correspondence file, Hunter wrote, "Drury tried for President but Ross and I stalled that." On July 10, Richardson formally wrote Beatty, thanking him for his help "in connection with amalgamation of East and West Airways."

In his letter to Blake Wilson of Burns & Company, Vancouver, on June 20, 1930, Richardson tried to persuade Wilson to become part of the board of directors.

> Both railways have decided to take part ... The Government at Ottawa feels very friendly to this development. They do not want to let air mail contracts out to a lot of different companies that do not fly their mail on time ... Moreover, it is realized that from the point of view of efficiency, economy and service it is good business to encourage the development of one strong company across Canada. Unofficially several members of the Cabinet have assured me of their desire to encourage the development of civil aviation and to give out more work than they have done in the past.

Interest in the "new" Canadian Airways Limited was not confined to Canada. Sir Eric Geddes, chairman of Britain's Imperial Airways, delicately inquired of Beatty on September 3 whether there would be a spot for Imperial Airways in the Canadian Airways setup. "The papers say CN and CP have taken an interest in Western Canada Airways and

I am wondering whether there is any possibility of co-operation to the mutual benefit of Canada and the British Empire, between Canadian Civil Aviation and Imperial Airways ... We are a child of the British Government ... we are in no sense Government controlled ... It seems a pity that my Company, Imperial Airways, which is attaining a unique position in the Empire, should be out of touch with your great Dominion."

Copying Richardson, Beatty responded to Geddes on October 13. He pointedly made no reference to any joint cooperation with Imperial Airways and simply stated that the two railways "will only have a moderate and very minority interest in the new company, and its policies will be controlled by a Board of Directors over which it is expected Mr. James Richardson will preside." Geddes took the hint and did not broach the subject again until two years later, when Canadian Airways' fortunes had changed.

The CNR finally received permission from the government in November 1930 to invest in Richardson's company. Canadian Airways Limited was incorporated on November 25, 1930. Although the name "Canadian Airways Limited" initially caused some confusion because the eastern company with that name was still operating, Richardson believed the name best represented the idea of the transcontinental system that he hoped to establish. It took over the assets of Western Canada Airways in the West and the Aviation Corporation in the East. Richardson held 72,677 shares of the initial total issue of 127,088 shares. Canadian Airways was originally capitalized at $3,177,200; this financial burden was mainly Richardson's. As Richardson reported later:

> It was thought desirable to have a Board for the Canadian Airways that would impress American interests with the fact that the Company was financially in an impregnable position. A number of Directors came on to our Board through the interests of the companies that were acquired. The others were largely the nominees of either Sir Edward Beatty or Sir Henry Thornton, as men who would be interested in helping Canadian aviation and would give the national company at this time the kind of front it was desirable for it to have.
>
> My thought was that all of these gentlemen would have become interested in the Company in a very substantial way but by the time

the new Canadian Airways were all set up, very few, who were not shareholders before, were disposed to make any substantial commitments. The result is that the burden of the Company still rests on the shoulders of those who have pioneered the enterprise.

James Richardson was appointed president, and Sir Edward Beatty of the CPR and Sir Henry Thornton of the CNR were appointed vice-presidents. Each railway invested $250,000 in the venture. The board of directors represented little or no financial interest; it was chosen primarily to establish an even balance of power between the CNR, the CPR and the private subscribers and to give the whole country representation on a geographical basis. Some of the men were chosen simply for their financial position, so as to "impress American interests." The list of directors *was* impressive; it included the leaders of Canada's top financial and business institutions. (See the Appendix.)

Canadian Airways' head office was located in Montreal. Richardson continued to live in Winnipeg and control affairs from there. Working out of the Montreal office were Mulock, appointed assistant to the president; Wilfred Sigerson, comptroller; and C.G. Drury (brother of Victor Drury), secretary treasurer. Richardson assumed the position of acting general manager. The repair shops remained in Winnipeg, because that city was seen as "the hub of all activity."

Canadian Airways was separated into two divisions, Canadian Airways Limited, Eastern Lines (the companies formerly owned by the Aviation Corporation) and Canadian Airways Limited, Western Lines (formerly Western Canada Airways). Western Canada Airways retained its name until November 1931. In August the Pacific Lines division was created, with boundaries south to the United States, east to Alberta, north to the Yukon and west to the Pacific Ocean. Each division had its own assistant general manager, comptroller, secretary treasurer, operating manager, maintenance manager, pilots and clerical staff.

Functionally, the company was divided into three sections: operations, finances, and accounts and control. The line of communications was upward through each one of these groups, and through the head of each to Richardson. Canadian Airways was set up to operate from coast to coast. Very quickly it began operating in every province, although East and West were not yet connected. Figuratively and literally, Canadian Airways was off to a flying start.

As he did with Western Canada Airways, Richardson ran his new company according to definite operating guidelines. Mulock sent out notices covering a variety of operational matters. Richardson emphasized safety as well as a reputable service. For example, pilots flying the mail to the Magdalen Islands could do so "only on days when weather conditions are perfect, and machines are to obtain a very high altitude before proceeding across the open sea ... Pilots are to take responsibility for accepting passengers and not to accept a passenger if he is intoxicated because he could be a hazard or be objectionable to other passengers."

Richardson wanted his people to be thoroughly conversant with all aspects of the service and to promote the company. "Superintendents for each district are to fly their district as pilot or passenger at least once a week and they must visit with Post Office officials on the cities on their route." Richardson was known as an employer who strived to provide good equipment and a good working environment. He established a technical library at head office for the general use of any employee "to encourage the desire for definite knowledge on aviation and aeronautics in general."

Canadian Airways had the support of the politicians and civil servants alike. Enthusiastic as he might be over the potential of aviation, Richardson was too wise to move into the national picture without the blessing of government. There was too much at stake. He first ensured that his actions were approved by the federal government. Politically untutored, Richardson never asked for a letter spelling out the details of the verbal understanding that Canadian Airways would become Canada's chosen instrument for national and international airways development. He assumed that written legal air mail contracts and a "gentleman's agreement" (the way he often conducted his business on behalf of James Richardson & Sons) were more than adequate. Unfortunately, he would later find that memories were short and selective. But that is another chapter.

The formation of Canadian Airways Limited marked the close of a distinct phase in the history of civil aviation in Canada. Until 1929, airways development had been confined almost entirely to northern areas and had been carried out by many small companies. Now one large company controlled almost all of the air transport business in Canada. Aviation had moved into the realm of big business, and James

Richardson represented the new type of leadership that the industry needed so badly to give it an air of respectability.

Previously, the government had viewed air transportation as supplementary to other methods; now it was seen as a legitimate mode of transport. Aviation had come of age. The CNR's $250,000 investment symbolized a change in the government's attitude. It was now prepared to support the development of commercial aviation in Canada. The CNR participation, airfield construction and the air mail contracts represented the start of a continuing program of assistance to Canadian Airways. The nucleus of the trans-Canada airway was now in place. Canada was making up for lost time.

Besides taking steps to institute a national company, the government initiated the flying-club movement in 1927 to deal with the shortage of pilots. It also encouraged municipal governments to provide airports. The idea was to have local communities build a chain of municipal airports across Canada for a scheduled airline service. The public embraced both projects. From the man on the street to local groups of businessmen, everyone got into the act. Even the stodgy Canadian Chamber of Commerce came up with catchy phrases, "Keeping Canadian Aviation Canadian" and "Acceleration of Travel Means Acceleration of Business," to help promote "the flying age." Spurred by the excitement of air travel, Halifax, Moncton, Toronto, Winnipeg, Regina, Edmonton and Vancouver, to name a few, began building airports and establishing flying clubs. By 1928 there was a chain of airports from coast to coast.

With Canadian Airways as its agent, the government began extending air mail services in late 1929. The most spectacular achievement, and one that attracted worldwide attention, was the Fort McMurray–Aklavik service, nearly three hundred miles beyond the Arctic Circle, inaugurated on December 10. The principal development, however, was the inauguration of the daily prairie air mail on March 3, 1930. By flying the mails overnight between Winnipeg and Calgary, a twenty-four hour saving in the transcontinental journey could be made. The Montreal–Toronto service was extended to Detroit via Hamilton, London and Windsor.

Next came an experimental service between Montreal, Saint John and Moncton. Arrangements were made with the U.S. air mail service to convey mail between Detroit and Pembina, North Dakota, so that there was a through connection by air between Moncton and Edmonton by the spring of 1930. There was twice-weekly service from Quebec to Seven Islands, a weekly service from Moncton to Charlottetown and, during the navigation season, a service from Ottawa through Montreal to Rimouski, connecting with the incoming and outgoing Atlantic mail steamers. In February 1931 a service between Winnipeg and Pembina was established, connecting Canada's postal services with American services to St. Paul and Chicago. Matters were moving swiftly, and everyone seemed happy.

Post Office official George Herring told Mulock that "the western mail was running practically 100% and [he was] more than pleased with the whole operation." Coolican wrote to Brintnell in June 1930, "From daily reports ... regarding the prairie air mail it would seem that you are rapidly approaching the 100% perfection mark." Government reports, which earlier had been dismissive, now boasted of air mail development. "Air mail service in Canada has already assumed a major importance in the life of the Canadian people," wrote the deputy postmaster general in August 1930.

Route expansion, however, brought problems for Richardson. Even before the formal amalgamation, he heard rumblings of monopoly or takeovers from some of the smaller companies. Typically, he did not take advantage. "I understood that Commercial Airways are anxious to sell out to us. I would be willing to deal with them fairly and take on any of their personnel," he instructed Mulock by telegram on December 15. Senator W.A. Griesbach, writing on behalf of Commercial Airways to Prime Minister Bennett on January 23, 1931, disagreed: "Commercial Airways, a small local company, is being shouldered out of the field by Canadian Airways, which is a large and wealthy company with headquarters in the East."

Bennett, unmoved by the letter and subtly refuting that Canadian Airways was an eastern company, replied on January 28: "The Winnipeg company is now conveying the mail to Calgary via Lethbridge ... In view of the fact that the President of the CNR is now a Vice President of the Company and the President of the CPR is a Vice President, I think you will agree that we are endeavouring to create a real service with great benefit to the country as a whole."

There was no indication that the government was concerned about the monopoly that Canadian Airways would enjoy. According to Gordon Lawson, former senior vice-president of James Richardson & Sons, both Mackenzie King and R.B. Bennett considered the presence of "high-powered people" on Canadian Airways' board of directors and the inclusion of the presidents of both railways to be sufficient to quell any accusations of monopoly. Bennett's reply to Commercial Airways supported Lawson's statement; it can also be viewed as a government stamp of approval for Richardson.

Competition from the Civil Government Air Operations, however, remained a problem. Despite the numerous letters Richardson wrote to ministers, deputy ministers and DND that Canadian Airways could fly officials more cheaply, General McNaughton would not withdraw his men from what Richardson considered commercial operations.

DND and the Post Office did support Richardson's efforts to make international connections. It could be argued that Richardson, with their approval, was already acting as Canada's chosen instrument. In early 1929, he requested permission to hook up with Northwest Airways of Minneapolis. Coolican replied that he would "be glad to see you to discuss this service." Concerned that Imperial Airways and Pan Am might make a deal, Richardson contacted Sir Eric Geddes. On December 1, 1930, John Wilson wrote Richardson to say "how regrettable it was that Imperial Airways was talking to Pan Am. I hope that Sir Eric Geddes keeps you advised. This matter has not come before this Department officially so far as I am aware but I think that you could count on our support in any movement towards better liaison with other Empire services."

At the Imperial Conference Civil Aviation Committee meeting, held in London on October 20, McNaughton had bragged that "a well-balanced largely self-supporting and varied program of air operations is in effect throughout Canada and the formation of a sound and economic development [was] laid recently. The close association of the existing transportation and financial institutions with aviation in Canada should bring to aviation a wide outlook and influence."

These international connections were vital to Canada. Coolican's December 13 report explained that the Winnipeg–Pembina service provided a direct connection between the Canadian and the United States,

Mexican, Central and South American air mail systems. It also kept out American competition, establishing "the principle that United States operators stopped at the Border and the balance of the flying was continued by Canadian operators," according to Coolican.

John Wilson became braver and started warning the government about becoming complacent. The first red flag was raised by Wilson in the report he wrote for the minister of national defence to present to the governor general. Although it was a year-end "good news" report for the new Conservative government to present to the public, Wilson took the opportunity to insert a message. There were two drafts on file; the first was dated December 18, 1930, and titled "Air Services," and the second was dated December 26 and titled "The Development of Airways and the Carriage of Mails by Air in Canada." Both were written by Wilson and signed by the minister of national defence, Donald Sutherland.

There was little difference in the two versions. Both were upbeat in tone and spoke glowingly of the advances Canada had made in developing its air services. Wilson concluded by recommending that authority be given to extend the air mail service (steamer) from Rimouski to the Strait of Belle Isle; to begin construction on the airfields between Montreal and Moncton and between Lethbridge and Vancouver; and to begin the survey of the route between Winnipeg and Montreal and Toronto.

Undoubtedly Wilson soft-pedalled the tone, since the report was going to the governor general. However, the message was there for anyone who cared to read. "The increased use of air mail throughout the world requires that the position of the Dominion in regards to the carriage of mail by air, both as an internal question and one affecting world communication, should receive consideration so that a policy may be developed which will ensure the Dominion full benefit of our geographic position."

There was no mistaking his second message: Canada held the key to the world's most important trading route and had better do something about it. "The North Atlantic Ocean is the most important of the world's trading routes, strategically, financially, industrially, socially and politically. The shortest line of communication between North America and both Europe and Asia lies within Canada or adjacent to our coasts. The question of trans-Atlantic flying is now being seriously considered ... This proposal [by the U.S. government] to divert trans-Atlantic traffic from its natural northern channel makes it urgently necessary that the Canadian route should receive attention with a view to its immediate development." Wilson added, "A fully developed airways leading from there [the Maritimes] to Montreal is an essential part of this development."

Wilson then discussed the importance of linking East and West. He acknowledged the value of Canadian Airways carrying the mail from Pembina but cautioned that though "this service will give direct communication by air with Montreal and Toronto [it will be] through a foreign channel and by a somewhat longer route than by passing direct through northern Ontario. Nationally and strategically the link through northern Ontario is of great importance but its immediate construction is not so urgent since the alternative route is now available." Unfortunately, this last phrase weakened his argument. The message that he needed to get through to the politicians and bureaucrats was the necessity of building an all-Canadian route *now*. Wilson also reminded officials that mail for the Orient used Canadian ports and steamships but that future air routes to Asia would be over Canadian territory. He concluded by recommending the extension, building and surveying of a number of airways.

At the very least, the final report would have been read by the prime minister and the minister and deputy minister of national defence before it was sent to the governor general. As events were to progress, it is difficult to understand how it could have been so blatantly disregarded. Perhaps Wilson was too subtle in his admonition to government that it still had no aviation policy and that this failure had serious national and international repercussions. The problem was that the report, while it raised a few red flags, also had a self-congratulatory tone. In essence, Wilson was saying that Canada was doing very well in airway development. The good public servant did not want to embarrass either the new government or long-time aviation officials.

Within four short years of *The City of Winnipeg*'s first flight, James Richardson had realized his dream. From a service into Canada's northland to open up and develop the natural resources, he had now put in place the infrastructure for a coast-to-coast air service. He had worked hard to balance the interests of the public and private transportation systems and had given the government direct access to Canadian Airways through the inclusion of CNR's president on his board. He had provided responsible financing, good management and safe aircraft to build an efficient and reliable service that would move Canada into the modern era of airway travel. Canadian Airways was unique in its development; no other national service in the western world operated without direct government funding. It relied solely on air mail contracts to give it financial stability. James Richardson and Canadian Airways were poised to develop one of the great airway systems of the world. Already Richardson's eyes had turned to the Atlantic, the Pacific and the overland route to Asia.

In a letter to New Brunswick Telegraph's Howie Robinson early in 1931 he wrote: "We have been looking a long way ahead. We enjoy geographically some very important advantages owing to our position in latitude. Canada will be on the future high-speed world trade routes. As Canadians it is small credit to us if we do not take advantage of what Nature has given us." Undoubtedly he had spun the globe in his library many times while planning his routes.

CHAPTER FOUR

The Air Mail Crashes

I T WAS ALL GOING SO WELL for Canadian Airways. Then, early in 1931, without warning and bit by bit, pieces of the air mail contracts were eliminated or the rates "adjusted." Rumour had it that the whole air mail service would be shut down. One of the most serious effects of the Great Depression was its check of Canada's progress in the air. The purse strings were pulled tight; a policy of economic retrenchment reigned.

The first hint that something was amiss occurred on February 17, 1931, when the government asked Canadian Airways to bid on the contracts it already held for Montreal–Rimouski, Quebec–Seven Islands, Seven Islands–Anticosti and Moncton–Magdalen Islands. Quite naturally, this outrageous request sparked a letter of indignation from R.H. Mulock to the Post Office. He also wrote the prime minister on March 30, delicately inquiring about the rumours going around. "Naturally the whole matter is of paramount importance to the aviation industry. Due to the ramifications of Aviation in the Domestic, Foreign and Empire situation, I believe that no reductions in any Air Estimates should be considered or made without a complete inquiry."

Then, without further beating around the bush, Mulock told the prime minister that the transcontinental air mail service would pay for itself within three years of being operational, reminded him that England had asked for cooperation from Canada in speeding up the mail via the Strait of Belle Isle, and warned that the United States was spending money to establish itself in Canada. "The United States realize that their air mail system must go through Canada for world connections, and there are already many indications that they are using every means in their power, openly and sub rosa, to force the issue and retain at the same time control of an inter-continental system." There is no record of a response from Bennett.

As the rumours flew, municipalities across Canada became concerned that their airfields would be deserted and their business communities left high and dry. Their letters to the prime minister were similar to Mulock's. On April 9, the secretary treasurer of St. James, Manitoba, reminded Bennett that St. James and other municipalities had built airports at the suggestion of the government. "The Town Planning Scheme of St. James has been centered upon the airport, and the future industrial development of St. James will depend very largely upon its continued operation ... The discontinuance of the air mail service from the Stevenson Field will seriously retard, if not entirely destroy, for years to come, the progress of aviation ... as far as this airport is concerned." He asked the government to reconsider its decision.

On April 14, the city clerk of North Battleford wrote Bennett with much the same message. "This city has incurred heavy capital expenditures for an Airport ... to accommodate air mail planes, which would be practically useless if the air mail were discontinued. The cities of the West have done and are doing their part towards the development of aviation and have been almost entirely influenced in this by the inauguration of the air mail service, but there is not yet nearly sufficient private and commercial flying in this province ... to justify the construction and maintenance of proper accommodation at the airports if the mail is discontinued."

A.W. Merriam, Bennett's private secretary, responded to these two letters on April 15 and April 20, respectively, with a perfunctory "Your letter will receive the consideration of the Government." In the Maritimes, on April 30, the Saint John city council passed a resolution protesting the cancellation of the air mail service to and from the Maritimes.

Meanwhile, Richardson was marshalling his arguments. On April 10, 1931, he sent a set of figures to the prime minister, showing the cost to Canadian Airways of retaining its organization and personnel in the event that mainline operations were discontinued. There were four points in particular of which Richardson wanted Bennett to be aware. First, the general popularity of the air mail service. Second, that the cancellation "militates sharply against the effort we have been making to build up a larger poundage with the idea of getting it more self-sustaining." Third, if the government would not support Canadian Airways, the company created to run the air mail, why had it asked B.C. Coastal Airways to submit a tender when it was not even in business? "I am at a loss to understand why the government in these times encourage a new company to start up, particularly when backed with American money. We have done everything possible to meet the wishes of the government and keep our organization together. We are not looking for dividends ... but want to keep our machinery oiled and greased and improve our service," said Richardson almost despairingly. His final point was a plea for government to cut back on its own air service. "The government will save much money by encouraging commercial operators rather than extending their own civil operations."

Questions were also being asked by members of Parliament. On April 14, C.R. McIntosh of North Battleford asked point-blank whether or not the government would continue the prairie air mail. McIntosh was told his question was not in order, that it was too close to a request for a declaration of policy by the government. On the following two days, he tried again, with no luck. On the third day he stated, "To be or not to be, that is the question," to which the postmaster general answered, "The question is under consideration." The government refused to be drawn into a debate. Government memoranda show that it still had no clear idea where it was going; ad hoc decisions were the order of the day.

Coolican also exerted pressure. On May 8, he wrote his political boss. Unfortunately, Coolican never had the larger picture in mind and offered only short-term solutions. He should have pointed out that the trend of intercity air mail finances showed that revenues would far outweigh the expenditures within a relatively short time and that overseas revenues would show a profit from the start. Instead he recommended that he be given permission to renegotiate some of the contracts at much lower figures—ignoring the fact that Canadian Airways, unlike the government air services, could not run indefinitely at a loss. Almost casually he advised that the reductions in the estimates meant that the Montreal to Saint John and Moncton, Toronto–Buffalo, Montreal–Ottawa and Bissett–Lac du Bonnet services would all be eliminated. How Coolican could be so obtuse about the ramifications of allowing the Montreal–Maritimes airway to be cancelled is hard to fathom.

Narrow-minded Coolican might have been, but shy he was not. Receiving no response to his letter, he ignored protocol, bypassed the postmaster general and wrote directly to the prime minister on May 29. Again he based his argument on eliminating services and reducing prices. His solution suited Bennett, who was desperately seeking ways to reduce expenditures, and his line of reasoning was accepted. On May 28, Coolican confirmed in a memo to the postmaster general that on the prime minister's instructions, he had entered into negotiations with Canadian Airways to continue the present services at reduced rates and the contracts would be let for a four-year period from June 1, 1931—although even that agreement was wiped out within the year. This was false economy. It was undoing the work of the previous two years and putting Canada back to where it was in 1928–29, with the Americans ready to pounce.

Richardson tried again. Unfortunately, his June 6 telegram to the prime minister was too mild. "I told Coolican a few weeks ago that Canadian Airways was most anxious to cooperate with the Post Office in any reasonable way in connection with readjustments that may now be thought necessary. I am sure you appreciate that our equipment and planes are based on our contracts." Richardson made a huge mistake, first in not stating that Canadian Airways' financial stability rested on the air mail contracts, and second, in not pointing out that the air mail would generate needed revenues for government coffers. Bennett saw the air mail only as an expenditure, a luxury the country could ill afford when he had to deal with homeless and hungry people. Clearly Richardson was operating under the assumption that the "readjustments" he was negotiating were simply temporary measures, and he was prepared to ride out the lost income.

Richardson refused to become excited despite the rumours from Parliament Hill that the signed contracts were to be thrown out. Even when Beatty became disturbed, Richardson remained confident. After all, Canadian Airways had fulfilled all the terms of the contracts; he knew the prime minister and considered him a trustworthy associate; and if the rumours were correct, the Richardson family were long-time supporters of the Conservative party. But the bottom line, as far as Richardson was concerned, was that he had four-year signed contracts and he never believed that the government would wriggle out of them.

The uncertainty about what was going to happen made it exceedingly difficult for Canadian Airways to plan properly. Coolican too argued for a decision on the fate of air mail. He wrote the postmaster general on June 9, and when he received no answer, he wrote again on June 15. This memo was short and to the point.

The following is the situation in regards to the air mail service:
1. Services discontinued June 1.

Toronto–Buffalo	Winnipeg–Calgary
Montreal–Moncton	Quebec–Seven Islands
Montreal–Detroit	Seven Islands–Anticosti
Moncton–Magdalen Islands	

2. Contracts cancelled as from July 15.

Winnipeg–Calgary–Edmonton	Montreal–Rimouski
Montreal–Albany	Winnipeg–Pembina
Montreal–Detroit	

3. Services on which no action taken.

McMurray–Aklavik	Amos–Siscoe
Sioux Lookout–Red Lake	Amos–Chibougamau
Peace River–North Vermilion	Leamington–Pelee Island

These services to remote and difficult areas, which are being left undisturbed, involved little or no additional cost over land and water services which would be slower, more uncertain and less satisfactory, especially during winter months.

On June 25, Mulock tried again. To the postmaster general he tactfully wrote, "The time is slipping by and if any changes are contemplated, we will require a certain amount of time to arrange for them ... Submit that this whole question be settled at as early a date as possible." There is no response on file. Now Coolican wrote again to the prime minister on July 3, once more reminding him of the value of the international connections and the competition from the Americans. The uncertainty continued. The effect on morale was taking its toll.

Stymied by the silence from Parliament Hill and in a desperate attempt to shut out potential competition, Richardson decided in June to double Canadian Airways' service between Vancouver and Victoria "because of threatened competition and as an emergency measure." As he explained to Beatty on July 14, Western Canada Airways had been providing a Victoria–Vancouver service with a Boeing flying boat, a five-passenger plane, once a day. He wanted to increase it to two round trips a day because he was concerned that the competition would start its own service. Beatty replied the same day, "No objection to increasing service if regarded as experimental, to be reviewed by railway companies if found necessary within 30 days. Thornton concurred."

Still the government dithered. Meanwhile, the American firms were watching and planning. Two Pan Am representatives visited Ottawa and informally discussed matters with DND and Post Office officials. No sooner had they returned to the United States than Juan Trippe of Pan Am made his move. He applied to open a line between Boston and Halifax, beginning August 1, 1931. He also requested the name of a company that DND thought suitable for cooperation with this project, since the Post Office felt that a Canadian company should carry the mail one way. Wilson told Trippe to contact Canadian Airways.

Trippe wasted no time. He immediately went to Montreal and phoned Mulock, who arranged for Trippe to meet with Beatty, Thornton and some other Canadian Airways directors on July 16. Trippe's proposition was simple. He wanted Canadian Airways to take the contract and sublet it to Pan Am. Mulock telephoned Richardson, who said he would only consider a 50–50 fully autonomous partnership: Canadian Airways on one side and Pan Am on the other. This was not satisfactory to Trippe, who proposed again that Canadian Airways take the contract and sublet it to Pan Am. Richardson, concerned with Trippe's persistence and the government's casual handling of its external affairs, directed Mulock to go directly to the prime minister and impress upon him the necessity of protecting Canada's interests. In a terse letter to the prime minister on July 20 (with Mulock signing on his behalf), Richardson pulled no punches.

> We believe that this is the narrow end of the wedge which may affect the air commerce of Canada and the Empire in the near future ... This whole movement should be analyzed by your government to protect the interests of Canada and the Empire. We would like to make the following suggestions–
>
> 1. That you, Sir, alone should approve of any air mail contracts of an international nature only after a thorough analysis to see what the final objectives of our American friends are.
>
> 2. That with the present operation of Pan American Airways being carried out on August 1, our country should have a clear understanding with the United States government that we will only allow this service to be carried on as an experiment, and that the whole situation be laid open for investigation before the operation will be allowed to be repeated next year, or continued permanently.

Mulock also prepared a very detailed memo on Pan Am and enclosed it with the letter. His memo clearly stated the danger of Canada's indecision.

> You will have noticed in the Press that Pan Am is starting an international air line between Boston and Halifax. It is with some concern that we note this peaceful penetration by American interests ... As the carriage of mail is the forerunner of trade and commerce we believe that the Canadian Government should not enter into any long term periods for the carriage of mail over Canadian territory by American companies and paid for by the American Post Office.
>
> This type of penetration we are referring to, would gradually put the United States in a paramount position as far as flying over Canada is concerned ... Pan Am is really a most effective tool of the United States Department of Commerce for the furtherance of American foreign trade ... Unless Canada watches her step we might discover that our American friends are gradually in a position that they will control the routes to Europe and Asia via Canada to the detriment of Canadian and British interests.

There is no reply on file.

To say that Richardson was disturbed over the government's laxness would be an understatement. The facts were plain to him. Canada was in danger of losing control of its own airway system as well as any international routes. To those he thought might have some influence, he would quite literally take them by the hand to his library and explain the international airway picture. "'Come, look at this,' he would say, and twirl the globe before him. 'Not so long and it will be "North to anywhere" and what does that mean?'" He was exasperated over what government officials would not or could not see.

Coincidentally, Wilson had written his deputy minister a few days earlier, on July 16. His letter was even more explicit than Mulock's. He painted a picture of a powerful Pan Am already operating all the airways in the Caribbean and with lines running down the east and west coasts of South America. "This corporation is the recognized instrument through which the United States Government develops its foreign air transport lines ... It should be clearly realized in considering the proposal of Pan American Airways that the stake at issue is the development of the world's greatest intercontinental airway."

Contrary to what General McNaughton would later say, Wilson admitted that Canada had not even discussed this development with the appropriate authorities. He wrote that Canada must either co-operate with American companies or allow them to fly into Canadian territory. A few years later, Lester Pearson of External Affairs would say that he was "thoroughly disillusioned with respect to External Affairs department. Our foreign policy is 'do nothing.'"

The matter did not end there. Upping the ante and adding to the urgency, Wilson also reported that the Americans were fully aware of the potential of another route over Canadian territory. This was the route north from Chicago to Sault Ste. Marie, James Bay, Hudson Strait, Baffin Island, Greenland, Iceland, the Faeroes and Scotland. The only part of Canada that Wilson saw as secure from American penetration was the West. "A fully equipped airway is in operation from the Canadian boundary at Pembina to Edmonton and a skeleton service then north via the Mackenzie Valley to the Arctic Coast. The Canadian portion of the airway connecting North America and northern Asia is, therefore, ready to accept traffic should the United States authorities ask for an Alaskan connection."

Ironically, before Wilson even finished typing his memo, he was forced to add a postscript: "Mr. Trippe telephoned from the office of Canadian Airways in Montreal, with whom he was conferring in regard to the operation of the proposed Boston–Saint John–Halifax service. This shows his desire to cooperate and meet our wishes in every way." This was stretching the truth. The government had no policy; how could Trippe cooperate? Wilson correctly concluded that the project was too important to be shelved and that if Canada could not do its share it would not be practicable to prevent others from undertaking this development. He suggested that a first step would be the approval of the *Policy Report to Council* of December 1930.

Wilson must have spent all of July writing memos because in less than a week, on July 27 and July 30, 1931, he sent off two more, again to the deputy minister. In the first memo, Wilson wasted no time with small talk on government's supposed achievements. For once he got right to the point: Pan Am had now requested permission to erect its own radio stations at the Halifax and Saint John airports for its proposed Boston–Halifax service. This would mean a considerable expenditure and was evidence of the importance that Pan Am attached to the route. Wilson was very concerned.

> The principle at stake is an important one, namely whether the Government is prepared to depart from the policy adopted heretofore of considering the provision of aids to air navigation a function of the Dominion Government. If this permission is granted it means that a precedent is created whereby an independent company and in this case, a foreign company, is permitted to establish, at considerable expense, aids to air navigation on what will undoubtedly be a very important Canadian airways of the future ... If this company is allowed to establish, not only their own air service but their own radio communication and weather service, for this is also implied in their request, it will mean that Canadian planes flying over this route would be at the mercy of a foreign company for these services ... It is recommended therefore that Pan Am be advised that the Department does not consider their request can be granted at present.

In his second memo, he stated that Pan Am had just received a ten-year contract for the Boston–Halifax service. "It is a matter of surprise," wrote Wilson, because both Juan Trippe and Mr. Winslow of Pan Am had assured DND that the service would be purely experimental. "Mr. Winslow was emphatic in his statement that the present service had no ulterior motives, that they did not contemplate an extension beyond Halifax and that their proposal was in no way connected with trans-Atlantic flying or an approach to it. It was purely experimental and future developments would depend on the experience gained this year."

The memo does not ring true. Wilson's previous memos all raise the warning bell that Pan Am was preparing itself for trans-Atlantic flight. Thus, to pretend that the contract was a surprise was false. Also it was highly unlikely that Trippe or Winslow would admit their true objectives. Would a fox at the henhouse door tell the hens what his real objective was? If Wilson really was taken in with Pan Am's assurances, then he was very naïve. Why would anyone in DND think that Pan Am, with tentacles already into South America and acknowledged as the United States' chosen instrument for international airways expansion, would not reach into Canada to be well placed for the world's most strategic airline route?

When the deputy minister of national defence, G.J. Desbarats, learned of the contract, he shot off a letter to O.D. Skelton, undersecretary of state for external affairs. He sang the same song as Wilson. How ludicrous that the deputy minister of national defence would believe that Pan Am only wanted to set up an experimental service and that the service had nothing to do with flying the Atlantic. Why else would Pan Am want an outlet in the Maritimes, if not for trans-Atlantic flight? Far more likely, the memo and letter writing by Wilson and Desbarats was simply a way to cover their backsides. If they could suggest that Pan Am had not been telling the truth, then no one could blame them when the Canadian airways system fell into American hands.

A year later, Desbarats wrote to Skelton about Pan Am's exploration and development work on the Arctic route. He remarked that it certainly showed the determination of the Americans to find a solution to flying across the Atlantic one way or another. Desbarats confessed that Canada's position regarding the direct route was weak and that it would be fairly simple for foreign interests to develop this route without consulting Canada, provided that Newfoundland and the Irish Free State were agreeable. Desbarats was very aware of Pan Am's motives.

Mulock was also concerned about this issue and had written to the prime minister on July 9, 1932, suggesting that Canadian Airways run a small triangular service between Saint John, Moncton and Halifax because the traffic on Imperial Airways was steadily increasing and that with the added activity of Pan Am, Canada's position was in jeopardy. Mulock warned the prime minister that Pan Am intended to fly across the Maritimes to Newfoundland to meet Canadian steamers and Imperial Airways once they began flying the North Atlantic route. Not only did Pan Am's Boston–Halifax service checkmate the Canadian Belle Isle airship operation, but it was possible that Pan Am might secure rights on the Boston–Newfoundland route. Mulock believed that the triangular service would block Pan Am and put Canada in a position where it would hold the key for flying between Europe and North America.

Mulock, who seemed to be the fly on the wall at many meetings, later reported that the prime minister strode up and down his office and vowed, "The Americans can fly on their side of the Line but we are capable of doing all the flying in or over Canada." Mulock also stated that Skelton "was told off, from that day, as watch dog for the Premier on matters of this description."

Temporarily blocked, Trippe wrote Richardson on July 30, 1931, suggesting cooperation between the two companies. Richardson played it close to his chest and said nothing, forcing Trippe to come to him again. Trippe telegraphed Richardson a month later, and Richardson responded laconically that he would likely be in New York in the fall and they could "have a visit" then. Undoubtedly Trippe's impatience was whetted because he knew that his rival, E.G. Thompson, president of Trans-American Air Lines, had also beaten a path north to Canada and had talked with Mulock and Wilson. In August Mulock advised Bennett of a talk he had "with one of our American friends." Mulock was referring to his meeting on August 19, in Ottawa, with E.G. Thompson. The topic: possible cooperation in developing international routes and the possible creation of an international company. If the government was doing nothing about protecting Canadian air routes, Richardson was doing his best to stay one step ahead of the Americans. With two strong American companies eagerly panting at the door, the fat was in the fire.

Still the prime minister made no move. Nothing seemed to make an impression on him. Revenue and expenditures were all he was interested in. Was he not air-minded enough to comprehend the significance of Canada losing control of its domestic and international air routes? Why are there no memos from McNaughton to the prime minister on file? McNaughton, as chief of the general staff, had the prime minister's ear and could have made a powerful case.

That Richardson was sincere in his statement that Canadian aviation must remain in Canadian hands was evident when he refused to play with either Pan Am or Trans-American. Both airlines were offering "real" money, and either would have given Richardson the financial security he needed. According to an Ottawa insider, at a time when civil aviation had been assigned "to the soporific care of the military power, Jim Richardson represented, in himself, the only nationally unifying force in air planning in the country." Richardson later reported to one of his directors on the sequence of events during those months. He wrote with his usual simple directness.

> We discussed our problem with the government on the broadest possible lines and stated that we wanted no consideration that was not good business for the Dominion of Canada ... The Pan-American is not going to give any consideration to the interests of Canadian Airways ... We are going to try to look after those interests ourselves and while we must always be willing to work together on any reasonable basis, where international matters are concerned we should be very jealous of any business that nationally belongs to us because should we approach them with a suggestion that we participate in any business that nationally belonged to the United States I think they would be suspicious that we had gone somewhat mental and ring for an alienist.

Meanwhile, the fate of the Canadian air mail was still in limbo. Indecision continued to mark the government's response. On August 15, 1931, George Herring wrote Canadian Airways, advising that flights to Regina, Moose Jaw, Saskatoon and Edmonton would cease that day. On August 18, Coolican sent a copy of Herring's letter with the comment that "authority has been given for the continuation of the service between Winnipeg and Calgary and its extension from Calgary to

Edmonton from August 16. Service between Regina, Moose Jaw, Saskatoon, North Battleford and Edmonton to be discontinued August 16."

Richardson wrote Bennett again on November 26. Unfortunately, he used the wrong approach, telling Bennett that Canadian Airways had just taken delivery "of a giant air freighter, the largest single-engine aircraft in the world." This was the big Junkers JU-52, CF-ARM, "the flying boxcar." Richardson proudly wrote, "There is nothing similar to this plane on this continent and there are only a very few of these in the world. Our maintenance man has been in Germany the last two months watching the construction of this ship and consulting in connection with special attachments that we require for our work in the Far North."

That Canada had the world's largest single-engine aircraft was of no interest to Bennett. As a member of Parliament observed, "It just got me down here. Jim Richardson always reminded me of that line in the story book, a great, clean beast who'd wandered into a swamp and got netted. He just couldn't believe what his senses told him and, instead of making some kind of a deal with experienced lobbyists to gnaw the cords, he just kept on crashing and fighting in the direct way of the frontier."

That same day Richardson wrote to Sir George Perley, the acting prime minister. He used the same approach, explaining how Canadian Airways was serving Canada. "Even in these days of depression and trouble Canadian Airways believes that one of Canada's greatest assets lies in her wonderful natural resources. The country north of steel is full of possibilities. Fast and cheap transport is holding up this development ... Canadian Airways has now purchased one of the largest freighting aircraft in the world." He concluded by saying he would be stopping in Ottawa and hoped to see Perley and the prime minister. Like his letter to Bennett, this one showed Richardson's earnest distress, his honest faith that no one who knew the good things that Canadian Airways had done and was capable of doing would deliberately undermine the company. He, who had so much pride in Canadian Airways and in being Canadian, could not understand how others could not see the situation as he did.

Why did Richardson not seek advice and do some strategic planning? Where was Sir Edward Beatty, whom his biographer said was a friend of Bennett's? Why did he not exert pressure on Bennett? Where was General McNaughton, who wanted a "chosen instrument" and should have been concerned from a military point of view about Canada losing control of its airways? Why did the government begin dismantling the new air mail system when all government memoranda warned of the dire consequences of doing so?

On November 27, 1931, Wilson wrote another memo, "Airways Development, Maritime Provinces–Montreal." The eight-page memo was a strong one. Wilson began by recommending that the air service between Montreal and the Maritimes be re-established immediately because it speeded up mail delivery and, even more importantly, it was the western terminal for "the world's most important airway." He warned that other countries were eyeing Canada's Atlantic coast and that Canada should waste no more time and begin developing a policy for both domestic and trans-Atlantic flying. Typically, Wilson tried to deflect the blame from the government by saying that if officials had realized the consequences of cancelling the Montreal–Moncton air mail service, they would have given it more thought.

Wilson then wrote that government officials did not know that the United States was interested in the development of the northern route at that time. This was not altogether true. Yes, Canada did not know *when* the United States would look to the northern route, but all DND and Post Office correspondence since the late 1920s emphasized the importance of the route and stressed that it was only a matter of time before Pan Am would make its move. The Montreal–Maritimes airway had been developed to begin the Canadian connection. Wilson was making excuses.

Although the decision on the air mail was left hanging, Richardson was powerless to stop the march of events. It must have been an unbelievably tense time for him. Finally the axe fell. On February 17, 1932, Coolican sent a registered letter to Canadian Airways stating that the air mail between Winnipeg, Calgary and Edmonton would be cancelled on April 1 because "of a material reduction in the appropriations for air mail services for the year 1932–1933." The next day, Wilfred Sigerson, Canadian Airways' comptroller, telegrammed assistant general manager Tommy Thompson to say that the radio beacons on the Prairies were to be discontinued on March 1 and the lights would be shut off on March

31. "As far as Ottawa is concerned, when we are out of sight we are out of mind ... This looks very much like washing out the prairie mail is definitely decided" was his gloomy conclusion. The prairie air mail had crashed.

Bennett was not a newcomer to politics or unfamiliar with the political ramifications of the air mail. He had been elected leader of the Conservatives in 1926, and as leader of the Opposition he was not coming in as a political neophyte when he formed the government in 1930. Thus, he should have grasped the essentials of the December 1930 report: first, that Canada had to take steps quickly, so as not to be swept completely into the American airline orbit; and second, that the development of national and international airway routes offered the promise, or at the very least the hope, of dramatic future growth and a way out of the despair of the depression. In other words, the future for

The cancellation of the prairie air mail evoked this response in the *Winnipeg Free Press*. (*Winnipeg Free Press*, March 9, 1932, Arch Dale)

air mail was very promising in December 1930; all indications showed that it would have provided financial relief for the government. Yet the reductions and cancellations began in 1931.

DND and the Post Office's rationale for cancelling the prairie air mail and the eastern intercity services was that they "served only local needs." Thus while Canadian Airways' mail contracts were slashed, Canadian Colonial Airways, an American company, flew happily through the government's estimates with barely a penny cut. The government's explanation was the observance of international good faith: the two international services were left intact because DND was afraid that the Americans would move in if Canada withdrew. In view of this statement and all the memoranda Wilson had written in the previous four years about the dangers of American penetration, it is difficult to understand how McNaughton and Coolican could have overlooked the consequences of cancelling the Montreal–Moncton and intercity services in the Maritimes. For no sooner had the Maritimes service been cancelled than Pan Am stepped in with a request to extend its New York–Boston service to Saint John and Halifax, with the option of extending it to Sydney and St. John's, Newfoundland. Pan Am was given a contract allowing it to operate a two-month summer service beginning in 1931.

By allowing Pan Am to participate in Canadian domestic traffic, the Canadian government was violating the principle that only Canadian registered aircraft could carry on a commercial business in Canada and setting a precedent for the operation of similar services elsewhere. And Pan Am, having been granted one concession, now asked for more. Canadian Colonial Airways, then operating the New York–Quebec route, also requested an extension from Quebec to Ottawa, and North West Airways wanted to move into Winnipeg and Vancouver.

Why did Bennett not wait for the report of the 1932 Royal Commission on Transportation and take direction from its recommendations? As it turned out, the commission recommended that the government support the development of a national company, that the company be formed in cooperation with the railways and that government assistance be in the form of five-year air mail contracts. The commission also suggested that Canada take immediate steps to safeguard its position in trans-oceanic flying. Why did Bennett not wait to see the results of the upcoming Imperial Economic Conference, which he was hosting in

Ottawa that July? He must have known that trans-Atlantic flying would be on the agenda. Sure enough, a Trans-Atlantic Committee was appointed and recommended that Canada, the United Kingdom, the Irish Free State and Newfoundland "actively encourage" the development of the direct route. DND obviously still looked upon Canadian Airways as its unofficial chosen instrument, because McNaughton requested a Canadian Airways representative to sit in on some of the Trans-Atlantic Committee's discussions. Both these reports confirmed what Wilson had been saying for years. Did any of Wilson's memos reach the prime minister's desk?

In truth, as far as trans-Atlantic flying went, the Bennett government had undermined its own bargaining powers when it withdrew its financial support from Canadian Airways. Canadian Airways, with no assurance of steady support from the government, had withdrawn from the Maritimes and was in no position to discuss future developments with Imperial Airways. Acutely aware of Canada's vulnerability, Wilson again recommended that the government inaugurate air services in the Maritimes and a ship-to-shore service. The government did nothing.

It is hard to understand why Bennett, who needed new sources of revenue, did not capitalize on the potential moneymaker of the air mail, unless the case was never properly presented to him. Who was to blame for this? McNaughton's memos show that he was concerned, for nationalistic reasons, about Canada's lack of airways, but they also show his overriding desire to keep the air force flying. The prime minister seems to have received mixed messages. It appeared that McNaughton, like Coolican, allowed his personal agenda to jeopardize the larger picture.

Bennett undoubtedly saw the air mail program as an expensive novelty rather than as part of an overall plan to develop a trans-Canada service. It is highly probable that if McNaughton and Coolican together had argued the case for air mail more cogently, Bennett would have rescinded the order to cancel. Since it was McNaughton, Wilson and Coolican (under Mackenzie King's government) who had supported and encouraged the creation of Canadian Airways, they should have made it clear to Bennett that, by cancelling the air mail contracts, he was wiping out the nucleus of the incipient trans-Canada airways system. The Post Office should have pointed out that the trend in air mail revenues showed that within a reasonably short time the air mail would not only be paying for itself but making a profit. In fact, the Post Office's figures for the last six months of service showed air mail revenues were already 58 percent of the expenditures and rising.

Did Bennett listen to anyone? Historian Blair Neatby observed that "Bennett could be an arrogant bully. His cabinet ministers were rarely consulted on major policies and their opinions carried little weight. One of the stories going the rounds in the 1930s was of the tourist who saw R.B. Bennett walking alone towards Parliament Hill from his suite in the Chateau Laurier, talking to himself. He asked a bystander who it was and got the reply that it was the Prime Minister holding a cabinet meeting. Bennett dominated his government and his party while in office, and when the party was shattered and defeated he was loaded with all the blame." This is a partial explanation.

What was Bennett's alternative? He had come to power at the beginning of Canada's worst economic crisis. The whole of his tenure as prime minister was overshadowed by the Great Depression. Historian Michael Bliss noted that every area of Canada was hit: "By the summer of 1931 Canada was staggering under the double burden of a mounting trade deficit and huge foreign debts. The price of grain had fallen below all levels known to modern times. The wheat pools were hopelessly over-extended and were being carried by the banks ... 1932 and 1933 were the worst years of the Great Depression." Perhaps the talk of international airway control was too esoteric for a prime minister who soon would have three thousand unemployed workers on Parliament's doorstep and "Bennett buggies" appearing across the Prairies. Would Bennett's actions have been so unreasonable if he had been properly briefed?

In 1930, no one could have forecast the intensity of the economic disaster that would befall Canada. Very quickly after he was elected, Bennett provided $20 million for relief. This was a radical step, because until then municipal or provincial governments accepted unemployment responsibilities. The assumption in 1930 was that the economic recession was temporary and emergency measures were sufficient for the short term. But the recession got worse and was compounded by drought. In towns, men found themselves out of work and by mid-1931 half a million had no jobs. The numbers grew, hitting a low point in 1933, when three-quarters of a million were unemployed.

Responsible men, Conservatives and Liberals alike, believed in balanced budgets. Bennett attacked the depression along traditional lines: a reduction of public expenditures and retrenchment all along the line. However, if McNaughton, Wilson and Coolican had worked together, they could have produced figures showing that the air mail, both domestic and international, would provide money within a relatively short time. Money coming in, not going out, was the argument that Bennett needed to hear. Unfortunately, McNaughton, Wilson and Coolican all had different agendas, and Bennett never heard a convincing argument until the system had collapsed.

General McNaughton must bear the largest proportion of blame. He was one of Bennett's chief advisers. So too must "the Ottawa men, the civil service mandarins." J.L. Granatstein noted that in the 1920s and 1930s, "Canadian public servants dealt almost entirely with events from an Ottawa context. The capital was the centre of their existence." Not for many decades did politicians become uneasy about the influence of these men or the close links between the Liberal party and the senior bureaucracy, who were not answerable to anyone.

James Richardson must also bear some of the blame. He never harnessed his board of directors to lobby the government. With this powerful board, he could have applied the necessary pressure. He did not present Canadian Airways' case in strong enough terms. Nor did he make clear to Bennett that Canadian Airways' financial security rested on the air mail contracts. This was Richardson's strongest argument, for Bennett was to say later that he did not realize this and thought that, with Canadian Airways' powerful board of directors, Richardson had unlimited funds behind him. The more important issue, however, is why Richardson allowed the government to get away with cancelling the contract.

With two years still remaining in its contract with Canadian Airways, how had the government escaped its legal obligations? The contract between Western Canada Airways and the Post Office contained a clause that allowed the postmaster general to annul the agreement on thirty days' written notice if, in his opinion, the public interest required it. Richardson was aware of this because he had taken the precaution of having a law firm examine the contract. The firm had commented on "the very exceptional powers that the government reserved for itself" of

"Man of the North." James A. Richardson, president of James Richardson & Sons, Limited, 1919–39. A photograph taken around 1925. *Inset, top:* Canadian Airways Limited Canada goose logo. *Inset, bottom:* Western Canada Airways Canada goose logo. THE ARCHIVES OF JAMES RICHARDSON & SONS, LIMITED

Above: Al Cheesman, Rod Ross, Bernt Balchen and Fred Stevenson made history, flying Canada's first major airlift in the winter. This photo was taken in Hudson, Ontario, in 1927. CANADIAN AIRWAYS COLLECTION, PROVINCIAL ARCHIVES OF MANITOBA #411-1

Facing page, top left: John A. Wilson, controller of civil aviation, Department of National Defence. NATIONAL ARCHIVES OF CANADA PL 117438

Facing page, top right: General Andrew McNaughton, chief of the general staff, Department of National Defence, was a factor in Canadian Airways' fate. CANADIAN FORCES PHOTOGRAPH ZK274

Facing page, bottom: Competing railway presidents worked in harmony as Canadian Airways' two vice-presidents: Sir Edward Beatty, president of the Canadian Pacific Railway, and Sir Henry Thornton, president of Canadian National Railways, in 1923. Note how the photographer has placed Thornton one step down from the shorter Beatty, to give the impression that both were equal in all ways. CITY OF TORONTO ARCHIVES

Above, left: Leigh Brintnell *(right)* with de Havilland 61 Giant Moth, G-CAJT, in 1928. Brintnell was Western Canada Airways' second general manager. He left to form rival Mackenzie Air Services. CANADIAN AIRWAYS COLLECTION, PROVINCIAL ARCHIVES OF MANITOBA #128

Above, right: Pilot Punch Dickins, who joined Western Canada Airways in January 1928, was one of the best-known pilots in Canada and one of Richardson's top men. He was loaned to the CPR during World War II to assist the trans-Atlantic ferry service. Upon its formation, Canadian Pacific Airlines appointed Dickins its first general manager and vice-president in 1942. This photo was taken in 1933. THE ARCHIVES OF JAMES RICHARDSON & SONS, LIMITED

Facing page, bottom: Pilot George A. (Tommy) Thompson with Avro Avian G-CANQ, at Cranberry Portage, Manitoba. Thompson joined Western Canada Airways in February 1928. He was a superb administrator and manager, and Richardson appointed him general manager after Leigh Brintnell left. THE ARCHIVES OF JAMES RICHARDSON & SONS, LIMITED

Above: Western Canada Airways'
Boeing B-1D with a prospecting group
at Vernon Lake, Vancouver Island, in
1929. Western Canada Airways used the
flying boats mainly for fishery patrol,
although they were also used for the
Vancouver– Victoria–Seattle run. They
cruised at 95 mph. CANADIAN AIRWAYS
COLLECTION, PROVINCIAL ARCHIVES
OF MANITOBA #82

Facing page, top: The Fokker Super Universal G-CASP, transporting goods to
remote communities in Manitoba and
northwestern Ontario. This photo was
taken in Cold Lake, Manitoba, in 1929.
THE ARCHIVES OF JAMES RICHARD-
SON & SONS, LIMITED

Facing page, bottom: Pilot Fred
Stevenson accepts the first batch of
newspapers, the *Winnipeg Tribune,* for
delivery to Red Lake in June 1927. This
was the first time that the mining area
would receive up-to-date news. The
Fokker Universal, G-CAGE, *Fort
Churchill,* now on floats, is the aircraft
in which Stevenson lost his life in
January 1928 at The Pas. Winnipeg's
municipal airport was named Stevenson
Field in his honour. THE ARCHIVES OF
JAMES RICHARDSON & SONS, LIMITED

"The spirit of adventure." James A. Richardson, president of James Richardson & Sons, Limited, 1919–39. A photograph taken around 1925. THE ARCHIVES OF JAMES RICHARDSON & SONS, LIMITED

imposing fines or of terminating the contract before the contractual period was up. There is nothing on file recording Richardson's thoughts about the clause, but evidently he either believed that the government would never resort to such a measure or thought that the risk was worth taking, for he had signed the contract.

Although he firmly believed that the government had a moral and legal responsibility to honour the contract, Richardson felt that Canadian Airways' position would be better served by not making a public issue of the cancellation or forcing the issue with the prime minister. According to Gordon Lawson of James Richardson & Sons, Richardson did not want to embarrass Bennett. He was dead wrong in accepting the prime minister's decision and unwisely waited two years before reconsidering the matter.

Richardson should also have challenged the legality of the government breaking its contract. As later correspondence showed, he had a strong case. He could have made it uncomfortable for Bennett if he had pointed out to the public that the government had broken Canadian Airways' contracts but not the international contracts and that these were maintained, at a much higher rate, at the expense of the domestic routes. Richardson was too much the gentleman. A 1927 *Financial Post* article, subtitled "Great Grain Man of West Known for Good Sportsmanship on Field of Play and in Arena of Business," described Richardson's character aptly. "At Queen's University, the boys used to say of him that in addition to playing a good game, he played a 'square' game ... While he is now accounted one of Canada's rich men, he has earned his wealth shrewdly but not at the expense of his fellows ... He plays the game squarely." Perhaps Richardson should have played politically.

The year 1932 was a dismal one for Richardson. The business decline was progressive, and its effect was cumulative. The intercity air mail structure had all but collapsed, and the government seemed unconcerned. With the financial basis of his organization gone, Richardson had to decide whether to carry on or shut down. It was a difficult decision. In no other country in the world had air transport been able to carry on without subsidy. Richardson realized he would face heavy losses and perhaps bankruptcy if the government did not come to his aid. But it was very rare for Richardson to give up; he had a great sense of commitment and personal responsibility. More importantly, he did not see the airline as a speculative project. He decided to keep Canadian Airways flying.

In his annual report to the shareholders in 1932, Richardson stated that he felt an obligation to carry on the bush services. He believed that air transport in the North was of vital importance to the continued development of the country; without it, progress would be delayed by many years. It was later said that there was no single factor more important in bringing Canada through the depression than its mining industry, which could not have had its phenomenal development without air transport. Although this acknowledgement pleased Richardson, it did not alleviate the fact that he personally lost over $3 million by keeping his company flying during the "dirty thirties."

Philanthropy aside, Richardson quite naturally wished to protect his investments and maintain his leading position. When the government reinstated the air mail, Richardson wanted to be first in line, with an organization administratively and technically capable of giving the service. However, the strongest inducement was that he truly believed the government would recognize its moral responsibility to Canadian Airways, either by reinstating the contracts or by compensating the airline for its lost revenue. Richardson trusted his "gentleman's agreement."

Unfortunately, the cancellation of the contracts had left the company with equipment and other liabilities that it could not legally get rid of. Canadian Airways had been formed to provide a transcontinental operation; in order to carry out its obligations and on the strength of its four-year air mail contracts, it had incurred heavy capital expenditures. Canadian Airways had bought special mail planes and radio equipment, leased or bought airfields, built hangars and rented office space, with the leases running concurrently with the air mail contracts. Not only did Canadian Airways need the full four years to write off its equipment, but also a large part of this capital outlay was unproductive and entailed expenditures for mortgage reductions, taxes, maintenance, repairs and general carrying charges.

Richardson explained his dilemma in a letter to S.L. Campbell, assistant manager of the Bank of Commerce in Montreal, on September 16, 1933. "Canadian Airways has been steadily losing its cash position and this has not been due to any miscalculation or errors in its policy, but the fact that the government stopped its main source of revenue ... The future of the Company depends upon some recognition by the Federal Government, both of its contractual obligations to the company and the national character of its business, and discussions on this matter are taking place again this Fall ... There is not much likelihood of a market for Canadian Airways stock for some time to come." Campbell's reply was hardly encouraging. "It seems clear that if this rate of retrogression keeps up, it is a matter of only a very short time until the entire working capital of the Company will disappear."

Burdened with excessive overhead charges, surplus operating personnel and the maintenance of inactive aircraft, Canadian Airways had to find ways of cutting costs. The first step was to reduce personnel. For Richardson, this was a heartbreaking process and he agonized over these decisions. "I was forced to release more than a score of faithful employees," he later wrote.

More than sixty years later, "Punch" Dickins recalled how Richardson called a meeting of some of the senior people in his office. "Mr. Richardson told us that the situation was critical as there would be little money available for prospecting or developing and that we were to economize in every way we could. He asked us if we would take a 10% reduction in our base pay and no one objected. He said we would have to cut down on staff but we must keep married men, especially those with families and those who had 'proven their worth' (to use his words) and if we all worked together, we would survive the depression. Well, we did."

Another long-time Canadian Airways employee, Don Whellams, spoke movingly about how hard Richardson tried to keep the company intact. Nevertheless, Richardson was forced to cut; positions were combined, and all expenditures not considered essential were deferred. At the end of 1932, total wage and salary payments were 26 percent less than in 1931, and total operating expenses were down 22.8 percent. Despite these economies, the operating expense per productive mile increased by 13.1 percent.

Meanwhile, Mulock met briefly with the prime minister and followed up the meeting with a letter the next day, on March 31, and another on April 2, 1932. In his March letter he stated that there were more than $3 million invested in Canadian Airways and one-quarter million dollars each by the CNR and CPR. He then placed blame for the company's predicament on the government. "In good faith we purchased air mail equipment, kept on employees as requested by the government last August. We have built up a nation wide organization in the belief that when the Government requested operations we were justified in spending the investors' money ... We recently re-equipped the Toronto–Detroit Division with very fast mail planes, which are of no use for other purposes, and having always operated this route and having purchased the special equipment necessary, this line should be operated by our Company." Wilson confirmed that the Post Office had insisted that Canadian Airways purchase three special air mail planes.

In his April letter, while acknowledging that the RCAF could initially operate at less cost, Mulock pointed out that the figures government was using presented an inaccurate picture of costs because they did not include wages, which were charged to the RCAF, or take into consideration the depreciation or insurance of aircraft; these were picked up by another government department. Mulock next moved to "good faith" issues. He pointed out the huge sums invested by the private sector in capital structures at the government's request. Aircraft and engine manufacturers alone had invested $4.7 million; municipalities across the country had spent $4.3 million in building airports, and Richardson himself had sunk $3.2 million into Canadian Airways. "If aviation is to go to the wall in Canada the aircraft and engine manufacturers will have to shut down, and if Canadian Airways are forced into the corner it is doubtful if private capital will ever take an interest in operations again," he wrote to the prime minister.

Mulock then reminded the prime minister that many people would be thrown out of work. The aircraft industry employed some two hundred people, and Canadian Airways, as of February 1932, employed 193, already some seventy men less since the cutting of the air mail contracts. Did the prime minister wish to see even more skilled personnel on the bread lines? Mulock also warned that if the municipalities were forced to close their airports, the RCAF would be unable to move either east or west of its main station at Camp Borden. "Considering that the Air Force, from a defence point of view, should be the most mobile unit, it is very interesting to those of us in Commercial life, that without any cost to the Government we have built up an Airways on which alone the Air Defence of Canada can move."

The bottom line was that Canadian Airways had been born in troubled times. The market crash of 1929 resulted, in the next year, in a 50 percent reduction for all classes of air traffic, freight, express and mail. Western Canada Airways' excellent financial position carried the newly organized Canadian Airways into 1931 with a healthy working capital of $881,112 and $426,790 cash in hand. The main factor in offsetting the reduced traffic was the revenue from the air mail contracts. But when the government began cutting Canadian Airways' contracts in February 1931, in an effort to lower government expenditures, it spelled the beginning of the end for Canadian Airways.

In response to the initial cuts, Canadian Airways pursued an aggressive policy of extending the company's lines and expanding its survey and photographic work, so despite the reduced air mail revenues and the purchase of a $78,000 aircraft (the flying boxcar), it had a working capital of more than $1 million at the end of 1931. However, by March 1932, the government had cancelled four-fifths of Canadian Airways' intercity air mail contracts, more than three million revenue miles, which if flown would have grossed Canadian Airways $2.5 million. Total air mail revenues declined 74 percent from 1931 to 1932, making any net profit from air mail impossible. Canadian Airways' air mail contracts were now limited to casual runs and a few daily short scheduled runs.

The immediate outlook for the company was uncertain. The cancellations disastrously affected its financial basis and its monopoly of air mail contracts. Although James Richardson was forced to retreat, he rallied his people. He believed in his Canadian Airways so deeply that he was convinced it was only a matter of time before he would be flying the continental route again.

CHAPTER FIVE

Growing Pains:
The Developing Air Transport Industry

THE YEARS 1930 TO 1942 were critical for Canadian Airways and the air transport industry in general. The reduction of government expenditures for civil aviation placed the company in a precarious financial position, and throughout the 1930s it struggled to maintain itself. An influx of newcomers often disregarded safe flying practices and indiscriminately quoted low rates, bringing the whole rate structure down. Cutthroat competition became the order of the day, and the Post Office in particular took advantage of the situation to force down the rates even more. Competition from the government also continued. By 1939, the industry was on the verge of bankruptcy. The individual companies finally came to realize that they must cooperate in some fashion, and the government came to the reluctant conclusion that it must provide controls for the industry. This period was an important one; the cumulative events of the time resulted in a government-owned airline, the first positive legislation dealing with some of the industry's problems and the formation of what would become Canada's second major airline.

All evolving industries experience growing pains. However, many of the aviation industry's problems could have been alleviated if the

government had established a policy in the early 1920s, when it established the Department of National Defence. Shoving commercial aviation under the strong arm of the military, which had its own agenda,
harmed Canada's air industry. Its problems ran the gamut, from the
nuts-and-bolts problems of a new industry, to the lack of rules and regulations monitoring the number of companies flying in a particular area
(repeating the mistakes of the railway woes) and inadequate enforcement of the few existing rules, to the total disregard for making policy
decisions about commercial airways development. Ad hoc reactions by
government were the order of the day.

The air transport industry was so new that insurance and equipment
obsolescence assumed large proportions of its operating expenses. The
manufacture of aircraft, engines and navigational aids was still in an
experimental stage, and adequate provision had to be made for depreciation and obsolescence. Development in the 1930s was so rapid that
any large aircraft was almost out of date at delivery time. Improvements
were constantly being made in accessories, such as propellers and instruments. Obsolescence costs ran as high as 33⅓ percent per year, compared with 15–20 percent for depreciation, making it difficult to justify
the purchase of new aircraft when the old were not fully depreciated.
All these charges increased the cost of operations and were charges that
the operator had to bear if it was to meet competition. They could not
be passed on as higher rates to the customer, and as a result obsolescence costs continually ate into Canadian Airways' reserves and were
one of the reasons why it did not show a profit.

Canadian Airways' accountants divided air transportation costs into
three categories: overhead, depreciation and obsolescence, and direct
operating expenses. This knowledge of costs and James Richardson's
directive that they be incorporated into the costs quoted to the customer set Canadian Airways apart from most of the other companies.
Overhead and depreciation depended on the volume of flying. Direct
operating expenses included gas, oil, aircraft, engines, accessory maintenance, public liability, property damage and passenger insurance.

Traffic volume from 1927 to 1930 had been sufficient to allow Canadian Airways to base its rates on its overhead and depreciation costs.
However, in 1930, traffic shrank nearly 50 percent because of the business recession. The obvious answer was to raise the rates, but this was

not feasible in depressed times. The solution seemed to be a lowering of rates to try to increase the volume of traffic. But on the scheduled services between the railhead and the northern communities there was little express, mail or passenger travel, so lowered rates were not the answer. There seemed to be little choice between dropping rates to get business or letting aircraft sit idle. Richardson knew that to fly for less than cash costs was suicidal, so he made the decision to drop rates reluctantly. They were not lowered indiscriminately.

Compounding the loss of revenue from the air mail contracts and the lower rates for other traffic was increased competition. Initially the depression had wiped out most of the aviation companies, leaving Canadian Airways with a relatively free field for expansion. The situation changed in 1932–33, when prospecting and mining activities picked up and drew attention to northern air transport. Flying freight and passengers seemed to be an easy way to make a dollar, and newcomers flooded the industry. Because there were no government regulations controlling the number of operators or the rates to be charged, anyone with a licence and an aircraft could set himself up in business, fly where he wished and charge what he wanted.

Most newcomers were pilots, not businessmen, and neither knew their true operating and maintenance costs nor understood business management. They were satisfied if they obtained money from a flight to pay out-of-pocket expenses for gas and oil. To draw traffic from Canadian Airways they quoted lower rates, which did not cover overhaul, insurance, depreciation or obsolescence costs. Although many of these "fly by night" operators soon went out of business because their low rates could not sustain them, the constant influx of newcomers dragged the whole rate structure down to an uneconomic level. By 1933, both passenger and express rates in the Red Lake mining district were down 50 percent from 1932 prices. The situation in eastern Canada was just as critical.

Northern air transport was almost entirely dependent for its welfare on mining development and prospecting. Mining development depended on an active and buoyant mining market in Toronto, because the necessary funds came mainly from public offerings of penny stocks. When the market became very active in 1933–34, it was not difficult to raise funds for new ventures into northern air transport. As competition increased greatly in Manitoba and the Northwest Territories, rates in those districts began to fall. By mid-1934, however, less money was available for prospecting and northern development generally.

The decline in traffic in the North increased competition, and air rates dropped still lower. More competition in northwestern Ontario, Manitoba and the Northwest Territories resulted in increased flying hours, far out of proportion to the volume of business. Many operators flew with reduced loads and lost money for every hour flown. By the winter of 1934–35 passenger fares had dropped 25 percent, package express rates by 55 percent and planeload lot rates by 50 percent in central Manitoba. Rates also dropped in the Mackenzie River district. It was not long before the mining companies and the Post Office took advantage of this intense competition and began playing off one operator against another.

Significantly, it was Canadian Airways that made the major effort to put the air transport industry on a firm footing. As the rates continued to tumble, it attempted in 1933 and 1934 to put rate agreements into force among the operators. In the fall of 1934, Tommy Thompson organized a conference in Ottawa for aircraft operators and manufacturers from all across Canada. His idea was to have a round-table talk to impress upon both the operators and the government the need for some kind of rate enforcement to stabilize the industry. He asked DND to chair the meeting. John Wilson was agreeable to DND participation but not anything more, saying that the private operators "for 15 years have solved their own problems without government assistance and are prepared to continue to do so."

Wilson was mistaken; DND had been asked to attend because the operators and manufacturers wanted the government to play a more active role in solving some of the problems that the industry was experiencing. Wilson acted cowardly and hypocritically. In a 1932 memo, "Civil Government Air Operations," to the deputy minister of national defence, Wilson had made an analogy to the railway situation, making it very clear that in the air industry, the commercial operators would not be stable until DND's attitude and policy changed. Typically, Wilson said one thing to his peers and something else in public. In an internal memo, he argued for the government to intervene; but when Thompson asked him point-blank to have DND chair a conference to try to resolve the destructive competition, Wilson wrung his hands and pretended that the commercial operators were doing just fine on their own. Thus, with little help from DND, Canadian Airways organized the conference.

Attending were the minister of defence (Grote Stirling), the deputy minister (L.R. LaFlèche), John Wilson and nine other DND representatives, four National Research Council representatives and forty-one representatives from the aircraft operators and manufacturers. The only major operator not in attendance was Leigh Brintnell, former general manager of Western Canada Airways and now one of Canadian Airways' most bitter competitors. Little was accomplished except agreements among the operators to work together. Unfortunately, most of the agreements were short-lived; discounts were hidden, overloading was flagrant and other manipulations made a mockery of them. In 1935, Thompson told Richardson that he had had enough of the "gentlemen's agreements"; to be of any use politically, there must be documentary evidence that Canadian Airways had tried to cooperate with the smaller companies.

The cutthroat and unrestricted competition that characterized the 1930s affected all phases of Canadian Airways' business. Whether competing for casual passenger traffic or mail and freight contracts, the firm often found itself in competition with other companies who obeyed no rules and took advantage of lax government inspection. As a businessman, Richardson expected competition. But he also expected everyone to play by the rules and the government to enforce existing regulations. Richardson was concerned that the present practices would destroy the fledgling air transport industry, and he had every reason to be worried. Not only was the competition destroying the financial basis of the reputable companies; it was causing many of the more unscrupulous air operators to fly in dangerous ways. An example was the practice of overloading.

Aircraft are licensed for a maximum gross load, which must not be exceeded, in the interests of safety. This load is, however, usually much lower than the aircraft is capable of carrying under normal conditions and can be increased by as much as 25–50 percent. As a result, unscrupulous operators used overloading as an inducement to customers on charter flights and tonnage quotations. As Thompson explained, "If an operator is prepared to carry 25% or even 10% more load for the same charge between two points than another operator will carry, the customer will give his business to the carrier who will take the large load."

Time and time again, Canadian Airways cited specific cases of overloading to civil aviation officials. Wilson's retort to accusations of slack enforcement was that he did not have enough inspectors to check loads on a regular basis. In any case, the inspectors were so well known that when they appeared in a district all the pilots made sure their planes were not overloaded. Wilson was correct; but there is also truth in Canadian Airways' complaints that Wilson could have used the RCMP more and that he was more concerned with being friendly with all the operators than with enforcing the regulations. What particularly irked Canadian Airways was the fact that DND appeared to be unnecessarily harassing *its* pilots with checks, while ignoring the competition a few yards down the shoreline.

Canadian Airways also accused DND of doing little more than lightly reprimanding or temporarily grounding pilots caught overloading. "If the Department had made an example of the operators by grounding the implicated aircraft or by imposing heavy fines, the results might have been effective. This reprehensible practice of overloading had its climax in northern Quebec, where an aircraft licensed to carry a pilot and five passengers crashed, killing the pilot and six passengers," wrote an angry Tommy Thompson, referring to a General Airways plane that in 1936 crashed because of overloading, killing pilots and passengers. The Civil Aviation Branch took no disciplinary action. When Canadian Airways questioned this, it was told by A.T. Cowley, superintendent of air regulations, that DND had decided not to worry about overloading anymore but to let the operators find out for themselves that it did not pay! As Thompson remarked, it was "a most astonishing statement for any director of air regulations to have made."

He also cited another case, in which an aircraft with all on board was lost on the Pacific coast, leaving no trace. According to Thompson, no disciplinary action was taken toward the operator; instead, the Post Office, in full knowledge of the accident, awarded the company a lucrative air mail contract. In a letter to M.P. James L. Bowman on April 10, 1934, Richardson wrote that the "Controller of Civil Aviation made no really worthwhile effort to compel our competition to live up to the Regulations" and that Canadian Airways' adherence to the regulations was "one of the chief reasons" for its poor revenues.

Competition from the government remained a major problem for all air operators. Lack of a government policy for aviation was the culprit. All the operators suffered from the overuse of the Civil Government Air Operations and the encroachment of the RCAF into commercial activities. Although General McNaughton initially supported the development of Canadian Airways, Richardson now believed McNaughton was against strong companies because they detracted from the government air operations and took jobs away from civil servants.

Outspoken in his criticism of the Civil Government Air Ops, Richardson described them as "wasteful and extravagant" and accused them of never worrying about having to bring in a dollar for every dollar spent and of absorbing money that should have gone into building up commercial companies that would become self-sufficient. In a succinct and biting letter to R.J. Manion, minister of railways and canals, on April 16, 1934, Richardson warned that commercial companies must be encouraged or there would be no private investment in aviation and that a permanent curb must be placed on the government air operations or "we will surely be landed with another CNR."

Richardson had assessed the situation correctly. Even John Wilson, controller of civil aviation, agreed, although typically he did not voice his opinion where it counted. In the early 1920s Wilson had warned against the mushrooming government air operations, and in 1932 he was still complaining about the "over-extension and over-elaboration" of government air operations—this at a time when government was in the process of cancelling air mail contracts and contemplating giving them to the RCAF.

Wilson's January 1932 memo, "Civil Government Air Operations," was a repeat of much of what he had written many times in the 1920s: "It is not too much to say that from 1925 to 1930 'the tail of Civil Operations wagged the Air Force dog.'... Operation after operation was proposed which involved the transportation of men and supplies to the districts now serviced efficiently by commercial operating companies, who have done all the pioneer work, without mention of the possibility of patronizing their services."

Perhaps Wilson rattled a few cages; perhaps Richardson's comments were heard in the East. At any rate, the situation was discussed by DND officials and the suggestion was made that government withdraw from commercial operations. Unfortunately, wrote Wilson, "this wiser policy received no recognition." Once more, McNaughton's wishes ruled the day: he wanted to keep the air force flying. To Wilson's credit, he did not hide behind his usual cloud of reassuring words but bluntly stated the damage the military was doing. "There is grave danger that a situation may arise, if it has not now arisen, similar to that which exists in the railway world today, where the company which pioneered railway development is now faced with Government competition, and the consequent duplication of services to the extent of bankruptcy of both services. The commercial operator cannot live in competition with freely given service, without regard to expense, from this Department. He needs all the traffic the government can give to augment his work and make it profitable so that he may improve its efficiency."

Wilson certainly understood Canadian Airways' dilemma. The uncertainty about what constituted government work and what was the preserve of the private companies made it risky for Canadian Airways or any other company to expend large sums of money on special aircraft or to undertake long-range planning, because it could not be sure that the government would not step in and take away its business. Sure enough, in April 1932, the RCAF took over Canadian Airways' Quebec–Seven Islands–Anticosti and Moncton–Magdalen Islands air mail contracts. In the short term, the RCAF could carry the mail more cheaply than could a private company. Although he reversed this decision eight months later, McNaughton had set a dangerous precedent. The RCAF took over a number of contracts previously held by Canadian Airways. "We were bush pilots in uniform," recalled one officer.

On March 31, 1932, General McNaughton, P.T. Coolican, Group Captain J.L. Gordon (director of Civil Government Air Operations), Wing Commander G.O. Johnson (assistant director of Civil Government Air Operations) and J.A. Wilson met in Ottawa to consider some of the air mail services. The group decided to leave the international services in place to prevent foreign interests from entering the field. The other services were to be taken over by the RCAF.

To their credit, the group acknowledged that the displacement of private enterprise was only a temporary economy. They realized that not only would the RCAF put civilians out of work, but in the long run, a military operation would be more expensive. They also recognized that millions of dollars had been invested in Canadian aviation by private enterprise, much of it encouraged by government, and that any move to replace private effort would discourage the further investment of capital. "Our aim should rather be to encourage private effort by judicious assistance where essential and so broaden the basis of our air development," they reported.

In November 1932, to regain the North Shore service on the St. Lawrence, Canadian Airways told DND that it was beginning a passenger and freight service. The Eastern Lines superintendent, F.T. Jenkins, met with McNaughton and Coolican to discuss the situation, with the result that they recommended that the RCAF withdraw and the air mail contract be returned to Canadian Airways but at a "substantial reduction of the previous rates." Rubbing salt into the wound, McNaughton also said that the RCAF would be taking over Canadian Airways' photographic aerial survey work in another area.

Coincidentally, while McNaughton held his March meeting, Mulock was writing to the prime minister about many of the points McNaughton was discussing. He argued two main points in his March 31 memo: the huge private investment ($4.6 million) in the aviation industry and the fact that air mail revenues would soon overtake expenditures, so it would be unwise to wipe out this potential cash cow.

The discriminatory practices of the Post Office were another major problem for Canadian Airways. Like most of the industry's troubles in the 1930s, they resulted from no overall policy regarding air mail or airways development. Postal officials considered it their duty to get the mail carried as cheaply as possible, without concerning themselves about the effect on the industry.

Tommy Thompson, who rarely spoke a disparaging word about anyone, raged, "The all important question in their minds seems to have been how to drive down the air mail rates to pile up profits for the Post Office Department. One official boasted that Canada is the only country in the world that makes a profit out of its air mail ... The Postal Department feels at liberty to gouge what it can out of operators forced to carry the mail at loss or give up the air routes that bring them their traffic."

Air mail revenues were an important part of the airline rate structure, and the steady reduction in the Post Office rates throughout the
1930s placed the whole industry on the verge of bankruptcy. Postmaster
General Arthur Sauvé generally left the air mail services to his departmental officers, who were more interested in seeing how low they could
force the rates than with developing a sound air mail system. They did
not understand the economics of an airline company and were not prepared to learn. Richardson offered more than once to open Canadian
Airways' books to them. Adding insult to injury, they awarded contracts to companies that openly disregarded the air regulations or were
in financial difficulties.

After 1932, when the Post Office began to re-tender casual intercity
and bush air mail contracts, it followed a variety of practices, moved
more by political whim or patronage than by any definite policy. The
Post Office Act stated that contracts were to be awarded after calling
for tenders. The Post Office often ignored this ruling. For instance, in
1935, without calling for tenders, without the contractual period having
expired and without warning, it took away Canadian Airways' Sioux
Lookout–Pickle Crow air mail contract and gave it to Starratt Airways.
In 1937, again without calling for tenders, the Post Office awarded Grant
McConachie of United Air Transport a contract for an Edmonton–
Whitehorse service—a potentially lucrative route for the eventual airway
to Asia. Neither Canadian Airways nor Edmonton-based Mackenzie
Air Services, both with experience in northern British Columbia and
the Yukon, were asked to tender. In June 1938, asking only Northern
Airways and Ginger Coote Airways to tender, the Post Office awarded
the Vancouver–Fort St. John air mail contract to Ginger Coote, a company involved in many accidents and then under investigation for the
loss of an aircraft with all on board.

Politics was definitely at play. Richardson was out of favour in
Ottawa. Among other things, he was not a lobbyist, he did not play
"the game," whereas the genial, smooth-talking and very likable Grant
McConachie knew where to pour the oil. McConachie, who would go
on to become president of Canadian Pacific Airlines, was a graduate of
the hard school of flying frozen fish. In his early days of flying, McConachie would do almost anything to obtain work. He was not above
stretching the rules until they broke. He began early—his biographer

says that McConachie charged passengers for flights to help him cover his flying lessons while he took his commercial licence!

It was well known that the Post Office was friendly to McConachie, who was negotiating to take over Ginger Coote Airways. Richardson felt helpless against this blatant disregard for proper tendering procedures and was disturbed over the awarding of a contract to a company with such a bad safety record. The loss of a contract was bad enough; the damage to the developing air industry concerned him more.

The Post Office, taking advantage of the intense competition, played off one company against another. In the mid-1930s, it began awarding contracts on a short-term basis or with only a verbal agreement. Neither arrangement gave Canadian Airways the security it needed for long-term planning. Sometimes the Post Office refused to pay the total costs for an air mail service. Occasionally it paid for only a one-way service when Canadian Airways' contract called for a two-way service, claiming, as its excuse, that the firm was overpaid in other areas. Once it tried to get the mail carried free on the almost two-thousand-mile southbound route along the Mackenzie River, saying that it could not pay poundage rates because there were no scales in the district.

Richardson also had a running argument with postal officials on good business practices and on what constituted safe flying. When Canadian Airways received the Vancouver–Seattle air mail contract in 1935, it asked the government to provide navigational aids and weather services before it undertook the contract. The often foggy conditions, the many unscheduled flights and the two daily scheduled services operated by United Airlines presented a potentially hazardous situation. The Post Office turned a deaf ear to Canadian Airways' requests; if the company wanted the contract, it would have to operate the service without any additional aids.

By 1935 Canadian Airways had no air mail service that was running at a profit, and most barely covered operating expenses. By the late 1930s, the intense competition for all traffic had forced air mail rates so low that many companies accepted contracts at less than operating costs. Services like the Vancouver–Victoria one, which operated at a loss, were kept intact mainly to keep Canadian Airways' name before the public or to prevent another company from moving into the area.

Richardson worked tirelessly but unsuccessfully to have the awarding of the air mail contracts and the fixing of the air mail rates taken out of the Post Office's hands and placed under the jurisdiction of an independent body, such as a board of transport commissioners. Although John Wilson was sympathetic to Canadian Airways' plight, he was unable to effect any change.

The most likely explanation for the government's inaction was that, after the creation of the Interdepartmental Committee on the Trans-Canada Airways in May 1933, it was assumed that an early decision on all airways matters would be made. This, however, was not the case; the government continued to waffle. Neither the creation of the Department of Transport in 1936 nor that of the Board of Transport Commissioners in 1938 solved Canadian Airways' problems with the Post Office. Not until 1939 did the government formally hear Canadian Airways' case on the air mail situation, and even then nothing was done. On January 25, William Euler, the acting postmaster general, admitted to Richardson that "there is no hard and fast rule governing the procedure of awarding contracts for the conveyance of mails by air."

By awarding contracts to the lowest bidder and accepting bids that were patently below the costs of the service, the Post Office contributed to the destructive competition among the aviation companies and to the bankrupt conditions of the industry by mid-1939. It saw only an opportunity to make enormous profits at the expense of a new industry—ignoring the fact that if the companies went bankrupt, the whole air mail structure would collapse. Wilson had written numerous memos stating that the Post Office made "a handsome profit" on its air mail service. In his "Brief on Transportation" to the government, Thompson explicitly stated that the Post Office's profit was 125 percent on the air mail. Ironically, when the government-owned Trans-Canada Air Lines was created, P.T. Coolican complained to Thompson that now the Post Office would not make any profit.

Other problems related to the development of a new industry concerned the technical and operating side of an aviation company. From the start, Canadian operators were handicapped by having to purchase aircraft from other countries and adapt them at considerable expense to Canadian conditions. Canadian operators also were not allowed to import secondhand equipment. They had to pay the full list price in the United States plus duty, sales tax, exchange and delivery charges.

American operators, on the other hand, could pick up secondhand aircraft in the United States and, with a very low capital investment, operate at prices far below those of the Canadians.

Canadian aviation and aircraft-manufacturing companies had to pay heavy duty on the raw materials or special accessories that were not manufactured in Canada. Aircraft operators were further penalized by having to pay higher prices for aviation gas and oil than did their American counterparts. As a result, Canadian Airways lost a number of air mail contracts to American companies, who could submit a lower price. In 1934, it lost two charters to Alaska Airways alone for this reason.

Formal instruction for air engineers and advanced pilot training were difficult to obtain in Canada. On-the-job training was the usual method of learning for aircraft mechanics. Canadian Airways tried numerous times to have the government initiate courses. When R.H. Mulock contacted A.T. Cowley, superintendent of air regulations, in November 1933 to ask the government to institute training courses, Cowley replied that it was "not considered that Departmental Officers were the proper people to give such a course." The RCAF at Camp Borden offered the only refresher courses or advanced instrument training programs. Only a limited number of places were available to commercial pilots each year. Canadian Airways was unsuccessful in having the RCAF increase the number of openings for commercial pilots, and in the fall of 1935 it was told that there were no spots for Canadian Airways.

Competition also came from U.S. companies. Again, it was the absence of a clearly defined Canadian aviation policy that allowed this to happen. The looseness of the international agreement between Canada and the United States allowed American companies to operate in Canada. What usually happened was that the U.S. company formed a subsidiary or "dummy" Canadian company with a "Canadian-sounding" name. One example was Canadian Colonial Airways, which was a subsidiary of Colonial Air Transport. Canadian Colonial had been formed in Maryland and had held the Montreal–Albany air mail contract since 1929. Once the Canadian subsidiary established itself between an American and Canadian city, it requested a further extension into Canadian territory. If a Canadian company was not operating in the area, DND usually granted the extension.

Richardson wanted the government to secure a more comprehensive ruling on the awarding of Canadian air mail contracts, so that Canadian companies were not competing with American companies. Canadian Airways had lost a contract to an American company because DND and customs officials had been slack and allowed that company to illegally bid on a job. Worse still was the fact that U.S. companies were being subsidized in Canada.

Richardson, who believed strongly that aviation in Canada must be controlled by the Canadians, kept a close watch on Pan Am and American Airways, because he did not trust the government to do the job. When he heard rumours that American Airways wanted a foothold in Canada, Richardson secured a commitment from American Airways in September 1933 that it would not establish itself in Canada without first discussing the matter with him. Not until 1939, when Canadian Colonial threatened the government-owned Trans-Canada Air Lines' air mail services, did the federal government finally begin to crack down on the Americans.

Despite all these problems, during the depression aviation saw its greatest expansion until World War II. Northern air services continued to grow, and in 1937 Canada led the world in air freighting. Canadian Airways was carrying more passengers and pounds of freight and mail. Nevertheless, by 1939, the destructive competition and low air mail rates had brought not only Canadian Airways but also the other major aviation companies in Canada to the brink of bankruptcy. During its lifetime, Canadian Airways never paid a dividend to its shareholders or made sufficient profits to build up a reserve to cover depreciation; it lived off its working capital.

By 1940, the company that had been instrumental in opening up the northern mining areas and providing other public services was virtually insolvent because of the government's neglect of the commercial operators. While earlier methods of transportation had been helped by the government, the northern air transport operators, the backbone of commercial aviation in Canada, were never materially assisted.

"An Air Policy Wanted":
The Trans-Canada Airway

A S THE SOUL of Canadian Airways, James Richardson valiantly struggled on. He doubled the volume of flying in 1932 but drew only half the revenue of 1931 and reported an operating loss to his board of directors. He persuaded himself and others that it was only a matter of time before Ottawa would declare an airways policy. Richardson's energy, driving force and enthusiasm convinced his people to hang on. He was so earnest in his belief that he assumed the importance of the airways question would be obvious to those in power. Unfortunately, he never understood the power of lobbying or that of calculating, cautious civil servants, who more often than not chose the path of circumspection as the road to success, if not to glory.

Vigilant but cautious, John Wilson did his best to push the government to declare a policy. "This country is at a disadvantage so long as there is no strong nationally recognized and supported operating company to act as our agent and meet, on equal terms, the other national airway companies ... hence our desire for consistent support of Canadian Airways," he wrote to the deputy minister of national defence in 1933. However, only Wilson rose above departmental turf protection and said what needed to be said; but no one listened to him.

The stakes were high for Canada: control of world airways development and of one of the most lucrative trade routes in the world. The trans-Canada, the trans-Atlantic and the trans-Pacific airways were up for grabs in the early 1930s. However, when Prime Minister Bennett clipped Canadian Airways' wings in 1932, he destroyed the assured income that Richardson needed to attempt an expensive and risky route development. Thus, Juan Trippe and Pan Am won the lead in international airways development while Richardson and Canada were back in the bush. Through government bungling, Canada lost its chance to become a leader in aviation. In fact, Canada almost lost control of its own airways. It happened this way.

Before the development of long-range aircraft, Canada's location was of great importance to the world's airways. The Department of National Defence knew it, and Richardson knew it. The "great circle" track, the shortest line of travel joining Chicago, the centre of North America's transportation systems, with Tokyo, Shanghai and Hong Kong, passed through Winnipeg, northern Alberta, Dawson and Nome, crossed the Bering Strait and skirted the coasts of northeast Asia. In 1927, the American airlines had tried to move into Canada and had been stopped by Richardson's intervention. In 1932, Canada was vulnerable again; this time the Americans moved into Canada to begin to develop the airways of the future. Pan Am was particularly aggressive.

By late 1932, Pan Am was exploring the possibility of extending its lines to Whitehorse to build an airport at the railway terminus there. This would make Whitehorse an important air base, the jumping-off point for the interior of the Yukon and Alaska. This was part of a much larger scheme—the airway from North America to Asia. Pan Am already controlled Chinese National Airways and had a stake in Japanese commercial airways. It also controlled flying in Alaska and was already making connections across the Yukon. The Canadian government had received proposals from Pan Am during the past few years for an airway through central British Columbia, to connect the U.S. airways with those in Alaska.

As early as 1929, Richardson already had his eye on the Orient. With Western Canada Airways' route across the Prairies to Edmonton and down the Mackenzie River to Aklavik and then to the Yukon, Canada had had the opportunity to beat the Americans. The cancellation of the prairie air mail section put an end to that development. Ever alert, Wilson had written the deputy minister in January 1933 that the Americans were proposing an alternative route through British Columbia and the Yukon and then across the Pacific. Wilson was ignored. He and Richardson had, however, kept on top of the matter, and Wilson and Mulock drew up a "Draft Outline of Possible Co-operation between Pan American Airways and Canadian Airways" on October 11, 1933. The company referred to in the draft was Pacific Alaska Airways, "a company of the Pan American Airways System."

Finally, on October 26, 1933, the deputy minister of national defence, L.R. LaFlèche, wrote to O.D. Skelton of External Affairs, advising him that John Wilson had suggested that Pan Am contact Canadian Airways to strike a deal. LaFlèche told Skelton that DND did not think that Pan Am should be allowed to build airfields or install radio or other navigation aids in Canadian territory. DND's solution was for the government to support a Canadian service from Whitehorse through the Yukon to Alaska, to connect there with the Pan Am system.

On November 2, Wilson wrote again to the deputy minister, stating that James Richardson should make this counter-proposal directly to Pan Am's president, Juan Trippe, and that this would allow Canadian Airways to control the terminal airport at Whitehorse and Pan Am to control the other terminal at Fairbanks. Richardson wrote Trippe on November 3, concluding matters to their mutual satisfaction and obviously to the Canadian government's approval, for Skelton wrote to LaFlèche on November 16 that Canadian Airways' counter-proposals were reasonable and should safeguard Canada's interests. Wilson wrote Mulock on December 1, thanking him for the copy of the deal and his cooperation. In good faith, Richardson assumed that Canadian Airways was acting as Canada's "chosen instrument," albeit in an unofficial capacity.

Through all of this, General McNaughton was remarkably silent. There is only one memo from him on file. On September 28, he wrote to Skelton, "I have a feeling of considerable anxiety at the situation which has been created whereby an American private company under thin guise has been permitted to come into Canada and set up an airway complete with visual and radio beacons, landing fields, etc. and to place their own men in charge ... I am fully convinced that the precedent which has been created will be followed up by requests and demands for the establishment of like privileges by other Americans operating companies elsewhere, for example, Pan Am in British Columbia, all of which will be very embarrassing." McNaughton's first reference was probably to Canadian Colonial Airways, a subsidiary of American Airways. Why he should be raising this concern now is hard to understand—Canadian Colonial had brought Richardson into the national picture, and he had been warning DND of American intrusion since 1928.

By this time, flying the Atlantic was becoming a commercial possibility. Here too, Canada was to lose its geographic advantage. There were three routes across the Atlantic: the Arctic route, via Labrador, Greenland and Iceland (Montreal–London, 3,625 miles); the direct route, via Newfoundland and Ireland (Montreal–London, 3,270 miles); and the southern route, via Bermuda and the Azores (Montreal–London, 5,625 miles). Canada had long recognized that the direct route was most advantageous to its interests, since the logical North American terminal would be Montreal. The United States and the United Kingdom preferred the southern route, with the terminal in New York. The United Kingdom, however, was prepared to work with Canada to keep the lucrative Atlantic traffic within the British Empire. But Canada did little to develop the direct route. When U.S. plans to develop the southern route fell apart in 1932, Pan Am made the bold move in 1933 of operating an airway through Canadian territory, with the ultimate aim of controlling the direct Atlantic route. How had this happened?

Under Prime Minister Mackenzie King, Canada took its first step to speed up the delivery of trans-Atlantic mail in the summer of 1927, when pilots flew the mail from Montreal to Rimouski to connect with the ocean-going steamers. This lopped off 330 miles of slow steamship travel. The service had operated every year since, between May 1 and November 30. The next attempt to speed up mail delivery was in 1930, when flights between Montreal and Halifax were initiated. This saved more than twenty hours from the previous connection by train. Also in 1930, in an attempt to make almost one-third of the trans-Atlantic trip by air, a trial flight met the mail steamers in the Strait of Belle Isle, more than 1,000 miles east of Montreal. This combination of air and steamer meant that mail could reach Montreal from London in only four days.

If Canada could maintain this service it would establish the St. Lawrence route as the "high-speed communication route between Europe and North America." However, the St. Lawrence River was not open the full year for navigation, so seasonal changes meant that mail steamers used three different routes: the winter service, December 1–April 20, when Halifax was the port of transfer; the spring service, April 20–July 1, when steamers entered the St. Lawrence via the Cabot Strait; and the summer service, July 1–November 30, when the steamers entered the St. Lawrence via the Strait of Belle Isle.

The winter route made airway services to the Maritimes critical to the Atlantic airway. This had been one of Richardson's key arguments for maintaining Canadian Airways' route from Montreal to Halifax when the government began cancelling contracts. Any expenditure for air navigation facilities or air mail on this route would help consolidate the Maritime position for the eventual all-air service by a Canadian route. In 1931, representatives from Canada, the United Kingdom, the Irish Free State and Newfoundland met and agreed with Richardson on the importance of the Montreal–Halifax connection. On August 19, McNaughton told Richardson that he expected the prime minister to reinstate both the eastern and prairie air mail services shortly. Bennett, however, did nothing.

In July 1932, Ottawa hosted the Imperial Economic Conference, and in its report on civil aviation Canada admitted that it had curtailed its domestic air mail development and had done nothing about an international hookup. The United Kingdom was not pleased; flying the Atlantic was a live issue. A committee on the Atlantic service was struck with representatives from the United Kingdom, the Irish Free State, Newfoundland and Canada, the four governments that controlled the approaches to the direct route.

McNaughton, who evidently still considered Canadian Airways to be Canada's chosen instrument, telegrammed Mulock on August 8, asking him to come to Ottawa for the formation of an air committee. Richardson, also assuming that Canadian Airways would be officially named as Canada's chosen instrument, authorized Mulock to speak for the firm. The committee agreed that all four governments would give every possible preference to the direct route and that they would not support the development of any other route or give privileges to any foreign government without consulting each other.

If the recommendations from the conference were not enough to push the prime minister to action, the just-released draft report from the Royal Commission on Transportation should have been. It recommended that a national company be formed in cooperation with the railways and that the government support its development by postal contracts. It noted that American aeronautical research was progressing more rapidly than anticipated and that an all-air route across the Atlantic was likely in the not-too-distant future, which would make Canada's air-to-ship service obsolete before it even began. It warned government that the Americans, who wanted the right to construct air navigational facilities over Canadian routes, were not likely to take no for an answer if Canada were not going to provide these facilities. It recommended government take action now. Nothing happened.

Tired of waiting for Canada, Britain's Imperial Airways ignored its government agreement to work with Canada and secretly began talking with Pan Am about the southern route. Aerospatiale of France also approached Pan Am. Meanwhile, Lufthansa of Germany was flirting with the Irish Free State. Even more of a threat was Pan Am's order in December 1932 for six Clipper-type luxury aircraft. With these, Juan Trippe expected to dominate intercontinental air transportation. Richardson and Beatty warned External Affairs and DND that Canada could not stall any longer. Any chance of holding the supremacy on the trans-Atlantic route was fast slipping from Canada's grasp.

Instead of firing off an urgent letter to the prime minister and mobilizing his department, McNaughton whined to Sir William Clark, the high commissioner for the United Kingdom in Canada, that the Americans were not talking to him. "We have never received any authentic information ... All our information on this subject has been gleaned from conversations with officers of the United States or representatives of their commercial aviation companies. Our feeling is that when trans-Atlantic flying is discussed ... we should interchange information so that we can both be fully advised as to what is developing and so that the United States interests will not secure a position from which they can play us off one against the other." McNaughton's ego was bruised; his pettiness was plain.

Wilson didn't waste time complaining; he simply did what he

always did and wrote another memo. Dated December 29, 1932, it recommended that Canada immediately implement its share of the airway. Wilson laid out the estimated costs for the airway and navigational aids; most importantly, he stressed that the revenue from overseas mails would very quickly overtake expenditures. He also pointed out that these revenues would be augmented by domestic and American air mail revenues. Nothing happened. Where did Wilson's memo go? Did it reach the prime minister?

In 1933, when it looked as if the Canadian position would be further weakened by Newfoundland granting Pan Am the right to operate aircraft to Newfoundland and to construct bases and other air navigation facilities, Canada was given another chance to pull up its socks. A conference on trans-Atlantic air services was held in Newfoundland in July, and representatives of the United Kingdom, Canada, Newfoundland, Imperial Airways and Pan American participated. Imperial Airways agreed to cooperate with Canada on the institution of an air–steamer mail service on the direct route. Newfoundland agreed to give Imperial Airways operating rights in Newfoundland and permission to construct ground facilities if it did not do so itself. Similar rights would be granted to a Canadian company nominated by the Canadian government. Imperial Airways could, with the approval of the governments of Newfoundland and the United Kingdom, assign its rights wholly or in part to Pan Am.

All in all, however, the many attempts Imperial Airways made from 1930 to 1933 to cooperate with the Canadian government met with failure. Six years had passed since the first ship-to-shore air mail experiments; twice Canada had come close to losing out to the Americans and twice the United Kingdom made allowances to her Dominion, but Canada never carried out any part of the agreement. O.D. Skelton obviously did not consider international airways development as being important to Canada's external affairs.

Wilson wrote another memo on the trans-Atlantic services on July 25, 1933, in which he was quite blunt about Imperial Airways' feelings about the lack of Canadian cooperation. As usual, his warnings were ignored, although McNaughton would often remark on how he and the Canadian government had cooperated with Imperial Airways. Another year slipped by, and with it Canada lost control over the Atlantic airway.

It seems incomprehensible that the Canadian government could not make up its mind what to do about the trans-Canada airway, much less the trans-Atlantic or trans-Pacific. Considering that Canada had recently been involved in a world war and that McNaughton himself had been overseas, the government's inability to grasp that policy making must embrace international concepts is difficult to fathom.

Government officials could not even settle the question about developing an airway from Montreal to the Maritimes or establishing the air–ship service on the St. Lawrence or building navigational aids in Newfoundland. Even the question of what should be carried on the trans-Canada airway caused dissension among departmental officials, and a ridiculous amount of time was spent arguing about this. If DND had asked a few questions about what other airlines in the United States, the United Kingdom or Europe were doing, it would have had an answer. Richardson had stated emphatically that to be viable, a company must be able to carry mail, passengers and cargo; it could not be restricted to mail.

Canada was in fact in a weak position in the early 1930s to assert itself against or to cooperate with either Imperial Airways or Pan Am. Trans-Atlantic flying had become a commercial possibility in 1930, just at the beginning of the Great Depression. The Canadian government's cancellation of Canadian Airways' contracts in early 1932 virtually destroyed Canada's only large aviation company, the company formed to become Canada's chosen instrument. From then on, when its own future was so indefinite and with no assurance of steady support from its own government, Canadian Airways was in no position to discuss future developments with Imperial Airways or anyone else—although Richardson did not share this opinion. Ever the optimist, he continued to maintain contacts with Imperial Airways and Pan Am as well as his belief that Canadian Airways would take its proper place in the scheme of things.

Though a staunch Britisher, Richardson was as determined to protect Canadian routes from the British as from the Americans. "Our company, Canadian Airways, is quite capable of handling any work of a domestic character within Canada and this includes the Transcontinental run from the Atlantic to the Pacific seaboard ... As far as international flying is concerned ... Imperial Airways and Canadian

Airways must work together ... but they still have their old dream of the Imperial Airways operating all trunk lines in the British Empire including Canada ... I can see no advantage ... to us in having Imperial Airways financially interested in the Transcontinental or domestic situation in Canada," Richardson wrote somewhat testily to Beatty on January 22, 1933.

However, try as he might, Richardson could not push the government to define a policy. It was mid-1933 before he finally captured Bennett's attention. To Bennett's credit, mired as he was in other issues, he immediately set in motion a process that should have resulted in government making a quick decision on air policy. Unfortunately for Canada, not to mention Richardson, the players at the table would not give clear direction, and as a result, government continued to act on an ad hoc basis.

Like Mackenzie King before him, Bennett waited until circumstances forced him to act. The decisive factor in prodding the prime minister was Richardson. On March 21, he phoned Bennett, and the next day he sent a personal letter. This plea from Richardson at last aroused Bennett; something must be wrong. Richardson's March 22 letter covered all pertinent points; unfortunately, his writing lacked its usual punch. He began almost apologetically, which was not the way to approach Bennett. "I appreciate very much the time you were good enough to give me on the telephone last night after I know what must have been a very tiring and trying day in the House. I did feel, however, that it was very necessary that I should get through direct to you some of the financial problems of the Canadian Airways, about which I am very much disturbed, and I would like to review in this letter the matter of our conversation."

Richardson had not yet learned what it took to keep his planes flying in Canadian skies. It never occurred to him that what he might see clearly, others might not. To him commercial aviation was an asset to Canada's growth, and Canada must retain control of it. His letter to the prime minister should have stressed the national importance of Canadian Airways and the financial benefits that would accrue to the government if the firm stretched its wings nationally and internationally. Instead, Richardson proudly wrote of Canadian Airways' accomplishments. Pride, however, cut no ice with Bennett. "The Airways were never doing a more useful job at any time than now and never doing it better. We have not hesitated to try and do our full job in opening up the North."

It would have been more effective to bluntly tell Bennett that the company had run out of money and that its board of directors had little financial investment in it. (Bennett later said that he thought Canadian Airways' powerful board of Canada's top financiers had plenty of money to put into the company.) Instead Richardson spoke of how he was trying to cope, an argument that would not sway Bennett. "We have cut our operating and administration expenses to the bone consistent with being able to supply the government with information they require and keeping together the character of organization we have. Our men are all working overtime and are not complaining, but we must have more volume and a little more margin if we are going to be able to carry through."

Richardson did not emphasize strongly enough the danger of Canada not having its own national airline. To Richardson, who had so accurately assessed the situation, the danger was obvious and thus there was no reason for him to do more than gently remind the prime minister. "I believe we are on the verge of large developments in air transportation. Canada occupies a key position ... I believe we have a highly efficient organization and highly competent personnel worthy of that support and consideration which I now ask."

For all his gentlemanly ways, Richardson was no pushover, and his correspondence, particularly his private notes, shows that he had a dry wit and a way with words that delivered whatever message he wanted. Unfortunately, this letter did little for his case. His telephone call to McNaughton on March 22, however, pulled no punches. He emphasized Canadian Airways' serious condition and indicated that "unless some definite policy is developed under which [the company] can accept mail contracts with something better than the bare cost of oil and gas, it will be necessary for them to close their doors."

McNaughton, realizing the gravity of the situation, wrote the same day to R.K. Finlayson, the prime minister's private secretary. "This would be a very serious and unfortunate condition for us as Canadian Airways is the only Company owned and controlled in Canada to which we can look for the important operations which are bound to develop in the very near future. With Canadian Airways out of the picture the field is open to aggressive American Companies and the control of Canadian aviation passed to New York. The situation is so serious that I have asked the Controller of Civil Aviation to outline it in full in a memo, copy to you … I think you should let the Prime Minister know."

This letter suggests that McNaughton still supported Canadian Airways. Finlayson passed the letter and memo on to the prime minister, and Bennett immediately asked Wilson to prepare a memorandum on the state of affairs in aviation. Wilson's March 17, 1933, memo, titled "Air Transport Policy," began by justifying the government's actions. "The stoppage is not general and … has so far affected only one small phase of aviation, i.e., airway development and intercity air services in Canada." To say that intercity services was only "one small phase" was the height of hypocrisy. The cancellation of "one small phase" had destroyed the entire underpinning of the incipient national system as well as the connector with the world's airways.

Wilson contradicted himself in the next paragraph, when he stated that a "difficult situation is arising because of our stoppage of progress in intercity airways—a) Penetration by United States air lines and b) The disorganization of Canadian operations." Again he minimized the damage by describing it as only "a difficult situation." Points a) and b), however, clearly showed the seriousness of the government's actions. In spite of Wilson's initial tiptoeing around the seriousness of the situation, his memo was very significant.

Wilson confirmed Richardson's declarations that Canadian Airways had been formed with the government's encouragement to operate the trans-Canada airway and be the contractor for international flying. "Control of the eastern Canadian airways was only defeated by the timely action of the Canadian group now interested in Canadian Airways Limited, who, with the moral support of the Government, stepped into the breach, took over the financially weak Canadian companies and formed them into a strong group." Twice more he confirmed the government's support of Canadian Airways. "The formation of a strong national company in Canada and its support by the Government, through the Post Office and this Department, led the Canadian Pacific Railway to favour participation in Canadian Airways." He also acknowledged government support "through the investment of a quarter of a million dollars by the Canadian National Railway in Canadian Airways ... In this way, by gradual evolution, a strong national Canadian company was built up, with the support and encouragement of the Government."

Wilson next identified all the contracts that Canadian Airways held and its widespread operation. "The magnitude of these scheduled operations called for an extensive organization for their proper financial and business management, very different from anything hitherto required in Canada." This was an important point; later, McNaughton, Coolican and C.D. Howe, minister of transport, would try to portray Canadian Airways as an insignificant bush company.

Wilson courageously criticized the Post Office's practices in tendering, stating that they were pushing the aviation industry into bankruptcy, and if Canadian Airways were forced to shut down, "the result will be deplorable ... Canadian aviation ... will not recover for many years." He made ten recommendations, most of them pertaining to Canadian Airways and the support that government should give it. He recommended that the government recognize Canadian Airways as its "chosen instrument" and protect it from "cutthroat competition." He also recommended that the Post Office give it more air mail contracts and that those already held by Canadian Airways be renegotiated "at equitable rates." He sent copies of his memo to DND and Post Office officials.

Meanwhile, Richardson was waiting patiently for an answer to his March letter. On April 5, 1933, he wrote again to the prime minister. Naïvely he said, "I sincerely hope that it will always be possible for Canadian Airways to be kept free of politics and carried on, on a business basis; with the approval and support of the Government ... I sincerely hope that you see your way clear to make the matter of the support of the Canadian Airways a matter of government policy." This letter prompted the prime minister to call McNaughton on April 18. McNaughton recorded the conversation in a memo.

McNaughton's memo was important. First, it showed that he still supported Canadian Airways and that he approved of the RCAF carrying the mail as an emergency solution only, "because I thought that as a matter of national policy we should have a strong Canadian company which could handle this and other work for us." Second, and most importantly, he stated that the prime minister had directed him to formulate a policy regarding Canadian Airways and the aviation question in general and wanted a full report and "considered recommendations" before the end of May. Thus directed by the prime minister, McNaughton, Wilson and Coolican formed themselves into a committee in early May.

Typically, the committee's first move was to have Wilson write a memo, "Government Policy on Aviation"—a rather ironic heading, since Wilson acknowledged that there was no government policy: "As long as there is no government policy the Post Office Department will take advantage of the situation to reduce costs." This April 20 memo was probably Wilson's shortest, but it said a great deal. The first sentence set the tone. "Civil Aviation as an Industry has advanced in nearly every country except Canada, notwithstanding the depression. Progress has been made by means of private companies selected and subsidised by the Government. In England—The Imperial Airways; in the United States—The Pan-American; in France—Aero-Postale; In Germany—Luft-hansa." Wilson reaffirmed that Canadian Airways had been formed to be the national operator, that there was no aviation policy and that the Post Office was reaping the benefit. Nothing appears to have happened as a result of the memo.

Sir Edward Beatty was concerned enough to write Richardson on April 15. "There seems to be a gradual whittling down of the use by the Government of Canadian Airways services ... Obviously the Company cannot continue to function unless the Government recognizes its existence and ceases the practice of letting out these services to mushroom companies at rates which are not remunerative." Richardson called a board of directors meeting on April 28 and finally put his board to work. He appointed a special committee to look into the problems confronting Canadian Airways. The committee moved quickly, and by May 6 Richardson had a covering letter and confidential report ready for Bennett.

The letter was written with dignity but also with a touch of desperation. It should have been written a year earlier. "Canadian Airways Limited is rapidly approaching the time when unless aided it will have to close down its operations. The available and realizable working capital will be, by the end of June, reduced to some $85,000 ... The company's present financial position is not due to any errors in its policy, but to the fact that the Government stopped its main source of revenue by cancelling the Air Mail Routes and Contracts. All possible economies have been enforced without destroying the organization or affecting the quality and reliability of the service rendered. The Company would welcome an examination by representatives of the Government of its books and records."

The committee reminded the prime minister that the government had invested $250,000 in Canadian Airways and observed that "there is not enough business in Canada to support more than one organization." Richardson had argued this point from the start, and it was the reason he included both railways in Canadian Airways. Furthermore, aviation was subsidized in all other countries and Canada should do no less. Finally, "private capital had provided nearly $3,000,000.00 in cash to develop and organize an all-Canadian airways service. It is a foregone conclusion that no additional capital can be secured from private investors for the continuation of these operations." This statement should have struck a chord with Bennett, who did not believe in government intervention.

The committee suggested five alternatives to the drastic cancellation of services. Its first recommendation was that the government recognize Canadian Airways as its "Air Mail Contractor." Its second, third and fourth recommendations dealt specifically with air mail payments, fishery patrol contracts and a recommendation that the commercial work being handled by the RCAF be returned to Canadian Airways "at a fair price." The fifth dealt with payment for services in the North. The letter was signed by Richardson, Charles Gordon (president, Bank of Montreal), Beaudry Leman (general manager, Banque Canadienne Nationale; vice-president, General Trust), Morris Wilson (vice-president, Burns & Co.), T.A. Russell (president, Willy-Overland Ltd.) and V.M. Drury (president, E.B. Eddy Co.).

Richardson, hoping to plead his case in person, personally delivered the letter to the prime minister. But Bennett was in no mood to discuss airways problems. As Richardson later reported to his committee, "The Prime Minister was under considerable stress and strain at the time in connection with getting away for the Economic Conference, and I was unable to make any definite progress with him."

Bennett did suggest that Richardson see the minister of railways, R.J. Manion, who was sympathetic and took Richardson's suggestion that his deputy, Valentine Smart, go to Montreal to check out Canadian Airways' books and discuss its problems. "Smart came to Montreal and we provided him with all the figures and information he wished to have."

There was a flurry of memos in this period. Coolican finally responded to Wilson's March memo on May 15. There was no mistaking his message: he disagreed with almost everything Wilson said. He denied that Canadian Airways had been formed with DND's or the Post Office's encouragement. He rejected Wilson's contention that the postal rates and short-term contracts were inequitable or injurious to Canadian Airways' financial stability. He stated that Canadian Airways should not be the trans-Canada operator because he was not satisfied with its past performance. He was vague in his criticism and obviously had forgotten his earlier words of praise for the prairie air mail service.

Coolican took a shot at Richardson at the same time. "Canadian Airways organized and extended their operations of their own free will, without any government encouragement, in fact all their activities seem to have been actuated by the desire to reap immediate profit and to crowd every competitor from the field." He chastised Wilson for not considering a government-owned trans-Canada operator and concluded by saying that if Canadian Airways were chosen, then it should be controlled by the two railways.

The antagonism that marked the relationship between the Post Office and Canadian Airways was clearly evident. What Coolican's motives were can only be speculated. In all likelihood, he feared the growth of a large company that had the blessing of the government, knowing that this would put an end to the Post Office's opportunity to make large profits on air mail contracts. If he could divide DND and Post Office officials in their choice of the trans-Canada operator, this would delay the selection and allow the Post Office to retain some supremacy in airway matters.

The result of McNaughton, Wilson and Coolican's deliberations was another memo by Wilson, "Civil Aviation Policy," on May 24. The memo defined the committee's concept of the trans-Canada company and its recognition that there were two kinds of services in Canada:

"bush operations" and "scheduled intercity operations." The committee showed its ignorance of bush operations. It stated incorrectly that bush companies were self-supporting and needed no subsidy, nor did they require much in the way of navigational aids or weather services. The committee absolved itself and the government of not helping these companies and recommended that this policy be continued! It glossed over the destructive competition, the low rates paid by the Post Office and the fact that the government competed unfairly with the commercial companies. Wilson knew better but allowed the statements to stand. To the uninformed, such as the prime minister, these were innocuous words and gave no indication of the major problems in the air transport industry.

In discussing intercity services, the committee admitted that Canada was the only country in the western world where government had given no financial assistance, and then it piously absolved the government. "No premature action has been taken to encourage uneconomical and unnecessary airways and for ten years after the Armistice this field remained untouched deliberately." It conveniently ignored all of Wilson's memos over the past six years that begged the government to take action. The committee also exaggerated the state of readiness of the trans-Canada airway. Disregarding the fact that only the prairie section of the airway could be considered ready for operation and that the funds for building the rest of the airway were not available, it stated that the only major remaining problem was to decide whether the trans-Canada company should be private or government-owned. The committee reversed itself later on this point, and McNaughton himself contradicted the committee when he stated that the status of the airway was more important than the choosing of the operator. Of interest, however, was the committee's reference to a government-owned company; this was the first time this possibility had been raised.

Finally, the committee got around to discussing how the trans-Canada airway was to be operated. It suggested two alternatives, "one by state operation, the second by operation under contract with a strong aircraft operating company given such support by the state as may enable it to operate successfully until the traffic returns are sufficient to pay for the cost of operation." It admitted that if the first option were taken only the RCAF could do it, but conceded that the air force did not have "the elasticity to meet the conditions of competitive services and the varied and diverse requirements inherent in their operation." McNaughton did not want his air force "deformed" to carry out commercial operations.

If the second option were chosen, the committee saw two alternatives: the creation of a new company or the selection of an existing organization. If a new company were formed, it should have representation from both railways. The committee figuratively tripped over its feet when it remembered that the CNR and CPR were already working with Canadian Airways. "Both railways now have a large stock interest in Canadian Airways and it would seem that for the protection of these interests the new company would have to eventuate from a reorganization of Canadian Airways ... The danger is that Canadian Airways might pursue a policy independent of the railways, competitive rather than co-operative and supplementary." This statement was a red herring, likely thrown in by Coolican to undermine Richardson. Richardson had involved the railways in Canadian Airways from the start and had declared that he would continue to work with them.

The committee acknowledged that Canadian Airways was the only existing company capable of performing a transcontinental service. It took twenty-three points and nine pages before it finally recommended that Canadian Airways be entrusted with creating a national air transport system.

Point 24 recommended that one director be appointed to the board of management and that both railways take an active role. Also, if the government gave Canadian Airways "continuous support over a period of years through air mail contracts," there was little reason to doubt that it would become efficient and self-sustaining. "Such a company would be in a position to participate on equal terms in the development of the international airways, in which Canada is directly interested and deeply concerned."

Point 25 confirmed that Canadian Airways was formed to conduct the trans-Canada service. The committee also recognized that the company, formed at government's request, was now in financial trouble because of the government's withdrawal of its air mail contracts and that Canadian Airways should be given financial security until the depression was over.

Point 28 summarized the preceding points and made seven recommendations. The most important was the first one: "The government should recognize Canadian Airways as the instrument through which they intend to operate the trans-Canada airway and should give the necessary steady and consistent support to enable the company to organize these services as conditions warrant." The second recommendation was that postal rates be equitable; the third, which would be very contentious, was that Canadian Airways should relinquish its bush operations and confine itself to scheduled flying because it would have its hands full with the trans-Canada operation. Unspoken was the committee's fear that the government would be accused of creating a monopoly of air services for Canadian Airways. The rest of the recommendations were in line with the items discussed in the body of the memo.

This committee meeting was very significant in being the only one that resulted in a clear statement of recommendations. It would not happen again. Although Coolican criticized Canadian Airways, there was consensus that it should be recommended as Canada's national and international operator.

The committee was evidently prepared to implement its recommendations immediately; appended to the memo was a draft "Heads of Agreement" drawn up for Canadian Airways, the CPR, the CNR and the government to sign. The concise three-page agreement covered six issues: the parties, purpose and period of the agreement (eight years from April 1, 1934), and the obligations of the Dominion government, Canadian Airways, and the CNR and CPR. Reference was again made to the international situation and Canadian Airways' withdrawal from its bush operations "to the extent the Government may decide," since it would be guaranteed three thousand miles of flying.

McNaughton submitted the memo and draft agreement to the prime minister on May 30, 1933, with the request that the committee be given authority to negotiate an agreement with the four parties concerned. Clearly he supported Canadian Airways and wanted to resolve the airways situation immediately. Bennett also wanted to settle the question. McNaughton stated in another memo that the prime minister directed him to have the committee proceed with negotiations.

In a "secret memo" to himself on June 1, 1933, McNaughton detailed his conversation with the prime minister about the draft agreement.

"I told him that ... if I were authorized so to do I felt that I could approach the Railway Companies and Canadian Airways and negotiate a draft agreement with them which would satisfactorily meet the situation; that there would be no commitment to the Government of Canada unless and until this agreement had been approved ... The Prime Minister then said that he thought a draft agreement of this sort might be made without Privy Council authority and in Dr. Skelton's presence he authorized me to proceed in the matter."

This last sentence is extremely important: it showed that the prime minister gave McNaughton authority to act. McNaughton, however, did nothing. The finger of blame has long been pointed at Bennett for allowing the problems of the industry to escalate. Should O.D. Skelton have stepped in at this point and "reminded" McNaughton to get moving, or should he have discreetly alerted the prime minister that McNaughton was not carrying out his directive? Considering the urgency of the situation and his own request to begin negotiations immediately, it was inexplicable that McNaughton waited a month before informing Wilson and Coolican of the prime minister's directive. More damning is the fact that he subtly altered the prime minister's orders. Instead of the four principals coming in as equals and working out the management and financing, McNaughton, without any authority from his minister or the prime minister, changed the configuration and told Wilson that the railways would be in charge.

From the vantage point of more than sixty years, it appears that McNaughton wanted the draft "Heads of Agreement" to die a quick death. He had turned against Richardson; he had turned away from recommending private enterprise to wanting government control. That being the case, he wanted the whole process slowed down, knowing that every month of delay was a hardship for Richardson and lessened Canadian Airways' chances of being confirmed as the chosen instrument. McNaughton no longer supported Canadian Airways, but Bennett carried the blame.

History has many "what ifs." If McNaughton had followed Bennett's orders and brought together the four principals and negotiated the draft "Heads of Agreement," and if the prime minister had implemented the committee's recommendations, as it seemed he was prepared to do, it is highly unlikely that Trans-Canada Air Lines would have been created in 1937. However, history unfolded differently.

McNaughton, knowing that Bennett was due to leave for an economic conference in England, delayed calling a committee meeting, probably to ensure that Wilson had no opportunity to speak with the prime minister about the change in direction. It was unlikely that anyone would ever have known about McNaughton's devious tactics if McNaughton had not written a secret memo to himself and if Wilson himself had not written a "Memorandum for File, 'Operation of Scheduled Airways in Canada'" on June 28, 1933. Wilson's memos were usually directed to his deputy minister or to McNaughton; this memo was directed to the filing cabinet. Perhaps Wilson smelled a rat and wanted to cover himself.

In his memo, Wilson stated that McNaughton told him that the department's view had changed: the government should rely on the railways to participate in the new organization's management. This significantly altered the committee's recommendations as expressed in Wilson's May 24 memo, which the prime minister had approved. The new direction gave control to the railways. It was most unlikely that Bennett would have given his approval; he had so little faith in railway management that he had called for a royal commission on transportation.

More to the point, Wilson was the controller of civil aviation and part of the three-man committee appointed to make the airways recommendations. He was privy to all departmental meetings and was meticulous about recording meetings. Yet he was unaware of any departmental meeting that had recommended a change. The most likely answer is that it was not a departmental change but a "McNaughton change." Ever the good public servant, Wilson did not betray McNaughton. McNaughton knew his man and knew he was safe.

Wilson was most circumspect in his memo. "The Chief of the General Staff explained that since the preparation of a memorandum dated May 24th, 1933, for the Prime Minister before his departure for England and on which he had given permission for negotiations with the railway companies and Canadian Airways, leading to a new set-up, the Department's view had been modified and it was felt that the Government must look principally to the railways to control the new organization and actively participate in its management."

McNaughton was a good strategist. Knowing that Richardson had met with Manion and that Manion was sympathetic to Canadian Airways, McNaughton took steps to paint another picture of Canadian

Airways to Manion. On June 26, he wrote the minister of railways, "I have now some doubt as to the practicability of making use of this company. It is for consideration whether it might possibly be better to leave this company out of the Trans-Canada Airways picture and to set up an entirely new organization wholly owned by the Canadian National and Canadian Pacific Railways. I will develop this point further when I see you."

Obviously, McNaughton had no intention of carrying out the prime minister's directive to begin negotiations with Canadian Airways, the CNR and the CPR. Instead he lobbied the minister of railways to bring him on side with his plan to have the railways in control. Politically astute, he spoke personally to Manion on the day he told Wilson of the "modification." Manion, who had little if any knowledge of airway matters, was likely in awe of the powerful chief of staff and flattered that McNaughton was briefing him; he asked no questions. Manion, however, had just met with Richardson and saw nothing wrong with Canadian Airways' organization. In fact, he was so impressed with Richardson's arguments that he had sent Smart, his deputy, to Montreal to go over Canadian Airways' books. Clearly, Manion was easily swayed and no match for a heavyweight such as McNaughton. Wilson wrote, "The Minister [Manion] fully concurred that the lead in active management should be with the railway companies so as to ensure complete coordination of the air services and railways rather than destructive competition."

At the very least, this statement was misleading. There had never been any friction, much less "destructive competition," between Canadian Airways and the railways. Richardson and his two vice-presidents got along just fine. Moreover, S.J. Hungerford, the CNR's new president (Thornton had resigned after the Royal Commission on Railways) was on record as saying he was not interested in becoming overly involved in the airways situation because he had too many problems with the CNR. Manion had certainly not told Richardson he wanted railway control. Bennett would have vetoed railway control, saying it would be a surefire way to spell the doom of the new company. Even the deputy minister of railways, Valentine Smart, had expressed concern that the railways would not be innovative enough and might stifle airways development. Somebody was not telling the truth.

Bennett, of course, was in the dark. Preoccupied with a multitude of other matters, he would not check for some time to see how the negotiations for the draft "Heads of Agreement" were going. By then the damage would be done. McNaughton would have changed the composition of the committee and the terms of reference. In fact, McNaughton assumed the chairmanship and enlarged the committee into the very official sounding Inter-Departmental Committee on the Trans-Canada Airway (TCA Committee). He also ensured that the members would be under his control. He allowed another month to go by before calling another meeting and successfully dragged out the meetings for another two years, never bringing the committee to a consensus; the May 1933 consensus recommendations were conveniently forgotten. An election intervened and the government fell, with no action on the May 1933 recommendations to negotiate an agreement with Canadian Airways and the railways.

Interestingly, McNaughton's biographer, who wrote the first volume while McNaughton was still alive and had the advantage of having McNaughton proof everything, lays the blame of the long-drawn-out meetings at Richardson's feet. He wrote, "In view of the heavy subsidies demanded by Richardson ... the discussions proved protracted." At no time had Richardson asked for heavy subsidies. On the contrary, he did not want the air mail to be a drain on the public purse, and he and Mulock were shortly to discuss this very fact. Interestingly too, McNaughton's biographer wrote, "The operation of the airway was the chief concern," and two pages later wrote, "the actual operation of the airway was not so urgent as the construction," not realizing the significance of McNaughton's change of face.

As stated earlier, McNaughton well knew that determining the operator was the most important matter because that decision also impinged on the international scene. However, once McNaughton decided not to back Richardson, it was to his benefit to focus on the construction of the emergency airfields and allow the selection of the operator to dangle. Ironically, McNaughton would be praised as one of the key players in implementing the trans-Canada system. Indeed, he would brag that he was the mover and shaker behind the trans-Canada airway.

The two-year delay was a death sentence for Canadian Airways. Bennett, on the other hand, would wear the blame for allowing

Canadian Airways to wither and for Canada's loss of premier status for international flying.

McNaughton's letter to Manion showed his shift in thinking. As the powerful chief of the general staff and chairman of the TCA Committee, McNaughton would control the airways discussion. Because there was no member of the committee with any practical knowledge of commercial aviation or any understanding of the economics of business, McNaughton would successfully mould the committee to his point of view. By the end of June, the committee had mushroomed. If three members had difficulty agreeing, there was little hope that six to ten members would ever come to agreement. Interdepartmental rivalry would be in full swing. In attendance were numerous DND representatives plus Wilson, Coolican, Manion or his deputy, and Lester Pearson from External Affairs. Canadian Airways' destiny was in danger.

McNaughton called a meeting of the committee for July 4 to discuss strategy. Present were McNaughton, Coolican, Cowley and Smart. They decided that the requests in Canadian Airways' memo to the prime minister were "unreasonable." Wilson was directed to write Richardson, asking him to provide the committee with "any reorganization contemplated and what assistance they would need from the government."

From the start of these meetings McNaughton played games with Richardson. For instance, he delayed calling a full meeting until July 11, and he waited until July 8 before inviting Richardson to attend. (There was no direct air connection between Winnipeg and Ottawa.) McNaughton led not only Richardson down the garden path, but also most of the committee. Only Manion knew that McNaughton intended to write Canadian Airways out of the picture and that McNaughton was simply going through the motions.

McNaughton was an ineffective chairman. Only once did he bring the committee to a consensus position, and that was the original three-man committee of Coolican, Wilson and himself. He bullied committee members to his point of view and allowed interdepartmental turf protection to override the larger purpose of defining a national policy. On at least one occasion he did not act on the prime minister's directive, and on another he undermined the committee's recommendations by writing secretly to the prime minister, reversing the committee's recommendations. Even when he left the committee for the National

Research Council in the summer of 1935, McNaughton kept his finger in the trans-Canada airway pie and could not resist interfering and muddying the waters. With his committee at odds with each other, it was understandable why Bennett did nothing.

In June 1934, Senator J.A. McDonald assessed the state of aviation in Canada. His comments gave little if any credence to McNaughton's claim that he had performed a valuable service. "Canadians pride themselves on their high standard of living, yet Canada alone among countries of importance made practically no progress in the development of aviation during 1933, and it is the only country of moment whose citizens have not at their disposal the privilege of travel over regularly scheduled air routes."

Copies of the confidential minutes of the Trans-Canada Airway Committee meetings are in McNaughton's and Wilson's papers; copies of the minutes of the meetings attended by Canadian Airways are in the Canadian Airways Papers. Reading the minutes, McNaughton's private memos and Richardson's letters to various cabinet ministers and the prime minister reveals a tale not yet told.

Present at all meetings, unless otherwise stated, were McNaughton and Wilson from DND, Coolican or Herring from the Post Office, and Smart from Railways and Canals. In addition to these regulars were two to five others from DND and Pearson from External Affairs. In September 1934, W.C. Clark, deputy minister of finance, was asked to join the committee. When invited to attend, the Canadian Airways representatives were usually Mulock and Sigerson or Richardson and Thompson. Beatty and J.O. Apps, his assistant, represented the CPR, and Hungerford of the CNR came on behalf of his company.

On July 11, 1933, McNaughton held a meeting. Attending were Richardson, Mulock and Sigerson from Canadian Airways, and McNaughton, Coolican and A.T. Cowley from DND. Although the meeting was called ostensibly to discuss Canadian Airways' March 1933 memo to the prime minister, McNaughton told Richardson that the TCA Committee could not consider the memo until it knew who the trans-Canada contractor would be. Richardson was annoyed that McNaughton had deceived him about the purpose of the meeting, but he could do nothing to correct the situation.

Discussion quickly bogged down on the committee's proviso that one company could not handle both the bush and transcontinental operations. Richardson led off. "We are very much interested in the trans-Canada air service, but it is very questionable in my mind whether any other company would be in a position to give good service in the way of opening up the bush country. We are in a better position to do it than anyone else. We have been carrying on bush operations with all our energy ... The bush operations are not entirely self-supporting. They must get help either directly or indirectly ... air mail is one of the most satisfactory ways to meet that situation."

Sigerson suggested that Canadian Airways could reorganize itself into two departmental lines for the two jobs but, for the sake of economy and efficiency, use the same workshops, maintenance and overhaul shops and administrative office. Coolican refused to accept this, stating that "we have already suffered from exclusion and monopoly" and that "dissipation of energy [and] ideas in the past [have] helped to get us into the state we are." As usual, Coolican's remarks were more inflammatory and baseless than helpful or concrete. Although he kept harping on "monopoly" as the problem the aviation companies were currently having, there was no basis for his comment. Richardson finally challenged Coolican: "What are your other motives for desiring to have a separate company operate the two jobs?" Coolican responded, "Politics and economics." To which Richardson replied, "As far as economics is concerned, the fewer the organizations, the more economical it is, and the better the service provided." Coolican countered, "Theoretically that is true, but I doubt if that would work out in practice."

Coolican returned again to the issue of monopoly, implying that it had been the practice of the past few years and that it certainly had not worked out. He was, however, wrong; unrestricted destructive competition had been the problem. Richardson acknowledged that competition in the bush operations was good but it had to be handled properly. McNaughton answered, "We think the task is too big for common management." Retorted Richardson, "If we were to consider dropping our bush operations we would stand to lose a great deal, such as equipment." Richardson explained that he could not substitute aircraft between the two operations and that he would have to sell all his equipment, hangars and so on at a loss and did not believe he should be penalized for carrying on the services during the last three years. "We have been carrying on this work for six to seven years. We have done very useful work. We have a good organization, it is well set up." He asked once again if the committee had any problem with the bush operations being considered as auxiliary to the trans-Canada operations. McNaughton refused to answer. The only point agreed to was that the company must be Canadian owned and operated. The meeting disbanded with nothing accomplished.

Some time after the meeting (there was no date on the letter), Cowley wrote to Richardson. He (mistakenly) indicated that the intermediate landing grounds on the trans-Canada airway would be ready by September, and thus it was urgent to settle who the operator would be. He told Richardson that the committee believed it should be "left to private enterprise under such regulation as is necessary to provide adequate safety to the general public, to ensure that equitable rates are in force and that the service is developed in harmony with and as a necessary supplement to the rail and steamship services now operated by the Canadian railway companies."

Cowley's letter was significant in showing that McNaughton had not confided in him that he wanted the railways in control or had written Richardson out of the scheme. Cowley undoubtedly was sincere when he concluded his letter to Richardson by asking whether he wished his company to be considered and, if so, "what reorganization would you be making and what kind of liaison would you have with the CPR and CNR and the Finance?" Although Cowley expressed urgency and asked Richardson for a quick answer, McNaughton did not bother to call another meeting until late September.

In the meantime, officials from Canada, the United Kingdom and Newfoundland met in Newfoundland in July. There the Ottawa Agreement, made the preceding summer, was reconfirmed and preliminary plans for a trans-Atlantic service were made. Imperial Airways was in control of the situation because Canada had done nothing about its share of the agreement. Imperial Airways, impatient with Canada's inaction, demanded that Canada state what its contribution to the trans-Atlantic service would be. Canada had few options. It had neither the aircraft, a developed aircraft industry nor an operating company that could provide the service between Canada and Newfoundland, much less across the Atlantic. McNaughton, hindered by tunnel vision, did not help Canada's position when he told Imperial Airways that Canada could not commit itself to anything until it chose its transcontinental operator.

McNaughton's recollection in later years was different. He presented himself as having saved Canada's place in international flying. "With her rights protected, Canada could patiently await the development of suitable long-range aircraft by other countries, while going ahead with the development of her own internal airway. A Canadian company—TCA—would eventually be formed, ready to take a place in transatlantic flying that had been held open for it by the acumen of McNaughton," wrote his biographer.

The minutes, however, indicate that it was Wilson, showing much more foresight, who recommended that Canada provide all the ground facilities necessary in Newfoundland, because this would keep the door open for Canada to participate more actively at a later date. Richardson, fully informed, found these talks as inconclusive as the trans-Canada discussions. Sir Eric Geddes of Imperial Airways was obviously as unimpressed as Richardson was with McNaughton and the Canadian government, and he approached Beatty and Richardson again.

Beatty, annoyed with Canada's lackadaisical attitude, informed the prime minister of his conversation with Geddes and warned Bennett that Imperial Airways was expanding its vision—not just across the Atlantic, but across Canada if Canada did not name its operator. In an August 1, 1933, letter to the prime minister he wrote, "Sir Eric Geddes believes the overland route through Canada should be operated by his Company or a Company closely affiliated with the Imperial Airways." He said that Geddes would be asking Bennett the name of the Canadian contractor, and if none were named, Imperial Airways was prepared to run the service itself. These were bold words. Still Bennett stalled.

By August, Canadian Airways was in desperate financial circumstances. Richardson had a cash surplus of only $104,898, and at the September meeting of his executive committee he told them he could not carry on beyond the following spring. In spite of the uncertain future, Thompson had reported on August 31 that "the morale of the personnel, both pilots, engineers and agents, has never been higher." By the fall Richardson was able to report, "All our operations in the field are now carried on at an operating profit and our problem is to increase our volume, which would entail no additional overhead expense."

This was not enough, and on September 9 Sigerson sent, by code, the following telegram to Richardson: "I cannot help but make the conclusion that a showdown discussion by you with the Prime Minister with the assistance of the Vice-Presidents ... at the earliest possible moment is absolutely essential ... Bennett will otherwise continue to stall indefinitely ... I reach this conclusion not only because of increasing difficulty in raising transport prices but also raven [code word for the Post Office] is continually chiseling down rates for services in process of being renewed instead of raising them to help us."

On September 11, Richardson wired Mulock to say that he had had a "very satisfactory talk with McNaughton yesterday." Trusting as always, Richardson offered reassuring statements, such as, "[McNaughton] states that he thinks it desirable to clean up and come to an understanding on the general question covered in the Committee's letter before some of our more pressing problems can be dealt with ... I am satisfied we will be able to get together on all of the fundamentals. I know the reaction you get from the Ottawa officials but I am sure these gentlemen are thoroughly seized of the fact that we want to carry out the Trans-Canada service for which we were set up."

Richardson continued to believe McNaughton. Richardson's own patent honesty made him too often and too long unsuspecting of others' motives. But he was not the only one led astray by McNaughton; so was Bennett. As far as the prime minister was concerned, Richardson and Canadian Airways were still the main contenders. Obviously acting on the assumption that Canadian Airways would be Canada's chosen instrument, Bennett asked Mulock to attend a luncheon he was hosting for Sir George Beharrell of Imperial Airways, who was in Ottawa in early October. Discussion concerned the trans-Atlantic airway. The prime minister, still overburdened with economic problems, paid little if any attention to the deliberations of the TCA Committee. Those in the know, however, were very aware of the sparring interests of the different departments. An Ottawa insider later wrote: "Since all proceedings were secret and confidential, Ottawa was currently and reliably informed as to what was happening. The word was that a battle royal was on. General McNaughton was determined to make the military the dominant air arm."

McNaughton called a TCA Committee meeting on September 30 and asked Richardson to attend; Mulock attended in his place. Nothing conclusive came of the meeting. Another meeting was called for October 18. Beatty, Hungerford and Richardson attended and found themselves outnumbered by eleven departmental representatives. In the hour and a half that McNaughton had allotted for the meeting, he went over much the same ground as he had at the July meeting. He stated he could do nothing about Richardson's March memo. He spoke about how hard and how long government had been working on the "Trans-Canada Airway" and he praised the government for protecting Canada's interests in international flying.

Tired of listening to McNaughton spout empty platitudes, Beatty asked him point-blank what the government's policy was for the Canadian end of the trans-Atlantic system. John Wilson was forced to admit that Canada still had no policy. Undeterred, McNaughton then boasted about his putting unemployed men to work clearing for the intermediate airfields. "By the 30th of September next year we have every reason to expect that all the intermediate landing fields and ground facilities will be in a fit state to operate high speed aircraft from Halifax to Vancouver." (The trans-Canada airway was not completed until 1939.)

Even McNaughton's claim that he initiated putting unemployed single men to work on the trans-Canada airway may not be entirely correct. In a letter dated October 11, 1932, to James Richardson, R.H. Mulock related a discussion he had with government officials the previous winter. "We were looking for ways and means to capitalize on the depression and the unemployed to the benefit of aviation." When nothing materialized, Mulock wrote the prime minister on January 16, 1933, before he was due to meet with the provincial premiers. "Any funds that could be used for the development of an Air Highway across Canada would be very well spent from the National point of view ... In all cities there are a large number of single men without any permanent homes. These men followed construction enterprises, and drifted wherever work was available ... These men are commonly known as 'floaters' or 'drifters.' They are the best type of labour, and although some may have radical views the majority are only too willing to work if given the opportunity."

Discussion finally moved to Canadian Airways. McNaughton told Richardson he would have to abandon the bush services. Richardson was not about to give up easily. It was to be a contest of wills. "What we want is more business. The rates that you give us in Canada, going the way Mr. Coolican suggests, probably would not amount to a very large amount of money ... The bulk of the revenue of the Imperial Airways came from the British Government." Knowing full well that government needed to subsidize intercity airway development, McNaughton blustered, "We are doing something, Mr. Richardson, that the British Government never did for Imperial Airways. We are actually building the landing fields."

McNaughton was stretching the truth. It was not the federal government but the municipal governments and private interests, such as Richardson, who had built the majority of airports in every major city in Canada. The "fields" McNaughton referred to were being built as a result of unemployment relief programs, and they were emergency fields only. These fields were never used because by the time Trans-Canada Air Lines was formed, aircraft of longer range were in operation.

Richardson tried to pin down McNaughton, who, as usual, refused to make any commitment, saying only that the proposed company should include the two railway companies, Canadian Airways and possibly a minor interest by Imperial Airways, and that one director should be appointed by the government.

Richardson's blood must have boiled with the reference to Imperial Airways. Carefully, McNaughton made no suggestion that the railways should be in control. He allowed Richardson to assume that he would be in control. McNaughton then asked Richardson for a detailed plan of operations and estimates for a trans-Canada company. His parting comment was, "I think it would be a very bad thing to attempt to combine mail and passenger services at this time." His ignorance of airline economics was evident.

An October 16, 1933, memo written by Richardson to Beatty alternated between optimism and despair and showed that Richardson, while trying to put the best face forward, was also grasping at straws. "Relatively we are making some progress ... We are doing a fine job in opening up the mining areas ... Even today money outside of Canada could be found for our operation ... from Imperial Airways, from American companies and Imperial Oil. But ... our whole object was to keep this a 100% Canadian show and there has been no camouflage used any place ... We can possibly make an arrangement with Taschereau and Quebec regarding photographic work ... Unfortunately, General McNaughton is anxious to get the photographic work back under DND."

Canadian Airways officials meanwhile were busy working up the trans-Canada airway cost figures. Sigerson produced an exhaustive list that showed how prepared and able Canadian Airways was to undertake this huge operation. He telegrammed Richardson on November 23, "Four of us working here night and day to get figures ready." To ensure that they were not missing out on anything and were working their costs according to good airline practices, Richardson also directed Sigerson to check with some of the principal operators in the United States.

The situation was complicated by the progressive openings and expansion of various routes. As Sigerson explained in a November 4 letter to Mulock, "Since volume is all important in connection with unit costs determination ... unit cost will be one figure when only part of the complete run is being operated and an entirely different figure when we are operating straight across the country." Having no understanding of how costs were calculated and how the volume of business could affect costs, government officials would quibble over Canadian Airways' figures.

On November 10, Bennett finally asked for a progress report on the trans-Canada airway project and the Atlantic connection. McNaughton's response on November 14 was a masterpiece of convoluted writing. "Discussion has been proceeding intermittently as opportunity offered since May 1st last with a view to evolving proposals, properly coordinating the several interests involved ... discussions ... purely exploratory ... no commitment ... the views of the members of the Inter-Departmental Committee have been developed to the point that we can now indicate the general line on which we think action might best be taken to safeguard the public interest, hope shortly that you will have an interim report." In effect, the TCA Committee had accomplished nothing since the prime minister had asked McNaughton on

May 1 for a recommendation. Clearly, Bennett had forgotten his approval of the May 24 recommendations or McNaughton had somehow talked those recommendations and draft "Heads of Agreement" out of the picture.

Meanwhile, Imperial Airways and Pan Am were not standing still. Mulock wrote Richardson on November 13, stating that he had heard that two companies were to be formed in connection with the Atlantic mail service. "One will be on the British end and one on the Canadian end. The one on the British end is to be formed by a interest each of Great Western Railways, Imperial Airways and the CPR. The one on the Canadian end is to be formed by a ⅓ interest each of Canadian Airways, the CPR and Imperial Airways."

On November 15, McNaughton wrote another confidential memo to himself. There seemed to be no purpose for this memo unless he wanted to ensure that someone later interpreted history his way. The memo covered old ground and seems to be an attempt to cover himself in case the committee made a recommendation. More than once, McNaughton assured the unseen reader that he had informed all committee members that all discussions were "purely exploratory and involved no commitment of any sort."

By now totally frustrated with the inaction from McNaughton, Richardson appealed to the newspapers for help. On November 25, the *Winnipeg Free Press* ran an article titled "An Air Policy Wanted." Not surprisingly, Wilson and other DND officials reacted by calling the story "unfair." Still with no word from McNaughton and disturbed about his insistence that Canadian Airways divorce itself from bush operations, Richardson felt he had no choice but to contact the prime minister again, asking for an appointment "of a few minutes anytime Wednesday." On November 29, he wrote a frank and very detailed letter to Bennett.

> I am greatly disturbed and upset over the Airways picture and feel that it is urgent that I should have a little time to cover the matter with you. Mr. Beatty tells me he feels that he does not think I could ever have put the whole Airways proposition up to you properly, referring to the fact that the Air Mail contracts to Western companies and Eastern companies were given out before your Government

came into office and that the Canadian Airways was put together on the basis of these contracts and for the purpose of keeping Sir Henry Thornton from going into an extensive aviation program ... or he would have been into the aviation field, inviting wasteful competition between the two railroad companies ...

With the cutting off of the Air Mail we had to lay up our Mail planes and we endeavoured to take care of ourselves by buying additional bush equipment and prosecuting this end of the work with all our energies. Progress has been very gratifying from the point of view of the contribution we have made to the opening up of the country, but it is impossible to make it stand up on its own feet ...

Following the memorandum presented to you last May I understand a Departmental Committee was appointed under the chairmanship of Major-General McNaughton ... they advised us that they had no authority to deal with the question of policy contained in [the] Memorandum to the Prime Minister, but they wanted to make recommendations in regard to who was to carry the Trans-Canada Air Mail from coast to coast. They thought this should be done by a separate company and that whoever did carry this Mail should not engage in bush work ...

One of the thoughts brought out at this meeting was that not only should a separate company be formed but who was going to manage it. I think this was very unusual, because if we were going to undertake to guarantee the speeds and schedules we surely would require to engage executives, which I think we are thoroughly competent to do ... Colonel Smart, who went to Montreal and made a study of our company, told me afterwards that he was quite satisfied our set-up was entirely proper for handling the Trans-Canada Air Mail and that he saw no need of a separate company, and that he thought the Committee did not feel so strongly on this as they did ...

The Committee asked us to give them costs ... there is no interest or profit factor embodied in the figures ... In view of the fact that the Committee say they have no authority to deal with the whole problem of the Canadian Airways I do not see how anything can be closed up between Mr. Beatty, Mr. Hungerford, myself and the Committee ... The Company needs consideration in the meantime.

If you feel justified in naming the Canadian Airways exclusive carriers for His Majesty's Air Mail, it would seem as if our problems would be much simpler and we are prepared to work hand in hand with the Government.

Richardson put his heart on his sleeve with his last paragraph. "We do not expect to make large profits but we do want to keep alive an organization into which has been put over $3,000,000 and which is performing, in my humble opinion, one of the best constructive jobs being done in the Dominion of Canada, and to which I have given a great deal of time during the past 7 years, without any remuneration or compensation of any kind, in the belief that I was doing something very much worthwhile." The whole experience must have been a very unpalatable one to Richardson.

His letter was hand-delivered to the prime minister, and to Bennett's credit, he reacted quickly by directing McNaughton to see Richardson immediately. It is too much of a coincidence that Richardson, who was in Toronto, received a telegram from McNaughton that very day advising him of a committee meeting the next day, November 30, at 10 A.M. Neither Beatty nor Hungerford could make it on that short notice. Richardson, Mulock and Sigerson attended. McNaughton began with, "We are as yet in the discussion stage and . . . neither the transportation companies nor we ourselves are entering into any definite commitment. Today we are to hear from Mr. Richardson." McNaughton's words and actions were a typical bureaucrat's response: hold a multitude of meetings, keep telling everyone that nothing definite can be promised and let the months drag on.

Richardson pressed his case tactfully. "The present set-up of our company enables us to start out now and carry on at any time with progressive success. We have in our own service, at the present time, 160 personnel who have been with our company for seven years, and I think we have accumulated a wealth of experience in flying. Mr. Sigerson has worked on these figures exclusively for a couple of weeks, night and day. He has brought his working sheets with him and Colonel Mulock is here at the disposal of your Committee, and we are prepared to assist you in any way we can . . ."

McNaughton, baiting Richardson, demanded to know if Richardson had discussed "the form" of the company with the two railway presidents. Clearly he hoped that Richardson had not talked with Beatty and Hungerford, so that he could "use" the omission to show that Richardson was not prepared to work cooperatively with the railways. Suppressing his anger, Richardson politely replied, "We have discussed that, and our position is that we have to conform to the policy of the government ... We would like to carry it on as a Trans-Continental part of our service ... but if the government decides that it is to the best advantage to operate as a separate Company, we are quite willing to conform to that ... The costs we have submitted here are based on an independent company as you requested us to do."

Richardson submitted the detailed costs for each progressive stage and gave costs for both the transcontinental and ship-to-shore service. The schedules were all supported by Canadian Airways' worksheets. Richardson said he was prepared to give the details of every item of cost and to note that his figures gave little if any profit margin. "We are prepared to supply this service on a cost basis, or on any basis which can be mutually worked out satisfactorily, and I may say that we are here to work one hundred percent with whatever may be the established policy of the government." When asked by Wilson if the figures were actual costs, Richardson replied, "These costs include no profit or interest. They are the bare costs as we see them today. The people who prepared these figures are responsible for them, and they are quite prepared to come here at any time, in person, and discuss them with you."

Wilson then asked if the figures were endorsed by Beatty and Hungerford. Richardson answered in the negative, explaining that they had not gone over the figures but were well aware that Canadian Airways was working them up for presentation. Sigerson, sensing where Wilson's questions were going, asked, "Mr. Wilson, may I ask you a question? Were Mr. Beatty and Mr. Hungerford present at the last meeting of the Committee as Railway Presidents or as Vice-Presidents of Canadian Airways?" Wilson replied, "As Presidents of their respective Railway Companies."

At this point Smart spoke up, on behalf of Canadian Airways. "I do not see how the Railway people can say whether the figures are right or wrong. We asked Canadian Airways to put these figures up." Wilson obviously was annoyed with Smart running interference for Richardson and retorted, quite out of character, "That is beside my point. The question is whether they were here as representatives of the two Railway Companies, and whether they, as such, are prepared to endorse these figures." Committee relations were visibly on edge if the normally unperturbable Wilson had his feathers ruffled.

With absolutely no qualms, Richardson submitted Canadian Airways' very detailed working sheets, plans and figures to the subcommittee of Smart (chairman), Herring, Wing Commander Johnson and Wilson. These plans represented more than seven years of operating experience and, more importantly, the layout for a national airline. They were given with the assumption that the contract would be given to Canadian Airways. Richardson could do no less—otherwise, he would have been seen as obstructionist—but essentially he gave away the house. The government now had the figures, schedules, costs and indeed the blueprint for a national airline at its fingertips. It did not need Canadian Airways any more.

The meeting was adjourned, and Coolican wasted no time before complaining. In a letter to McNaughton on December 8, 1933, he said, "I was rather struck with the attitude adopted by Mr. Smart with regard to the necessity of protecting the capital already invested by the Canadian Pacific and Canadian National Railways ... One thing had to be perfectly clear and that was that the Post Office Department had absolutely no interest in such an investment and consequently it would not be taken into consideration as affecting the picture in any way ... Might I add also that Mr. Herring made it clear that the figures to be submitted were not to be regarded as constituting a regular tender, neither was it to be understood that the submission of figures by the Canadian Airways Limited in any way implied that they would become the eventual contractors."

There were three more meetings, on December 4, 7 and 11. Sigerson and Mulock were invited only to the last two. At the December 4 meeting Herring showed both his lack of business savvy and his ignorance of aeronautics. He said there was no need for a second pilot for high-speed aircraft, that the costs of engine maintenance and fuel consumption were excessive, and that the concept of productive and unproductive miles was irrelevant as a business factor. Wing Commander Johnson disagreed with Herring on all matters relating to flying, and Smart played the role of mediator. As the weeks and months of negotiations progressed, Smart would show himself the most willing to learn about the air transport industry and the most able to look beyond his own department.

The differences between the estimates prepared by Canadian Airways and those done by the government were great, and no agreement was reached as to whose were correct. While all agreed that Canadian Airways should have a profit, neither Wilson, Smart nor Herring could agree on how it was to be calculated. The most contentious item was Coolican and McNaughton's demand that only mail be carried—no passengers. This was a factor in the differences of cost figures because Canadian Airways had based the figures on aircraft that could carry mail, freight and passengers. At this point, Wilson backed up Richardson and said that Canadian Airways should be encouraged to build up an express business.

Herring also quibbled over what Sigerson termed "productive miles," which he explained were the miles for which they expected payment, so they did not include mileage flown without mail, such as the ferrying of aircraft, test flights or the completion of trips cancelled because of weather. Mulock explained that the actual air miles flown would probably exceed the productive land miles covered by up to 30 percent and that this should be taken into consideration in comparing any of the operator's cost figures with those of a corresponding government service that counted the total hours flown in arriving at a cost-per-hour figure for overhaul or maintenance. With no agreement reached on anything, Mulock and Sigerson were asked to leave the meeting.

With Canadian Airways gone, Wilson, sounding as if McNaughton had coached him, stated that "it was highly desirable that the railways should take an important, if not a controlling interest in the new company so as to avoid the possibility of competition between the Airways and the Railways." Smart again showed that he was his own man by stating, "In my life long experience of railway management and operation I cannot subscribe to the theory that control by railway men would avoid competition. In my opinion control of an airway system by the railways would strangle the system ... What is needed is independent control over all forms of transportation—rail, water, road and air." Smart had vision; even more than Wilson, he saw that the air transport industry could not be hampered by the railways or the military. He would prove to be a good advocate for the industry, but McNaughton would later muzzle him and he would not speak out again on behalf of Canadian Airways. Worth noting was Smart's recommendation in 1933 for a federal department of transport. McNaughton would later take credit for recommending this.

A subcommittee meeting was held on December 13; present were Smart, Wilson, Johnson, Herring and McLean. Its purpose was to consider the draft report that was being prepared for the main committee. The meeting was short; Smart led off the discussion by saying, "Airways operations should be controlled by an administration which [has] the welfare of air transportation solely at heart. If the airways are under the railways, administration and control would suffer through the lack of interest on the part of railway personnel." Nothing further was discussed, and the meeting was adjourned.

Richardson, ever suspicious of government costs, was concerned that government requirements would be so onerous that the costs would be excessive and the whole program scrapped. Mulock too "was afraid that when the two figures came together on the Prime Minister's desk (i.e., operating figures from the Post Office and capital and maintenance figures from DND) he might be inclined to put the whole matter off another year and so started scheming to find ways to make the final figure more attractive." In his letter of December 14, Mulock explained further: "The total cost to the government or taxpayer is a figure that needs a lot of thought on our part ... The government is struggling to maintain Canada's credit ... The cost of the Trans-Canada operation falls into two divisions: a) Operating (Post Office) and b) Airways (DND). As far as 'a' is concerned I think the figures arrived at are as low as possible and therefore we cannot relieve the taxpayer in this plan. Under 'b' I think there is a possibility of considerably lowering the burden on the Treasury." Mulock suggested that a subsidiary company be formed that would finance the airways completely; thus the cost to the government, especially capital costs, would be much less.

Herring was not happy with the prospect that Canadian Airways might be the national operator. He must have spent Christmas Day thinking about it, because on December 26 he wrote a five-page letter to Coolican complaining about Canadian Airways. Contradicting his earlier comments that Western Canada Airways had been performing a service at almost 100 percent perfection, Herring now wrote, "Their record on the Trans-Prairie service was such as to create a definite doubt as to their ability to undertake a scheduled operation of much greater magnitude and importance than any they have undertaken in the past." He was vague in his complaints. Herring also took exception to Wilson's charge that the Post Office had not played fair ball. "The Canadian Airways have been treated in a most generous manner by the Post Office Department." He rationalized some of the low rates by saying that the RCAF could have done it for a much lower price! He too did not realize that if the cost was not picked up by the RCAF it would be charged against another government department and, in the long run, was not cheaper. "All in all, the Canadian Airways Limited should feel satisfied that everything possible has been done by the Post Office Department to give them adequate opportunity to carry on."

Coolican, fired up by Herring, wrote McNaughton on December 27. Like Herring, he never spelled out what was wrong with Canadian Airways. Contradicting Herring, he said, "Experience has amply demonstrated the fact that private operation is the more economical. You will gather from this that if I were forced to declare myself I would cast my vote for private operation. But I would want it clearly understood that I regarded the whole question purely from a Postal Service point of view, without any regard whatever for other factors which might affect the situation from a National point of view."

Meanwhile Richardson, ever on the outlook, expanded his holdings again. In December 1933, Canadian Airways acquired Spence McDonough Air Transport. However, despite bringing in another competitor and making economies all along the line, Canadian Airways was unable to maintain its previous rate structure. By the end of the year, Richardson had to borrow $400,000 from the bank to keep Canadian Airways flying.

Nevertheless, in the Christmas spirit, Richardson sent McNaughton an airway pass, to which McNaughton responded on December 3, "I assure you that we highly value the close co-operation which we continue to have from yourself and the other officers of Canadian Airways and that we look forward with you to the important developments which are bound to come in the near future." Richardson, encouraged by the TCA Committee meetings and the outward friendliness of McNaughton, sent a telegram to all officers and staff of Canadian Airways, along with his Christmas greeting, "We must tackle the new year with renewed courage and energy."

"A Case of the Blind
Leading the Blind"

"WE, OF COURSE, have been living in hopes of the restoration of the air mail," Richardson reported to his board of directors. But on January 4, 1934, when the Trans-Canada Airway Committee filed its confidential report, it did not recommend Canadian Airways as Canada's "chosen instrument." Bennett refused his old acquaintance's request for a copy—a sad irony, since it was Canadian Airways' technical knowledge and Richardson's collaboration that had made the report possible. Rumour ran rampant. What would James Richardson do? With the company's future looking so dismal, selling seemed to be the smart answer. But Richardson believed in what his company was doing for Canada and felt that, given time, the prime minister would see the value of Canadian Airways.

If given the total picture, Bennett most likely would have made a different decision. Hamilton newspaper editor F.I. Ker assessed the prime minister correctly when he advised Richardson to lay all the facts on the table for Bennett. "I do not think the personal element counts for much with him in this or any other case, which is as it should be.

I do think, however, that if this case is put up to him concisely and on its merits the Prime Minister would do the just thing, and justice is, after all, the only thing that the Canadian Airways is after."

Unfortunately, Richardson waited three more months before definitively describing the complete Canadian Airways story. By then it was too late. Bennett's cabinet members knew little about the aviation industry and its importance to Canada's national and international growth and could give no wise counsel to their leader. As the commissioner of the Ontario Securities Commission, George Drew, wrote to Richardson:

> I am satisfied that we will get nowhere until the control of civil aviation is taken out of the hands of the Department of National Defence. I did not know until you told me today that Manion and Guthrie had been appointed as a committee to deal with this matter. I am sorry Guthrie was appointed, because he not only knows nothing about the air, but is unsympathetic. I have a very vivid recollection of meeting him in Calgary, just after I had returned from my jaunt to the Arctic, and his only comment was, "My God! George, haven't you taken enough chances with your life already without going on a damn fool trip like that?" Manion is more receptive, but unfortunately knows very little about the air and has not to my knowledge made any use of air transportation in his work. In fact, so far as I know, the only member of the Cabinet who ever uses an aeroplane is Sir George Perley, who has discovered that this is a fine way of getting to his fishing camp, and uses Air Force machines for that purpose. I am honestly afraid that in this committee, it is a case of the blind leading the blind.

The civil servants, whom the prime minister should have been able to count on and who did know the full story, were busy protecting their own departmental interests or were overshadowed by the military. "Aviation was treated as if it were wholly military," Wilson was to write more than once. Not the least of Richardson's problems was the fact that Bennett's departmental TCA Committee was ignorant of airline economics. Richardson, playing "the square game," could not compete against the rival interests within and without government, who used whatever tactics were necessary. Without a copy of the TCA Committee's report, Richardson did not even know exactly what he was fighting. He was behind the eight ball from the start.

The confidential draft report that committee members met to discuss on January 4 demonstrated the committee's lack of any in-depth understanding of the subject. Six pages of twenty numbered paragraphs comprised the report. There was no sense of urgency in its tone, and indeed the committee danced around for fourteen paragraphs before getting to the main issue of who was to be the trans-Canada operator. Even then it made a weak recommendation, which was further undermined by McNaughton, who sent a confidential letter to the prime minister and minister of defence contradicting the committee's key recommendation.

The report summarized domestic airway development, the effect of the proposed trans-Atlantic and trans-Pacific airways on Canada, and the organization, schedules and costs of the trans-Canada airway. It acknowledged Canadian Airways' assistance, and the firm's influence was seen in the majority of the report's recommendations. The committee studied the report paragraph by paragraph; Squadron Leader Cowley of DND recorded the comments. These minutes, attached to the report and covering four pages, are important, for they show where dissension occurred and who controlled the committee.

Only two points generated any real discussion: railway control and the separation of Canadian Airways' bush operations from the trans-Canada service. Most members believed the railways should be in control, except the deputy minister of railways, who disagreed and was not afraid to say so. Cowley recorded, "Mr. Smart gave as his opinion that it was important that the control should not be placed in the hands of the railways. The railways had huge investments and should a conflict of opinion come at any time between the railways and the airway their inclinations would naturally be to sacrifice the airway."

Canadian Airways came under attack for its claim that it could handle both the trans-Canada airway and bush operations. Wilson stated that the two operations were different, implying that one company could not deal with both. Smart saw the economics of having one company manage both and challenged McNaughton and Wilson. Cowley recorded: "Mr. Smart asked if there was any inherent difficulty in having the same corporation operate both bush and scheduled operations.

He stated that the railways had different services which were all carried out under the one control. It was agreed that there was no reason why an institution such as Canadian Airways could not carry out both operations provided that the management was kept entirely separate." The committee agreed, until McNaughton intervened. Cowley wrote, "General McNaughton stated that the objection to having one corporation in charge of both bush and scheduled operations was primarily political."

Paragraph one stated what was happening worldwide. It did not admit that Canada was the only major country with no intercity development. Tucked away in Appendix E was the truth: "Canada seems to be alone in the lack of definite Government support in the development of air traffic ... The establishment of no less than three highly efficient air lines from Great Britain, Holland and France to the Straits Settlements and Dutch East Indies seriously threatens the supremacy of the Canadian route and this threat is intensified by the constant development and extensions of these air lines." These comments should have been in the body of the report, not hidden away in the appendices.

Paragraph two admitted that Canada had no intercity airway. However, the spin put on the words lessened the seriousness of the situation and made it seem as if Canada had been busy elsewhere in airways development. "Today, only three major airways remain to be organized —the Trans-Canada, the Trans-Atlantic and the Trans-Pacific."

Paragraph three, referring to Appendices A and B on the transAtlantic and Pacific, also belied the gravity of the matter. "These [appendices] show the progress to date and the alternative plans now under discussion for the development of these great services." The phrasing made it sound as if Canada had made progress and had alternative plans in place. Nothing could have been further from the truth. The next sentence contained a more revealing phrase: "if Canada continues to refuse her cooperation." The committee's use of the word "refuse" refutes McNaughton's statements that Canada had cooperated with the United States and Great Britain.

Paragraph four admitted that four transcontinental airways paralleled the international boundary and that American companies were diverting mail from Canada and seeking entry into Canada with feeder lines. The committee saw no reason to be alarmed. "So far, Canada's attitude has been to avoid American participation in the development of aviation activities in the Dominion with a view to safeguarding the field for Canadian operators." The committee was stretching the truth; Richardson had warned that the cancellation of the air mail contracts had wiped out not just his company's financial basis but the Canadian operator needed to preserve the airways against American intruders. The committee continued to whitewash government actions by talking about its "policy of exclusion," but the government had no policy; it was simply sitting on its hands. Canadian Airways, acting on its own, had maintained, at a financial loss, its international services to keep out the Americans.

Paragraphs five and six gave general statements about the trans-Canada airway, remarking specifically on the prairie air mail, "This section was operated successfully from the 3rd of March, 1930, to the 31st of March, 1932." Post Office officials would later deny this. Paragraphs seven, eight and nine discussed the number of airfields required, their status and cost. The numbers were there for anyone who read carefully, but the committee cleverly did not say outright that most fields were not built and that twenty-nine had not even been located. Paragraphs ten and eleven discussed the air mail, its revenues and inauguration. The committee admitted, as Richardson had long pointed out, that air mail revenues should soon exceed expenditures. The committee, ever optimistic, then went on to say that the airway should be in operation by April 1, 1936.

Paragraphs twelve and thirteen referred to the estimates submitted by Canadian Airways and the advantages of using this airline. Despite the committee's agreement with Smart that one company could handle both the bush and transcontinental services, McNaughton, using his position as chairman, again overruled the committee. Cowley wrote that the operating management of the trans-Canada airway must be separate from any other air operations.

Smart's ability to look beyond the narrow confines of his department to the broader question of all transportation systems can be seen in paragraph fourteen, which recommended a department of transport (his suggestion). Hidden away in the last part of the paragraph was the important recommendation for an independent company to operate the trans-Canada airway, as long as there was a separate controlling department over all forms of transportation to prevent destructive competition between air, rail and steamship travel.

After months of deliberations, the committee sat on the fence and came up with a brilliant deduction in paragraph fifteen. "Two alternatives present themselves—(a) A company closely affiliated with existing transportation interests. (b) Operation by the Dominion Government. Both methods have their advantages and drawbacks. The committee incline towards operation by an independent company but recognize that questions of high Government policy may make the retention of complete control in the government's hands desirable." The committee's choice of words made this a half-hearted recommendation. Significant was the reference to a government-controlled air service.

Paragraph sixteen suggested that Imperial Airways be involved, that both railways be represented and that the government appoint one or two directors. Paragraph seventeen said little. Paragraph eighteen talked about mail schedules, and paragraph nineteen discussed the ship-to-shore service.

Paragraph twenty made eight recommendations. These were the meat of the report: construction should continue on the trans-Canada airway as an unemployment relief measure, more land should be acquired for airfields, provision should be made in the estimates for the maintenance of the airway and for air mail contracts, the contract should be given for ten years, the principal officers of the company should be British subjects living in Canada, and equipment should be Canadian built, if possible.

Of interest was Appendix F, on costs of operations, which acknowledged another of Richardson's arguments, that the bulk of the revenue came from traffic other than air mail and that government had supported all other forms of transportation in Canada. "The construction of the trunk airways and their maintenance should not be considered as a charge against the air mail but rather as a national undertaking, just as improvements to the St. Lawrence waterway, with its dredged channels, lighted systems, wireless, signal and weather systems have been provided for as national considerations warranted, without reference to the cost of the mail services using the facilities." The appendix also reported that municipalities and private investment had spent $4 million in building airfields.

The report, dated January 18, 1934, was signed by McNaughton, Pearson, Wilson, Coolican and Smart, with Cowley signing as secretary. McNaughton waited until January 30 before delivering the report and his secret letter. If the prime minister was unsure about appropriate action before, McNaughton's letter would further confuse the issue. "In [the committee's] reaching the tentative conclusion that a private commercial company should be set up ... it may be found expedient [in McNaughton's opinion], so far, at least, as the transit of H.M. mails is concerned, to retain complete control in the hands of the Dominion Government."

McNaughton's recommendation was not unexpected. Although he had told Richardson that Canadian Airways would be the basis of the national company, he had often said privately that the company should be government owned. What was unexpected was McNaughton's deceitfulness to Richardson and the committee. Richardson, described by so many as always acting scrupulously, assumed that McNaughton was "an officer and a gentleman" and would act accordingly. But in his letter McNaughton wrote that it had "clearly emerged from the discussions with designers and operators, that so far as the main lines of the Trans-Canada are concerned it will be necessary, in order to keep to the schedules required, to have separate aircraft to carry the mails, and while some express matter may be carried in these machines, it will not be practicable to use them for a passenger service."

Nothing in McNaughton's, Wilson's or the Post Office's papers confirms that designers and operators had stated this. On the contrary, operators, Richardson in particular, argued the exact opposite—and experience in other countries showed that manufacturers had to design aircraft that could carry mail, freight and passengers to ensure a viable company. The minutes of other TCA Committee meetings make clear that McNaughton did not understand airline economics and had no wish to learn, and more importantly, his main desire was to keep the air force flying. If the mail were to be carried separately, then the air force could fly it.

McNaughton, like Coolican, was obsessive in his belief that mail must be carried separately from passengers and freight. He may have felt that the ends justified the means. His biographer, an admirer of McNaughton, did suggest that when McNaughton passionately believed in something, he would allow nothing to stop him. In this instance, McNaughton was far more interested in keeping alive his air force than in keeping alive a commercial entity. But here, Smart's argument made more sense, and McNaughton, unable to force the committee to agree with him, likely decided to go along with it, while already plotting a secret letter to the prime minister.

It would be interesting to know what Cowley did *not* record in the minutes. There was no reason for the prime minister to question why his chief of staff differed from his committee. McNaughton was known as Bennett's man. "During the Bennett years no man had been closer than he to the seat of power. He had sat on the box with Bennett and had often decided the road that the government should take ... He had become perhaps the most powerful public servant in the country," wrote his biographer, John Swettenham.

McNaughton, a good strategist, covered his tracks well regarding his thoughts about Richardson. In his letter to Bennett he implied that the committee talked minimally with Canadian Airways officials and only about a few items. He left the impression that while Canadian Airways' executives were pleasant, they had little to contribute. His only useful piece of advice to the prime minister was that he should make an early decision on the report so that action could be taken "to safeguard the proper interests of the government and the people of Canada."

All in all, the TCA Committee report accomplished little. Except for continuing to build the intermediate airfields, government did little. Undoubtedly McNaughton's secret letter to the prime minister, which strongly contradicted a weak recommendation, made it easy for Bennett to continue to procrastinate.

Richardson, meanwhile, was pinning his hopes on a personal meeting with Bennett. He finally saw him on February 16, 1934. The records do not reveal what took place. It can only be imagined what two powerful men, each with their own agenda, said to each other. Did either listen to the other, or were they both too intent on telling their own story? Richardson later described the meeting to Beatty, and reading between the lines, one can surmise that sparks flew. "Bennett said that Sir Henry Drayton had just been through the West preaching 'economy' and it would not do to open up the Prairie Air Mail. I told him the Prairies were very air-minded. He said this might be true of the cities and towns but some of the farmers would object. I wish Drayton had talked about 'efficiency in government' instead of 'economy in government.' You cannot have efficiency without economy, but you can have economy without efficiency ... in fact you can have economy that ruins efficiency."

Richardson's meeting with the prime minister proved to be a bust. McNaughton's influence was apparent.

> Mr. Bennett thinks it desirable to have the soldiers carry the Mail and to wind up our company. I told him that in order to keep our company afloat it would be necessary to restore the western Air Mail at our contract prices ... He asked me if I knew how many people that [$250,000] would feed. I asked him if he knew how many people had been supported by the opening up of the mines, in which we had been a large factor ... I asked him if he had any objection to our getting the money from the Imperial Airways ... and he said he thought this was undesirable, evidently feeling that it would commit the Dominion Government to action. I told him we could not drift on this matter any longer. He promised to discuss the matter immediately with his Cabinet.

Sir Edward Beatty replied on February 19. "My dear Jim, I discussed Airways affairs with the Prime Minister by 'phone yesterday. I found him, of course, definitely opposed to any subsidy because, he insisted, that the government could not afford to establish air mail services now and that it would be politically unwise to do so."

Beatty's lack of influence with the prime minister is hard to explain. According to his biographer, Beatty and Bennett were friends and often saw each other socially. If Bennett did not listen to Beatty in reference to the airways, neither did he agree with Beatty about amalgamating the CPR and CNR. Despite Beatty's disappointment in Bennett's lack of support for the CPR, he believed in Bennett's "good faith."

Meanwhile, back in Ottawa on February 16, John Wilson was busy writing another memo, "Air Developments and Their Effect on Canada," which went over the same ground as his previous memos of the past six years. However, extremely concerned with the continued inaction of the government, Wilson tried to shake some life into government officials, and his writing took on a brisker tone. He included slides of the European and American airways systems and of the North Atlantic and Pacific airways. Canada's neglect was obvious.

Wilson also added a new argument. He bluntly told officials that government had helped the railways, steamship services, telegraph and telephone systems and radio but had left the airways to fly on their own. Then he listed all the points where the Americans had tapped Canadian traffic: the Maritimes, Montreal, Toronto, Windsor, Winnipeg and Vancouver. His argument was clear: Canada soon would not need a national system; the Americans would have tapped the traffic at all vital points.

Wilson then discussed both coastlines and stated that the Americans were making an all-out effort for a trans-Pacific route. He was acting boldly for he was contradicting McNaughton, who had been dismissive about the trans-Pacific airways, saying that nothing would happen for many years. Wilson emphatically stated that the Americans had their eye on two routes: either the Winnipeg, northern Alberta, Yukon and Alaska route to connect with Asia to Japan, or the alternative coastal route from Seattle and Vancouver northward. He concluded by warning that Canada would lose the north Atlantic trade route to American interests.

Although Wilson's memo was very clear as to what government should do, McNaughton's actions were not. While the controller of civil aviation was trying to prod the government to form a national company, the chief of the general staff was recommending that the military carry the mail. Here is a recap of the sequence of events. McNaughton chaired a committee that recommended that a private company operate the national airway and then went behind the committee's back to secretly recommend a government-controlled company to the prime minister. Next he advised the prime minister to have the air force carry the mail in various areas, such as the Pacific coast, presenting it to the prime minister as vital to the defence of the coast. Since the 1932 Geneva Conference on disarmament, McNaughton had been concerned about home defence. But in 1934, of whom was Canada afraid? He also suggested that the Post Office pick up the costs. Smart man. According to his secretary, McNaughton had seen the prime minister on March 10 and pushed for defence on the Pacific coast in the form of aircraft for "reconnoitering purposes." He suggested that funds come from the Post Office because "the Army" would also carry mail. By hook or by crook, McNaughton would keep his men flying.

More complications arose when Billy Bishop, well-known World War I pilot and an admirer of Richardson, warned Richardson, on March 11, that the "Toronto group" had resurfaced and was trying to organize a company to bid for the trans-Canada contract. It was attempting to hijack the air mail contract, since the group had no intention of actually running an airways company; it simply wanted to obtain the contract and then "later be able to turn it over to the railroads at a good profit." This group of influential men had been loosely organized by Percy Parker, a Liberal fundraiser, and financed by Harry Gundy in the late 1920s to form British North American Airways, which had never operated. The group changed slightly year in and year out. For instance, E.P. Taylor, president of the Brewing Corporation of Canada, and the Hon. J.L. Ralston were said to be members in 1936. At any one time it represented a powerful group of about fifteen businessmen, civil servants and politicians of both major parties.

The group wanted Bishop to join them but he declined, believing that Richardson had received "a dirty deal" from government and from some of the Toronto group speculators. Bishop went on to say that this group "was responsible for a good deal of criticism being thrown at the Airways." Bishop assured Richardson of "his 100% cooperation and support" and volunteered to stump the country on behalf of Canadian Airways. Richardson was now fighting mad. No way was he going to sit passively by and watch his company be shunted out of the picture by a group that was only interested in the airways on a speculative basis.

The only course of action, as Richardson saw it, was an all-out campaign to arouse public opinion and government officials on Canadian Airways' behalf. He personally carried Canadian Airways' case to newspaper editors and political, business and financial leaders across the country. Beatty and Richardson also pressured the prime minister into appointing a cabinet committee to look into the airways situation. Richardson also resurrected the cancelled contract as a first tactical step, which should have been done in March 1932. He asked Sigerson to contact the original lawyers, Brown, Montgomery & McMichael of Montreal, who responded on March 1, 1934, "We assumed that services were discontinued by you on April 1st, 1932, without protest, in other words that you accepted the stand taken by the Postmaster General's Department ... The Company ... has lost whatever residuum of legal right it might have had to impugn the validity of the annulment."

Richardson's personal friend and lawyer, James B. Coyne, thought otherwise: Richardson did not "acquiesce" in the cancellation, and while he did not press his legal rights in 1932, neither did he abandon them or agree to accept the cancellation "without compensation or deferred performance." In a "Memo for Mr. Richardson" dated April 10, 1934, Coyne wrote: "Cancellation based on a desire to save money at the expense of the contractor, when performance is otherwise satisfactory and without regard to his commitments and loss, is not a requirement of 'public interest,' but in fact and in intent amounts to bald repudiation. It does not supply the case necessary in order to give power to cancel ... Your consent, if any, was only to a 'stand still' arrangement. It would be well, I think, to recall on the record now your protest and non-acceptance."

Prominent Winnipegger J.A. Matheson said: "Surely one of our greatest national assets is that fundamental respect for a contract, once entered into, which is the cornerstone of our whole economic system ... If the faith and trust of the people of this country in the integrity of the government is shattered ... our whole commercial and financial system will be damaged."

Unfortunately, Richardson did not follow Coyne's advice, and his decision not to take legal action against the government was an incorrect one. He had nothing to lose and everything to gain. If Richardson had properly harnessed his board of directors to exert pressure on government and at the same time threatened legal action while the boards of trade and the western newspapers were clamouring for the reinstatement of the prairie air mail, Bennett may very well have bowed to pressure to reissue the air mail contracts. Later correspondence from Bennett showed that he was weakening.

One of Richardson's first calls was to Frank Ross, president of Saint John Dry Dock & Shipbuilding, who had good connections and lots of common sense. Ross met with the prime minister and R.J. Manion, who confirmed Richardson's suspicions that McNaughton was blackballing Canadian Airways. Wrote Ross, "McNaughton said that our organization was all wrong and that he certainly was not going to discuss Government business with an American book-keeper [Sigerson], that if we got any American money we could be assured that we would never get an Air Mail contract and if we got any money from the Imperial Airways we could be sure we would never get an Air Mail contract." McNaughton's reference to Imperial Airways was an example of how he vacillated about the national company. Manion assured Ross that he did not agree with McNaughton and that he, along with Bennett, believed that Canadian Airways was entitled to the first consideration when the contracts were given out. He also said that the prime minister was going to appoint a cabinet committee to study the aviation question and he would probably be chairman. "McNaughton's attitude was that he had himself done far more for aviation in Canada than everybody else combined, that he had done it when he built the transcontinental airways with unemployed men and . . . that the transcontinental should be kind of a memorial to him."

There were many comings and goings in Ottawa. The controller of civil aviation unexpectedly dropped in to see Mulock. Although Wilson had nothing but praise for Canadian Airways, "he thought it was politically unwise that the company who flew the transcontinental air mail should engage in any other business. It is rather surprising that men in his position feel that it is up to them to settle the Government policy," Mulock reported to Richardson. "He, of course, is just a mouthpiece for McNaughton, his only direct interest being that if there were a lot of small companies his job would be more important." Richardson, by now having lost all faith in McNaughton, responded: "The Civil Government Air Operations and National Defence are dead against a large private company . . . McNaughton, unquestionably, would like the government to fly the mail across Canada, although he does not like to say so."

Two could play the game. On March 21, 1934, Richardson called upon Wilson. Undoubtedly he hoped that Wilson would report their conversation to the prime minister. However, although Wilson wrote a memo recording the meeting, it appears that he told neither McNaughton nor the prime minister of Richardson's visit. Even more unusual, the memo was not addressed to anyone and was unprofessionally typed—it looked as if Wilson had typed it himself. It gave only the bare facts of Richardson's visit. Perhaps Wilson was so disturbed with the airways situation and so reluctant to openly confront McNaughton that he could do no more than record the bare fact of Richardson's visit. The memo revealed Richardson's deep disappointment in how matters were unfolding. Richardson accused the government of having taken advantage of its privileged position "to break contracts in a manner which would not have been possible by a private commercial company ... He was very bitter," Wilson wrote.

Wilson ended the conversation by sanctimoniously telling Richardson that "this Department has never been anxious to step into the field of commercial aviation except insofar as might be necessary to pioneer new developments and to do work such as survey and air photography which could more advantageously and efficiently be done directly under the auspices of the Government." For Wilson to trot out those comments to a man who was about to lose close to $3 million and be forced to shut down his company because of government's actions was particularly hypocritical—he was aware that Richardson knew otherwise. Richardson, accustomed to saying what he meant, must have felt the hopelessness of the situation as he listened to Wilson's platitudes. Wilson was reacting true to form, rationalizing government actions when someone criticized them.

The letters and memos that Richardson wrote during this period are heartbreaking. All the hopes and dreams he had in 1929, the patriotic feeling that he was doing something good for the country, had come to nothing. The feeling of being "used" by politicians and bureaucrats must have preyed on him. Knowing that McNaughton had deliberately misled him was a bitter pill, and the knowledge that the prime minister was receiving his advice from a biased and purely military perspective was galling. Financial losses, economic collapse and business reverses he could deal with, but finding himself betrayed by those he thought were honourable was almost impossible for a man of his integrity to understand.

Richardson appealed to the prime minister once more. His draft memo of March 20, 1934, showed his distress and his honest faith that no one who truly understood the whole story of Canadian Airways could do other than the just thing. "In justice to a distinguished Board of Directors it will be necessary to tell the full story to the people of Canada, so that there will be no reflection on the people who have put up their money to assist aviation in Canada ... If the Government, through failure to carry out their contracts, abandons this company now, it will be nothing short of tragedy."

It is doubtful that he sent that memo. Too much the gentleman, Richardson decided it would not further his cause if he publicly embarrassed the prime minister. He now decided to write a memorandum outlining Canadian Airways' history, its achievements and its present situation. He spent most of the Easter weekend pouring his heart into the "Easter Memo," ten pages of comprehensive information and good ammunition. Originally intended for his board of directors to use in exerting pressure on the government, copies of the memo were soon sent to newspapers, the mining community, prospectors, boards of trade, chambers of commerce and any individuals whom Richardson thought could help Canadian Airways' cause. The kid gloves were off.

Touching all bases, Richardson personally called on C.P. Fullerton, chairman of the CNR board of trustees, emphasizing that the CNR would lose its quarter-million dollars if Canadian Airways folded. Fullerton promptly wrote to the prime minister, asking what could be done. Bennett replied on March 24, "I see no likelihood of our being able to do more for the Canadian Airways Limited than we have already done. I realize, of course, that this imperils to a considerable extent the investment of the Canadian National Railways, but on the other hand we have reached our limit."

Richardson armed his friends with facts and figures and asked them to bombard the prime minister and their MPs and senators with letters and telephone calls. The outpouring of support, especially from the West, was strong. The press, too, took up the cry. The *Vancouver Daily Province* wrote a particularly pungent article on April 17, 1934. "We never had a complete transcontinental air mail system in Canada but we had the nucleus of it. It was discontinued in the depths of the depression, not because it was inefficient but because it was not paying for itself and because economy till it hurt became the ruling passion of statesmanship at Ottawa." In the East, F.S. Chalmers, editor of the *Financial Post*, wrote to Richardson on April 26 that he too was prepared to help.

Winnipeg, in particular, supported Richardson. The April 14 *Winnipeg Tribune* carried an article describing the benefits of commercial aviation to Canada's development. Richardson asked the *Tribune* to mail copies of the article to every Canadian newspaper. The Winnipeg Board of Trade sent a strongly worded telegram to the prime minister on April 17, emphasizing how mining development had helped the West. Many business groups wrote Bennett; his reply was the same to all. "The Dominion of Canada is not financially in a position to help ... having regard to the campaign carried on by the Canadian Chamber for economy and the very proper desire to balance the budget, do you suggest that we should ask the Canadian taxpayers to pay subsidy to this undertaking?"

The *Winnipeg Free Press* editorial on April 25, titled "The Mysterious New Air Unit," referred to National Defence's condemnation of the British government's policy of giving all air mail contracts to one private company (Imperial Airways); the military's bias against private enterprise was plain. The editorial also wondered aloud who the new operator was to be and recalled that three-quarters of a million dollars was spent on the now-worthless airship base at St. Hubert, more than was spent on the air mail service. The *Edmonton Journal* on April 20 cried, "Definite Air Policy Needed." Canada required "a healthy commercial air service."

F.I. Ker, of the *Hamilton Spectator*, responded with a long letter, offering useful insights and suggestions. His letter also gives a sense of the character of those who were prepared to follow Richardson's lead because they believed that they were genuinely doing something good for their country.

> I feel no concern whatsoever about the money I put into it, but, as a Canadian citizen deeply interested in the progress of civil aviation in this sparsely settled country of ours with its immense distances and rich resources lying beyond the reach of our other means of transportation, I am disappointed and disgusted that all the money that has been put into it by yourself, the Canadian National, the CPR and the other stockholders, and all the thought, worry, and hardship of the operating officers, the flying men, and the ground forces during the past six years has been spent in vain either because of the

indifference of the government to the safe and sound development of aviation in this country and its willingness to let the enterprise perish, or its fear of making itself a target for political criticism on the eve of an election by coming to the assistance of an organization with such a strong board of directors, even though such assistance was nothing more than the carrying out of contractual obligations incurred by a previous government ...

Not many people realize what a struggle it has been to get commercial aviation in this country out of the haywire operation stage, and that the Canadian Airways is the result of an enormous amount of thought, worry and negotiation on the part of men like yourself, and others who were persuaded that it was a worthwhile, patriotic undertaking, and were interested in it as such rather than from the prospect of financial returns. The fact that the component companies could have been sold out to American interests at a large profit in 1928 is some measure of proof that there were other things in mind than the mere making of money ...

If you think it would do any good, I am quite willing to send a copy of this letter to the Prime Minister. He may be arbitrary sometimes but I believe, given the facts, that he is fair.

Richardson's notes, letters and memos for this period attack McNaughton and the Civil Government Air Operations as being the root cause of commercial aviation's problems. "There is no doubt but that the successful operation of our company ultimately challenges the existence of Civil Government Air Operations ... We certainly cannot build up civil aviation in Canada if the government is going to compete with us and give free services."

James B. Coyne, president of the Manitoba Aviation League, saw McNaughton's manouevrings in this way. "With Canadian Airways out of business, McNaughton would start his new 'national' organization upon a basis denied to you, and which if granted you, would enable you to continue. McNaughton clearly wants to run a big show ... If you agree to the restriction, the departments would have the whip hand and would use it until you gave up."

By mid-April, just weeks before Canadian Airways' annual meeting, Richardson increased the pressure on Bennett and some of his ministers.

On April 16, he wrote a four-page letter and enclosed the Easter memo to R.J. Manion, minister of railways and canals. In the letter he commented: "If this Company is to carry on there must be a policy on the part of the Government recognizing it as their Air Mail carrier. If Canada is to have a worthwhile Air Mail Service it must be with a through line, with feeder services. McNaughton's view that the Air Mail line across Canada should be run by a separate company that is not allowed to engage in any other operation will not appeal to any business man who has been well-trained in sound economics of business. McNaughton's plan is an effectual way of killing Canadian aviation."

He sent the same letter to Arthur Sauvé, postmaster general, and Donald Sutherland, minister of national defence. On April 18, Richardson sent the Easter memo with a covering letter to the prime minister. He requested a decision from Bennett immediately, since Canadian Airways' annual meeting was to be held on April 26. He also made three proposals. One, that the government give to Canadian Airways the prairie mail run and Montreal–Rimouski run. Two, that government regulate the rates, enforce civil aviation regulations and bring the aviation companies under the authority of the railway commissioners. Three, that if government decided against one and two, it should compensate Canadian Airways for its cancelled contracts.

What effect all the lobbying had was hard to determine. On the one hand it seemed to help, since the Post Office awarded Canadian Airways the Montreal–Rimouski contract, which had gone to the RCAF the year before. Some interpreted this as a hint of government policy to follow. On the other hand, it seemed to provoke McNaughton to become more vocal in advocating a government-run company. Frank Ross wrote to Richardson on April 22: "I saw McNaughton about a month ago in Ottawa ... He thought that the equipment and personnel of Canadian Airways was unsuitable to the handling of the mail service and he could not recommend to the government any alliance between Imperial Airways and Canadian Airways. Through your personal efforts since that date, in my opinion, the Government has had a complete reversal of policy ... they have laid down the policy of carrying the air mail by private contract instead of by DND. That in itself is no small accomplishment. I would suggest you go to Ottawa in a conciliatory mood ... Receiving the Rimouski contract is the evidence of their [government] willingness to assist with what means lies within their power."

Ross also wrote to Manion, on April 24, 1934. While pointedly putting his finger on one of the root causes of commercial aviation's problems, he tactfully said, "The question of civil aviation ought to be taken in hand by a Cabinet Minister, one who has had the necessary commercial and executive experience to deal with such a situation and the matter not left to the discretion of military officials who view matters in an entirely different light from those of us who have had to bring back a dollar for every dollar spent plus some profit."

Manion responded to Ross on April 26: "Guthrie and I are both very friendly to giving some assistance but, so far, have not succeeded in making the Chief see it that way because of the financial difficulties of the country ... Both Guthrie and I are going to try and press the matter further and endeavour to get something done."

On April 26, the prime minister answered Richardson's letter. For the first time there was a difference in tone. Bennett appeared to be leaving the door open; he was not as adamant in saying no. "I do not see how the Dominion of Canada can provide further for an airway service." These words were not as final or negative an answer as Bennett had previously given. The prime minister had written similar words to James Coyne on April 25, and Coyne had picked up the slight change in nuance. He responded with another letter to Bennett on April 30. "To your concluding sentence, 'I do not see how we can expend further sums on this service,' may I say this: The cost of resumed trans-prairie air mail service is comparatively small and will continually diminish ... It is important to maintain confidence in the continuance of government contracts where definite periods are stipulated." Coyne gave the prime minister the basis for a change in policy; unfortunately, the prime minister did not take it.

Bennett continued to be bombarded by letters demanding that he assist Canadian Airways. On April 28, the presidents of the young men's sections of the Winnipeg Board of Trade and the Vancouver Board of Trade wrote to Bennett. Both advocated that the government develop an air policy and give assistance to Canadian Airways. They also lambasted the government for expensive government air services and spoke about preserving "for Canada its place in the establishment of international air routes." To the Vancouver Board of Trade, Bennett replied: "This country is not in a financial position to grant any subsidies. You cannot urge economy one week and expenditures the next."

The prime minister also received pressure from the Senate. On June 7, Conservative senator J.A. McDonald spoke at length on the "unsatisfactory position of aviation in Canada." He ridiculed departmental answers. "I asked, 'What is the government doing to encourage the establishment of inter-city passenger services?' The department answers: 'Inter-city services are the business of the operating companies.' ... Again the answer is evasive. Why not frankly say 'nothing.' ... The department is badly informed when it states that the commercial operations in Northern Canada are self-sustaining."

McDonald strongly criticized the RCAF for taking work away from commercial operators, saying it "should be maintained solely as a military unit and should not participate in commercial operations." He wanted a special committee of the House formed to study commercial aviation needs. "Apparently the Civil Aviation Branch is convinced that it knows all there is to know of the conditions and problems of the commercial operators. The information I have before me is to the contrary ..."

McDonald was a good orator and brought in every argument possible.

> Russia, a country which many Canadians consider beyond the pale, is wide awake to the value of air transportation, and has extended its organized air mileage to a distance of approximately 32,000 miles. During this year a Trans-Siberian air route, covering a distance of 5,500 miles, has been put into operation. The Russians are flying this route daily, using 5-motor air-liners capable of carrying 36 passengers, while we in Canada have not in operation one aeroplane which compares in any way with these large Russian air-liners ...
>
> Practically all the flying that is done in Canada is carried on in the remote areas of its new north, where the aeroplane has played an important role in exploration, in mining development and in fire patrol ... yet Canada, perhaps more than any other country, needs a network of airlines.

Finally the Canadian Airways special committee, composed of Richardson, Beatty, Hungerford and Sir Charles Gordon, met with the cabinet committee, Hugh Guthrie (minister of justice) and R.J. Manion. Richardson described the meeting to H.R. Drummond-Hay. "They gave us a very sympathetic hearing and did not hesitate to say they thought the government owed the Airways a moral obligation and we concluded that they felt quite emphatically that our contribution to mining was such that it would never do to have our services withdrawn."

By June 23, 1934, however, Richardson conceded in a memo that matters were at a standstill.

> The representations that were made to Mr. Bennett and the Ottawa government this Spring were all without avail. Mr. Bennett takes the stand that the Government have no money for Air Mail and that as far as our work in opening the mines is concerned this is a matter entirely of private enterprise and if we did not do it somebody else would ... Mr. Guthrie stated that we certainly had a very strong moral claim ... nothing ever came of this ...
>
> The position seems to be that it is quite all right for the Dominion Government to repudiate contracts with the Canadian Citizens but it is not good business to repudiate contracts with American citizens, because this would be a breach of international good faith. This is logic that I am not capable of following myself, but no doubt it is all clear to a great legal mind like Mr. Bennett's ...
>
> Mr. Bennett is disposed to be vindictive and I do not think that there is anything to be gained by our company going into a public controversy on the subject at the present time ... Mr. Bennett appears to have closed and locked the door on us.

Surviving the Cuts:
"Keep the Show Going"

ERHAPS THE GREATEST BLOW to James Richardson's buoyant faith occurred when Prime Minister Bennett shut the door on his hopes of the resumption of the air mail contracts. But he was not one to hold a grudge. Some months later, when Bennett was to be guest of honour at a function in Winnipeg, Richardson came home to change into black-tie attire and found Mrs. Richardson unwilling to go. "Why, he's Prime Minister whether he should be or not: he's the first Minister of State, we've got to go," he exclaimed. James Richardson had a resiliency of spirit that made him the happy master of his fate. It was never more evident than in the next few months.

Instead of folding up Canadian Airways' wings, Richardson rallied his directors to ride out the weather, explaining, "We decided that if we let go most of our Head Office organization and reduced salaries and compensation all through the organization, that with increased business it might be possible for us to keep the show going, making all the reductions in the staff in our offices but keeping our full personnel in the field at work." It was a sense of doing, of beating the odds, more than hope of profit that drove him. Men like Richardson are rare: such single-mindedness and devotion to a cause are exceptional.

Consolidation and retrenchment, and simplicity and economy of operations became Richardson's watchwords. When Canadian Airways was formed in 1930, its operation and administration were conducted through an executive office in Montreal; Eastern Lines, with a general office in Montreal; Western Lines, with a general office in Winnipeg; and Pacific Lines, with a general office in Vancouver. After the 1932 cancellation, the set-up had been retained in anticipation of the renewal of large-scale air mail operations and start-up of the transcontinental operation. Now, with the future of air mail "at present indefinite and obscure," according to Richardson in a press release, changes were necessary.

Over the years a large volume of freight, express and passenger business had been built up in western Ontario, central Manitoba and the Mackenzie River district; this traffic represented approximately 75 percent of the company's total revenue. Winnipeg was the centre of the company's business; it was also Richardson's home. There was no change in the board of directors. Wilfred Sigerson was appointed general manager and comptroller, and Tommy Thompson remained assistant general manager. The survey–photographic department remained in Montreal. Winnipeg was to be headquarters, and actual transport operations would be controlled from six bases.

The six operating bases and superintendents were:

Maritime Provinces (Moncton)	Walter Fowler
Quebec and Eastern Ontario (Montreal)	Romeo Vachon
Western Ontario (Sioux Lookout)	A. Westergaard
Central Manitoba (Norway House and Ilford)	H. Hollick-Kenyon
Mackenzie River area (Edmonton)	C.H. "Punch" Dickins
Pacific Coast (Vancouver)	Don MacLaren

Along with consolidation came cuts in personnel and salaries. It was not an easy decision for Richardson to make. He had never considered Canadian Airways as a dividend-earning machine. It was still "his baby," to which he had given heart and soul. It was with regret that on June 1, 1934, he sent around a memo on compensation adjustments. "The reorganization has resulted in the release of more than a score of faithful employees of the company ... Rather than resort to further reductions in personnel which would necessitate decrease in field personnel working directly on transportation operations, we have decided the following." Pilots would receive no mileage bonus until seventeen hundred productive miles were flown in a month, but their base salaries would remain unchanged. Air engineers except for apprentices would take a cut of 10 percent, and "all other personnel except those receiving $100.00 per month or less would have a 10% reduction. I regret doing this . . . it is the only way to assure continued operation of the company."

Not everyone agreed with Richardson's arguments; his pilots, who earned between $2,700 and $3,000 a year, were upset. (Were they aware that many Canadians counted themselves lucky if they made $2,000 a year?) "Punch" Dickins went to bat for his men, writing to the assistant general manager and sending a copy to Richardson and the board of directors. Dickins's argument was based on the life of the pilot and mechanic. The letter gives a good description of a bush pilot's life.

Every labourer is worthy of his hire, and this certainly applies to us in the field. Not only are we giving services but we are actually giving something out of our lives for which no sum of money can compensate. Visualize last winter's work—Pilots, engineers, agents, getting up at five o'clock, in the dark, and getting out to start fires to heat oil, to start torches for heating the engine, then remaining out in the cold all day, rushing to get the engine going before it freezes up again, flying, landing, refueling, delivering mail, express, passengers, at temperatures from thirty to seventy below zero, and these are the official Dominion government temperatures. Probably through flying about five then another hour's work draining oil, fastening down ropes, setting skis on blocks to prevent freezing down and then refueling to be ready for next morning. This not just one day but every day, Saturdays, Sundays, holidays for four long winter months, that Canadian Airways schedule can be maintained.

Operations this last winter were carried out in sixty and seventy below zero weather for a week at a stretch. I doubt if any of our executives have ever been out in sixty below zero and will have a hard time visualizing conditions, but from our viewpoint it means frost blisters as big as twenty five cent pieces on fingers, nose, chin and cheeks black and peeling skin all winter, and in some cases frosted lungs caused by exertion such as carrying oil pails, or pushing on the tail in the full slip stream of the propeller, to free up skis stuck on frosty snow . . .

I have not worked as hard in the field as most of our men but I did operate the Peace River Vermilion mail service last winter in addition to filling in on the Mackenzie service, and carried on office work, correspondence and made an average of nearly fifty calls per week on prospective customers. In three years I have had two weeks holidays, including Saturdays, Sundays, holidays, and even Christmas, same as the rest of the men in the field.

Once one man is lost from the organization it will be impossible to reassemble it and there is only one way to keep it . . .

Undoubtedly Richardson was hurt by Dickins's letter. He had done his best to keep his people working throughout the depression, not just with Canadian Airways but with James Richardson & Sons. Richardson keenly felt the responsibility of his position as one of Canada's leading businessmen. He saw Canadian Airways not as a mere business corporation but as an entity performing a valuable service for his country. He wanted to keep the airline flying and as many employed as possible. On June 12, Richardson telephoned Dickins. What he said is not known, but no doubt it followed closely the letter Richardson sent to Dickins on June 13.

This company has always resisted, insofar as it was able to, any reduction in compensation to its officers and employees . . . I am well aware that the boys on the Mackenzie have gone through a particularly hard and severe winter . . . but any feelings they have in this respect should be directed not against the company but against those organizations which have paid lower salaries and have cut prices and have done everything possible to destroy our price structure, which would enable us to pay the compensations that we would like to do.

I think our boys should know the salaries paid by the other companies in Canada and by private operators, and I have asked Mr. Thompson to write you what information he has on the subject.

I think this would be satisfactory proof that the Canadian Airways have not been the company that has tried to pull down salaries ...

I am prepared now and always to go as far as I can to retain a happy family in the Canadian Airways organization, and I hope that we will all be able to see this show through together into smoother waters.

Richardson wired Dickins again on June 15, advising that he could not make any definite commitments at the present, "but I can assure you I will be glad personally to discuss this whole proposition with you in six months' time or any time." Dickins responded on the same day: "You can count on my hearty co-operation ... Some announcement to the effect that this arrangement would be reconsidered at end of six months would be very heartening to all."

Perhaps because of Dickins's memo, Richardson sent a personal letter to all staff, explaining more fully why the company was undergoing massive reorganization and retrenchment. He entreated his employees not to leave. In his letter to pilot Archie McMullen of Fort McMurray, Alberta, on June 1, he wrote:

We have at the expense of risking the complete extinction of our capital investment, decided to carry on. To do this it is necessary for us to cut our expenses and increase our revenue so that we may operate without any cash loss ... We have made economies in many directions and reductions of salaries all through the organization. The President of this organization has never received any salary or compensation of any kind from aviation since he first formed the Western Canada Airways nearly eight years ago. The General Manager of this company has suggested a reduction of salary for himself very much greater than anybody else in the organization and he naturally expects everyone associated with him to co-operate in meeting our present problem.

I have been in Montreal for some little time, making a thorough study of all our problems here and I regret extremely that it is necessary to make any reductions anywhere. I believe we have in our organization the cream of the flying men in Canada. Our pilots have, I believe, always been paid considerably more money than the pilots of any independent company in Canada and I believe our pilots have made more money than any pilots flying their own planes. This is something that I want to see continue ...

I know that the company has your loyal support and may I call on you now to extend every courtesy to our customers, to do everything in your power to increase the company's traffic, to do everything you can to hold up our price structure on a sound commercial basis and to get as many full loads as you can in every day ... With the cooperation that we know you and every other pilot in our service will give us we feel that we will be able to maintain the Canadian Airways as a permanent national institution and one which we hope you will be proud to be associated with.

In late July, further cuts were necessary. Richardson made them in management. Having let Mulock go in May, Richardson now asked Sigerson to leave. Sigerson was devastated, yet to Richardson he wrote: "I have spent five years of happy slaving for a man who I had come to love just as a father or brother ... And still I do not regret the happy days of working together, the inspiration of your visits to Montreal and my visits here with you, including the many wonderful visits in your home in company with a noble wife and interesting children ... I hope that you will in the future afford me the opportunity of further serving you and this, of course, without any further compensation than your friendship and goodwill." The loyalty Richardson inspired in his people was evident.

Richardson's plan was to concentrate on bush operations, but securing the trans-Canada contract still remained his most important objective. To that end he advised all personnel to give the impression that Canadian Airways would be the transcontinental operator. Richardson put all his effort into expanding Canadian Airways into every corner of the country and beyond. He instructed F. Jenkins of the Maritimes and Photographic Department "to stir up business in the Maritime Provinces and in Newfoundland." Richardson wanted to get a jump on Imperial Airways, which was covetously eyeing Newfoundland. Leaving nothing to chance, on August 4 Richardson wrote personally to Jenkins, giving him the ammunition to promote the company. Richardson's dry sense of humour was apparent when he spoke of Canadian Airways' good safety record.

I feel that we have been rather modest at times in not emphasizing more the fact that we have been carrying on these operations ... in every Province of Canada, the North West Territories and the Yukon, and we are flying in the East Arctic and the West Arctic, and that over a period of eight years we have flown nine million miles and never seriously jarred any passenger who bought a ticket with us into the north ...

Nothing is more distasteful to me than blowing one's own horn, but I do not think you will misunderstand me if I enclose to you a copy of a 'Who's Who' pamphlet showing my business affiliations ... you might find some of my affiliations or associations helpful in your discussion with the Commission ...

In talking to the Newfoundland Commission I think it would be well to impress on them the great contribution that the Canadian Airways have made in opening up the mineral wealth of Northern Canada and that it is generally conceded by mining people that we have pushed this country ahead twenty years and that we would like the opportunity of seeing if we could not make a similar contribution to Newfoundland.

Richardson also wanted to keep Imperial Airways out of Labrador and asked Jenkins to drum up business there.

Richardson was reaching farther than Newfoundland. In June, Thompson wrote Parry, Leon & Hayhoe, travel and tourist agents, asking them, among other things, to represent Canadian Airways in South Africa. Richardson was also trying to regain the Mackenzie River contract. Since the late 1920s, he had seen the advantages of this area as a route to the Orient, and he did not want it to slip permanently from his control. Unfortunately, when Leigh Brintnell left Western Canada Airways, he lost no time in establishing himself in Edmonton and securing the Mackenzie River contract by undercutting Canadian Airways' prices. He next obtained American financing to help him purchase aircraft, so Richardson's efforts to regain control of the area were unsuccessful.

In October 1934 competition came unexpectedly from Clarke Steamships, who decided to start using aircraft. This was a blow to Canadian Airways, who had pioneered the air mail service along the North Shore of the St. Lawrence and had kept it going through the depression and hoped to reap any benefits once regular trans-Atlantic flights or the ship-to-shore mail service began. Thompson felt that Canadian Airways had no choice but to cooperate with Clarke. As he explained to Richardson: "Clarke Steamships is a powerful organization of old standing having a virtual monopoly of transportation along the North Shore, are well-thought of by the Post Office and are powerful in Ottawa. An association like this would strengthen our hands in obtaining government contracts, particularly in Quebec."

Wisely, Thompson also suggested that the new company not operate under Canadian Airways' name. "If Quebec Airways is used this will give Quebec a feeling that it is their company, thereby obtaining their goodwill." A few telephone calls between Desmond Clarke and Richardson in early November settled the question, and Quebec Airways was incorporated in December. The fleur de lis was chosen as the company's logo and appeared on all its aircraft. Canadian Airways owned all the preferred shares and 7,500 of the 10,000 common shares. The remainder were held by Clarke Steamships. Quebec Airways was separate from Canadian Airways and operated under a Quebec charter; Hungerford of the CNR was one of its directors.

Quebec Airways represented a new policy. Since his acquisition of the eastern companies, which along with Western Canada Airways had formed the basis of Canadian Airways, Richardson had bought two more companies, Commercial Airways in May 1931 and Spence McDonough Air Transport in December 1933. These companies had lost their identities and had been absorbed into Canadian Airways' structure, for Richardson's plan had been to centralize management to stabilize the new industry. Now, with charges of monopoly being levelled at Canadian Airways, Thompson's suggestion, that any new additions to the company be allowed to retain their identity, made sense.

In November 1934, Richardson believed Canadian Airways' luck was finally going to change. "I had dinner with Mr. Bennett on Tuesday night and he told me it was his understanding that all contracts now being given out for Air Mail were coming to us," Richardson wired to J.O. Apps, Beatty's executive assistant, on November 29. He did not say how Bennett had come by this information, and it was incorrect.

Significant, however, was the fact that the prime minister was still under the impression that Canadian Airways was the front-runner.

Not so convinced were McNaughton and Wilson, who opposed Canadian Airways' receiving the transcontinental contract if it continued to handle bush operations. "Postal authorities agree with this policy and I think it is one of the reasons why they will not renew our bush mail contracts for periods of more than a year. If this policy is put into force and Canadian Airways is awarded the transcontinental air mail, all our pioneering effort in the bush will be lost unless a subsidiary company or companies are formed to take care of this work," Thompson wrote to Richardson in mid-October after seeing McNaughton and Wilson in Ottawa.

The subject of the flying boats had surfaced again at DND in March 1934, when Imperial Airways repeated its July 1933 offer of two flying boats to Canada. Wilson's memo, this time on the ship-to-shore service, bluntly stated that Canada had done absolutely nothing to carry out its share of the 1933 Newfoundland agreement. "If this generous offer of cooperation and assistance is now refused and Canada takes no action in the matter, it is clear that Imperial Airways will have no alternative but to continue their cooperation with Pan American Airways on both routes, to the exclusion of Canada." Wilson emphasized that the government needed to make a decision that very week. Bennett remained silent.

The prime minister's inaction twice forced McNaughton to submit revised costs and schedules to Bennett for the opening of the trans-Canada airway. McNaughton appeared concerned with the delay, yet inexplicably, when the prime minister gave McNaughton the green light to formulate a policy on air matters, McNaugton waited four months before calling a meeting. On September 18, McNaughton wrote the deputy minister of finance, W.C. Clark, asking him to be a part of the TCA Committee. In briefing Clark, McNaughton wrote "that as a result of many meetings a report was made to the Prime Minister in May 1934 when it was agreed that the matter had reached the point that the Committee might form a definite policy to govern the action of the Dominion Government."

McNaughton, like Wilson, was meticulous in recording meetings and reports. It seems unusual that there is no other reference to the report in Bennett's, McNaughton's, Wilson's or Canadian Airways' papers. Was McNaughton trying to make it seem as if the prime minister had waited until May 1934 before requesting a policy? This may well be the explanation, because McNaughton also neglected to tell Clark that the committee had made a report a year earlier, in May 1933, and another in January 1934, both with recommendations to formulate a policy.

On October 23, 1934, McNaughton finally called a committee meeting. Considering the urgency of the situation and McNaughton's earlier letters to the prime minister chiding him for not making decisions, McNaughton's delay is difficult to explain. The October meeting was the only record of a TCA Committee meeting since January 1934. McNaughton's agenda was to hear a progress report on the construction of the trans-Canada airway and to consider a program for 1935–36 and the method of operation of the airway. The last item was hard to fathom. The question had been settled in May 1933 and again in January 1934. What was it doing on the agenda again?

Nothing was accomplished at this meeting. Issues that had been discussed innumerable times in the past and supposedly settled were rehashed. Once again, the question as to who should operate the transcontinental service was raised. There was no indication in government papers that the prime minister was dissatisfied with the committee's recommendation (weak though it was) that a private company operate the transcontinental service. Thus there was no reason for the committee to debate the issue again. McNaughton seems to have wanted to discuss it in hopes that he could persuade the committee to recommend a government-owned company.

The landing fields were discussed. McNaughton stated that 75 percent of them were either completed or well in hand, and McNaughton and Wilson recommended that until the whole Montreal–Vancouver section was completed, there was no sense in opening the Winnipeg–Vancouver section. Canadian Airways disagreed. It advised opening the airway in stages. Wilson stated that the Winnipeg–Vancouver fields would not be ready until July 1936. Did anyone ask why it would take another two years if 75 percent of the landing fields were presumably complete or "in hand"? Wilson said the Montreal–Maritimes section would not be complete until July 1937. Again, the same question could be asked.

Good strategist that he was, McNaughton then moved swiftly to the crux of the matter. Who was going to fly the airway? "Now there are certain things to be done next year. We must provide for two experimental machines in next year's estimates. We have got to find out where they may be obtained and what they cost. We can have the Air Force try them out for us. We will leave it to the Department to decide from what vote they are to be provided." McNaughton smoothly insinuated that the RCAF try out the aircraft on the trans-Canada airway. No one asked why experimental aircraft were needed or why the RCAF should be involved in flying what would be a commercial enterprise. McNaughton continued, "I think we should provide for two machines, if not three ... There is another thing. Mr. Wilson's staff has got to be increased."

Now McNaughton's reason for asking the deputy minister of finance to be a part of the committee was apparent. He needed the government to underwrite increased staffing and the purchase of experimental aircraft. His motives were becoming clearer. When it was assumed that Canadian Airways would handle the service, it was also a given that Canadian Airways would finance all personnel and equipment costs. The handwriting was now on the wall. As James Coyne had predicted, McNaughton wanted the trans-Canada airway to be "his show" and he needed the support of the deputy minister of finance. McNaughton then reverted to landing fields and admitted that some of the fields on the Prairies needed work. That would cost approximately fifty thousand dollars, which he also wanted the committee to approve.

Valentine Smart, quiet until now, once more recommended that all forms of transportation be under one organization. McNaughton, sounding as if he had never heard the topic raised before, asked, "You think that we should have all transportation controlled under one head?" Wilson replied, "We have always advocated and tried to work in close cooperation with the railway companies." Smart said, "That is not what is worrying me. I mean a controlling body that will administer a true economic system." McNaughton was not interested in Smart's comments and turned the discussion back to the money required for purchase of aircraft and additional staff.

McNaughton briefly discussed the ship-to-shore service but did not tell the committee of Imperial Airways' offer of two flying boats. Herring warned, "We should do something before Pan American does.

I think we should get busy as soon as possible." McNaughton abruptly cut off Herring and adjourned the meeting with the comment, "The other subject was the question of the set-up of the Airway Operating Company. That is a long debatable subject and there is no special hurry about it."

For McNaughton to halt discussion on the ship-to-shore service before it was settled was an astonishing move to make. For him to say there was "no special hurry about" the decision of the operating company was equally surprising. However, it was not surprising if McNaughton wanted to ensure that no decision was made. He wanted the RCAF to carry the mail because it would be an easy matter to turn Civil Government Air Operations into a government-run service. It may also have been a delaying tactic to force Canadian Airways out of business. If Canada's major airline closed its doors, it would be much easier to recommend a government-owned and -operated company. Whatever his motives, McNaughton appeared oblivious to Canadian Airways' financial problems and showed no concern for Richardson's position.

Why he cut off discussion on the ship-to-shore and trans-Atlantic service is harder to explain. As the top military man in the country, he knew that Canada could not continue to delay its international hookups. He also knew that Imperial Airways was chafing at the bit and Pan Am was lying in wait to run the service itself. Although the trans-Atlantic airline may have been discussed as a cooperative venture, Juan Trippe was determined that the United States, that is, Pan Am, should be in the forefront.

Richardson had wisely remained in touch with G.E. Woods-Humphrey of Imperial Airways and had made a point of seeing him on September 26, 1934, when he was in England, no doubt prompted by a letter from W.B. Burchall of Imperial Airways. On September 10, Burchall, writing to Richardson about another subject, also said, "I went so far last year as to tell John Wilson if the Canadian government were to leave Canadian Airways high and dry it would give everybody else cause to proceed with great caution in putting money into aviation at the present time in Canada. I hope your reorganization has put you into a good position so when the time comes for the Trans-Atlantic service to be established our two Companies will be able to cooperate."

Richardson kept McNaughton informed about his discussions with Imperial Airways. Subterfuge was not part of Richardson's makeup. Although he could have made things uncomfortable for McNaughton by not doing so, he visited McNaughton after his return from England to relay Imperial Airways' concerns. McNaughton recorded Richardson's visit in an October 31 memo. Richardson had told McNaughton that he had lunched with Sir Eric Geddes, Sir Ashley Cooper and Sir George Beharrell of Imperial Airways and discussed airways matters. Richardson also informed McNaughton that Geddes had complained that he had received no cooperation from Canada and that Geddes had suggested that a company jointly owned by Imperial Airways, the CPR and the British railways be formed and that the Canadian end of the service be operated by a company jointly owned by the CPR, Imperial Airways and Canadian Airways.

Richardson then asked the all-important question as to whether there was any decision about the Canadian operator. McNaughton wrote, "I told Mr. Richardson that at the moment no decision [was] yet reached as to the method of operation of the Trans-Canada Airways; that we were still busy with the preparation of the aerodromes and intermediate landing fields, and that we had not yet felt the need of knowing what the operating organization would be." Once again he was contradicting himself; for years, both he and Wilson had been saying that it was urgent to choose the operator.

On November 12, McNaughton received a copy of a confidential document covering the Empire Air Mail Scheme. He called another meeting of the TCA Committee for December 11 to discuss "proposed Airways machines," proposed estimates for 1935–36, the British government's proposals for an Empire Air Mail Scheme and the trans-Atlantic service, including the ship-to-shore service.

Indecision and squabbling marked this meeting. Again, issues that had been previously decided were raised for discussion. There was debate as to what was more important, the trans-Canada airway or the ship-to-shore service. Wilson, who had earlier recommended that Canada institute the ship-to-shore service first, now felt that Canada should concentrate its efforts on completing the airway. The rest of the committee wanted to inaugurate the air–ship service. McNaughton offered no guidance and, indeed, tried to explain away the committee's indecisiveness by saying that the government had given it no help, that there were only a few individuals in DND who could devote any attention to airway problems and that there was a limit to what DND could do.

Herring, as usual, approached the problem from a narrow and shortsighted viewpoint. In his anxiety to have Canada included in the Empire Air Mail Scheme, he overlooked the fact that the equipment used for the air–ship service would not be suitable for the eventual all-air service. Clark straddled the fence and recommended completing both services.

It was becoming very apparent that McNaughton was simply looking for ways to keep his men flying. He pushed for agreement to purchase three aircraft and then said he must have money to train personnel to fly the aircraft. Clark, from Finance, was upset that McNaughton was ignoring what had been decided at the previous meeting and wanted to discuss the ship-to-shore service. Wilson thought it was better to concentrate on the national airway. Clark responded, "Don't you think you are taking a chance on the other countries getting ahead of you?" Only Clark seemed to have any anxiety that Canada was going to be left out in the cold. The discussion continued to meander. Finally McNaughton, totally reversing himself, said, "With the public demand today as it is, I cannot help but feel that it has become a matter of urgent policy to go ahead with the Trans-Canada."

Canada's place in the Empire Air Mail Scheme was significant by its absence. The United Kingdom had not included Canada in its plans for the very good reason that there was still no "Canadian connection." In spite of Canada's promises in July 1933, the Canadian government had done nothing about the ship-to-shore service or chosen its trans-Canada operator. McNaughton had seen the Empire Air Mail memorandum; he had no excuse for saying Canada still had a year in which to choose its operator.

On December 22, Wilson wrote a memo, "Empire Air Mail Scheme, Canada's Position," whose main point was that both the United Kingdom and the United States had made rapid developments in long-range aircraft that would make Canada's plans obsolete regarding the trans-Atlantic service. Why did he not raise this point at the meeting, where it might have shaken the committee to act in harmony instead of squabbling among themselves? Typically, he did not confront McNaughton, but waited until after the meeting and buried a very important piece of information in a memo that probably went nowhere. And so 1934 passed, with no positive action being taken on the trans-Canada airway except for the building of some intermediate landing fields.

The rumours flew during the early months of 1935. "The powers have committed themselves to the air mail and I believe it will be in operation by late Fall unless the election has an upsetting influence. According to present plans it is intended to let each division to a different company," wrote J. Deering of the Ford Motor Co. of Canada to George Hutchins of James Richardson & Sons on January 22. However, Canadian Airways was very concerned with DND's public announcements, promoting DND at the expense of commercial aviation. For instance, when Brigadier General Lindsay Gordon of the RCAF addressed the young men's section of the board of trade in Winnipeg in February, he talked about the importance of the RCAF and Civil Government Air Operations. Meanwhile, the January 1935 DND monthly newsletter indicated that the RCAF would have an increase of $700,000 for re-equipment.

By this time aeronautical development in the United States and Great Britain had progressed so rapidly that commercial long-range aircraft were in the offing. The Americans were well ahead of the British, and Pan Am planned to test-fly a trans-Atlantic aircraft in February. If the tests were successful, Pan Am would begin a trans-Atlantic service in the summer of 1935. The realization that they could not offer an all-air trans-Atlantic service explained the anxiety of the British to see Canada establish the ship-to-shore service. Canada's proposed service would be outdated before the bickering TCA Committee had even made a final decision.

There was also the question of the trans-Canada airway. Would cabinet authorize expenditures for developing both the trans-Canada and trans-Atlantic airways concurrently? Compounding the problem was Pan Am's request on November 2, 1934, to operate a service through the Maritimes, so as to be favourably situated for trans-Atlantic flights. The government had still not answered Pan Am. The committee could not afford to waffle any longer. Thus McNaughton's comment of "no special hurry" depicted a chairman who either did not care or did not understand the significance of the larger aviation question.

Smart and Wilson seemed to be the only committee members capable of regarding Canada's "aviation question" from a variety of viewpoints. Unfortunately, Smart, who had been outspoken in earlier meetings, was remarkably subdued at later ones. Wilson, more often than not, stood lock step with McNaughton at committee meetings. As usual, on paper he was strong; he showed foresight and strength when he was hiding behind his memos. For example, on January 23, 1935, in a very forthright but confidential memorandum to the deputy minister, Wilson condemned the Canadian government for its "laissez-faire programme in aviation," for being "the only country which has reduced expenditures on civil aviation materially" and for placing its air services "on a care and maintenance basis."

Wilson described the progress in airways development in other countries, commented on Canada's poor development and blasted bureaucrats and government alike for placing civil aviation under military control. "That a re-organization of the Air Services has been necessary every three years since they were started surely shows either lack of a clear understanding of the problem or a refusal to face the facts ... Because the Air Force and Civil Aviation both use aircraft is no better reason for their common administration than for a common administration of the Navy and the Merchant Marine, which both use ships," he pungently wrote. He recommended immediate corrective action. Why did Wilson not say this at TCA Committee meetings?

Recognizing the necessity for a reorganization of government services, including civil aviation, the prime minister, on December 10, 1934, appointed a secret committee, chaired by McNaughton and composed of Finlayson, C.H. Bland (commissioner, civil service) and W. Arthur Steel (commissioner, Canadian radio broadcasting). On January 24, 1935, in a confidential report to the prime minister, the committee recommended that telegraph and telephone, radio broadcasting, meteorology, surveys and civil aviation be combined into one department to be called the Department of Communications. The committee saw civil aviation "more closely related to 'communications' than to 'transportation.'" It also submitted a draft for a revised Aeronautics Act and suggested that the act be introduced at the same time as the new Defence Act.

The legislation for these changes was never introduced. McNaughton later wrote that one of the reasons he had not presented this legislation

James A. Richardson, president of James Richardson & Sons, Limited, 1919–39.
A photograph taken around 1925. THE ARCHIVES OF JAMES RICHARDSON & SONS,
LIMITED

Above, left: An intrepid woman passenger climbing early "airstairs." The four-passenger Boeing 40 B-4, CF-AIM, was used on the western air mail service in the early 1930s. Note that the pilot sits in an open and lonely cockpit. CANADIAN AIRWAYS COLLECTION, PROVINCIAL ARCHIVES OF MANITOBA #99

Above, top right: James Richardson believed in marketing his company. In 1930, the huge billboard at St. Hubert Airport advertised mail, passenger and freight service to anywhere in Canada. CANADIAN AIRWAYS COLLECTION, PROVINCIAL ARCHIVES OF MANITOBA #1721

Above, bottom right: The Canadian Airways headquarters building, Marion Street, on the river at the foot of the Norwood Bridge in Winnipeg. This photo was taken in 1934; the building is now owned by Poulin's Exterminators. CANADIAN AIRWAYS COLLECTION, PROVINCIAL ARCHIVES OF MANITOBA

Facing page, bottom: The Junkers 52, CF-ARM, getting ready for its first flight on floats, at the foot of Brandon Avenue, Winnipeg, in 1931. Known as the "Flying Boxcar," CF-ARM operated on wheels, floats and skis and cruised at 100 mph. THE ARCHIVES OF JAMES RICHARDSON & SONS, LIMITED

Right: CF-AVD, a de Havilland 84 Dragon, at Gold Pines in 1936. The Dragon was used for flying over water because it had two engines. It cruised at 110 mph. CANADIAN AIRWAYS COLLECTION, PROVINCIAL ARCHIVES OF MANITOBA #152

Below: Canadian Airways' Junkers W-34, CF-AQV, was purchased in 1935. It is here seen at Colby's Landing, Ontario, in July 1938. Its cruise speed was 100 mph. THE ARCHIVES OF JAMES RICHARDSON & SONS, LIMITED

Facing page, bottom: A 1940 photo of Canadian Airways' Fairchild Super 71, CF-AUJ. The aircraft had large access doors, which made for the easy loading of large and bulky items, but the pilot sat behind the cabin, which limited visibility. THE ARCHIVES OF JAMES RICHARDSON & SONS, LIMITED

Left: The drafting room of the aerial surveys division in Montreal. CANADIAN AIRWAYS COLLECTION, PROVINCIAL ARCHIVES OF MANITOBA #2376

Bottom: Canadian Airways' Beechcraft 18, CF-BQQ, at Winnipeg in 1941. Three were purchased in 1940 for service in the Maritimes. Note the logo on the nose and the new uniforms worn by the pilots. The 18 was a light twin designed to take two pilots and six passengers. Its cruise speed was 205 mph. This model first flew in 1937 and remained in production until 1969. THE ARCHIVES OF JAMES RICHARDSON & SONS, LIMITED

Facing page, bottom: Richardson purchased two Lockheed 10A Electras in 1936. This was the aircraft he intended for the trans-Canada service. It was the most modern airliner in Canada. It featured two engines and a retractable undercarriage, carried two pilots and ten passengers and cruised at 190 mph. CF-BAF is at Stevenson Field, Winnipeg, in 1937. Note the Canada goose logo. It must have been difficult for Richardson to watch his logo being scraped off and replaced with Trans-Canada Air Lines' name. THE ARCHIVES OF JAMES RICHARDSON & SONS, LIMITED

Muriel Sprague Richardson (1890–1973), wife of James A. Richardson, in the 1940s. She became president of James Richardson & Sons, Limited on the death of her husband in 1939 and assumed responsibility for Canadian Airways Limited. Muriel Richardson was president of the company for 27 years, longer than any other president since the founder. THE ARCHIVES OF JAMES RICHARDSON & SONS, LIMITED was that, under the proposed plan, aviation would have been handed over to the railways and, therefore, would have been in danger of being "suppressed and made subservient to the interests of the railways." McNaughton was talking out of both sides of his mouth. He had been the main advocate of railway control over the airways and had chaired the committee that had produced that very recommendation. For McNaughton to use that reasoning as an excuse simply does not wash. Significant also was the fact that Smart was not appointed to this committee, probably because McNaughton did not request him, knowing that Smart would recommend that civil aviation be transferred to a newly created department of transport. McNaughton did not agree, preferring to see civil aviation tucked away with communications; that would leave the military dominant.

In a March 20 memo directed to no one, McNaughton admitted, for the first time since the late 1920s, that Canada was in trouble. "In consequence of the lack of through airway facilities, not only is Canada not benefiting from these possibilities but the developments which have taken place elsewhere have resulted in the diversion to foreign airways of high class traffic of value and urgency which had previously been carried by Canadian railways and steamship connections. This diversion is ... a matter of serious concern." McNaughton must have been very worried to have admitted this, even in a private memo. This memo, of course, contradicts his committee memo that there was no hurry to choose a Canadian operator or to re-establish the Montreal–Halifax connection.

The TCA Committee met twice more in 1935, on March 14 and July 5; but McNaughton now seemed to have lost all interest in airway matters. He was not particularly concerned about Canada's exclusion from the Empire Air Mail Scheme or the collaboration between Imperial Airways and Pan Am, nor did he try to prevent Pan Am from establishing a service from New York through the Maritimes to Newfoundland.

The July 5 committee meeting had only four participants: McNaughton, Wilson, Norman Robertson from External Affairs, and A.S. Deaville from the Post Office. Words like "immediate action" were used in connection with the trans-Atlantic service, and references were made to Imperial Airways, Pan Am and Newfoundland and their requests to Canada for action. No one on the committee remarked that it continually discussed the same matters each time, each year, and that members seemed to be simply warming a chair when turning up for meetings. McNaughton said nothing. At the end of June, he left DND for the National Research Council, although he retained his chairmanship of the TCA Committee. He chaired only one more meeting.

McNaughton believed that he had more than fulfilled his job as chairman. In a "private and confidential" letter to Woods-Humphrey of Imperial Airways on July 18, 1935, written as he was on the verge of leaving for the National Research Council, he smugly wrote of the part he had played in the construction of the trans-Canada airway and how secure Canada's position was regarding international matters. He conveniently chose to ignore his March 20 memo and all of Wilson's memos that strongly urged the government to make policy decisions. Understandably, he would not have wanted to admit Canada's lack of progress, but he should have known that Imperial Airways was aware of what Canada had *not* done.

The letter reveals more about McNaughton's personality than it does about the status of Canada's airways. McNaughton was, in fact, responding to Imperial Airways' concern over the American penetration of Canada. Wholly satisfied with himself, he wrote, "Everywhere our own interests have been carefully and fully safeguarded." Did he really believe that Canada was covered, or was he too full of himself to properly evaluate the situation? In what was obviously a swan song letter, McNaughton continued: "The progress made with our airways in the last few months has brought the time of commencement of operation of a trans-Canada air mail service within sight ... The key fields between Halifax and Vancouver will be usable for experimental flights in October this year." It would be four more years before the Halifax–Vancouver connection was finished.

McNaughton told Woods-Humphrey that every penny for which he asked to hire staff, do experimental radio work and do "certain other work on the airways" was given. He patted himself on the back with the comment, "At last we can consider that we have an approved policy and we can now proceed along the path we have mapped out with every confidence. As regards the Atlantic connection ... we have been content to leave this development to your initiative in the present, because we felt we could best cooperate in the general scheme by driving forward our own internal arrangements ... Our airways in Canada are definitely moving forward."

Under McNaughton's leadership, the TCA Committee produced little that was concrete except a mass of memoranda. To be fair, McNaughton was responsible to a prime minister who saw commercial aviation as a nonessential item. However, the result was that under Bennett, with McNaughton as the chief adviser, commercial aviation in Canada stagnated. McNaughton never promoted the advantages of commercial aviation to Canada's national and international economic development. Was this deliberate, or was it through ignorance? McNaughton's biographer, John Swettenham, wrote that "McNaughton controlled all the essential strings." Unfortunately for commercial aviation, McNaughton pulled few if any strings for its advancement, with the wider ramifications that Canada lost the lead it once had.

McNaughton permitted interdepartmental rivalry to delay committee decisions. He himself vacillated on critical issues. However, the most damning comment on him was his "selectivity" in what information he passed on to the prime minister and to his own committee members. McNaughton's biographer used the word "manipulate" in describing how McNaughton worked: "Here we see McNaughton at his best— manipulating one of his functions to the advantage of the second, and with a by-product of benefit for a third. And all was directed to the provision of the airway and the general good of Canada." His biographer relied a great deal on personal interviews with McNaughton for this period, and McNaughton's memory was selective about the airways question.

McNaughton was very clear about the important role he played for Trans-Canada Air Lines. His biographer wrote that TCA began its operations "on the basic lines that McNaughton had recommended." The records show that at least once, McNaughton countermanded his committee's recommendation and that more than once, he delayed carrying out directives from the prime minister. His actions were detrimental to Canadian Airways and ultimately to Canada. His treatment of Richardson also calls for censure. For well over a year, he let Richardson believe that Canadian Airways was in the picture.

The puzzling part in all of this is that McNaughton undoubtedly would have described himself as a man of integrity. Did his lack of the most elementary business sense so distort his thinking that he truly believed that Richardson had little to offer? Or did his overwhelming desire to keep his air force flying blind him to the larger picture? If either were the case, it might explain his actions and the lengths to which he was prepared to go to attain his objective. Once McNaughton decided upon a course of action, nothing could stop him—after all, he was doing it "for the good of Canada." This unwavering belief in his own "rightness" so warped his judgment during World War II that he was relieved of his command and brought back to Canada.

When McNaughton later entered politics, he was also seen as switching sides. His biographer defended him. "Although it would seem to those with no knowledge of the background that he had been a turncoat twice—first when he had deserted the Conservatives to join the Liberal government and now, having been the arch-apostle of voluntary methods, he had stolen the position of the Tories to advocate conscription—such was not the case. But appearances were against him ... The derision, scorn and fury which the Tories had felt for McNaughton since he had saved King by joining his government ... poured down on the man they considered their betrayer." James Richardson, if he had been alive, would probably have concurred.

McNaughton believed that he had done more for airway development in Canada than anyone else, and he was not shy about dropping hints about his role. In reality, he, more than anyone, hindered the development of commercial aviation in Canada. His influence was huge, and if he had worked with Wilson and Richardson, he could have ensured that Canada was in the forefront of airway development. Instead, his preoccupation with the air force and Civil Government Air Operations clouded his judgment. He did not understand, nor would he listen when others tried to tell him, that a strong and viable commercial aviation industry would put dollars in the government's treasury, and that would mean money was more likely to flow to the air force. McNaughton, as the saying goes, cut off his nose to spite his face. A good soldier and scientist he undoubtedly was; a statesman he was not. He let his prime minister and his country down.

Meanwhile, Richardson kept re-jigging Canadian Airways. At the April 1935 annual meeting, the board of directors appointed G.A. Thompson general manager. Richardson's address to the shareholders focused mainly on government. His bitterness was apparent.

General McNaughton, the Chief of Staff, unquestionably a man of ability, appears to have no interest or sympathy with the kind of work we carry on, but he is anxious that his department should dominate the radio all across the north, regardless of how much this costs the Dominion Government or how inefficient their service may be. He also is set on his Department doing all the photographic work in Canada and if public opinion would permit he would also like to fly the Air Mail. We asked him if he would also like to take on the responsibility of looking after the so-called bush work and he said he certainly would not have anything to do with that, somebody else could do that.

Richardson's contempt for civil servants who frittered away tax-payers' money on foolish projects was clear in this extract of a letter. "I expect that people who have never done anything really constructive or useful in their lives will continue to be prominent in advocating schemes for the expenditures of public money, confident in the belief that our governments have inexhaustible stores of money on which to draw, and at least they are confident themselves that if anybody has to pay for these expenditures it will fall on someone other than themselves."

In May 1935, to strengthen the board of directors, Richardson asked Noah Timmins of Canada Cement to join. In his letter to Timmins thanking him for joining the board, Richardson's frustration with the government, politicians and civil servants alike, was evident. "The present Government has no policy in regard to aviation and the only work given out is by the Post Office, who state that in the absence of a government policy their departmental duty is simply to get their mail carried just as cheaply as they possibly can."

Richardson had reason to be bitter and concerned. Canadian Airways had no air mail contracts in which the revenue covered the costs of the operation. Its sole reasons for accepting these contracts, as Tommy Thompson explained to J.O. Apps of the CPR, were:

1. To retain the favour of the government in the hope of receiving a trans-Canada Air Mail contract some day.
2. To eke out the revenue from the mining fields on such bush air

mail services as run along or closely adjacent to the routes to the mining fields.

3. To keep in employment equipment on which capital expenditure has been made.

Anyone who knows much of business conditions must be aware that concerns are run at a loss in the hope of better days. In no country, even in good times, has commercial aviation been attempted on a large scale without government subsidy. The conditions in Canada are favourable, but no air transportation operator has yet retired with a fortune. Many have retired.

Anticipation that money might be forthcoming for a Canadian air mail service was in the air, and there was much jostling among companies. Famous World War I pilot Roy Brown, who was with General Airways, approached Canadian Airways with the offer that he would manage Canadian Airways. Beatty asked Richardson's opinion. Honesty was more apparent than tact in the reply. "The facts are that Brown has nothing to sell except that he was fortunate enough to get on Richthofen's tail during the War ... Brown has no control of his pilots. All of them have a free hand to make any rates they like ... Their pilots fly planes when they are the worse for liquor."

When that alliance did not materialize, Dominion Skyways tried to make a deal with General Airways in an attempt to draw business from Canadian Airways. That too went nowhere. Tommy Thompson, who had a pulse on all that was happening, suggested that their three companies try to work out a stabilization of rates. As he explained in his letter to Richardson: "I have for some time felt that the only solution for the small operators in the long run is for them to combine ... The main difficulties to the successful accomplishment of this in the past has been jealousy on the part of the operators themselves, lack of adequate finances and lack of a sufficiently able mediator."

What Thompson did not want was for Dominion Skyways and General Airways to join. A combination of this nature could give Canadian Airways strong competition with the mining companies. Not only that, with the companies' varied interests, they would be able to wield considerable influence at both the provincial and federal level of politics, regardless of what party was in power. The situation was potentially dangerous for Canadian Airways. Thompson recommended that they try to halt any such combinations and work instead to stabilize the rates to the benefit of all.

Still operating under the assumption that Canadian Airways would receive the main air mail contracts, Richardson did all he could to ready his company. One of his first moves was to send pilot Z. Lewis Leigh to California to receive instrument training (known as blind flying) from the Boeing School of Aeronautics. (John Wilson had told Thompson in September 1935 that there was no space for any Canadian Airways pilots to receive instrument training from DND at Trenton.) Lewis Leigh then set up a training program for Canadian Airways pilots.

In August, Thompson suggested to Richardson that, using the nucleus of the aircraft department of Canadian Vickers, he form an aircraft-manufacturing company to produce aircraft for the trans-Canada air mail service. "From its inception commercial aviation in Canada has been handicapped through having to purchase aircraft produced in foreign countries and adapt them at considerable expense to Canadian conditions ... When the time comes where is Canada going to obtain suitable machines in a reasonable time and at a price not loaded down with customs duty?"

There was a minimum of contact between Canadian Airways and the government in 1935. Canadian Airways was not asked to attend any TCA Committee meetings, nor was its advice sought on any airways matters. Since McNaughton had shown himself to be hostile to Canadian Airways and its relationship with the Post Office had deteriorated further, the firm saw little point in pushing its case in Ottawa. By mid-1935, Richardson had given up hope that Bennett would do anything for the company and was now pinning his hopes on Mackenzie King and the Liberals. It was said that James Richardson, believing that R.B. Bennett was totally to blame for his company's problems, cast his vote for the Liberals.

CHAPTER NINE

"Free of Politics": The Liberals and the Aviation Question

I N THE 1935 FALL ELECTION, R.B. Bennett's Conservatives were routed and Mackenzie King's Liberals were swept back into power. They came to office at a fortunate time. Canada had begun to pull itself out of the Great Depression, and the government could afford to ease the purse strings. The Liberals, committed to the completion of the trans-Canada airway, moved quickly to establish a framework for the development of civil aviation. Within a year and a half, the government enacted legislation that had an immediate impact on Canadian Airways and far-ranging results for commercial aviation in general. The negative policy or, as officials preferred to call it, "non-participation" that had characterized Canada's aviation "policy" was soon to end.

The similarity to conditions in 1928 was noticeable. Again, external pressure forced the government to implement a program for the inauguration of the trans-Canada airway. In June 1935, Canada's hand was forced. The French government proposed that the United Kingdom, the United States and France collaborate in developing the trans-Atlantic service by the southern route. To prevent this and to encourage development of the direct route, the Canadian government had to take action. The necessity for carrying out its trans-Atlantic agreement made it vital that the government immediately establish a national airline. King appointed a subcommittee of council to study the trans-Canada airway situation and requested a memorandum from the Trans-Atlantic Committee to bring him up to date.

Valentine Smart, the deputy minister of railways and canals, was chairman of the Trans-Atlantic Committee. With him were Loring Christie, counsellor, External Affairs; John Wilson, controller of civil aviation, DND; P.T. Coolican, assistant deputy postmaster general; John Patterson, director, meteorological service, Marine Department; and W.C. Clark, deputy minister of finance. Of interest in the report was an attached letter to the secretary of state for external affairs from his counterpart on Downing Street (J.H. Thomas) on August 9, 1935, in which Thomas bluntly stated that Imperial Airways and Pan American Airways had been working together for some time to develop a trans-Atlantic service. It was a direct challenge to Canada to start cooperating or be left out.

The report reviewed international airway developments since 1931. It covered the same ground as most of the previous reports and made many of the same observations—that Canada was the only major country with no national airway and no obvious plans to do anything about its trans-Atlantic connections. The implication was clear: Canada had not carried out any of its airways promises. "Canada must decide to what extent it will participate," the report stated unequivocally. The committee recommended that Canada should participate in an experimental trans-Atlantic service by the direct route and maintain all navigational aids in Canadian territory.

In late November 1935, representatives from Canada, the United Kingdom, the Irish Free State and Newfoundland met in Ottawa, seven times, to discuss the trans-Atlantic service. Their main recommendation was that a joint operating company be organized and run by these four governments. More discussions were held in Washington in early December among the United States, Britain and Canada. The main concern of the Canadians and the British was to formalize an agreement with the Americans before the French formalized their verbal arrangements with the Americans on the development of the southern route.

Side deals, however, were going on all the time, which made it doubly imperative that Canada declare its intentions. If not, it would find itself in the position of South America, where the banana republics ran their little air services but Pan Am carried all the through traffic. If Canada did not move immediately, the Americans would be so far ahead technically and so well established on the traffic side that any new Canadian service would face an uphill battle even to get back the mail loads, which were being transported by the American carriers. Since Imperial Airways hoped to be operating to Newfoundland in 1936, Canada had to take a stand or run the risk of finding itself in a last-minute rush to cooperate and getting the leftovers when the most desirable contracts had already gone to subsidized American services.

During the government's "non-participation" years, James Richardson had taken the precaution of maintaining close ties with Imperial Airways. On October 5, 1935, shortly before the fall election, he asked Senator W.H. Dennis, who was on his way to London, to speak with G.E. Woods-Humphrey of Imperial Airways. Richardson gave Dennis a letter of introduction to Woods-Humphrey in which he made it very clear that he and the government were prepared to cooperate with Imperial Airways "in an around-the-world service and as soon as they can get to Newfoundland or to our Atlantic seaboard we want to be ready with a fast air mail service to the Pacific ... We are anxious that no arrangements should be made with Pan American which will affect co-operation between Canadian Airways and Imperial Airways. We want to do everything possible to cement the Imperial ties and the All Red Route." Richardson's words were not hot air; two years earlier he had made a formal connection between Canadian Airways' and Imperial Airways' traffic departments to prepare for the day when an international hookup became viable.

Richardson was anxious that Canada should not lose out. "During the next 25 years developments in aerial transport will result in a large international trade being developed by air, and looking to our future it is most essential that we should take full advantage of our position in latitude ... We should consider the extension of our operation either on our own account, or in co-operation with the Imperial Airways," he stated to his directors at their April 1936 meeting. "We may have the most economical route, but if we do not develop it, and southern routes are built up ... there will be all kinds of entangling arrangements set up to hold trade in these channels ... We must not overlook the great advantage we enjoy through the short cut made possible through our being able to hop over the top of the world."

On the home front, Richardson lost no time in meeting with the new prime minister, Mackenzie King; J.C. Elliott, the postmaster general; and C.D. Howe, the minister of railways and canals. According to Richardson, Howe told him he could do nothing about the trans-Canada company until the airways came under his jurisdiction but assured him that Canadian Airways would be Canada's "chosen instrument," that Canadian Airways would be the "backbone" of the trans-Canada company. To his directors, in April 1936, Richardson reported that Howe stated that "it is his desire that they should become the Imperial Airways of Canada." There is no documentary evidence from Howe or King to corroborate this, but Gordon Lawson of James Richardson & Sons remarked that there was no reason not to believe Richardson's claims. Richardson and Howe were "very friendly" at the time. Howe had built a number of grain elevators for James Richardson & Sons and the firm was pleased with Howe's work. More to the point, Lawson observed that Richardson often conducted business with a handshake and that he considered a man's word as binding as a legal document.

Fearing that King would base his plans on the TCA Committee's January 1934 report, Richardson asked J.O. Apps of the CPR to try to obtain it. With difficulty, Apps managed to wrangle a copy, without the appendices. He sent it to Richardson, asking him not to let anyone know that he was in possession of it. Richardson passed it on to Tommy Thompson for his scrutiny. In an October 19, 1935, letter to Richardson, Thompson spelled out some of his concerns about the report. Noting that no one on the committee had any practical knowledge of commercial aviation, he observed that the committee "picked to pieces Canadian Airways cost estimates without any opportunity of defending it."

Thompson suggested that Richardson invite "a responsible party in the Post Office to investigate our costs as shown on our books and passed [by] our auditors ... High officials in the Post Office and Government should know the true costs of a sound commercial operation

rather than take their figures from would-be experts or smaller operators." Not surprisingly, Thompson disagreed with the committee's conclusion that one company could not handle both the transcontinental
and bush operations. He reminded Richardson that Canadian Airways'
Survey Division was separate from the rest of the company and that the
bush division could be handled on a similar basis. Thompson also met
with J.C. Elliott and C.D. Howe on November 21, 1935.

Although more skeptical than Richardson, Thompson also assumed
that Canadian Airways would obtain the main contract. "With our
nation-wide organization and through our association with the railways, we hold a preferred position," he wrote, but he left nothing to
chance. In a letter to Richardson on November 12, 1935, Thompson
recommended that when Z. Lewis Leigh returned from his instrument
flying course at the Boeing School of Aeronautics in California, he
establish a similar training program for Canadian Airways. "This would
not only provide ourselves with competent pilots for the mail when
ready, but what is more important, would show the authorities that
Canadian Airways realize the importance of being ready."

Ominously, Thompson added, "The Royal Canadian Air Force in
Winnipeg have instituted an Instrument Flying course. I do not like
this as it may mean that when the trans-Canada air mail is inaugurated,
the RCAF wish to be in a position to say they have the only trained
pilots available, with the intention of using this as an argument to run
the first experimental service or else to force those pilots onto the contractor. I may be entirely wrong, but it should not be overlooked." The
cost of setting up the program was high "when there are no direct
financial returns, but I feel the urgency of the matter warrants it."

Thompson also recommended to Richardson that their pilots on
the Vancouver–Seattle service be outfitted with uniforms without delay
because they were constantly being compared with United Airlines'
smartly dressed pilots. Thompson enclosed his design for cap badges,
breast badges and buttons, suggesting that the buttons have Canadian
Airways' emblem, the Canada goose, embossed on them. He recommended that the uniform be a plain, double-breasted tunic with long
trousers made of blue serge, the same pattern as used by American
Airways, while the cap should be the ordinary peaked navy-blue uniform cap.

Richardson replied enthusiastically the next day: "I agree ... It is highly important that our equipment and personnel not be unfavourably compared to American lines ... There will also be the effect of generally improving the esprit de corps of our personnel and their pride in our company." He added that Coolican had told him that "we were on the spot on the Vancouver to Seattle run, that we were being critically observed by both American airways companies and Vancouver citizens, who were disposed to feel that perhaps they might be better served by United Air Lines ... Any slip on this service might detrimentally affect the standing of the company in connection with the larger issues which we may before very long have to deal with."

A month later a worried Thompson wrote Richardson that Cowley had told him that DND had insisted that Imperial Airways fly into Montreal. If this happened, Thompson said, it would cut off the trans-Canada air mail route from Montreal to the Maritimes. Clearly DND officials did not understand the significance of controlling the total transcontinental system.

Rumours and deals were in the air on the international front also. Apps wrote Richardson on October 7 that C.H. Clendining, of the Irish Trans-Atlantic Corporation, wanted to meet him to discuss the route from Londonderry, Ireland, to Sydney, Nova Scotia. On December 10, Clendining wrote to Richardson, referring to their conversation in Montreal, and enclosed a copy of the secret agreement signed between the government of Newfoundland, Imperial Airways and Pan Am. He also enclosed for Richardson's confidential information a copy of his letter to the secretary of the Department of Commerce, Belfast, regarding his visit to Canada and the United States.

Clendining was very concerned that Imperial Airways and Pan Am would make a deal to create a monopoly on the North Atlantic route, which would cut out Ireland and Canada. He told Richardson that he had spoken about this to Canada's minister of national defence, the minister of trade and commerce, and two CNR trustees, who assured Clendining of their support for the air terminus at Sydney. Covering all bases, Clendining met also with the mayor of Sydney to stir up enthusiasm there.

Despite the work of Richardson, Apps, Clendining and various individuals from Imperial Airways, the Canadian government had been hopelessly lax for too long, and the secret agreement between Imperial Airways and Pan Am appeared to be too far along for the Canadians to do anything about it. The result, as Richardson and Wilson had many times warned, was that Canada was out of the picture.

Meanwhile, Thompson was busy trying to ensure that Canadian Airways was the front-runner. On October 29, 1935, he discussed a number of important route connections with Richardson. He confirmed that Canadian Airways had received the Vancouver–Seattle contract (begun October 1) in the face of stiff opposition from United Airlines, which had the U.S. mail contract between Seattle and Los Angeles. To obtain it, Canadian Airways had to hand over to Northwest Airlines the mail contract between Winnipeg and Pembina. Thompson's choice was a good one because the Seattle contract was double the daily mileage, its passenger component was greater and, even more importantly, it would help to prevent American penetration into British Columbia and, through B.C., into Alaska.

But Thompson was concerned that Canadian Colonial Airways, now a subsidiary of American Airways, held the feeder line between Montreal and Albany; this meant that the Americans had two feeder lines while Canadian interests had only one. Richardson later wrote that the Vancouver–Seattle operation was run at a loss and Canadian Airways had thought of cancelling it, "but we had such a howl from the Vancouver Board of Trade and other organizations that we felt the goodwill of Vancouver, which we might later need, was of sufficient importance that it was undesirable for us to discontinue the run."

Thompson considered the Maritimes routes the most pressing problem because of the probability of Imperial Airways inaugurating an experimental trans-Atlantic mail service via Newfoundland during the next twelve months; thus the question of a connection between the Maritimes and Boston became even more important. The newspapers were full of Clendining's visit to Canada, and the public was well aware that he was also looking for a connection with an American airline, likely Pan Am, that would be interested in connecting with any trans-Atlantic schedule. Thompson was worried about the Boston–Maritimes route because there was nothing in the international agreement governing flying in Canada by the Americans, except the provision that only international traffic could be handled.

The inauguration of the Vancouver–Seattle mail run consolidated Canadian Airways' position on the Pacific coast, but so long as the route between Halifax and Saint John was open, Canadian Airways' (not to mention Canada's) position in the Maritimes was precarious. The situation was aggravated by the possibility of Clendining making an agreement with an American line to connect at Sydney (even though he was also talking with Richardson). Thompson recommended to Richardson that Canadian Airways immediately institute a public-awareness campaign in the Maritimes on the importance of air mail. He was adamant that they must launch a sustained promotion of air mail and secure the support of the local business and service clubs and newspapers.

Matters finally began to move. King appointed a subcommittee of cabinet to deal with aviation, composed of Ian Mackenzie, minister of defence; J.C. Elliott, postmaster general; and C.D. Howe, minister of railways. The departmental committee was composed of Smart, Cooli-can, Herring and Wilson. On November 22, 1935, the departmental committee recommended to the prime minister that Canada cooperate in the direct service by Imperial Airways. Edward Beatty immediately relayed this information to Richardson and advised that a more detailed memo would be sent to the subcommittee of cabinet.

Of incidental interest was a letter from W.F. Lough, district director of postal services in Winnipeg, to Richardson on October 8, 1935, advising him "that the Winnipeg Postal District was now handling about 70% of the entire air mail transported in the Dominion."

Although 1935 ended with no official resolution regarding the trans-Canada airway, the *Financial Post* had no doubts, and on January 11, 1936, it stated emphatically, "Canadian Airways Limited unquestionably will be the nucleus." On January 23, the *Winnipeg Free Press* ridiculed DND and the Post Office's contention that the mails must be carried separately. "This order is contradicted by world practice ... Woods-Humphrey, Managing Director of Imperial Airways, says, 'No mails-only service has as yet paid its way on the air mail surcharges ... The separation of passenger services from the mails means that the costs of both must rise.'"

Ever optimistic, but with a tinge of concern, Richardson said to his friend F.I. Ker on January 24, "I am hopeful that the Trans-Canada Air Mail problem will be dealt with on its merits and in the interests of Canada regardless of any other considerations—if government does not listen to political influences with axes to grind."

Working to Canadian Airways' advantage was the fact that federal officials were finally coming to realize that the railway issue was a national transportation problem and that the rationalization of the railways could not be accomplished without rationalization of all competing and ancillary forms of transportation. The proposed Department of Communications would be dropped in favour of the better-conceived Department of Transport.

Now that the government seemed prepared to take action, Thompson began work on scheduling, cost estimates, equipment and personnel requirements, administration and capital investment for the operation of the trans-Canada airway in January 1936. Thompson wanted Canadian Airways to be ready. Imperial Airways expected to have a North Atlantic service in operation by 1938, and it was imperative that Canada have a transcontinental service in place. He envisioned the service going into operation in four successive stages: Winnipeg to Edmonton, Vancouver to Lethbridge, Montreal to Winnipeg, and Halifax to Montreal. He worked out the cost estimates to coincide with each of these stages.

In early January, Thompson wrote Richardson about a possible merger between Dominion Skyways and Canadian Colonial and suggested that Richardson contact Hartland Molson personally and ask him not to combine with any other company until he spoke with Canadian Airways. A few days later, Thompson recommended that Richardson prepare a memo regarding the inauguration of the trans-Canada airway, before Parliament opened, and send it to all members, along with a personal covering letter.

Richardson travelled to Ottawa in early February and met with C.D. Howe and S.J. Hungerford of the CNR. He followed up with a letter to the prime minister, reminding him that

we were entrusted with this work by your previous administration. We have suffered, as a company, great hardship through Mr. Bennett's action in summarily cancelling our contracts, without cause.

I am hopeful that at an early date it will be possible for the government to declare their policy in regard to the Trans-Canada Air Mail, at least insofar as the organization which will be entrusted with the work. Our officials have the experience to render very valuable service in this connection, and stand ready at any time to put themselves at the disposal of your officials at Ottawa for any discussions in which they may be helpful.

Richardson also wrote Howe on February 6, giving a brief history of the company and some vital statistics: Canadian Airways had been operating almost ten years, operated twelve radio stations in the North, had one hundred oil and gas stations distributed across northern Canada and provided an air service into every section of Canada. "We have one hundred and seventy-four people now in the service of our company, and we are thoroughly capable of planning, organizing and carrying out a Trans-Canada Air Mail service that will be creditable to our company and to your Government." He bluntly told Howe that he hoped that the government would establish its policy quickly and that "the policy will be that the Canadian Airways, in cooperation with the two railroads, will be entrusted with carrying the Trans-Canada Air Mail, and the major Air Mail routes in Canada."

His letter to Hungerford was much the same, although he bared his soul a little more when he wrote: "I am concerned that the question of policy be settled . . . One of two small competitors are demanding these contracts be thrown to open tender . . . We cannot afford to have any revenue, however small, taken from us." He concluded by asking Hungerford to put pressure on the government to settle upon a policy quickly.

Richardson's main theme in all his letter writing at this time was to reinforce the notion that Canadian Airways had been established to carry mail and passengers across the country and to be the international carrier, and to impress officials that the company had the facilities, personnel, knowledge and experience to undertake the transcontinental contract. As an extra, he often threw in the observation that no polar expedition had been undertaken since 1929 without seeking advice, pilots and mechanics from Canadian Airways. His letters usually concluded with the strongly worded, "Canadian Airways Limited wish to cooperate with the two railways (who both have a substantial interest in Canadian Airways) and the Government of Canada to work out a Trans-Canada operation. We see the urgency of making an immediate settlement of government policy regarding aviation. We would like to be assured that it is the Government policy to entrust the Trans-Canada air mail service to our Company and the two railways."

Mackenzie King responded to Richardson on February 11, "As soon as we are in a position to take definite steps I have no doubt that Mr. Howe will wish to communicate with you." The next day, Howe wrote: "Every consideration will be given to the past experiences of Canadian Airways Limited ... The Estimates for civil aviation, which have now been tabled in Parliament, contain a substantial increase over previous years." The *Financial Post* on February 22 noted: "The King government [is] definitely committed to the completion of the transcontinental airway and the launching of an air mail service ... This is the first time money has been appropriated for this purpose since the western air mail service [was] abandoned in 1931."

On February 25, Thompson sent Richardson a handwritten note from Manitoba MP James A. Glen (whose son was a Canadian Airways pilot) warning that Herring (chief superintendent of air mail) was bad-mouthing Canadian Airways. He asked Richardson to destroy Glen's note after reading it. Thompson urged Richardson to lobby in Ottawa and prepare a report for Glen to read in the House about the lack of cooperation from civil aviation officials regarding overloading. Thompson was counting on Glen to carry Canadian Airways' case in the House of Commons, for he supplied Glen with additional information. In a letter to Glen on February 25, he stated that the Post Office was basing its cost studies on those of the American airlines, which flew many more miles per day than any Canadian operation could expect to do, and that the Post Office ignored the fact that the cost of gas, oil, engines and aircraft plus the tax on equipment was much higher in Canada than in the United States.

Thompson was fully aware of the pressure that would be exerted on Howe and knew it was unlikely that Canadian Airways would receive the trans-Canada air mail contract easily. Whoever received the contract would have a virtual monopoly on Canada's main airways. It was highly probable, therefore, that the trans-Canada company would not be chosen on its own merits and that the whole question would turn into a straight political issue. In this respect, the "Toronto group" constituted Canadian Airways' most serious competition. Its resurrected British North American Airways board of directors was composed of politically powerful men. So confident, or so full of bluff, was the group that E.P. Taylor, its president (succeeding Percy Parker, who died in April 1936), wrote to Woods-Humphrey of Imperial Airways that it had the trans-Canada contract "in the bag."

Fortunately the close relationship Richardson had with numerous Imperial Airways people paid off. Woods-Humphrey confidentially contacted Richardson to alert him of Taylor's letter stating that the Toronto group would be given the contract. On April 20, Richardson thanked Woods-Humphrey and added: "The activities of these people have been inspired by a man named P.C. Parker ... C.D. Howe, who is now the Minister of Transport, advised me personally that he had told Mr. Parker he would not discuss the matter with them at all and recommended that if he had anything of interest to discuss in connection with the matter he should take it up with me."

American aviation interests were active too. C.D. Howe told J.O. Apps that Lucius Manning, the Chicago representative of American Airways, was working with the Toronto group to finance a trans-Canada company. J.L. Ralston, former minister of national defence, was said to be the attorney for American Airways, in addition to working in alliance with the Toronto group. Ralston also submitted an application for the trans-Canada contract on behalf of Canadian Colonial Airways, the subsidiary of American Airways that held the Montreal–New York air mail contract. Errett L. Cord of Pan Am was also involved with Canadian Colonial and was trying to extend that company's operations in Canada. The connections between the various groups were many and confusing, and the degree of politicization was high.

To protect Canadian Airways' interests, Thompson suggested that in addition to lobbying, Richardson also prepare a memorandum in which he presented Canadian Airways' case as forcibly as possible for the "influential members of the House of Commons and the Senate." However, Richardson seems to have done little along these lines except to send the personable Don MacLaren, superintendent of the Pacific Lines, to Ottawa in the spring. Again Richardson made a major strategic mistake in spurning political pressure in favour of merit only. He had been burned more than once, and someone should have advised him that Howe had earned a reputation for making rash promises and allowing flattery to cloud his judgment.

On March 24, Thompson wrote Richardson that the Post Office had just awarded Wings Limited a contract without tendering. "We are at present in an impossible position maintaining a national organization at considerable loss in the hope that we will receive recognition as the government organization for the carriage of mail." He asked Richardson to use his influence in the East to have the government do something about the unfair tendering practices.

Richardson wrote to his good friend Norman Lambert that MP Glen had told him that Canadian Airways' weakness in Ottawa was that it did not lobby and that there was a great deal of misrepresentation of their position. For instance, Glen informed Richardson that Herring (not knowing that Glen was a friend of Richardson) had told him (and many others) that "we had an extremely high overhead, no idea of earning money and did not know the meaning of trying to economize." Richardson replied that the claim was ludicrous and that he would be glad to have an independent investigator audit his books and whatever else it took to convince government officials that their operation was run honestly and properly.

On May 6, Val Patriarche, Canadian Airways' general traffic manager, wrote J.O. Apps, general executive assistant of the CPR, detailing more problems with DND. "We have run across what appears to be serious discrimination against Canadian Airways personnel in the matter of issuing the new Public Transport pilots' licences."

Patriarche explained that Lewis Leigh, who had taken and passed the instrument training course at the Boeing School of Aeronautics in California and was probably the only pilot in Canada with the most up-to-date instruction available, had been refused the new public transport licence by DND because his night flying was inadequate—although his present commercial licence was already endorsed for night flying! Patriarche went on to explain a number of similar problems with other Canadian Airways pilots, including himself, and highlighted the fact that ex-RCAF pilots now flying with the Manitoba Government Air Service were obtaining the licence with no problem and fewer qualifications. "The appearance of the whole thing is that commercial pilots are to be prevented from obtaining the new transport rating while RCAF personnel are being given the required instructions. The attitude could then be taken that the only qualified pilots for mail operation are those of the RCAF."

By the middle of April, the situation was desperate for Canadian Airways. The decision to maintain operations on a national basis was purely political, but even that was now doubtful. The firm's policy of taking bush mail contracts at any price rather than letting them go to their competitors had played into the hands of the Post Office. Increasingly, the Post Office was awarding contracts with no tendering. Richardson did not want to abandon the contracts, however, because they added to the operator's prestige. In a memo to Richardson on April 14, Thompson admitted that Canadian Airways had inadvertently aided the Post Office and recommended that the company change its policy.

As the months slipped by, Richardson became more and more anxious to begin discussion with C.D. Howe on the organization of the trans-Canada company. However, since Howe still insisted that he would do nothing until the Department of Transport was created and he was made minister of transport, Richardson could do little but wait. The delay seemed interminable. In early April, Thompson suggested to Richardson that they engineer a series of editorials across the country in connection with the transcontinental mail. His recommendation was timely, because Kenora MP Hugh McKinnon told Richardson that "there was strong propaganda being worked at Ottawa for the purposes of building up a political opinion that any obligations owing to Canadian Airways through the wiping out of their contracts had been discharged by the local contracts that this company received in the last few years."

Always one to look at transportation as a whole, Richardson asked Thompson to begin negotiations for a controlling interest in Patricia Airways of Hudson, Ontario, which would enable Canadian Airways to quote on combined air, land and water operations in the Sioux Lookout district. They also knew that it would be harmful to Canadian Airways if someone like Starratt Airways bought it instead.

Although most newspaper editorials were very favourable to political newcomer C.D. Howe, the *Winnipeg Tribune* commented on June 5 that Howe's political inexperience and disinclination to listen to advice were already noticeable. "Mr. Howe is a newcomer in politics ... When he argues that the CNR can be made practically a department of government without coming under the influence of political patronage, he shows he simply does not know what he is talking about."

Others too were concerned about Howe's naïve outlook. MacLaren, who was in Ottawa on behalf of Canadian Airways, wrote to Thompson on June 16 that "Lambert agreed that Howe would like to deal with us direct but he still does not fully comprehend the political ramifications which attach to the letting of the Trans-Canada contract." A few days later, MacLaren wrote Thompson again, saying that Howe had told him "that we need have no fear that any representation from other groups would have any consideration by him." Howe was certainly not shy about making promises to various people about Canadian Airways.

At the beginning of June, Richardson again approached Howe on the question of the airway. "I had a very satisfactory chat with Mr. Howe ... Nothing adverse to the Canadian Airways interests would develop if I am away," Richardson wrote to Beatty on June 6. He told Howe that he was planning a trip overseas during July and August but would cancel it if Howe wished to talk with him. Howe informed him that he would do nothing until the end of the summer. Richardson, after meeting with Lambert in Ottawa in early July, wrote Thompson, "I think things will break all right for us, but we will have to keep our ear to the ground, take nothing for granted and try and not only hold our position, but strengthen it in every way."

Richardson received encouraging news from Frank Ross, who had just returned from a fishing trip with Howe. He wrote Richardson in early July that Howe "stated arrangements would be made with your company for service from Winnipeg to West this fall and next spring arrangements would be again completed with you for service from Halifax to Winnipeg. He states definitely nobody else will be considered as he has no intention of creating another railway competitor. In addition he states the government is under an obligation to you which has to be recognized. This is for your confidential information."

Feeling confident, Richardson left Canada for Europe the first week of July. He hoped to get in some holiday time and also to check out aircraft factories. Richardson had no sooner arrived in London than Howe and Wilson unexpectedly showed up in Winnipeg and requested that Canadian Airways turn over its soon-to-arrive Lockheed Electra to the newly formed Department of Transport (DOT).

DOT, created on June 23, 1936, brought together all forms of transportation under one minister. Civil aviation, for the first time, was accorded equal status with rail and marine services and was now completely separated from military control. Howe wanted Canadian Airways' Electra because he wanted DOT to begin testing the radio stations between Winnipeg and Lethbridge. The government did not have a modern, instrument-equipped aircraft to do this, and Howe was aware that Canadian Airways had ordered the Electra for its Vancouver–Seattle air mail service to comply with Post Office requirements. As he saw it, the Electra was the obvious choice because it would be suitable for the experimental radio work and for the actual operation of the trans-Canada airway. He therefore asked Thompson if Canadian Airways would charter its Electra and a pilot to the government for three months and implied that Canadian Airways' cooperation would benefit its chances for the trans-Canada contract. As Richardson later explained, "Mr. Howe stated that this would be our first step into the big picture."

Howe demanded an answer within twenty-four hours; this was to prove typical of his handling of the trans-Canada airway issue. More than once he rashly decided upon a course of action and then tried to ram it through without having carefully considered the consequences. In this instance, his ultimatum of an answer within a day placed unfair pressure on Thompson. Richardson was in London, Beatty and the rest of the directors were elsewhere, and Thompson needed more than a day to weigh adequately the implications of the request. Because Howe had personally requested Canadian Airways' cooperation, Thompson felt he had no choice but to cable Richardson, July 13, recommending the firm's compliance. Richardson agreed, and Canadian Airways put its pilot, Hollick-Kenyon, and its plane at DOT's disposal, under the direction of Squadron Leader Tudhope; but Richardson was not permitted to make any announcement in regard to the work.

On July 15, Thompson wrote to Richardson, advising him that Howe had also requested that he, Jack Tackaberry (comptroller of Canadian Airways) and Richardson meet with him as soon as he returned from Europe to discuss the operation of the Trans-Canada air mail with a special government committee. Things were looking good for Canadian Airways.

Nonetheless, the sequence of events from this time on is conflicting and vague. Richardson returned early to Canada, in mid-August, to see Howe. But Howe now sent word to Richardson that it was not necessary to meet, that he was "not yet clothed with the proper authority" and that "everything was working out along the lines of our previous discussions." Shortly after this, Howe asked Canadian Airways to submit a written proposal on the trans-Canada service.

On August 21, Richardson wrote to Norman Lambert, "I am a little disturbed recently by the activity of American Airways . . . Cord has got another Canadian charter for aviation." Cord wanted to acquire Canadian Colonial, which then operated between Montreal and Albany and had just received permission to extend from Montreal to Ottawa. It intended to sell out to Pan Am, which would give Pan Am the run of the Maritimes and allow it to hook up with Imperial Airways. How any of this could be happening was inconceivable to Richardson. Were the Post Office and DND not talking to Howe?

Thompson advised Richardson the next day that Smart had told him he was still waiting for the final recommendations from his committee. He commented again on the strong political connections that the "Toronto group," now headed by E.P. Taylor, had with the government. On August 24, Thompson told Richardson that Coolican felt that Howe was "inclined to underestimate the question of political expediency in connection with trans-Canada airway and might have difficulty in organizing it just as he would like."

More warnings came on September 4 from H.P. Robinson, who wrote Thompson (who in turn wrote Richardson the same day), "to put little faith in any promises made by the Minister of Transport . . . a Cabinet minister had told Robinson that Howe had prepared a Bill which if passed would give him complete control of all transportation systems in Canada and the Premier refused to sanction it." There are pencilled notes on file that appear to be Richardson's; unfortunately, they carry no date. The rough notes on yellow notepaper state, "This seems to be the period when Howe changed."

Canadian Airways' plan was delivered to Howe by Sir Edward Beatty the last week of September 1936. Why Beatty was chosen to handle the negotiations is unclear. According to a variety of sources, including Gordon Lawson and Jack Tackaberry, Beatty was often in Ottawa and more available for an impromptu discussion, and he was more used to dealing with the government than Richardson was. Howe's letter to Richardson on September 25 does not suggest that he was displeased at the prospect of having to deal with Beatty. However, nothing was as it seemed.

Richardson's earlier words, "I sincerely hope that it will always be possible for Canadian Airways to be kept free of politics and carried on, on a business basis," uttered fruitlessly to Prime Minister Bennett in 1933, came to haunt him again. This time he knew that the "aviation question" was not going to be settled on its own merits. Politics, as happened so frequently, now became the determining factor.

CHAPTER TEN

"Passing the Buck"

S PURRED BY C.D. HOWE, civil aviation and Post Office officials were busy writing reports for submission. On August 5, 1936, John Wilson submitted a "Memorandum on the Construction of the Trans-Canada Airway," which regurgitated much of what he had written before. Remarking on General McNaughton's secret letter to then Prime Minister Bennett (which contradicted the committee's main recommendation), Wilson diplomatically referred to it as McNaughton's "modification" of the report. He gave no rationale for drawing attention to McNaughton's "modification"; perhaps he was covering his tracks in case anyone should question why nothing had been done with the TCA Committee's 1934 report. Wilson referred to the "joint operating company," yet to be formed, between the United Kingdom, the Irish Free State, Newfoundland and Canada, saying once again that Canada's national company should be the "agent" to work with it.

The Post Office also filed its "Memorandum Submitted by the Post Office Department on the Subject of a Trans-Canada Air Mail Service" on August 5, and it too regurgitated most of the department's previous statements. "Canada seems to be alone in the lack of definite government support in the development of air traffic . . . Canada stands to profit to a much greater extent than any other country in the world from an orderly and economical development of air mail." The Post Office recommended that Canada immediately implement an air mail service.

The TCA Committee submitted its "Draft Report for Consideration by the Interdepartmental Committee on the Trans-Canada Airway" on August 10, an accompanying explanatory statement on the same date and a final report on September 4. The explanatory statement, written by Wilson, recommended that a national company be organized for both domestic and international operations but defined it vaguely. It suggested that the government put up 20 percent of the capital, each railway be asked to put up 20 percent and existing air operators be given the opportunity to subscribe for the remaining 40 percent of the capital. There should be no monopoly of air operations, and civil aviation should remain self-sustaining. Services in the mining areas should be provided by private companies assisted by remunerative air mail contracts.

The draft report outlined the estimates required and the stages in which the service would be inaugurated. It did not, however, come to grips with how the company should be organized, simply advising that "a company be formed to operate the system under contract with the Post Office Department." The report suggested that existing air companies might offer any suitable aircraft they had in operation in lieu of cash, and these subscribers could elect three directors to the board.

There was also a report, titled "Trans-Canada Airways (New Company)," which had no author, no date and no departmental name on it. It was in Valentine Smart's working papers but was likely written by Wilson; it was sent to Smart on August 21, 1936. The report provided a very elementary breakdown of cost estimates for personnel, equipment, land and office expenses, plus a suggestion that $3 million be authorized in capital stock initially and another $1 million be issued at a later date. Considering that Canada was not yet out of the depression and that most professionals were earning less than $6,000 a year, salary figures were high for the about-to-be-conceived company. For example, the president was to receive $25,000; the managing director, $10,000; the secretary treasurer, $6,000; pilots, $5,000; and the chief radio man, $5,000. The report also provided a sketchy breakdown of schedules, mileage, types of aircraft, life of aircraft, maintenance costs and a few other details for the actual operation. Whoever wrote this section had little knowledge of the complex task of working up a transcontinental operation.

On September 4, the TCA Interdepartmental Committee brought in its final report, "Trans-Canada Airway and Mail Service," an expansion of the suggestions presented in the draft report, with some variations as to control and operation. Neither TCA Committee report gave a strong recommendation as to who should be in control. It was obvious also that the practical aspect of the airline's establishment was beyond the committee's capabilities. As in 1933–34, committee member P.T. Coolican showed himself to be shortsighted. He disagreed that there should be a fixed air mail rate, that the company should develop a freight and passenger service in conjunction with the air mail and that the airway should be opened progressively in four sections. The recommendations that most affected Canadian Airways concerned the control of the trans-Canada company and the operation of the feeder services. The committee recommended that the company be jointly owned by private enterprise and the government. This report gave more control to the government than did the draft report: the government was to hold 25 percent of the stock, the CNR 15 percent, the CPR 15 percent and private aviation interests 45 percent.

The proposed set-up denied control to any single group, but the government, with 25 percent of the stock, and the CNR, with 15 percent, would form the strongest unit. The proposed board of directors also gave Canadian Airways cause for worry. There were to be seven directors: two appointed by the government, one each from the railways and three from the remaining shareholders. The chairman was to be elected by the directors, subject to the approval of the governor in council. The TCA Committee had, in effect, laid the foundation for a government-controlled company.

General McNaughton, who still kept a proprietary eye on the airway, may well have been the unseen power behind the set-up. A chance encounter between Howe and McNaughton may have tipped the balance and be one of the reasons why Howe became so receptive to a government-owned airline. McNaughton had attended a luncheon at the Rideau Club on July 21, 1936, at which John Wilson had been the speaker. Wilson's topic was Howe's trip over the prairie section of the trans-Canada airway in July—in Canadian Airways' Lockheed Electra. Also attending was the former prime minister, R.B. Bennett, who complimented his friend McNaughton on his work on the landing fields. Pleased, McNaughton went back to his office and wrote a private memorandum detailing Bennett's words of praise.

However, before he reached his office, McNaughton bumped into Howe. He included his conversation with Howe in the same memo. According to McNaughton, Howe too complimented him on the airfields. All of this would have been balm to McNaughton's ears, because he and Bennett had received a drubbing from the public and the Liberals about the unemployment relief camps (some of which had provided labour for construction of the emergency and intermediate airfields).

Howe, however, had a big mouth and did not stop there. (Howe's loose lips were verified by his biographers, Robert Bothwell and William Kilbourn, who wrote, "In his terse, utterly frank way, Howe liked to chat; and he loved political gossip: he eventually became one of the better retailers of cabinet secrets.") Howe revealed to McNaughton his plans to create a national company like Imperial Airways. Although Howe had a big ego, it was probably overwhelmed by McNaughton's. After all, McNaughton was a commanding figure: tall, austere and slim, he held the prestigious position of president of the National Research Council and was the former chief of the general staff. Undoubtedly Howe wanted to impress McNaughton and did so by divulging his plans about Canada's national company.

McNaughton, of course, was against this because he knew that Howe's choice would be Canadian Airways. Ever the good strategist, McNaughton did not bad-mouth James Richardson but spoke against the concept of a commercial company. "I told Howe I was doubtful if it were proper to hand the operation over to a commercial company . . . I assured Mr. Howe that I had been very deeply interested in the airway for many years . . . and in fact had advocated for a long time the transfer of civil aviation to a Department of Communications," he wrote in his memo.

Once again McNaughton fudged the truth. His reference to the

Department of Communications showed that his memory was conveniently selective. He had always resisted Smart and Wilson's recommendations to move civil aviation out of DND, and when he had the opportunity to create a Department of Communications, he recommended against it.

Two days later, on July 23, Coolican phoned McNaughton to ask him what he had heard about the airway. McNaughton also recorded this conversation in a private memo, again patting himself on the back when he told Coolican that Howe had praised his efforts and "that Canada could not have been provided with an Airway by any other method than construction under the relief projects." McNaughton told Coolican that he had warned Howe against setting up a company like Imperial Airways, which Howe favoured. "Mr. Howe had seemed to be impressed with my word of caution ... I then outlined to Mr. Coolican my thought that a *wholly owned Government corporation* should be set up to operate the airway as regards the carriage of mail. I pointed out that in any event it was not possible to combine mail and passenger services and I thought that the commercial operators should be well satisfied by having the use of the airway for passengers and freight at a nominal charge, leaving to the Government the handling of its own mail services" (emphasis added).

McNaughton extracted from Coolican the promise that he would call him after his talk with Howe and that the two of them should meet early the next week "to explore the possibilities." Clearly McNaughton wanted to be back in the picture. Evidently Smart had deliberately left him out of all discussions, and McNaughton was miffed. "I told Mr. Coolican that, in view of the fact that the Deputy Minister of Railways, Mr. Smart, had pointedly left me out of the Conference with the British authorities, I was not prepared to discuss matters with him and that I intended to give any advice on this subject which might be required direct to the Minister." McNaughton's vanity required that he be included in all airways matters; his pride was hurt that he was no longer considered vital. His remark about bypassing Smart, intended to show Coolican that he had the clout to go directly to the minister, indicates that McNaughton realized that Smart was no longer under his thumb.

After years of inaction, things began to move suddenly but disturbingly; Howe's intentions seemed ambiguous. On September 2, 1936,

Don MacLaren sent Richardson a coded telegram advising that Edward Beatty had told him that Howe had now prepared a trans-Canada plan and wanted either a re-formation of Canadian Airways or an entirely new company. "Howe intimated in favour of one company to handle main line Halifax–Vancouver; separate companies handle feeders."

Richardson phoned Beatty on September 2, saying that Howe had contacted him on August 25 and "advised that Civil Aviation would be transferred to DOT within two weeks and that the Council would determine a definite policy regarding two Trans-Canada Airways, by which I presume he means the through Trans-Canada Airways. I have been disturbed by the character of the new set-up that might be suggested and by talk of giving Main Branch Lines to companies who would ultimately be controlled in the United States." Richardson had become uneasy when Howe had added, "We have developed some rather definite ideas regarding the Trans-Canada Airways."

In early September Richardson tried to set up a meeting with Howe. Matters became more tense when H.P. Robinson told Thompson in early September to pay little attention to any promises made by the minister of transport. Apparently one of the cabinet ministers had told Robinson that Howe had prepared a bill that, if passed, would give him complete control of all transportation systems in Canada, but so far the prime minister had refused to sanction it. Thompson passed this information on to Richardson on September 4. "Mr. Howe might have difficulty in carrying out his wishes regarding the Trans-Canada ... Although Mr. Howe has told you on several occasions in all good faith that he would protect your interests, he finds now he cannot do it as fully as he would like. When Mr. Howe was in Winnipeg in July he gave me no intimation that the feeder lines would be run by a separate organization. The contrary was the case and his intention at that time was to form one large company with Canadian Airways as the backbone."

In response, Richardson wrote to Charles Dunning, the minister of finance, on September 5. "I hear things that give me reason to fear things are not working out as they should ... As I am advised that the policy recommendation may be to give out branch lines to different companies, I am disturbed, because if American companies get control of air lines and terminals, in populous parts of Ontario and Quebec, the traffic originating in and destined for this area will ultimately be routed through the U.S. and not through Canada."

Dunning replied on September 8, "My opinion is that your people are becoming unduly alarmed." Feeling he had been pawned off, on September 10 Richardson sent a coded telegram to Beatty that the situation had become entirely unsatisfactory and that they needed to meet immediately with Thompson to discuss strategy. Evidently Richardson and Howe met in mid-September, because Richardson wrote Howe on September 22 to say that he was glad that they had met and that he was sending Sir Edward Beatty the "complete information of Canadian Airways Limited." On September 25, Howe wrote to Richardson: "It seemed to me that Sir Edward Beatty is in an excellent position to work out a plan for the transcontinental service ... As soon as I receive his suggestion, I shall be prepared to discuss the matter further." Howe's words reassured Richardson.

Meanwhile, Canadian Airways finalized the blueprint for the transcontinental operation and organization on September 21. Beatty delivered ten copies of the plan on September 22. The fifty-page proposal, complete with charts and photographs of aircraft, was a detailed plan covering all administrative, financial and technical aspects of operating a transcontinental service. Included were complete schedules of the services to be operated and the men and equipment required, the four progressive stages in which the airway would be inaugurated and a complete breakdown of the financial costs for each segment of the airway.

Capital cost was $5 million, which was to be provided by Canadian Airways and the CPR, with the CNR's financial input left to its discretion. The board of directors was to represent the shareholders in the proportion of 37½ percent from each railway and 25 percent from Canadian Airways. To comply with the TCA Committee's 1934 recommendation of a separate bush and trans-Canada operation, Canadian Airways' proposal called for two companies: "Airways Limited," which would operate the bush services and take over Canadian Airways' assets and liabilities, and a "new" Canadian Airways Limited, which would operate the trans-Canada service. The proposal recommended that the government provide the intermediate airfields, lighting, snow removal, navigational aids and meteorology services.

Canadian Airways' plan was a good one—good for it and for the government and the people of Canada. It provided security for Canadian Airways because it called for an air mail contract of a fixed term (ten to fifteen years) at a fixed rate per mile and a definite period of depreciation for the aircraft. The proposal was an economical one for the government and the country. In addition, the plan set a limit on the profit the company could make, recommending that the company hand back to the government any profit in excess of 5 percent on the capital.

Of particular importance was the recommendation that if operating losses occurred, the company would meet them. The suggested cost of flying the mail was seventy cents per mile, and the proposal allowed for a periodic revision of the air mail rates because it was not known how long it would take to build up passenger and freight traffic. Once this traffic was worked up, the air mail rates would be revised downward, thus reducing the cost to the government.

Someone leaked the subcommittee's report to the *Financial Post*, which on October 10, 1936, ran the story that the committee had recommended a semi-public corporation: $5 million to be allotted, 25 percent to government, 15 percent to each railway and 45 percent to private interests. According to the *Post* the chief difficulty was the allotment of the 45 percent of the stock interest and the fact that the government would not give any stock allowances for goodwill or intangible assets. "It is learned that Canadian Airways Ltd. is regarded as having the greatest claim for preferment." As the *Post* pointed out, the extent to which the private companies would be interested in entering the picture was not clear, since the proposed set-up would deny to any single group control of the corporation. The *Post* also came to the conclusion that the Dominion government, with 25 percent of the stock, and the CNR, with 15 percent, would form the strongest unit.

None of this sat well with Richardson. Consulting with Beatty on October 14, it was decided that Beatty should meet with Smart as quickly as possible. There were mixed messages. Thompson, feeling optimistic, wrote MP James Glen on October 15, "The picture at present looks quite favourable." Richardson, feeling pessimistic again, wrote to Beatty on October 26, "Judging by reports sent by MacLaren to Thompson, Mr. Howe appeared to be decidedly unfriendly in so far as I was concerned." Howe, on the other hand, wrote Richardson on October 29, sounding as if he were in total agreement with him. He referred to Richardson's October 26 letter. "I had a long talk about aviation with Sir Edward and there is little difference of opinion between us regarding the development of the national service ... I am now ready to move in this matter."

If this letter can be believed, Howe still considered Canadian Airways to be the "backbone." Yet, when Richardson saw Howe in Ottawa and asked him what had happened to Canadian Airways' plan, Howe replied that there had been "an awful lot of lobbying done." To Richardson this was an unsatisfactory explanation. Howe had previously told him that he would refuse to talk to other interests, such as the Toronto group. Confusion reigned as Howe sent out conflicting messages.

Norman Lambert's diaries provide some explanation. Lambert, secretary of the National Liberal Federation and good friend of Howe, commented in his diary that when he played golf with Howe on August 23, Howe stated that he wanted to speak to Richardson about a proposition. However, in an entry for October 2, Lambert noted that Howe had criticized Richardson because he believed that Richardson had deliberately given him inaccurate mileage costs for the carriage of mail. Lambert, shocked by Howe's change of attitude toward Richardson, told Howe that he had never heard Richardson's integrity questioned before and that it was more likely someone from the Post Office who had misled Howe.

Lambert wrote in his diary, "When he [Richardson] left for England, C.D. Howe was going to make JR the Imperial Airways of Canada —and then quite without any warning he turned against him." On October 24, Lambert recorded in his diary that Howe had been heard "berating Richardson and saying he wouldn't be in the picture because he couldn't work with him." Lambert alerted Edward Pickering, King's assistant private secretary, "the PM should be told about the injurious political implications of Howe's free remarks about Richardson, and his proposed air policy." The next day Lambert wrote, "CD's breaches of faith" and listed five, one of them concerning himself. The third referred to Richardson: "Up to July 10 or 15, his assurances to JR [of] becoming *Imp. Airways of Canada* and in September without explanation becoming violently opposed to him."

Lambert felt that someone at the Post Office was responsible for misleading Howe, and even though he assured Howe of Richardson's ethical business dealings, the damage had been done. Howe dealt with Beatty from that point on and likely dismissed Richardson as a key participant. Yet it appears that Howe was prepared to accept Canadian Airways' plan, as evidenced in his October 29 letter to Richardson.

On November 26, Mackenzie King met with the senior members of his cabinet. According to King, they were agreed on the "inadvisability of it [the trans-Canada company] being publicly owned" but did not wish to "give it to a private corporation, particularly one in which Members of Parliament would be directly or indirectly connected." In addition, because of the duplication of facilities that would result in regard to the railways, they recommended as a compromise "having it placed under a Company representative of the two Railways."

Howe, who had earlier told Richardson that he had to protect railway interests, clearly preferred the cabinet's recommendation to that of the TCA Committee. In a secret memorandum to the prime minister on December 7, Howe outlined his proposal for the trans-Canada company.

I recommend that the trans-Canada aviation service be entrusted to the CP and the CN Railways jointly, with the provision that the Railways may obtain from existing aviation companies in Canada useful assets in the way of aviation equipment and personnel at fair market valuations in exchange for the stock of the aviation company ...

Its Board of Directors will include representatives of the two Railways and representatives of present Canadian aviation interests; the intention being to form a board that will be progressive and concerned about the development of aviation rather than the protection of the Railways. Operating personnel will be drawn from Canadian aviation circles, but, for a time at least, will include officers familiar with the latest developments in similar services in the United States and elsewhere ...

Private aviation interests have no basis for objection, as their present operations will not be disturbed in any way ... A choice of any of the private operating companies now applying for operation of the service could be made only by competitive tender, which would result in the abuses that have been evident in the United States' experience. *With a private company chosen by competitive tender, it would be difficult to protect the Government in the matter of a safe and adequate service.* Assignment of the service to the Railways will cause disappointment to private applicants, but less so than the choice of one of the private applicants. The nature of the service is such that one company must necessarily handle the service, thus precluding the possibility of dividing the work among several private companies. [emphasis added]

Was Howe, like McNaughton, using the "for the good of the country" argument to justify his ultimately government-owned airline? In the House of Commons, Howe would imply that he had been bombarded with applications, which made dealing with the individual companies impossible. On March 25, 1937, he said, "The question now arises: Have we invited the private interests to participate? That question was asked. May I say we did not need to invite them. They came from every part of Canada and the United States, and put on the most persistent lobby in Ottawa that I have ever seen. The only way we could make progress was to absolutely refuse to talk to them … How could we make a deal on the one hand with perhaps a dozen clamouring aviation companies … I have been living with this problem for several months."

His statements in the House contradict those in his secret memo to the prime minister, in which he wrote that he had received only seven applications, from the CPR and the CNR jointly; Canadian Airways; a group composed of men in Toronto, which had done no actual flying; Canadian Colonial Airways, an American company; a combination of three air transport companies from western Canada represented by Ross Gray, MP; a new company from the Maritimes and informal applications from some small companies. Howe was known to exaggerate, particularly when he was grandstanding in the House of Commons. He was a showman, and when on stage he knew how to dazzle his audience. In this case, he wanted to present a certain impression—that everyone wanted a piece of the action and that it was an intolerable situation he had to deal with.

However, there is something wrong about his letter. Why would the CP and CN apply jointly? It was highly unlikely that Sir Edward Beatty would apply on behalf of the CP and CN and not tell his good friend Jim Richardson. The more likely explanation was that Howe confused the application he received from Beatty as a joint railway application, not understanding that it was a tripartite application including Canadian Airways and the two railways. Beatty was known as a man of integrity, and it is inconceivable that he would have gone behind Richardson's back. Howe simply did not have his facts straight.

At the end of December, Beatty received a copy of the government's proposal. He wrote immediately to Richardson on December 30, voicing his suspicion that the committee leaned toward a government-controlled company and outlining his criticisms.

> I enclose a memorandum which he [Howe] handed to me and which he said summarized the views of the Cabinet, though no formal Order-in-Council has yet been passed. You will observe that the main difference between the present proposals and those which we tentatively accepted is in the allocation of the stock and the control of subsequent transfers by the Minister ...
>
> The reason for the change in the proposals is, of course, to prevent your Company holding the balance of power in the new Company, the Government apparently being persuaded that this was tantamount to Canadian Pacific control.

Attached to Beatty's letter to Richardson was an outline that Howe had sent to Beatty. The first sentence made it clear that Howe and the cabinet still envisioned "a private Company formed to operate an aviation service between Montreal and Vancouver, Montreal and Halifax, and such other interurban routes as may be designated to it by the Department of Transport." The government's plan differed substantially from Canadian Airways' proposal. Under the government's plan, 50 percent of the stock went to the CNR and such interests as it might name and 50 percent to the CPR and whomever it named.

Beatty believed that this provision was the result of pressure from the Toronto group because it gave them the opportunity to control, through the CNR, up to 50 percent of the stock. Beatty told Richardson that pressure had been exerted through Ian Mackenzie, minister of national defence, and the postmaster general, but Richardson wrote

Beatty a few days later, on January 2, 1937, with a slightly different story. Apparently Mackenzie and Frank Ross had passed through Winnipeg on their way to Vancouver. Ross wired Richardson to meet him at the train station.

> He told me that it was Mackenzie's opinion that Howe had made some promises to the Toronto people which were embarrassing, and that he was endeavouring to extricate himself from this position ...
>
> Mr. [Tom] Crerar has advised me that in his opinion Howe is definitely not in favour of introducing the Toronto people . . . He asked me if I was thoroughly satisfied with the proposal that Howe had made in regard to the 37½%–37½%–25% and I told him that I was, and he said that he was just as positive as he could be that it would go through this way, and that I could rest absolutely assured that there would be no Toronto promoters in the picture.

Another difference in the government's plan was in the composition of the board of directors and in the amount of power the government plan (the "Howe plan") invested in the minister of transport, who was to have control over any stock changes and could appoint one director out of nine. With the CNR having the right to appoint four directors (the CPR could also appoint four), the minister's nominee tipped the balance of power of the board in favour of the government.

Howe wrote a short note to the clerk of the Privy Council, Ernest Joseph Lemaire, December 29, 1936. "My government proposed to bring down a measure to provide for the establishment of a Trans-Canada air service ... [and expressed] the desirability of entrusting its operations to Canada's transcontinental railway companies in affiliation with private aviation interests, the whole to be under government supervision and regulation."

More changes in the government's plan in January 1937 undermined Beatty's and Richardson's power in the projected company. At the beginning of the month, Howe informed Beatty that another clause had been added that allowed the stock of the company to be purchased "by the Dominion Government at any time after notice and upon payment of its book value." Beatty immediately wired Richardson, commenting that this change meant that the minister of transport would have the right, by legislation, to take over the company and fix the basis of compensation for the portion of the stock held by the CPR and its interests. Richardson telegrammed Beatty on January 7, saying that he wanted the only stockholders of the trans-Canada airway to be the CPR, the CNR and Canadian Airways.

Howe sent Beatty the draft copy of the bill "to establish a corporation to be known as the Trans-Canada Air Lines" in early February. The bill incorporated Howe's alterations. Howe told Beatty that he would not submit the bill to council until he had received his comments. Enclosing a typewritten copy of the draft bill, Beatty wrote to Richardson on February 4, outlining his reasons for not agreeing with Howe's plan.

First, he could not consent to the provision that four directors were to be nominated by the CNR and the fifth (out of nine) by the minister of transport, "unless we were assured of the provision requiring a majority of the Directors appointed by CN and ourselves to agree as to any matter coming before the Board." Beatty said he had spoken privately to Howe about this, and Howe had assured him that this provision would be made in a bylaw. Understandably, Beatty was skeptical of Howe's promise and concerned that the bylaws might not be ready before the company was formed. This was why Beatty insisted that a clause be inserted in the bill to ensure equal distribution of power on the board.

Second, Beatty disagreed with Howe's suggestion that the general manager be the chief executive, stating that "the Bill attempts by legislation to invade the functions of the Board." Beatty felt that a general manager should report to a vice-president or president and that the board of directors should have the final responsibility for the organization of the company.

Beatty also questioned the right of the minister of transport to acquire all the private shares of the capital stock for their book value. He wanted the word "fair" substituted for the word "book" because the book value might not represent the real or fair value of the stock—the company may have built up goodwill and an earnings position that might not be reflected by the book value.

Beatty's final objection concerned the section allowing the minister of transport the right to determine what property (such as aircraft and engines) could be acquired for stock and on what terms. This provision allowed the minister not only to usurp the board's authority, it could adversely affect Canadian Airways. The understanding among Beatty, Howe and Richardson was that Canadian Airways would participate in the trans-Canada company either for cash, property or "in consideration of the transfer of a portion of [its] organization." Beatty wanted the wording changed to ensure that Canadian Airways would have this privilege. "I think it would be well if you would discuss the matter with your legal counsel and let me have your comments at the earliest possible moment."

Beatty wrote Howe on February 9 with his objections and recommendations and sent a copy to Richardson. He reminded Howe that he should ask for Richardson's comments. "With these changes the bill may be considered satisfactory to this Company, though, of course, I do not know what Mr. Richardson feels about it. In fairness to him I think you should receive any representations he cares to make because, while his Company is not mentioned in the Act, it is understood by all of us that it will be a participant."

Howe, furious, immediately wrote Beatty, disagreeing with most of Beatty's criticisms. "Any goodwill the company may have built up is due to the action of the government in assigning exclusive routes and in guaranteeing the Company against operating deficits. I do not think that the government should admit the item of goodwill in the very unlikely event that the public policy may indicate that the company should be taken over by the Government." For a former businessman to say this shows how stressed Howe was and how addled was his thinking. Interesting to note is his comment on the possibility that the company might become a government entity. How quickly Howe would forget that he had no intention of forming a government airline, and how soon he would brag about "my airline."

His total disregard for Richardson also deserves mention. Howe wrote: "Mr. Richardson has seen an earlier draft of the bill. Now that the bill is ready for submission to Parliament I can see no purpose in delaying matters to enable him to examine its final form . . . There may be some further changes before it is introduced."

These latest changes contributed to the CPR's and Canadian Airways' withdrawal from the proposed company. Howe was to say later that the two companies had unexpectedly withdrawn their support at the last moment, forcing him to revise his plan, and that he had offered a share of the company to them and that they had refused to participate. Both statements are half-truths and are examples of Howe's version of the creation of Trans-Canada Air Lines (TCA). Correspondence between Beatty and Howe shows that dissension between them had appeared at least three months before the Trans-Canada Air Lines Act was passed and that Beatty had strived to reach an agreement with Howe. In fact, it was Howe who shut the door on any further discussion. "If he [Richardson] is dissatisfied with the Bill he will probably be in the same position as all other companies now engaged in aviation," wrote an irritable and stubborn Howe to Beatty. It was evident that Howe was moving further and further away from Beatty and Richardson.

Upon receiving Howe's letter, Beatty replied the next day to clarify the question of control of the board of directors. He bluntly told Howe: "I would not be agreeable to the control of the Company's directorate being in the hands of four directors from the CN and one from the government. That would put the CP, with a 50% interest in the stock, in a minority on the Board, which, of course, is unthinkable." Beatty also argued strongly against the control that Howe was investing in the minister of transport and against Howe's interpretation of goodwill. "May I correct a misapprehension which apparently you are under. The goodwill of the Company will not be built up because the Government has given it a mail subsidy and allocated a route to it; it will be built up through other business which will be secured in consequence of the efficiency and safety of its operations."

Beatty was also angry with Howe for brushing off Richardson and lumping him with the other companies. He chastised Howe, "May I point out, too, that Mr. Richardson can scarcely be considered as in the same position as any other air service company in Canada, and any attempt to put him in that category will, I feel sure, be resented strongly by anyone who has knowledge of the history of civil aviation in this country."

Richardson, having received copies of these letters, responded immediately to Beatty on February 12. "I am entirely in accord with the criticism you make of the Bill ... Clause 9 of the Bill [which gave Howe sole authority over transfers of shares] is certainly highly objectionable to Canadian Airways ... I spoke to Mr. Howe about this some time ago and ... Mr. Howe assured me I need not worry ... because he would himself see that we were treated fairly. I regret to say, however, that experience has convinced me that Mr. Howe's word provides nothing very substantial to depend on." Richardson wrote a second letter to Beatty on the same day, suggesting that it might be desirable for him to appear as a witness before a parliamentary committee. Little did they know that Howe would ram the bill through and that Richardson would have no opportunity to appear before a committee.

Closely watching the situation was Woods-Humphrey of Imperial Airways, who had written Richardson about an article about Imperial Airways in the *Winnipeg Free Press*. Richardson replied on February 5:

> Confidentially I may say that Mr. Howe is a new man in public life and he has listened to all kinds of politicians ... Last Fall he brought into the Cabinet his proposals for the Trans-Canada ... which provided for allocations of the stock on the Trans-Canada and government participation. This was entirely different from our talks with Mr. Howe, and his proposals were ... thrown out by the Cabinet, for which he intimated to me he thought I was responsible ...
>
> The Minister of Transport will bring in his Bill in the next several days ... and it will likely provide that the whole service be handed over to the two railways and that they will select their own aviation partners ...
>
> I did not take up issue with the *Free Press* [which stated that Imperial Airways and Pan Am were annoyed with Ottawa's slowness]. The paper is a supporter of the Government and they simply have been a bit over-zealous in trying to shake the Civil Aviation authorities at Ottawa out of a deep slumber.

Distressed as he was, Richardson's wit was evident.

Woods-Humphrey wrote Richardson again on March 12, "It is a pity that the Railways will have such a predominant influence ... Such a set-up is likely to be prejudicial to the progress of the new company."

By now, newspapers across the country were commenting sarcastically about the government's indecisiveness. An article in the Prince Albert *Daily Herald* on February 15, aptly titled "Passing the Buck," noted: "The federal government, unable to make up its mind as to the set-up of the company to provide Canada with the Trans-Canada air mail and passenger services, is reported to be considering leaving this responsibility to the railways ... It is said that the government now considers it politically inexpedient to reach the decision on its own responsibility, that the buck is being passed to the railways ... Canadian Airways' record of service merits ... more consideration than it has received."

In March, after much discussion, a revised bill received cabinet approval. Beatty wrote Richardson on March 10 (enclosing a copy of the revised bill) and stated his concerns about the changes. Typically, Howe had indiscreetly revealed cabinet dissension. "The Minister told me yesterday that it had passed the Cabinet after a great deal of opposition, and you will see that it is different from the original bill in several respects."

The most detrimental change, as far as the CPR was concerned, was the one that gave the railway only three directors, instead of four out of nine, with the balance to be picked by the CNR and the government. As Beatty remarked cynically to Richardson, it was impossible to distinguish between the CNR and the government in matters of that kind, and if the bill went through, the CPR would have little voice even though it was providing 50 percent of the money.

> Another important amendment is that in Clause 7, which provides that, in the event of non-subscription of the shares by the Canadian National and the Canadian Pacific, they shall be offered for subscription to such other persons engaged or interested in aviation as are approved by the Minister ... I imagine that this latter amendment was put in in anticipation of the Canadian Pacific withdrawing and thus enabling the Minister to recognize his other aviation friends ...
>
> I have always felt that the Canadian Pacific should be in air transportation development in Canada ... we got, by amendment to our Charter in 1919, power to enter into air transportation, as well as to construct aeroplanes and their parts, but I must have regard to the future and to the possibility of our being linked up with a corporation politically directed, which might be very much to our detriment.

Consequently, on March 12, 1937, he wrote Howe "that it would be hard to justify to our stock holders the provision of $2½ million (or half the capital) in the Airlines when we would only have a minority vote in its administration. I would like you to realize my difficulty in attempting to reconcile assumption of one half the financial responsibility for the company without a corresponding representation on the directorate ... We are more than willing to be associated with the enterprise."

Howe responded on March 15, "The discussion in Council took the view that, as the Dominion government is accepting responsibility for all deficits in operation as well as providing airports, radio services and weather reports, its responsibility for the efficient operation of the Company is as great as or perhaps even greater than the owner Companies who will provide the capital under provisions that will at least guarantee reasonable interest returns."

Howe continued, "It is the intention of the government to appoint directors who are substantial business men interested in an efficient aviation service ... I cannot agree with your suggestion that Canadian National Railways is to all intents and purposes a department of Government. On the contrary, the Government maintains only a very slight contact with the railway. The government is obliged to meet the deficits of the Canadian National Railways just as it is undertaking to meet the deficits of Trans-Canada Air Lines, but it does not undertake to direct the policies of management of the railway company." Howe's first and last sentences meant little when the government controlled the board of directors, which controlled policy.

Howe effectively cut off any further communication from Beatty by concluding his letter with the remark that, while he would be glad to discuss the matter with Beatty, the government had now examined all phases of the bill thoroughly and it would be useless to attempt any further changes before the bill was introduced. As Howe appeared to be shutting the door (he would deny this later), Beatty felt that he had no alternative but to tell Howe (on March 17) that the CPR could not consider being a part of TCA on the terms proposed by the government. "I should appreciate it if, in the Bill as introduced, you would omit any reference to this Company." As Beatty said in a letter to Richardson the next day, "It is better ... that we should part company amicably now than run the risk of withdrawal after a series of difficulties in administrative policy."

Richardson now faced the truth: Howe's word was worth nothing.

Howe, the man he had trusted, had abandoned him. Anxious to show the country that he was a man of action, Howe was rashly forging ahead, forgetting promises but, more importantly, forgetting that he had a man and a company that were capable of establishing Canada's "chosen instrument."

The next few weeks were tense for Richardson. He expected that Howe would call upon him to appear before a parliamentary committee to explain Canadian Airways' plan. From a business point of view, he did not anticipate that members of Parliament would refuse to ratify a plan that cost the government nothing in capital and relieved the government purse of paying any deficits. James Richardson expected to be called by Howe to appear before a House of Commons committee. He waited in vain.

CHAPTER ELEVEN

"Double Cross"

C.D. HOWE was in a dilemma. He knew that both the CPR and the CNR had become a part of Canadian Airways with the government's blessing to form Canada's national airline in 1930. He knew this had been approved by two prime ministers, Mackenzie King and R.B. Bennett. Howe was also aware that when Bennett had cancelled the air mail contracts in 1932, James Richardson had maintained his organization intact, again with the government's approval, to be ready to proceed when it could provide money for a national service.

Indeed, Howe confirmed Richardson's expectations when he told Richardson, Sir Edward Beatty, Tommy Thompson and others (such as Norman Lambert), on a number of occasions, that Canadian Airways was to be the "chosen instrument, the Imperial Airways" of Canada. In fact, Howe had gone so far as to ask Richardson to buy an expensive, radio-equipped Lockheed Electra for DOT to use in checking out the radio aids on the transcontinental line, implying that the expenditure would not be wasted because Canadian Airways could use the aircraft on the national line. Howe had even asked Richardson to prepare a blueprint for the proposed new airline, which Richardson and his men did, delivering it to Howe in September 1936. The Canadian Airways men stood by, confident that no one could produce a more practical proposal. But Howe had also made promises to the politically and financially powerful "Toronto group." What was he to do? The first shoe dropped.

Contrary to Canadian Airways' plan, Howe's first draft of the airline legislation placed the CPR and the CNR side by side. The two railways were to be equally responsible for the capital. Howe's plan allowed him to save face with the Toronto speculators. Howe could say that he had given them the opportunity of participating, knowing full well that they would not, because all they could contribute was hard cash, and this would be unpalatable to them. According to George Hutchins, of James Richardson & Sons, the unnamed "chosen instrument" was still Canadian Airways, but Howe intended to bring it in under the wing of the two railways.

Disturbed by this turn of events, Richardson and Beatty were, nevertheless, prepared to work with Howe, likely because they assumed that the CNR, like the CPR, would choose Canadian Airways as its "instrument." They also assumed that the Toronto group, with nothing concrete to offer, would fade away. Then Howe dropped the second shoe. He began adding restriction after restriction, whittling away Richardson's and Beatty's power. The suggestion that the board of directors be controlled by the government was so absurd that negotiations broke down. It was obvious, Hutchins recalled, that this condition was put in for that purpose.

On March 22, 1937, Howe introduced Bill 74, "An Act to establish Trans-Canada Air Lines." His comments during the debates show that he lost control of the bill, allowing a company to be formed that was different from his original intention. Two minutes into his introductory speech, Howe declared, "The company contemplated by this bill is to be organized as a private corporation. It is not the intention of the government to own directly any stock in the company. The agency for organizing the company is to be the government's existing agency for the conduct of transportation business, namely, the Canadian National Railways."

The rest of Howe's speech was in line with the TCA Committee's recommendations regarding the terms of the air mail contract, profit, a guarantee against loss and an estimate of costs. Howe was desperate to get the bill passed quickly. To those who wanted more discussion or the whole matter sent to a special committee, Howe replied that there was no time, since trans-Atlantic flying was soon to come and the new company was to be Canada's agent for the hookup. "It is urgent to form this company and get the organization under way."

At the bill's first reading, only R.B. Bennett, leader of the Opposition, spoke against it. He immediately pinpointed one of the major flaws in the bill: that Howe proposed to ask the debt-ridden CNR to create and manage a competing entity. In addition,

> The minister ... says that the government will not itself own any of the capital stock of the enterprise, but that the Canadian National Railways will be charged with responsibility for the under-writing of the stock and that those who have heretofore been engaged in aerial operations will have an opportunity to subscribe for the share ... But I should like to see in great detail the conditions under which it is proposed to organize it. I confess that I have not been quite able to follow the minister in his statement that while we shall own none of the capital stock, the Canadian National Railways will be charged with responsibility for the underwriting of the stock, because under those circumstances it might well be that the control of the enterprise would pass entirely out of the hands of the government, and a franchise, the value of which cannot easily be over-estimated, would pass out of our control.

Bennett concluded in favour of having the bill introduced, but he could not resist adding, "I can conceive of a bill somewhat in the terms indicated by the minister as being objectionable for many reasons."

Howe's toughest critic throughout the debate was the imposing, clever and relentless Bennett. Although others saw flaws, it was Bennett who provided the most perceptive comments and the most constructive recommendations. Indeed, although Howe would claim the credit for creating Trans-Canada Air Lines—"my airline"—the company established by legislation was Bennett's, not Howe's. It was Bennett who pushed for government ownership.

For a bill of this importance there was amazingly little debate, probably because few MPs understood its importance and also because of

Howe's showmanship. Although not a good orator, Howe could be very convincing, in his brash manner. He was known as a shrewd businessman, and when he spoke of all the research he had done on airlines—as any good businessman would—MPs took him at his word. In Howe's favour was the pressure of time, which he constantly used to his advantage to cut off discussion. He introduced the bill late in the session and continually reiterated that it needed to be passed so that Canada could get her airline flying by summer! This was logistically impossible: the airfields were not complete, the radio and navigational aids were not constructed and the aircraft were not built. But Howe had no qualms about stretching the truth, and no one challenged him.

Fewer than half a dozen Opposition members spoke, and only Bennett kept returning to the issue again and again. His attack, however, was not merely political; he asked questions because he saw major errors in the bill that could be detrimental to Canada. His early charges were on the ambiguities of whether the company was private or government and who was to provide the money. The Opposition also questioned why Howe was proposing a company that the government did not own outright from the start, since it would be responsible for putting up the money and covering the deficits.

Debate resumed on March 25, when H.C. Green, Conservative MP for Vancouver South, objected to Howe's attempt to rush such an important bill through the House.

> This bill will set up a trans-Canada air line which will be without life, without any punch, and which will not be in a position to give real leadership. Really it will be just a sort of hybrid organization in which there will be none of the initiative we would get in a trans-Canada air line operated by a private company experienced in the business of air transportation ... We have Canadian Airways Limited, with a splendid operating record. The Canadian National and the Canadian Pacific each have invested $250,000 in this company.

Green then accused Howe of not knowing how the company was to be financed.

J.S. Woodsworth, CCF MP for Winnipeg North Centre, agreed with Green that "it does seem a very awkward arrangement to ask an already overburdened railway company to carry out the organization ...

However ... it is a service so intimately related to the whole life of the country that it seems to me it must in the long run necessarily come under government control ... Surely the lessons we have learned from railway building have taught us that the people, through the government, ought not only to retain control but maintain a controlling financial interest in the corporation."

Bennett now leapt into the debate. He began by listing what he called the "three principles" of the bill. First, the government was going to create a corporation, which was "to have a capital of $5,000,000, the provisional directors being employees of the crown at Ottawa ... The second principle is that the shares thus authorized by Parliament are to be sold by the corporation through indirect, not direct, methods ... Principle number three ... permits the Canadian National Railways to underwrite and dispose of the shares." Bennett attacked all three areas. He was merciless.

> First of all, the Canadian National and the Minister of Transport are one and the same thing to all intents and purposes. I am sorry to say that is so, but it is. There never has been a more complete domination of an enterprise than that of the minister over the Canadian National at the present time. That being so, he is offering to himself in another capacity the shares of the enterprise. He says: do you want them or not? ... That means the Dominion of Canada finds the money; that means the minister, as Minister of Transport, finds the money ... Is that a sound principle?
>
> I have asked myself a dozen times why the minister has not said at once that the Dominion of Canada is going to subscribe for these $5,000,000 of shares, instead of saying that five men in the public service shall be created into a corporation and they shall offer to the Canadian National Railways, which administratively is a part of the Department of Transport, the shares of the air corporation.

Bennett's reference to five men pertained to section 3 of the bill: "The following persons, namely, Valentine Irving Smart [deputy minister of transport], Robert Knowlton Smith, Charles Peter Edwards [also a civil servant with DOT], Edward Burton Jost and Findlay Malcolm Maclennan, all of the City of Ottawa, together with such persons as become shareholders of the corporation, are hereby incorporated under the name of 'Trans-Canada Air Lines.'" This was a most unusual provision. Bennett ripped to shreds Howe's method of disposing of shares, describing it as unfair and improper. He completely disagreed with the clause providing that government should pay any operating deficits.

Dunning answered that it was only for two years. Bennett retorted that this was exactly the story put up by Mackenzie and Mann (owners of bankrupt railway companies that the government took over and that became part of the CNR). Bennett stated, "If we are going into this air line business we should own it from the start, and not later." Woodsworth intoned, "Hear, hear."

Bennett continued his analogy with the railways: "One of the difficulties to-day about the railroads is that we had nothing to do with laying them out. They were laid out for contractors, and not for the public ... It is obvious that the Canadian National Railways cannot take over this enterprise except by paying for it money which we in the end will have to find ... I ask him [Howe] to revise this bill to provide that at the start, the ownership shall rest with us: that the shares and the capital stock shall be owned by the minister in right of the crown, in trust for the crown."

Although Bennett did not name Canadian Airways, he alluded to "the service" that both railways had invested in and suggested that its shareholders might serve on the Trans-Canada Air Lines board of directors, thereby obtaining their aviation experience. He concluded, "I plead with the minister ... to own the enterprise now, and sell it later if he so desires."

The MP for Kootenay East, H.H. Stevens, also lambasted Howe for creating a company that was a mixture of public and private ownership and for giving himself so much power.

Earl Lawson, MP for York South, raised the same objections, adding, "It leaves in his [Howe's] hands power to embark upon the expenditure of a huge amount of public money at some future date for the acquisition of something we now have."

A panicky Howe could keep quiet no longer. Worried that matters were not proceeding as he had anticipated, showman Howe stepped into the debate. He was like a steamroller, flattening opposition with tales of the trials and tribulations of making himself familiar with airline companies. In fact, his records do not show that he spent much

time doing that. After he was elected he was caught up in other matters, most recently, the creation of the Department of Transport in the
fall of 1936. His words, however, sounded very convincing. "I exhausted all available sources of information. I have ridden in every type
of equipment used on the mail routes in the United States; I have discussed the problem with the heads of all the successful trans-American
companies; I have had the privilege of discussing the problem with the
general manager of Imperial Airways and with officers of the British
air ministry."

The truth of the matter was Howe had almost no discussion in
1936 with Canada's premier airways man, James Richardson. Also,
although Howe implied that he had discussed matters with Imperial
Airways officials, neither Woods-Humphrey nor Geddes of Imperial
Airways ever told Richardson or Beatty, their long-time acquaintances,
that Howe had discussed airline matters with them. It is likely that he
rode around in some of the American aircraft and popped into the
offices of airline officials, but his involvement in any in-depth discussion is open to debate.

Howe belittled the suggestion that the government turn over this
airway to one of the private air companies. "The question which
immediately suggests itself is, which company? Well, perhaps there is
one company that by its experience and standing in the industry would
have a right to be chosen over other companies, but to-day that company is engaged in extensive services quite foreign to the services we are
going to develop here. I have not been able to decide how we could ask
that company to separate this trans-Canada service in an effective way
from the services operated by the same corporation in the north."
Howe was fudging the truth; Richardson's plan showed a separate company for the transcontinental operation.

Howe did not have the courage to name Canadian Airways; unlike
Bennett, who at least recommended that the government should consider "the service," Howe deliberately misled the House on Canadian
Airways' capabilities. Even more unworthy of Howe was the fact that
he never referred explicitly to Canadian Airways and its proposal.
Would members of Parliament on either side of the House have turned
down a plan that saw private enterprise underwrite all capital costs,
cover its own operating deficits and limit its profit? Howe did not give

them the chance to debate the question—an inexplicable strategy for a man coming from the business community.

Although Howe had come under heavy pressure from the Toronto group, its members had no flying experience and appeared to be backing off. James Richardson was one of Canada's most respected businessmen. He was known as a man of his word. If he said he could deliver a national service, he would; he had already secured the cooperation of both railways. He had already assured Howe, the prime minister and government officials that he would cooperate fully with government. Richardson had good contacts with the heads of Imperial Airways, Pan Am, Northwest Airways and United Airlines. He had all his ducks lined up; he was ready to go. He had the plan, 240 trained personnel and eleven years of flying experience.

While Howe blithely ignored the fact that the country had not recovered from the depression, Richardson and Beatty were offering a method that would not drain the public purse. They offered the service at a cost of seventy cents a mile for the air mail, to be reduced as passenger traffic developed, with a provision for a return of excess profits.

But Howe did not tell Parliament about Canadian Airways' proposal, much less that it had trained twenty-two pilots in the latest flying techniques, had bought two of the aircraft to be used, had already proven itself with the night prairie air mail in the early 1930s and had already worked up a blueprint for the entire operation, complete with all costs. Nor did he tell the House that Canadian Airways had consulted with one of the major American airlines and the Air Transport Association of America. Howe deliberately implied that Canadian Airways was a bush operation incapable of planning or running a transcontinental service. History would show that Trans-Canada Air Lines began its organization with Canadian Airways' aircraft, pilots and other personnel. The Canadian Airways men also believed TCA began with Canadian Airways' blueprint for operations.

It is likely that Howe did not tell his own cabinet colleagues about Canadian Airways' proposal. There are no copies of Canadian Airways' plan or any correspondence from Richardson and Beatty in Howe's files. Years later, TCA president Gordon McGregor asked Howe about the scarcity of material relating to TCA's beginnings; Howe pled ignorance. It seems highly probable that Howe deliberately destroyed all correspondence from Richardson and Beatty so that the story of "my airline" would be told from his point of view only.

Howe also misled the House when he said that it would take ten years to bring Canadian aviation up to American standards. This was not true; Canadian Airways was ready to fly with twenty-two pilots trained in the latest American flying techniques. Had Howe already planned to scuttle Canadian Airways as early as July 1936, when he borrowed its Lockheed Electra and pilot to test-fly the radio range but would not allow Richardson to tell the public whose aircraft and pilot were doing the flying? Why did Howe muzzle Canadian Airways? Was it because the company could have gained a great deal of publicity and support for flying the transcontinental?

When he was attacked about having the CNR assume the management of an airline company, Howe stated that United Kingdom officials had suggested railway cooperation to the TCA Committee. Again he was stretching the truth: this was an old recommendation and no longer valid. Woods-Humphrey had clearly pointed out in his recent letter to Richardson that he believed railway control would be detrimental to airline development. Howe slyly slid over the fact that cooperation and control were different things and that *no* airline in the United States was controlled by a railway; nor was Imperial Airways, for that matter.

Howe was caught in his own subterfuge. In caving in to the pressure of the Toronto group, he was forced to hide the Canadian Airways plan and to pass control to the railways. He thought the CPR and Canadian Airways would rescue him, but his appetite for power and his wish to control the board pushed the CPR and Canadian Airways out of the picture. *After* Parliament passed the bill, Howe went through the motions of inviting Richardson to participate by offering Richardson 49 percent of the shares. Richardson, however, was too canny a businessman to agree to be part of an organization in which the power lay with political appointees.

Howe obviously listened to the TCA Committee, which had no experience in running a commercial operation. He probably listened to General McNaughton, who also had no experience in running a business. Both recommended that the railways be in control. One of the ideas was that the airline could use their ticket offices and agents, so that if a flight were cancelled, the passenger could board a train.

Howe made one of his more absurd statements on March 25, 1937, when as one of the reasons for not wanting a government-owned airline, he offered, "As a minister of the government I shudder over the possibility of being responsible for the crash of a plane-load of passengers travelling on a wholly owned government air line."

Bennett would not let his quarry go, and Howe was forced to do some backpedalling. He implied that the drafters of the bill had not made clear that the CNR would retain at least 51 percent of the company stock. He tried to pretend that it had always been his intention that the CNR should have majority control. Howe said, "There is one point the bill does not make clear, but which it will make clear, namely that the Canadian National Railways will retain at least fifty-one per cent of the stock of the company ... so that at all times we would have government control." He had blundered in the first printing of the bill, and it was only Bennett's constant pressure that forced Howe to clarify the CNR's participation.

At the bill's second reading Howe concluded with, "I think we are getting the best features of government ownership without the obligation of direct government operation, which in the past has been troublesome." He spoke of the difficulties that the United States had with private air mail contracts—a problem of the early 1930s—and used this as an excuse not to go the private-company route. He conveniently neglected to advise the House that nowhere in the United States was there a government-owned company; all were private, and operating with air mail contracts.

Bennett seemed to be the only one not taken in by Howe's statements. On March 31, 1937, he led off the debate and, as usual, was cutting and dead accurate.

I suppose the minister is well aware that the bill of which he moved the second reading the other day, and the bill that is now before the House, are entirely different. He said that the printed bill did not express what the government proposed as its policy. It is now clear that the proposal is that the Canadian National shall own fifty-one per cent of this enterprise. As the bill originally appeared it was not in that form, but the minister indicated that change was proposed, and the reprinted bill indicates that it is the purpose of the administration.

I cannot think it is probable that the forty-nine per cent will be subscribed by the companies that are operating air lines in this country
... I had suggested that ... the Canadian National Railways and the
Canadian Pacific Railway might own the enterprise ... but the minister advised, I understand, that I should be informed that nothing
came of the negotiations which were carried on looking to some
ownership arrangement between the two railway companies.

Again Howe had not been telling the whole truth. Both Richardson
and Beatty were fully prepared to cooperate with the government.
Howe deliberately did not tell the House that the government had
demanded that the CPR put up half the money but was prepared to give
it only one-third control of the board of directors and that the balance
of power was tipped in favour of the minister of transport and the government. Howe implied that the CPR had backed out for no obvious
reason. It was also clear that Bennett knew nothing about the Canadian Airways, CPR and CNR joint plan when he said, "So the matter
stands in the form in which it is at present, and there are no suggestions before the minister that will enable any other view to be taken
than that which is expressed here."

Howe could have introduced Canadian Airways' plan at this point.
The plan could have been debated fully; if it had been discarded, Richardson and Beatty would have had a fair hearing. But Howe's silence
implied that no one in Canada was ready to come forward with a
feasible plan. Bennett twice more asked Howe to make Trans-Canada
Air Lines a government-owned company; he mocked Howe's suggestion that anyone would buy 49 percent of the shares and asked that the
whole matter go before a parliamentary committee "to hear witnesses."

Bennett was not convinced that Howe's proposal was the only
method available and wanted the opportunity to question those already in the aviation industry. For Howe's plan to succeed, Howe had to
block Bennett's request for committee hearings. "Witnesses" like James
Richardson and Sir Edward Beatty could scupper his bill. It was also
clear that Howe did not tell the House that the CPR and Canadian Airways were prepared to underwrite the $5 million cost of the airline and
to cover any deficits. How Howe in any conscience could say nothing at
a time when the government had little money to spare is inconceivable.

Howe's conscience must have been prickling him because he leapt to his feet and blurted out, "We expected almost until the day when we introduced this bill that our two principal railway companies would be shareholders in the enterprise. We learned at the last moment that the directors of one large company decided not to take up the enterprise, and therefore we had to make a very quick change in the bill." Again he was stretching the truth. Beatty had told him *before* the bill was printed that the CPR would not be involved, and in fact it was clear in early January that negotiations between Beatty and Howe were breaking down.

Howe blustered on and said things that, for a businessman, simply did not make economic sense. "I am unable to share my right hon. friend's doubts about aviation companies taking up 49 per cent of the stock. I have had a number of telephone calls since this bill was brought down ... I think there is nothing to fear about that feature. As to putting the bill before a committee and hearing all the interests which might appear, I feel that nothing of great importance would come of that; I have been in a committee for months now, listening to every one who cared to make representations."

Howe was not telling the complete truth. He had refused to meet with Richardson. According to his letter to the prime minister, Howe had received only seven applications. To brush off Richardson and his eleven years of experience with words like "nothing of great importance would come of that" shows how fearful Howe was that the truth would come out. He knew that Canadian Airways' plan was written with a background of years of experience and that Richardson would provide a first-class operation.

Howe also exaggerated the readiness of the airfields. This too was a deliberate ploy to play upon the so-called urgency of getting the corporation approved so that it could start flying immediately. He stated, "Our air fields are ready and finished; the whole organization is set up from Winnipeg west. Before this summer is over we expect that the entire system from coast to coast will be ready for operation as far as the main line is concerned." This was untrue, and Howe knew it. Wilson had been clear in his memo that it would be a number of years before the airway was complete.

On April 1, 1937, debate resumed. Once again Howe gave incorrect answers to questions about the readiness of the airfields: "At present we have airports at intervals of forty or fifty miles from Vancouver to Halifax." In fact, from Montreal east, there were few airfields ready for Lockheed Electras. Later he said, "Certainly we shall have these fields in operation early next year," but no one noticed the inconsistency in his statements.

Only a few more members of Parliament spoke. MP Thomas Church spoke at some length against a government operation, warning against "politics" being "rampant in the system just as it has been in the Canadian National ... Who wants to take stock in a concern like that, in which the government has 51 per cent, when they should own 100 per cent?" In answer to Church's question about an accident, Howe replied, "This will not be crown property." Soon, Trans-Canada Air Lines would be a crown corporation.

Bennett returned to the debate and challenged the legality of Howe's choice of words in some of the clauses. His comments were constructive and meant to keep government out of trouble. Howe, his ego badly damaged from the drubbing he had taken on his beloved airline bill, was argumentive and bombastic and was not about to let any lawyer tell him what various terms meant. He petulantly responded, "'Gross revenue' may have other meanings in other places, but for the purposes of this bill it means what appears in the definition." Bennett patiently tried to explain the legal meaning but soon realized that Howe was beyond listening and gave up. "I am not going to worry any more about it."

By now the House was going through the bill clause by clause. There was discussion again about how closely tied the CNR was with government. Howe denied this: "We are too prone to say that because we own the Canadian National Railways we operate it. That is not true." Bennett could not let that pass. "There are striking evidences of it."

Bennett returned to the original bill. "When this bill was drafted it did not provide for fifty-one per cent being owned by the Canadian National Railways." Howe responded, untruthfully, "That was always the intention; the unexpressed intention." Bennett was not about to be pawned off with Howe's facile answers. "It is these unexpressed intentions which give rise to the view that the Canadian National Railways is being run by the government. But the expressed intention of the government now is that fifty-one per cent should be owned by the Canadian National Railways. That was not so when the bill was given its second reading."

Bennett wanted a limitation placed upon the borrowing powers of the corporation. "It is usual in a company of this kind to make such a provision, and it would prevent the government from getting into trouble hereafter." Howe disagreed. How right Bennett would be.

In answer to questions as to what priorities the company would have, Howe responded, "It will be their object to get a full load of mail, first; passengers will come second, and freight third." As to the type of aircraft, Howe said, "I sincerely hope they will be sleeper planes, because that is a very comfortable way to travel." For all of his talk about the research he had done on airline companies, his answer was dated; the sleepers were going the way of the dodo bird.

With amazingly little opposition, the bill to form Trans-Canada Air Lines passed on April 6 and was given royal assent on April 10, 1937. The act called for an authorized capital of $5 million. The CNR was to underwrite the stock and could sell 49 percent to Canadian interests, upon approval of the minister of transport.

The terms of the act embodied many of the principles that Canadian Airways had recommended: security of a long-term air mail contract; equitable Post Office rates; and government provision of emergency landing fields, navigation aids and weather services. In addition, during the initial period (until December 31, 1939), Trans-Canada Air Lines was guaranteed a subsidy equal to any deficit, and air mail rates were to be fixed by a contract with the Post Office. After this period, air mail rates were to be set in conjunction with the postmaster general, the minister of transport and the governor in council.

Shrewd businessman that he was, Howe must have known that no business would opt to take stock leading to only 49 percent control with no hope of gaining more. However, he had a show to put on and the last act was yet to be played. He needed to be able to say that he had offered Richardson a part of the action. Accordingly, on April 3, 1937, Howe wrote Richardson and asked him to meet with Hungerford of the CNR and himself. Howe cunningly provided the lure of feeder lines if Richardson played along. What happened is revealed in Richardson's report at the company's annual meeting.

I asked Mr. Howe how the Canadian Airways could operate under the Bill and he told me that he did not think Canadian Airways could operate at all under the Bill. I told him that if they wanted to run a Government line and it was going to facilitate the business to get it under way right away, Canadian Airways would be glad to organize and operate the service between Winnipeg and Vancouver just as soon as the planes could be secured and the service put into effect, and we would be glad to do this for a management fee, so that the Government might have all the benefit without any participation in either profits or losses. Mr. Howe did not think this could be done under the Bill.

I asked him what was there then left for me to discuss and he said that I might go on the Board . . . and that if so desired Canadian Airways Limited would be permitted to subscribe for shares in the Trans-Canada Air Lines and might expect to receive some benefits by way of co-operation on "feeder lines" in the matter of routing passengers leaving Trans-Canada Air Lines for mining points.

Hutchins, the executive secretary, summed up the meeting. "Apparently Howe put on quite a show of pursuing Mr. Richardson to bring Canadian Airways into the picture." Richardson's offer to handle the western line under a management contract would have been beneficial to government because it offered a far lower risk than did outright ownership. From Richardson's point of view, it would have kept him in the picture and given him the lifeline he needed. Now, however, Canadian Airways was out of the trans-Canada picture.

"I remember my father saying that C.D. Howe did a 'double cross' on him," recalled George Richardson. That James Richardson was bitter and keenly felt that he had been betrayed by Howe is obvious in the first draft of his letter to Howe. Dated April 26, it read in part:

> I can only say that I feel very keenly the treatment accorded the Canadian Airways can have only one explanation, and that is that the Cabinet and House were not made properly aware of the character of the organization of Canadian Airways, the contribution they were able to make to a transcontinental air service and the basis on which their services were available, and this quite aside from the obligations due the company on unfilled contracts with the Dominion Government.

On the basis of assurances given to me by you many times that Canadian Airways were to be the keystone of the transcontinental service it is very difficult for me to understand the conclusions finally arrived at ...

I am sorry that you have seen fit to eliminate us. I consulted my Board and must decline the verbal invitation extended to me to join the Board of the Trans-Canada Air Lines. I do feel that I have had, during the past nearly eleven years, some background of experience in connection with airways problems and I could not consent to sit on a board where all the directors were, in effect, government nominees.

My conclusions are that as the new company will be governmentally controlled it will be subject to political influence and that I could have no effective voice in its direction. Under these circumstances I cannot well see my way clear to assume any responsibility, and under the present set-up I am not prepared to associate myself with the Trans-Canada Air Lines.

Ever the gentleman, Richardson concluded by offering his best wishes to Howe. However, realizing that his letter was pungent and revealed more of his feelings than he wished known, Richardson ran it by Beatty and Beaudry Leman, one of his directors. Leman suggested he tone down his accusations, and a watered-down version was approved by all.

The bite was gone. As Hutchins remarked to Richardson, "You will notice that he [Leman] has removed any possible 'sting' that there may have been in [the first draft] but that in doing so he has possibly removed some of the original intent." Unfortunately, Hutchins was correct. Richardson made a grave mistake in not sending the first draft. A damning letter accusing the government of a breach of faith might have forced Howe to play fair ball when it came to arranging the feeder services and, even more importantly, might have forced the government to define an air policy that was good for the country, not just good for TCA. Richardson's soft response allowed Howe and the government to wriggle off the hook. It also allowed Howe to tell the story of TCA as he saw fit.

Howe's response to Richardson's letter was masterly in denying that he played any part in forcing the CPR and Canadian Airways out of the national picture. Dated May 25, 1937, it read:

I have delayed reply to your letter of April 26 until I could look back over the file and determine where the present policy of the government has departed from your own views as to the organization of the proposed Trans-Canada air service ... We were in agreement up to the point that a new company would be formed to be owned jointly by the Canadian National Railways, Canadian Pacific Railway and the Canadian Airways Limited ... This plan could not be carried out owing to the fact that the Canadian Pacific Railway withdrew its participation ...

After the Canadian Pacific Railway withdrew, we undertook to work out a company owned by the Canadian National Railways and the Canadian Airways Limited in propositions to be determined.

This last sentence is untrue, but Howe had now convinced himself that it was the case. He appeared to have forgotten that he refused to have a full discussion with Richardson, and he never once in the House named Canadian Airways as one of the key partners. More to the point, he did not call upon Richardson until *after* legislation had decreed that private interests could have only 49 percent control. Did he think that no one would ever check the official record of Hansard and see that his statements were incorrect?

"I trust we can agree that your present attitude results from the withdrawal of the Canadian Pacific Railway and not from any action taken by this government. A study of the file indicates to me that this is the position." Howe cleverly did not refer to the correspondence that explained why the CPR withdrew or why Richardson refused to participate. "I am fully aware of the position of your company in trans-Canada aviation, and in drafting legislation I have tried to protect that position to the fullest possible extent. The Government is faced with the necessity for proceeding with an aviation policy in the light of present day conditions. Its policy has been drafted in such a way that full provision is made for participation of Canadian Airways Limited to any extent that it may desire." Did Howe really believe that Richardson would want to be part of an organization in which he had no effective voice but was committed to underwriting capital and covering deficits?

"It is a matter of regret to myself personally and to the Government that your company has decided not to participate in this enterprise. We have refrained from making any commitment to others until the extent of participation by your company could be finally determined." Howe ensured that *his* letter told the story as he wished history to record it.

What happened to make Howe shift so radically from his original plan? Why the breach of faith? The key players have all died, and Howe's papers are amazingly slim for the period leading up to the creation of TCA. There was virtually no paper trail left except what was in the Richardson files and Norman Lambert's diaries. There are few clues and no clear-cut reasons why Howe dropped Canadian Airways' plan, particularly when he stated unequivocally in his introduction of the TCA bill that he was not going to create a government-owned company. Howe was a complex man, and even speculation does not provide a satisfactory answer.

It may have been Howe's tendency to be swayed by political pressure that accounts for his abandonment of Canadian Airways' plan. Howe's practical political experience was less than a year old when he began planning the trans-Canada company, and he still believed that ordinary business procedures could govern his political dealings. Richardson and Beatty were not the only ones who commented on Howe's political naïveté and his propensity for "loose talk." Ian Mackenzie, minister of defence, had told Richardson that Howe had made "embarrassing promises" to the Toronto group—but Canadian Airways' proposal would have kept the Toronto group out of the trans-Canada company. The railway plan, on the other hand, was a compromise. It would allow the Toronto group to invest through the CNR and permit Howe to save face with that influential group. Beatty told Richardson in December 1936 that "the government wants Gundy, Lawson, McCullagh, Common, Odlum, Burns, Ralston to have an opportunity to subscribe for stock."

Fear of CPR domination of the proposed company may have been the chief reason for Howe's rejection of Canadian Airways' plan. However great its economic merits, political considerations probably ruled it out. Although there was concern during the 1930s that the CPR would take over the CNR, this was never voiced in the TCA Committee discussion, in the cabinet meeting on November 26, 1936, or in Howe's private correspondence. On the contrary, Howe welcomed CPR participation in the trans-Canada company to prevent destructive competition.

However, although Canadian Airways' plan appealed economically to Howe, the risk of eventual CPR control may have been too great.

At the end of the day it is hard to imagine that private interests would be linked with the CNR or that the CPR would have effective control. Undoubtedly Howe had made promises to Richardson that Canadian Airways would be the nucleus of Canada's airline. But the promises were made in his early days as minister—when he was more businessman than politician and before the glory of power had become so consuming.

Howe quickly discovered that he could exert even more influence once he got into the public sector. Historian Michael Bliss maintains that Howe was self-serving and ruthless. The role of the railways was crucial, and once Howe made the decision to split the deal between the CNR and the CPR, he may have been uncertain as to how these various enterprises would work together. Howe's biographer, Robert Bothwell, believes that Howe considered the CPR to be a conspiracy against the public.

The most superficial and most likely explanation for Howe's double-dealing is simply that as Howe became more caught up in politics, he wanted to keep control in his hands. In time, he would wield an unbelievable amount of influence. Opposition members soon complained about Howe's excessive appetite for power and the concentration of control in his hands. Howe went on to create more than twenty crown corporations. As "the Minister of Everything," Howe became the most important "public entrepreneur" of his time.

By this time, too, according to Gordon Lawson, Howe had become "enamoured" with the idea of a trans-Canada airline. Although Richardson had been fighting for years for such a company, Howe began to speak of it as if it were wholly his idea—"my airline." For Howe, TCA was to be Howe's creation, his baby, and he, as minister of transport, would retain control. Also by this time, Howe's ego had grown mightily. Howe was becoming known as a man who got things done. Canada was ready for its own airline, and Howe wanted the glory of that creation to be his alone. Thus Howe was probably truthful when he first told Richardson that Canadian Airways would be Canada's "chosen instrument." But the power of politics and the growth of his ego subtly changed the picture.

This does not, however, explain why Howe allowed a bill to be introduced that had so much ambiguity as to ownership. Did he believe that Beatty would reverse himself and be part of a government-controlled company? Although throughout the debates Howe is on record as saying that he did not want a government-owned company, biographer Bothwell claimed that Howe often "flew by the seat of his pants" and made contradictory statements. "His officials would sit in the gallery and hold their heads because Howe often said something that was wrong." Bothwell gave as one of his examples Howe's answer to a question in the House in 1945, as to whether Canada would make an atomic bomb. Howe answered in the negative—policy was made with Howe's statement, yet there had been no discussion at cabinet! Does this mean that we should simply dismiss his carelessness with the spoken word and off-the-cuff remarks as a quirk of his personality?

Howe's grandson, Bill Dodge, confessed that he had no explanation for Howe's motivation for muscling Richardson and Beatty out of the picture except, perhaps, "He was an engineer, a builder. He wanted his hands all over everything." Dodge believed that no one, including Howe's biographer, had been given the complete story because of the deliberate destruction of many files. Dodge also believed that Howe's private secretary, Bill Bennett, controlled the information he gave to Howe's biographer. "Bennett was the information control guy. He was a key person for the biographer. I think there was information he never led him through. It is questionable if he got the whole story," Dodge explained.

Bill Dodge tossed out another suggestion. Could considerations of national security and intelligence be a factor? His comment was based on a telegram that he had received from William Stephenson, the Canadian-born British spy better known as "Intrepid," who was responding to questions from Dodge about his grandfather in August 1985. According to Stephenson, Howe had asked him to form a Canadian airline. Apparently Stephenson had been involved with Imperial Airways and Qantas Airways. Although no date was mentioned by Stephenson, the time frame can only be 1936–37.

Why did Howe ask Stephenson to establish a Canadian airline? This piece of information, if it is correct (and there is no reason not to believe him), adds an unexpected wrinkle to the whole TCA question.

Stephenson also wrote that he and Howe "had many associations, both overt and covert." Within a short time Stephenson would be at the height of his influence, operating his intelligence network and providing detailed information to Churchill on Germany's war industry.

Stephenson was Canada's top intelligence agent during World War II. Did forming a government-owned airline have anything to do with Canadian security and intelligence? Was Howe part of Stephenson's intelligence network? Is this all too far-fetched to be contemplated? The simple answer may be that Howe approached Stephenson to be the general manager or vice-president of operations of TCA, after TCA was created. There is no whisper of contact between Howe and Stephenson in any Canadian records. The 1985 telegram from Stephenson to Dodge adds an interesting twist but gives no answers.

What must also be remembered was that the mindset in Ottawa was changing. The Great Depression had seen to that. Before 1937, only socialists and communists had pushed for government ownership of transportation. Now other people were beginning to look to government for answers to many of their problems.

Undoubtedly the pivotal reason for Howe's shift to a completely government-controlled company was the fact that his plan called for the government to assume financial responsibilities without having direct control. This point was forcibly argued by Bennett. When it looked as if the government would be responsible for the total $5 million, a government-owned TCA was a natural result. What the consequence would have been if the House had known about Canadian Airways' plan can only be surmised. Certainly Richardson felt that the outcome would have been different if he had been allowed to present the plan—and he said so in his letter to Howe on April 26, 1937. Canada had not yet recovered from the effects of the depression, and $5 million was an enormous sum. Thus it cannot be concluded that the House would have rejected a plan that was economical for the government and was offered by a company that was capable of performing a transcontinental service.

When the excitement of creating his airline died down, Howe in his private thoughts probably realized that he had betrayed Richardson. And so, he carefully crafted a letter to Richardson on May 25, 1937, giving his version of the events leading to his creation of TCA. Anyone reading it would think that Howe had bent over backward to have both Richardson and Beatty involved. If anyone was to blame, it was Beatty and Richardson. Howe denied that he did anything negative to prevent Richardson from being a part of Trans-Canada Air Lines.

Some years later, Howe put his version officially on record regarding why and how TCA came into being. It would be interesting to know if he really believed his own words. At any rate, on March 17, 1944, Howe, for the first time in the House of Commons, mentioned Canadian Airways by name. He was covering his tracks well, because not once in 1937 during the TCA debate had he named Canadian Airways. Howe's words in 1944 are not supported by the evidence.

> The intention of the government has been that of uniting the strongest transportation interests in Canada to undertake this new venture in transportation, and with that in view I approached Canadian National Railways, the Canadian Pacific Railway Company, and Canadian Airways, the latter being by far the strongest of the air transport companies then operating. These companies were invited to provide the needed capital for, and assume the ownership of, the airline company, the Government to assume responsibility for building adequate airports and the necessary communication system. Each of the three component companies was to share equally in the ownership of the airline, and each was to have two directors on a board of nine, the government to appoint three directors on account of its investment in airports and communications ...
>
> The Canadian Pacific Railway Company and Canadian Airways objected to having three Government directors on the board, and at the last moment these two companies withdrew their support, with the result that the Trans-Canada Air Lines Act provided for full ownership of the enterprise by Canadian National Railways. It is worthwhile stressing the fact, at this time, that the Canadian Pacific Railway Company and Canadian Airways were each offered one-third participation in the Trans-Canada Air Lines enterprise, and that both refused to participate in a company with the identical financial arrangements that now apply to Trans-Canada Air Lines.

Howe was not telling the truth. His secret memo to the prime minister, dated December 7, 1936, and the first drafts of the bill make it clear that each railway was to have 50 percent of the stock. It was not a one-third split, as Howe stated in 1944. What he actually proposed was that CPR put up 50 percent of the money and have only one-third of the vote on the board of directors. Nor was there any mention of Canadian Airways. In fact, with the exception of the board composition, what Howe was speaking of in 1944 was the Canadian Airways plan, which never saw the light of day. One need only read the debates in March and early April of 1937 to see that Howe never referred to Canadian Airways by name and certainly never acknowledged that it was prepared to put up half of the needed capital.

Where Howe came up with the CPR and Canadian Airways each having two directors is difficult to pin down. Certainly in each of the draft bills that he sent to Beatty, the numbers kept changing. In the March draft bill, Howe changed the board composition again. This time he gave the CPR only three directors out of nine, the balance being appointed by the CNR and the government. What Howe said in 1944 does not jibe with the facts. In addition, Howe never acknowledged the problem areas that Beatty tried to resolve.

Interesting too—now that Canadian Airways was no longer a factor in aviation—is how positively Howe now spoke of it: "by far the strongest of the air transport companies." In the debates of 1937, Howe never referred to Canadian Airways by name, and when he did allude to it he brushed it off as a company with little to offer. Was his conscience bothering him? More likely, Howe was simply rewriting history to absolve himself of doing in Richardson. Why he chose this particular moment to speak of a company that he had sent to its death is not known. Howe would say over and over again that he had invited both the CPR and Canadian Airways to be a part of the national airline.

Virtually all of Howe's papers regarding TCA for the period August 1936 to April 1937 are missing. The most complete record of the negotiations is found in Richardson's files. Twenty years later, the president of Trans-Canada Air Lines wanted to know the circumstances leading to the creation of TCA. On April 2, 1958, Gordon McGregor wrote to Howe to ask about the documentary record of "the planning and actions which led up to the formation of TCA and the chance given to the CPR to participate and its eventual status as a wholly owned subsidiary of the CNR. It seems possible that your personal records are the only source of such a history."

Howe protested ignorance. "I will lose no time in checking my files to see whether the necessary documents are there. If not, I will try to get them from DOT," Howe replied to McGregor on April 18. On May 9, he innocently wrote:

> I have been searching all my files for the necessary material. The simple fact is that these documents are not in my files. Herbie Symington says that he has a copy of the key letter from the CP giving a final turndown of the government's offer of a 50% interest. I think that what happened is that, when I turned over the DOT to Arthur Cardin, in 1940, I also turned over my private files relating to that Department. What happened to them after that is something I will never know.

McGregor responded on May 28, "Thank you for your efforts to locate the documents relating to the CPR's refusal to be a partner in the Trans-Canada enterprise." It is curious that the papers for this period are missing.

The original set-up of Trans-Canada Air Lines was in line with Canadian Airways' proposal but on a more lavish scale. The Canadian Airways men were convinced that TCA used Canadian Airways' plan as the blueprint for establishing itself. In the fall of 1936, Canadian Airways had submitted ten copies of its proposal to Howe. When it became apparent that Howe was adamant that the company be controlled by the government and that Canadian Airways and CPR would not be participating, Canadian Airways asked for the return of its copies. All but one were returned immediately. The outstanding copy was the one it had given to Don MacLaren, superintendent of the Pacific Lines. When it was finally returned four days later, it "was marked up in such a way that it was fairly obvious that it had been copied," recalled G.W. Hutchins.

Although it had no definite proof, Canadian Airways believed that MacLaren had sold his copy to the government in return for a position with TCA. MacLaren was the first Canadian Airways employee to go over to TCA. An August 12, 1937, letter from Richardson to Tommy Thompson records Richardson's feelings about MacLaren's departure: "While MacLaren feels the company has always done the right thing with him he has some qualms himself as to whether throughout our recent negotiations he has always done the right thing by the company ... I do not feel unfriendly to MacLaren, although I am a bit disappointed in him ... I thought that he should have stood up just a little better."

The Trans-Canada Air Lines Act marked an abrupt change in government attitude. It created a monopoly of air services on the main transcontinental line and replaced private effort with public funds. The complete burden of developing all aspects of the trans-Canada service was now the government's. Contrary to what Howe argued in the House, the terms of the act (only 49 percent of the shares were available to private interests) discouraged any investment of private capital. Political considerations were responsible for its creation. Unlike the founding of Canadian National Railways, the creation of the government-owned Trans-Canada Air Lines was deliberate.

Thus Canadian Airways, which had done most of the pioneering work in civil aviation and which had been maintained at a loss throughout the depression in anticipation of being the trans-Canada contractor, found itself back in the bush. What was particularly galling to Canadian Airways was the fact that TCA was established on all the principles and with all the safeguards that Canadian Airways had been requesting for years. As Beatty resignedly wrote to Richardson in July 1937, "How unfairly in the end we were both treated."

Back in the Bush

THE FORMATION of Trans-Canada Air Lines (TCA) resulted in an immediate loss of personnel for Canadian Airways. Lured by the security and higher wages offered by TCA and concerned that it would acquire all the profitable routes, Canadian Airways pilots, mechanics and technical, clerical and administrative staff began to leave within weeks of TCA's creation. TCA first went after those pilots who had just been specially trained in instrument flying. As Tommy Thompson bitterly remarked, Canadian Airways had spent almost twenty thousand dollars training pilots for TCA. This exodus caused serious problems for the company.

First, TCA gave almost no warning; it took a pilot with less than a week's notice, which left Canadian Airways with inadequate time to replace staff. By mid-June 1937, the Quebec area was left with no experienced Canadian Airways pilots. By July the situation was so critical that the company was unable to carry out its summer's work, and Thompson frantically wrote James Richardson, asking him to request TCA to give Canadian Airways one month's notice before taking any more pilots. TCA agreed but continued scooping up Canadian Airways' experienced pilots. Thompson was forced to contact TCA twice more before TCA showed any consideration for Canadian Airways' position. He appealed to Philip Johnson, TCA vice-president of operations, on July 30, and to Don MacLaren, now assistant to the vice-president, on August 18.

The formation of TCA also forced Canadian Airways to raise its salaries to compete with TCA's higher wages. Canadian Airways was still paying depression-level wages, and because of the insecure and unre-munerative air mail contracts and low passenger and freight rates, it had not increased wages in three years.

The third immediate impact was the loss of its last international service, the Vancouver–Seattle air mail contract. Although C.D. Howe declared in the House of Commons that the trans-Canada airway was ready, he knew full well that no section of the line would be in shape in the near future. Anxious to show his skill in quickly creating a national airline, Howe decided that Canadian Airways' Vancouver–Seattle service would be the first TCA operation. This being the case, Richardson asked, in his April 26, 1937, letter, that TCA buy Canadian Airways' two Electras at cost. It was to Howe's benefit to have the Vancouver–Seattle route and aircraft because it meant that TCA was taking over an established route and that Canadian Airways' pilots could provide the necessary pilot training.

As a result, Canadian Airways lost everything connected to the route. TCA took Canadian Airways' pilots, mechanics and aircraft as well as its tickets, order forms, pilot uniforms and even the vacuum cleaner from the Vancouver office. MacLaren offered to return the specially embossed brass buttons from the uniforms. Richardson was left with a handful of buttons to remind him of his vision of a national and international airline.

Even with the loss of the trans-Canada contract, Richardson had no qualms about continuing. Unlike 1932, when he lost the air mail contracts, the outlook in April 1937 was good. The January–April 1937 statistics indicated that 1937 would be a good year financially. Richardson optimistically assumed that he would overcome this latest hurdle.

The abandonment of Canadian Airways by so many long-term staff was tough on those who remained. Acutely aware of how demoralizing the situation was, Richardson turned his energy first to maintaining staff morale. On April 19–20, he hosted a staff conference to discuss problems and to obtain ideas from field personnel. In reading through the conference notes it was interesting to note that Richardson showed himself to be concerned not only with the bottom line of costs but also with staff health, "the vitality of the pilot." The number of flying hours was not yet regulated, and unlike so many of the owners who pushed their pilots beyond safe levels of flight time, Richardson recognized that it was "necessary to give each pilot some limit and to allow some time off for recreations, sports. Extra pilots will allow more intensive use of aircraft without over-working individual pilots."

Thompson followed up the conference with a memo to all pilots on May 6, subtly reminding them why they should remain with the company. He praised their importance to the company and referred to the cancellation of the air mail contracts in 1932 and the resulting drastic loss of revenue. Evidently Richardson was concerned about pilot morale, for Thompson wrote:

> The success of any aviation company depends very largely on its pilots. This is particularly true in the bush where the pilots are the chief contact with the customers, and consequently the chief salesmen ... By the same token untold harm can be done by being disinterested in or possibly unintentionally discourteous to a customer, or by some chance remark derogatory to company personnel or organization. It is only human nature to be upset or feel dissatisfied at times, particularly when tired, and if at any time you are this way or feel you are not being treated fairly, by all means let your officials know about it, but do not discuss it with outsiders. The writer wishes to assure you of a sympathetic hearing at all times and welcomes any constructive criticism.

Thompson meanwhile decided to close the Maritimes operation, and on May 4 he gave the order to Walter Fowler to "dispose of our equipment and contracts in the Maritimes but do it quietly, we need no publicity." This was a difficult decision. Thompson knew that it was only a matter of time before the Maritimes became a hotbed of aviation expansion, particularly the Moncton–Halifax–Saint John route. He had wanted to secure this run before TCA had its operation established to Moncton—C.D. Howe had announced that Moncton was to be the TCA's eastern terminal. But the Maritimes operation was run at a huge loss, and Thompson felt he had no choice but to pull out for the time being.

Aware that he needed to keep public confidence in his company, Richardson sent out a good-news release to the Dow Jones tape on October 4, 1937. "Canadian Airways Limited, the largest air transport company in Canada, announced that all their bases were experiencing the busiest season in years. The Surveys Division is exceptionally busy in British Columbia, Quebec, Labrador and Newfoundland. The Company has 211 employees, with a monthly payroll in excess of $25,000. The Company owns and operates 13 ground radio stations and has 42 active aircraft."

Meanwhile, having created his government-owned airline, C.D. Howe was still busy covering his tracks as to how this had come about. He wrote his version to both Richardson and to Sir Edward Beatty. It was a masterful remake of events. As it happened, Richardson and Beatty compared notes. Beatty wrote to Richardson to advise him of the story that Howe had concocted. Richardson, holidaying at Lake of the Woods, responded on August 14:

> I was interested in the last paragraph of your letter of July 29th in regard to Howe having taken the position that I was in entire accord throughout with his plans in connection with the Trans-Canada Air Services but had been influenced by you in finally refusing to have anything to do with the venture. Mr. Howe shifts his ground so often that it is not possible to keep pace with him. I am aware, though, that he has taken this position, as he referred to it in the last letter I had from him. I have been waiting until we finally got paid for our two Electra planes before replying to him on this point, when I will answer it very definitely.

Richardson also had the inside story on Howe's famous dawn-to-dusk flight, which took place on July 30, 1937. His version differed strikingly from Howe's and depicted a very foolish minister of transport and a very skilled pilot. The flight should never have taken place. However, Howe was caught by his own bragging. He had publicly stated that the first regular long-distance service would be in operation by July 1, 1937, but it was impossible for TCA to meet the deadline. The airfields were not ready, and the radio and navigational aids were not in place. It was not safe for TCA to carry passengers. July 1 came and went. Safety be damned—a blustery Howe decided he would make a dramatic dawn-to-dusk flight from Montreal to Vancouver to show off his new airline. The weather proved troublesome, and July slipped away. On July 30, Howe told Squadron Leader Tudhope to ready the plane. Tudhope told his good friend Tommy Thompson the details, and Richardson could not resist telling Beatty.

Howe arranged with Squadron Leader Tudhope to take him from Montreal to Vancouver on a daylight flight, and arranged to take with him Herby Symington and C.P. Edwards. The plane left St. Hubert field, early in the morning, but the visibility was bad and Tudhope returned to the field, put the plane in the hangar, and locked it up with no intention of ever taking it out again that day. A little while later Howe came around and told Tudhope to get the plane out, that they were going to go. Tudhope was well aware that it was a very unwise thing to do, but evidently the prestige of the Minister was such that he did as he was told.

The plane was able to get down at Gillies for fuel, but the visibility was so bad at Kapuskasing that they could not come down and they went right on. Tudhope was on his knees [praying] most of the time with the map, trying to figure out where they were, and just as they were about out of gas they found themselves squarely on top of Sioux Lookout. Tudhope was a very relieved man.

Thompson tells me it was a very fine piece of dead reckoning and that very few men in Canada could have done it; on the other hand Thompson also knows that there was a very large share of unadulterated good luck, because when one is flying without a beam and cannot see the ground it is quite impossible to make correct allowances for wind drift.

If their gas had given out just before they got to Sioux Lookout they would all have been written off, or if they had gone by Sioux Lookout a little to the north or a little to the south, or if the visibility had been a little poorer and they had gone right over Sioux Lookout, without seeing it, then we would have had in our morning papers the biographies of five gentlemen, namely, the Minister of Transport, a Director of the Air Lines, Chief of the Air Services, Squadron Leader Tudhope and his assistant.

It was altogether just a fool piece of business and something that could only be gotten away with the odd time. Philip Johnson was in Winnipeg when they passed through and he was very annoyed and upset about it. The Minister told him it was not a stunt, and he wanted to know if it wasn't a stunt what was it. Howe announced in Winnipeg that they had never had an uneasy moment on their trip. If you run into Symington some time you might ask him how he enjoyed it and possibly he will open up and tell you what he really thinks of it now.

This man Howe is the loosest talker of anyone I have ever met holding a responsible position. Why he should wish to advertise his ignorance on so many subjects is a bit difficult to understand.

Howe climbed out of the aircraft waving and smiling broadly, followed by very shaky, ashen-faced officials who were relieved to be safely on the ground. When questioned by the press, Howe implied that the flight was a piece of cake. Photos of his fellow passengers tell a different story.

Howe was unperturbed by Johnson's anger; he had achieved his goal. He had publicized his airline. The flight took over seventeen hours, many of them with no visual reference to the ground. It was Tudhope's skill as a pilot and sheer good luck that Howe had not wiped out his airline before its first official flight. Howe continued to have good luck with TCA, and TCA became Canada's beloved airline, with the "Minister of Everything" at its head. The public continued to be fascinated with the man.

Beatty responded to Richardson's letter on August 24. He too was concerned with Howe's version of events.

It would be pity if either of us were blamed for things which never happened. In looking back at the airways situation I cannot remember a single instance when you and I had different views or when either of us was under any influence from the other.

Your account of the 'non-stunt' flight of the Minister is extremely interesting, and I think he is to be congratulated on having successfully completed a thoroughly unnecessary and valueless trip without injury to himself or his companions.

Like you I do not understand the Minister or his attitude. Undoubtedly he is not friendly to the Company or to myself, and he puts it on the ground that I once wrote him a letter closing the correspondence we had had respecting our participation in the Trans-Canada plan. I assumed, of course, he meant what he wrote me, namely, that the Cabinet could not consent to anything other than he had suggested, i.e., a 50 percent split of the Capital Stock and a one-third representation to the Canadian Pacific on the Board. If he meant what he said, I had no alternative but to accept his decision and ask that our name should not appear in the Statute. I am quite satisfied that he would have continued it as in the original draft, and, therefore, would have added to the general misconception of our position and the reasons for it. Of course, if I had had any idea that his letter did not mean what it said, I would have left the door wide open.

Howe's trouble seems to be that the sudden acquisition of Cabinet rank and of power has gone to his head and he is not able to deal with ordinary individuals except on the basis of a superior being dealing with inferiors. However, he has undoubtedly been getting the "breaks" in many ways and as long as his luck holds out, we need not expect much change in him.

Howe could not keep his fingers out of TCA. After having indignantly told R.B. Bennett that the minister of transport would have little if anything to do with TCA, Howe turned up at the CNR's board meeting on April 23, 1937, full of suggestions. He recommended that the CNR should subscribe for the outstanding TCA shares and nominated three of his DOT officials to the TCA board of directors. CNR complied and then nominated its president, S.J. Hungerford, to the board, and he slipped easily into the president's chair of TCA. Howe then ensured that the CNR nominated three of his people to the TCA board: J.Y. Murdoch, Wilfrid Gagnon and Herbert Symington.

TCA held its first board meeting in May. Magically, Howe turned up, again full of advice. This time he told the board that there was no one in Canada capable of running the airline, and he recommended that TCA hire an American consultant; he even had a name to offer. Typically, no one challenged Howe. The man chosen was Philip Johnson, a former president of Boeing Airplane Co. and United Airlines. Johnson was well qualified, and when he insisted on his salary as well as those of the four specialists he hired from the United States being paid in American dollars, no one batted an eye. As the money flowed freely, TCA appeared to be modelling itself after the CNR. This was not unexpected, since they shared presidents.

TCA's second annual report, for the year ended December 31, 1938, stated that the company had 332 employees and 14 aircraft, even though the airline had not yet carried a passenger. Of the 332 employees, 37 were termed flight personnel, the remainder were "administrative officers, technical advisers, station, clerical and other, communications and dispatch, maintenance and overhaul." By way of comparison, Canadian Airways had 211 employees and 42 "active aircraft." The following year, D.B. Colyer moved into Johnson's position with a salary of twenty thousand dollars.

The Trans-Canada Air Lines Act laid down an aviation policy for Canada that would have long-term repercussions. It established a policy that was vastly different from that previously followed and was the antithesis of Howe's original intention. The act not only put the government into the actual business of operating an airline but also introduced a monopoly on the transcontinental line. Canadian Airways was now faced with a government rival that promised to be much more extensive than it was. TCA would unquestionably dominate the national scene. Prospects for expansion for the private companies were now limited to the North. It was back to the bush for Canadian Airways.

Canada's air policy was shaped to the advantage of TCA rather than to the airline industry as a whole. While creating the philosophy of monopoly for TCA, the act made no provision for the private aviation companies. The plan at the time was for TCA to operate only those feeder services that the government considered essential to the mainline operation. But TCA was uncertain which feeders it wanted, and this meant that everyone else operated in an insecure atmosphere, never knowing when TCA would take over one of its routes. Thus, while TCA held a protected position, the private companies were forced to scramble for business in the North. Unregulated competition and Post Office manipulations of air mail contracts continued.

By November 1937, Canadian Airways' fortunes changed and began their downward trend. The lack of regulations did not help. Although the formation of the Department of Transport (DOT) in November 1936 had provided an administrative framework for the coordination of meteorological, radio and civil aviation services, it had not supplied a remedy for the problems of the bush companies. DOT did not have the authority to provide economic controls for the air transport industry. In addition, the licensing system of 1937 covered only the interurban and international operations. Licences were not necessary for the bush routes, and the bush companies could still fly where they wished and charge what they wanted. Complicating the situation was the inability of DOT to name which feeder services would be operated by TCA and which would be available for the private operators. This resulted in vague and conflicting directives from DOT and made it difficult for the private companies to proceed with confidence with developmental plans for the feeder services.

For example, in May 1937, DOT requested the air operators to apply for route licences. Canadian Airways complied but then was told by DOT that no licences would be issued for the time being because the whole subject of scheduled air transport licensing was "under consideration." Quiet investigation uncovered collusion between DOT and TCA. When DOT received an application, it turned it over to TCA. If TCA wished to operate the service, then a licence was not granted to the private company. If TCA did not know if it wished the route, then the application was simply held in abeyance until TCA made up its mind.

Canadian Airways charged TCA and DOT with unfair collaboration. Conflict of interest was blatant. Two key DOT officials were also directors of TCA, and another TCA director was a Post Office official. Howe's man, Commander C.P. Edwards of DOT, John A. Wilson of DOT and George Herring of the Post Office were also all TCA directors. The TCA board of directors' minutes of the September 2, 1937, meeting show that Edwards was vigilant in protecting Howe's latest creation. Speaking as a DOT representative, Edwards stated emphatically that he did not want to make any commitments until TCA decided on its routes. This interference played havoc with Canadian Airways and the other companies;

they could do no long-term planning. There was no point in complaining to DOT since DOT and TCA walked hand in hand, with Howe monitoring the situation. DOT tended to promote TCA's growth at the expense of commercial aviation in general.

At the time, TCA had no interest in developing any of the feeder services, but it also had no intention of letting a potentially important feeder slip through its hands. TCA's board of directors' minutes of the November 10, 1937, meeting show that the question of territory to be serviced by TCA was again discussed. It was agreed that as a general principle the TCA "operations would be confined to those of a main line character" and that TCA would not operate on routes on which "traffic density does not warrant the use of Corporate standard equipment." It was felt that the feeder lines should go to the private operators, who could then make interline arrangements with TCA. However, TCA protected itself by saying it could also operate any lines that the government designated to TCA.

Here is what happened on the Edmonton–Whitehorse route. TCA recognized that this line might become important. However, the route was not fully developed, so TCA told DOT to give out a temporary air mail contract—until it warranted main-line status. Grant McConachie of United Air Transport desperately wanted the contract. It was worth thirty thousand dollars and would give him the leverage to buy better equipment and be taken more seriously. "You know, we used to be a little insignificant operator with dirty faces; you had to be Canadian Airways or Mackenzie Air Services. We were the poor brothers," recalled Sheldon Luck, one of McConachie's pilots. McConachie was "in" with the Post Office and was happy to have a temporary licence, because the route would give him a leg up on what would become one of the most lucrative routes in the northwest. Richardson was furious. Once again the Post Office had not tendered an important contract, and the government did not seem to care, either about the unscrupulous practice or that it was aggravating the problems of the northern operators.

To make matters worse, the outlook, which had been so promising in the early months of the year, had changed. By December 1937 the mining business had declined, Canadian Airways' stock had dropped from $7.50 to $3.50 a share, and it had loans amounting to $250,000 due the Bank of Commerce, secured by Richardson's personal guarantee.

Ironically, Canadian Airways' books for the first time in its history showed a small profit at the year's end.

Richardson's main concern now was the fate of the bush air mail contracts. He was afraid that they too would turn into a straight political issue. The Edmonton–Whitehorse fiasco was proof that there were no rules—who one knew was the main consideration. To better his chances and to cut his competition, Richardson decided to try to buy out the competition. It would not be easy; McConachie, who got his start flying frozen fish, now had his sights set higher. He now dreamed the same dream as Richardson—a route "over the top." Leigh Brintnell of Mackenzie Air Services also had his eye on the route to the Orient. Afraid of being pushed out by McConachie, Brintnell had suggested to him that they join forces. McConachie, a good poker player, was playing his cards close to his chest and did not say yes or no to Brintnell.

When "Wop" May approached McConachie about working together, McConachie was noncommittal, saying only that Brintnell had already approached him. Uneasy, May wrote to "Punch" Dickins:

> I think it would be a good idea to take this up with him [McConachie]. He is expanding his operations very rapidly and he advises me that he is equipping his aircraft with radio compasses and he is also putting wireless stations in at Fort St. John and Fort Nelson. He is operating 8 aircraft out of Edmonton. The majority of his machines are old and dilapidated but still he is getting away with it. His intentions are to specialize on the NW run from Edmonton to the Yukon. I would not like to see him get connected up with Brintnell in any way as I am afraid it would make a rather strong combination for this district.

The situation with the air mail contracts had deteriorated even more. All bush mail contracts in western Canada held by Canadian Airways Limited had recently been thrown open to tender, and two contracts had been awarded to others without calling for tenders. The two given without tender were the Edmonton–Whitehorse contract (to McConachie) and the Sioux Lookout–Pickle Crow contract (to Robert Starratt of Starratt Airways). On May 13, 1937, Thompson angrily wrote to MP James A. Glen of Russell, Manitoba, whose son was a Canadian Airways pilot.

The Postmaster General has seen fit to call for tenders on all the Manitoba and Northwestern Ontario air mail contracts, with the exception of the one from Sioux Lookout to Pickle Crow, which was taken away from us last winter and given to Starratt Airways without any tender, and without any notice to Canadian Airways Limited that any change was contemplated.

I am writing to ask if you would be good enough to write the Postmaster General and point out to him the services that have been rendered in Northwestern Ontario and Manitoba by Canadian Airways, and services which could have been rendered by no other organization during the darkest years of the depression when the development of the gold mines probably did more to assist the country than anything else. It is not as though we had taken these contracts away from other parties. We have carried the air mail in these two districts ever since it was inaugurated, and to the best of my belief have given excellent service.

Richardson was concerned about the feeder lines north of the TCA system. He was disturbed with the loss of the Mackenzie River air mail contract because that threw a monkey wrench into his long-term plans for a route to the Orient from Edmonton and Whitehorse. McConachie had won the first round, and he wanted to make sure that Brintnell did not win the second round by obtaining a licence to operate between Edmonton and Lethbridge. Thompson agreed and wrote Richardson in early July, "I consider the situation now developing at Edmonton is very dangerous to our interests and that we should take all means at our disposal to counteract it."

In August 1937, Roy Brown of General Airways approached Canadian Airways about working together, and in December he and Richardson talked. However, after looking at Brown's audited statements, Hutchins recommended playing hardball. "In dealing with Brown our opinion is that this suggestion be made on the basis of 'take it or leave it' because there is so much cash involved in putting this Company on a proper basis that maybe we should just take the money and buy new aircraft for ourselves and run him off the air." Brown never responded.

Undeterred, Thompson recommended that Canadian Airways pursue both General Airways and Dominion Skyways because those two companies would put the territory from Quebec to the Atlantic coast solidly in Canadian Airways' hands. They could then afford to sit back and let the independent operators in the West worry for a while and perhaps be in a more amenable frame of mind about hooking up with Canadian Airways. It was time to let matters jell a little.

Matters with the Post Office came to a head when Canadian Airways lost the contract into Red Lake, which it had held since December 26, 1926. The contract went to Wings Limited, which bid a few dollars less. Richardson, upset and angry about the unscrupulous practices of the Post Office and the shady practices of some of the other air operators, decided it was time to put some facts on paper and send them off to members of Parliament. His memo for Manitoba MP Thomas Crerar, the minister of mines and natural resources, dated July 14, 1937, covered the following points:

> Certain interests have been organized to take our mail bush contracts away from us. This is particularly noticeable in the case of the Mackenzie River contracts ... When this contract was again thrown open for tender we submitted a very low price, but it had been previously intimated to us that no matter how low a figure we submitted we were likely to lose this contract. We put in a very low tender on this work rather than lose it after our long record, and also because we ultimately expected to have our Edmonton–Lethbridge contract restored, which would have given us a run from the Canadian–American border to the Arctic Ocean.
>
> We are also interested in other runs into Alaska, but some months ago, without any tender whatever, the Post Office gave out a contract from Edmonton to Fairbanks, Alaska, to a man named Maconachie [sic], who has no substance or substantial equipment, and who, with the new contract, promptly secured $250,000 and set up as the United Air Transport. The Post Office have not only shut us out of all mail contracts on the Mackenzie River but they never gave us an opportunity of figuring on the Edmonton–Whitehorse run, which our men knew more about than anyone else and were better able to carry it out.
>
> To add to this it now appears to be the intention of the Post Office to give the Edmonton–Lethbridge run to the Mackenzie Air

Services . . . We hope that this does not mean that Brintnell has a preferred position in a run, the most of which was previously covered by a contract that we had with the Post Office, and which was cancelled without consideration.

On August 11, from Lake of the Woods, Richardson again wrote Crerar, covering the points in his memo and requesting his help. Believing that Crerar did not have the necessary backbone, Richardson also wrote to Norman Lambert, an influential Liberal, enclosing a copy of his letter to Crerar, briefly explaining the Post Office problems and concluding with "I feel that perhaps you could put the necessary stiffening in Mr. Crerar's back to have him accomplish [what is] necessary. Crerar has the right idea and I think the matter just needs another punch, but whether he will give the necessary punch or not I do not know." Richardson was learning to lobby.

In the meantime, Thompson, not trusting certain Post Office officials, was hand-delivering his air mail tenders to Ottawa, just minutes before the deadline. He now turned his attention to the Arctic and on August 19 put his ideas on paper for Richardson to mull over.

I am convinced that during the next twenty-five years, probably a great deal sooner, there will be established regular air services from England and Europe to the Orient via the Arctic . . . The logical people to pioneer this route are those who have through many years gained practical experience in Arctic flying, namely, Canadians and Russians. The Russians are already pioneering the route. The personnel are available in Canada, but if Canadians do not seize the advantage they now have, it will not be there forever. Might I suggest that steps be taken, possibly in co-operation with Sir Edward Beatty and Woods-Humphrey, to enable Canadian Airways Limited or a subsidiary company to take advantage of these coming developments.

Despite everything that had happened, Richardson was hopeful that Howe would keep his promise and award Canadian Airways most of the feeders as compensation for losing the trans-Canada contract. Thompson wanted to have Canadian Airways "recognized as the National Company to handle all the northern routes connecting with the International lines" and to develop the route to the Orient through northern Canada. In his letter to Richardson on August 19, he also stressed the need to safeguard Canadian Airways "to prevent any pioneering efforts from being exploited by others, as in the case of the Trans-Canada mail contract." As a final step to protect Canadian Airways, Thompson suggested that Richardson speak personally with both Mackenzie King and R.B. Bennett and "get their approvals and promise of support and protection, whichever party is in power."

In the fall, while in the East on business, Richardson tackled P.T. Coolican, "who laid himself out to be unusually friendly and maintained that the Trans-Canada set-up was a bitter disappointment to him because he had always fought for an independently operated company, where there would be some possibility of holding costs down ... I talked to him about the Edmonton–Whitehorse run and he said that this was only a temporary contract and could be washed out at any time. He thought there was a large chance of the Trans-Canada taking it over and that this was the logical line to take to the Orient."

Richardson also talked with Hartland Molson of Dominion Skyways and observed, "He is disturbed about the Skylines' competition, and wants to get our help in regard to zoning, and generally wants us to tell him how he can carry on successfully his airways, by co-operation or otherwise, or how he can extricate himself from his airways investment without losing whatever he has put up." In 1938 Richardson personally bought Dominion Skyways in Quebec and Arrow Airways in Manitoba. Both companies retained their identities and operated under their own names.

The Liberals had been in power for more than two years and had yet to do anything about the plight of the northern air operators. Howe and DOT seemed concerned only with TCA. Meanwhile the northern air transport industry was slipping closer and closer to bankruptcy because of the unrestricted and destructive competition. Tommy Thompson appealed to Howe's man, C.P. Edwards, chief of air services, on December 9, 1937. He told Edwards that he, "Punch" Dickins and Val Patriarche had drawn up a set of regulations based on American regulations but adapted for the Canadian North.

Richardson wrote to Crerar on February 10, 1938, that he had seen the prime minister in Ottawa the previous week, and "I believe that I convinced him that the Post Office had not played fair with us in the past and were not now playing fair with us." In a letter to Richardson on March 11, 1938, Beatty, obviously pleased that the corrupt practices of the Post Office were being aired, told Richardson that his conversation with the prime minister, J.C. Elliott and J.G. Gardiner "imputing dishonesty of two permanent officers of the Post Office Department ... was also repeated to others ... and is now widespread." Richardson replied to Beatty, adding that he had also "told the Prime Minister that I thought there was very objectionable political pressure used and I quoted what Coolican said to me."

Thompson was not convinced. In fact, he had come to the end of his rope—no more Mr. Nice Guy.

> We have to insist on seeing the tenders to prevent Herring from calling whoever ... We must make the Post Office practices public knowledge. Canadian Airways has nothing to lose. With regard to the Regina–Prince Albert feeder line, we need this to retain our other traffic. The only way I can see that we will get fair play is to have some of our friends call on Mr. Herring late on the afternoon of March 2 and insist on seeing all tenders that have been submitted. This will make it very much harder for Herring to call whoever his particular friends may be and tell them what to bid. I also suggest that we make public the Sioux Lookout–Pickle Crow tender. It would put the Post Office and Mr. Herring in an untenable position. We know we have nothing to lose by exposing as much as possible corrupt practices which are very evident in the Post Office Department, although we have no definite proof. I would also suggest that consideration be given to handing this information to the *Free Press* and as many other newspapers as would be willing to make a case of it. Canadian Airways are not the only ones in the aviation industry who are disgusted with the way contracts in general are being handled by the present government.

Financially, Canadian Airways was doing poorly. On March 15, 1938, Hutchins was forced to write to Richardson that "in the matter of finances this company will soon become a real problem and might better be considered in advance than left until its urgency became embarrassing. The Company requires at least $350,000 additional working capital and until such an amount or more is put up the position is unsound."

Canadian Airways was not alone in its troubles. Wings Limited, which received the contract from Sioux Lookout to Red Lake (under questionable conditions), now asked to be relieved of it because the rates were too low for it to continue operating the route on an economical basis.

Canadian Airways was still trying to work out something with TCA with the feeder lines. "Mr. Howe made great promises that our company would get most of the branch line runs, but whether these assurances are worth anything at all or not I do not know," Richardson wrote to Beatty in March. On June 7, Thompson wrote to Richardson that the "Vancouver to Fort St. John route is a live issue and it looks as if the Post Office will let this go without tendering. I suggest that we protest this vigorously." Clearly Richardson's February chat with the prime minister had not been effective. Canadian Airways broke openly with the Post Office when it awarded this air mail contract to McConachie without calling for tenders. This route would become the future northwest staging route leading to Alaska and allowed McConachie to bring in American money and expand greatly.

Richardson was heartbroken. As early as 1928 he had seen the possibilities of this route. In 1933–34 he had hoped to develop it; in late 1937 he had met with Vilhjalmur Stefansson of Pan Am, who had come to Winnipeg to talk with him, to discuss the possibilities of cooperating with Pan Am on the route to the Orient. This too had fallen through. In March 1938 Richardson made arrangements for Thompson to meet with Juan Trippe of Pan Am to discuss the route while Thompson was in New York. (He was also exploring possibilities in the West Indies). To lose the route through unfair practices was almost more than Richardson could bear.

Grant McConachie was not the only one he had to watch; Leigh Brintnell was up to his usual tricks. On August 18, 1938, Thompson wrote Richardson that "Brintnell is flying north from Edmonton almost every day with 1000 pounds of mail, which enables him to keep a daily service to Yellowknife; in order to pad the mail poundage Brintnell has subscribed to the *Edmonton Journal* and *Bulletin* for everyone in the NWT—a shrewd man."

R.B. Bennett, the leader of the Opposition, seemed to be the only politician prepared to ask questions. On February 24, 1938, in Parliament, Bennett asked who had received the mail contract to the Yukon. Howe answered that it was McConachie of United Air Transport. Bennett, a wily lawyer, was careful not to come out directly and accuse McConachie of anything underhanded. "I am not making any slighting observations with reference to him. On the contrary I would compliment him upon his ability to secure a contract by an act almost of legerdemain in pulling the rabbit out of the hat. You put your hand in, shut your eyes and pull out a mail contract to carry mails from Vancouver to the Yukon with the high approval of the Order-in-Council for which the Minister of National Defence must be partly responsible ... The wonders that such an active young man can accomplish." Anyone who has read Ronald Keith's biography of McConachie, *Bush Pilot with a Briefcase,* will know that McConachie would do almost anything to get business.

The situation for the bush companies was so bad by the end of 1938 that Richardson advocated the examination of Canada's air industry by an independent royal commission. Although it had created a national airline, the government continued to sidestep the question of national air development. Richardson accused the Post Office of making exorbitant profits (192 percent) on the northern air mail, at the expense of the bush operators, while running deficits on international flights. It would take a war for the government to turn its attention to northern air operators, the industry that had done so much for Canada during the depression years. Canada's air operators had carried more freight in the late 1930s than did those in any other country. Now they were being left to wither in the shadow of TCA.

Although they were bitterly fighting among themselves, the various owners finally realized that they needed to cooperate. Thompson asked *Canadian Aviation* magazine for help, and it agreed to publish five guest editorials, written by the airline owners, on the current state of aviation affairs. Richardson wrote the first editorial; the others were written by Leigh Brintnell, president of Mackenzie Air Services (August 1938); R.W. Starratt of Starratt Airways & Transportation (October 1938); Milt Ashton, general manager of Wings Limited; and Harvey Weber, president of Arrow Airways (December 1938). The editorials' titles describe their focus: Brintnell's "Northern Operations: A Constructive Government Policy Needed"; Starratt's "The Need for Co-operation"; Ashton's "Looking for Fair Treatment"; and Weber's "The Need for Regulated Operations." Between them they discussed the need for regulated operations, unfair Post Office practices, the licensing of routes, unfair competition by the RCAF, indiscriminate rate cutting, costs of aircraft and engines in Canada, and the stagnation of aviation in Canada. An excerpt from Harvey Weber's article gives one of the themes:

> Under present conditions an operator may pioneer a new area. Perhaps he will send an aeroplane over miles of wilderness at costs far exceeding revenue to stimulate some infant activity. It may be connected with fish, fur, mineral or some other commercial development. Under the stimulus of air transportation the new industry thrives and the volume of paying traffic increases. It reaches a point where the operator is in a position to profit from the venture and reduce rates so that a further volume of traffic may accrue. Then what happens? In comes the vagabond operator. He may be a pilot with more flying skill than business ability, financed by his admiring friends. He may bring in a surplus ship from some other organization heretofore working in another district, who find it easier when their business slacks off there to jump into some other territory rather than work a little harder searching for some traffic in their own. He has the scantiest of ground facilities. A shack on the shore of a lake and a plank to the aircraft with a barrel of gas lying in the mud is enough to carry on with but he feels sure that all he has to do is to cut prices and all the business will be his. He cuts prices but he does not get all the business. No one ever does. He may get fifty percent of it, which means that the volume of the original operator is now fifty percent of what it was before and his volume is just fifty percent of what it should be. Rate cutting would have very little effect if the volume of traffic could be maintained for both aircraft ... This sort of thing is not allowed in highway transportation ... Why is such a situation allowed to continue in this business of air transportation?

Milt Ashton minced no words: "Politics, too, has been a constant cause of worry and expense for most of the operators. It has been particularly evident in the tendering of air mail. Why is it that the Post

Office Department calls tenders in some cases and in others awards contracts without allowing bids? Why are contracts for photography and on services of national importance awarded without bidding and rates far in excess of what is reasonable—and profitable? ... The bush operator wants only fair treatment in return for a national service he performs. He does not want to feel that it is necessary to have 'a friend at court' in order to get equitable treatment."

Finally, on July 1, 1938, the Liberal government passed the Transport Act and proclaimed it in November 1938. The act placed the control of licensing in the hands of a Board of Transport Commissioners and brought a measure of stability to the industry but did not go far enough.

First of all, the Board of Transport Commissioners could not eliminate the duplication of services among the northern operators. The inclusion of the "grandfather clause" in the Transport Act meant that the board had to grant a licence to a carrier that had provided services in that area before the passage of the act. These grandfather rights benefited Canadian Airways, which had pioneered most of the routes and could therefore claim the right to a licence in most areas. But the board had no control over the number of aircraft operating in a district outside the licensed routes. Because the aircraft were equipped with skis and floats and could land practically anywhere, it was relatively simple for the unlicensed operator to circumvent the effect of any licence granted by taking off and landing just outside the licensed air route. The unlicensed operator usually granted concessions to secure traffic from the legal operator.

Second, the Board of Transport Commissioners had no control over air mail rates. While the TCA Act had provided for equitable air mail rates for TCA, the Transport Act made no such provision for the private companies. They remained at the mercy of the Post Office.

The Transport Act also introduced the problem of conflict between the executive powers of the minister of transport, under the TCA Act, and the judicial functions of the Board of Transport Commissioners, under the Transport Act. This happened because, when the Transport Act was passed, the TCA Act was amended to provide for the division of control of TCA between DOT and the Board of Transport Commissioners. This resulted in TCA being able to carry on whatever service it liked without reference to the minister of transport, as long as the service was not subsidized. In 1944 it was recommended that the Transport Act be amended to provide a clearer definition of the jurisdiction of the Board of Transport Commissioners over TCA operations. In practice, the board was limited to a passive role. It waited until it received an application before it acted. It did not concern itself with the development of policies designed to support commercial aviation.

While welcoming the legislation as an attempt to control unregulated competition, Thompson foresaw a number of problems with the Transport Act. He believed the application of the Railway Act to air transportation was not practicable and would result in at least a 25 percent increase in Canadian Airways' overhead, "entirely in the form of non-productive personnel looking after their records." He also felt that some of the operators would continue to file tariffs that were too low and was concerned that, if Canadian Airways protested, it would be accused by its customers of trying to raise the rates. Thompson recommended that Canadian Airways open its books to the scrutiny of the Board of Transport Commissioners to provide it with actual costs, so that it could accurately judge whether the rates submitted to it were at a level that allowed a reasonable profit.

In fact, on November 26, 1938, Richardson wrote to Howe and offered to open Canadian Airways' records to the board. Howe did not reply. Richardson also strongly recommended that the board's authority be enlarged and the Post Office Act be changed so that the board could participate in the setting of air mail rates. The government eventually incorporated most of Canadian Airways' suggestions, but too late to help Canadian Airways.

The Transport Act helped to prevent the formation of new companies but did little to alleviate the duplication of services and the low rates of the existing companies. Compounding these problems was a curtailment in mining activity because of the threat of war. This had an immediate effect on the volume of work available and on the whole rate structure. By December 1938, Canadian Airways' liquid position was so bad that Hutchins, the company's executive secretary, advised Richardson to discuss Canadian Airways' future with Beatty and Hungerford.

The annual report for the fiscal year ended December 31, 1938, showed a loss of $95,978 before depreciation, compared with a profit of

$107,925 in 1937. Working capital was decreased $156,547 and showed a deficit of $145,608. Canadian Airways was financed by a $300,000 loan from the Bank of Commerce, which was personally guaranteed by Richardson. Because CNR was unable to sell its stock after the formation of TCA, it still held shares in Canadian Airways. At this time, there were 129,753 shares outstanding, of which Richardson controlled 54.5 percent; the CPR and the CNR controlled 15.4 percent between them; and 410 shareholders held 30.1 percent.

There was little that Canadian Airways could do to improve the situation except persevere in its efforts to secure rate agreements with the other operators and to try to force the government to establish adequate controls for the bush companies. In 1938 Canadian Airways agreed to join Passenger and Express Air Services. This plan, proposed by J.L. Deering of Regina, manager of the Ford Motor Branch and interested in aviation, called for the formation of a central traffic organization to eliminate the duplication of traffic, offices, sales and commercial services among the companies.

Deering held two conferences in 1938 in an attempt to establish this organization. Twelve companies attended and initially accepted its principles. However, Leigh Brintnell refused to attend either conference, and his non-participation made it unlikely that the plan would work. By the end of 1938, most of the companies, except Canadian Airways and Arrow Airways, had dropped out.

During 1939, Canadian Airways concentrated on publicizing the plight of the northern operators. In early January, Thompson prepared a comprehensive sixty-page brief titled "Northern Air Transport" to give to MP James Glen and other members of Parliament as ammunition for them to plead for legislation for the bush industry. Richardson also arranged for a number of newspapers across the country to write about Canadian Airways and the financial problems of the air transport industry in general. His most significant effort was a memorandum, written by Thompson, to the Board of Transport Commissioners, recommending that all licensed carriers participate in any air mail contract in the district in which they were licensed, in order to take the awarding of air mail contracts out of the hands of political patronage. Thompson also recommended that the board institute a standard form of accounting and that it, like the air mail rates, be submitted for approval to a committee composed of representatives from DOT, the Post Office and the Board of Transport Commissioners.

Richardson, who was spending an inordinate amount of time on Canadian Airways business, wrote to the postmaster general, W.D. Euler, on January 7, 1939. His letter was crisp and to the point. He accused the Post Office of allowing political patronage to be the basis of its tendering, and he cited the awarding of the lucrative contract between Vancouver, Prince George and Fort St. John. Euler responded on January 17 with an unsatisfactory and political non-answer: "There is no hard and fast rule governing the procedure of awarding contracts for the conveyance of mails by air." Richardson showed the letter to Thompson, who responded on January 26: "We do not need Mr. Euler to tell us there is no hard and fast rule governing the procedure of awarding contracts. This is self-evident and is one of the principle [sic] reasons for this correspondence."

Richardson, in the East again, met Howe in March. To Beatty he wrote: "I also had quite a chat with Mr. Howe, who looked to be right on the edge of a physical breakdown ... He seems to be razzed on all sides. While he did not tell me so I understood he would like to quit but the Government will not let him out ... Mr. Howe said that the letting of the contract for the Prairie Airways had been very badly handled."

Then disaster struck. On June 26, 1939, James Richardson died suddenly of a heart attack.

CHAPTER THIRTEEN

"To Knit the Whole into a Profitable Operation"

"MOTHER ALWAYS SAID that the Airways killed him," recalled James Richardson's daughter Kathleen. Twice James Richardson saw his dream of a transcontinental airway system destroyed, and twice he was forced to turn back to the North to keep his company alive. Since the loss of the trans-Canada contract, he had been working around the clock on airways business as well as keeping on top of concerns at James Richardsons & Sons.

As the acknowledged leader of the air transport industry in the North, Richardson had put every effort into pulling the companies together to act in unison, hoping to force the government to listen. He had become their spokesman. It was to him that they looked to for guidance. His death from a heart attack was sudden but not wholly unexpected, considering the pace he kept. James Richardson's death left Canadian Airways without its guiding spirit and created a huge void in the industry.

Muriel Sprague Richardson, his wife, immediately and capably stepped into his shoes. As the long-time business confidante of her husband, she was familiar with all aspects of his various business concerns.

In 1939, she became president of James Richardson & Sons, a position she held for twenty-seven years, longer than any other president of the company. The co-executors of the Richardson estate were Muriel Richardson and George Hutchins, executive secretary of Canadian Airways. Hutchins assumed the administrative responsibility for Canadian Airways, assisted by Tommy Thompson (general manager), Jack Tackaberry (comptroller) and Gordon Lawson (senior vice-president of James Richardson & Sons). Sir Edward Beatty, while remaining as vice-president of Canadian Airways' board of directors, was soon to move into the presidency.

Canadian Airways' financial situation was so precarious that Hutchins lost no time in contacting Beatty. He bluntly told him that Canadian Airways had been financing its current accounts on the personal guarantee of Richardson through the Bank of Commerce and that the company was in debt to Imperial Oil to the tune of $100,000. He asked Beatty if he was prepared to become more involved. Beatty said yes. The decision to approach Beatty for financing marked the beginning of a closer alliance with the CPR. Little did anyone foresee that it would also mark the last chapter of Canadian Airways and the birth of another major airline.

Thompson carried on Richardson's goal of working out cooperative arrangements with the other companies. There was no necessity for pooling operations in the East, because Canadian Airways, Quebec Airways and Dominion Skyways were all controlled by the Richardson interests and had already worked out an agreement. Western Canada, however, was another story.

Leigh Brintnell proved to be a hard sell. Although he wanted an amalgamation of Mackenzie Air Services, Prairie Airways, Mayson & Campbell and Canadian Airways, he also wanted each company to operate only in a particular area or zone. Brintnell was convinced that there was room for only one company in each area and that decentralization was a solution. He wanted to take over the assets of Canadian Airways in Saskatchewan, Alberta and the Northwest Territories for stock in Mackenzie Air Services and to eliminate Canadian Airways' head office in Winnipeg.

Thompson wanted one controlling body: "Overhead in a large company, if properly organized, is a great deal less per unit than with a number of small companies in each district." He also felt the companies should continue to operate as separate units and more or less under their present management. He wanted to cut the duplication of services, terminal expenses, and the cost of maintenance and ground organization.

Hoping to make international connections, Richardson had been working to secure a contract in the Maritimes. It appeared that Howe was prepared to assist, for he had wired Richardson just weeks before his death, giving Richardson permission to start working out the details with TCA's Philip Johnson. Beatty, however, was twitchy about Howe's promises. "I'm a little nervous that Howe was undertaking this and that the contract might be considered a personal one and not considered binding to Canadian Airways and he felt we should close the contract," he told Thompson. In August 1939 Thompson took the precaution of meeting with the postmaster general, who gave him the go-ahead to negotiate a Maritimes air mail contract with Johnson, who had been told by Howe and TCA's board to do this. Thompson and Johnson drew up a draft contract but could go no further because the Post Office had not told TCA the exact routes, schedules or rates it wanted. "As you know, Post Office officials are definitely unfriendly to Canadian Airways and I am afraid they will hold up the contract as long as possible, and until it is signed there is a danger the government will change its mind," a worried Thompson wrote to H.P. Robinson of New Brunswick on August 29. With the possibility of re-entering the Maritimes, Tackaberry alerted Hutchins that Canadian Airways would need $1 million to cover the purchase of aircraft, the construction of radio stations and the training of personnel.

It was evident that Richardson's officials saw the CPR and Canadian Airways together obtaining control of the northern air operators. In a memo to Hutchins on August 8, Tackaberry outlined two recommendations. First, that they sell Airways Limited (established by Richardson in 1936 as a holding company for acquiring additional aviation companies) to the CPR and advise it to pick up the competing companies. Then, do a deal in which the Richardson estate and the CPR switched holdings, resulting in the Richardson estate controlling the bought-up bush companies and the CPR controlling Canadian Airways. Tackaberry's second recommendation was that the CPR buy the competing companies and lend $1 million to Canadian Airways, which needed this infusion to continue. Whatever plan was used, Tackaberry suggested that a management body be put in place for the efficient operation of all the companies.

Hutchins sketched a promising picture to Beatty. He estimated that it would cost only $600,000 to obtain control of Wings Limited, Starratt Airways, Prairie Airways, Yukon Southern Air Transport (McConachie's new company) and Mackenzie Air Services. Richardson's personal corporation, through Airways Limited, with total assets of $200,000, already owned Dominion Skyways, Arrow Airways and Quebec Airways. If the CPR was interested in obtaining control of the aviation picture in Canada, exclusive of TCA, it could do so for a price of between $1.5 million and $1.75 million. Hutchins was confident that "All companies could be put on a profitable basis overnight. Ask if this appeals to Sir Edward and if so, ask him to delegate someone to sit with us to work up a proposal for September. It would be like throwing money out of the window to put money into Canadian Airways to sweeten up that picture, unless the whole industry can be put on a profitable footing." As hoped, the CPR took the bait.

Over the next few weeks Hutchins, Thompson and Tackaberry worked furiously to come up with ways and means to approach the companies. Their comments provide an interesting glimpse into these companies. For instance, they judged that the three easiest to acquire were Prairie Airways, Wings and Starratt Airways. They thought highly of Dick Ryan, whose Prairie Airways was inadequately financed, and they felt a simple approach to its shareholders to finance it properly and give them a reasonable equity in the refinanced company would be a way to open negotiations. They estimated that it would require a cash outlay of $100,000.

As for Wings, Thompson was disparaging. "This company has no goodwill value, but from a competitive standpoint it has a nuisance value. Without control of the company, it is impossible to make any improvement in Canadian Airways' position in Central Manitoba." Wings also had mail contracts that would be valuable if the rates were adjusted; $60,000 would purchase 100,000 shares. Starratt Airways owed North Star Oil Company $70,000, and Thompson suggested gaining control by working through North Star Oil. Between 65 and

70 percent of all the air transport business in Canada was in the region between the Atlantic and Alberta (except that held by TCA). If Canadian Airways acquired Wings, Starratt and Prairie Airways, it would have control of the bulk of the traffic, with gross annual revenues of approximately $1.5 million.

"The goodwill of Yukon Southern Air Transport, if any, is questionable," continued Thompson. However, the company held mail contracts that had potential value. Thompson stated that Nesbitt, Thomson & Co., brokers in Montreal, were heavily interested in Yukon Southern, holding 70 percent of the stock as well as $50,000 of the bonds. Thompson estimated that $200,000 would buy this company. Acquisition of Yukon Southern was necessary because it was in a preferred position for any extension of the route to the Orient.

Brintnell was also anxious to acquire Yukon Southern. Thompson anticipated difficulty with Brintnell and believed that Canadian Airways would have better luck acquiring Mackenzie Air Services if it bought up the others first. "It would put him into a less desirable trading position if control of all other companies was acquired first. Brintnell is very aggressive, ruthless and will not be easy to deal with unless every possible step is taken to weaken his position. The cash required is $250,000. Mackenzie Air Services and Canadian Airways control about 25 percent of the total volume of traffic moving in the northern districts."

Hutchins felt the best tactic was for Canadian Airways and the CPR to acquire ownership or control of the principal companies in Canada as a first step. He wanted this done quickly to take advantage of the poor financial shape that most of the companies were in. Like Thompson, he wanted the government's blessing to offset any question of monopoly. His proposal to acquire control now meant that instead of requiring $1 million, Canadian Airways would require $2 million.

On September 6, 1939, Beatty wired Hutchins. "I talked with the Minister this morning and told him that CP has been asked to participate in the reorganization and that we would only do so if it had government's blessing. He said 'yes' and wanted us to consider a plan of zoning areas across Canada with operating individual companies confined to one or more zones. The government's sympathy is assured but we should not be stampeded into hasty and improvident action.

I think it is desirable that you and Thompson meet with [CPR treasurer] Unwin." Hutchins told Beatty that the CPR must decide quickly. "We will be bound to co-operate fully but before we do so it must be realized that the moment co-operation begins the opportunity to acquire competing companies on as favourable terms will doubtless be lost for all time."

Matters were progressing nicely when Canadian Airways received a notification in September that threatened to cripple its operations. DOT wanted to know how many pilots would be available immediately for air force service. This was bad news; a general response by pilots and mechanics from all companies would not only disrupt commercial air services overnight by grounding 80 to 90 percent of the aircraft but destroy Canadian Airways. Having the greatest numbers of personnel among the private carriers, Canadian Airways stood to lose the most, which would seriously affect its plans to acquire control of the other companies. Hutchins requested Beatty to offer Canadian Airways' services to the government but also to ask the government to show it some consideration by allowing it sufficient time to replace pilots and by withdrawing personnel from all companies on a pro rata basis.

Hutchins and Beatty continued their discussions. By December 1939 they had agreed that Canadian Airways and the CPR would work toward establishing a central traffic organization and forming separate companies to act as provincial subsidiaries of Canadian Airways. With the board's approval, Hutchins and Beatty reorganized Canadian Airways so that new capital ($600,000) could be brought in by the CPR. The refinanced Canadian Airways now was controlled with the Richardson estate holding 50.9 percent of the shares, the CPR 27.3 percent, the CNR 4.5 percent and "other" 17.3 percent.

The outlook for Canadian Airways was relatively good. At the end of 1939 it was still operating throughout Canada. The decline in traffic was not as great as it had been the year previous, although the announcement of war meant a drop in mining activity. In the Maritimes, Canadian Airways had started up another service in April 1939 between Moncton, Saint John and Halifax, hoping to counteract the growing influence of Maritime Airways and assure it of being awarded the Maritime feeder line contract from Moncton. The traffic in Ontario had picked up moderately. In Manitoba, Canadian Airways held all the major mining contracts and was doing the bulk of the business. Saskatchewan alone remained gloomy.

Traffic out of the Edmonton base decreased in 1939 but picked up in the Northwest Territories when Canadian Airways obtained the Eldorado Gold Mines contract at Great Bear Lake. The company also held the only two other contracts in this territory, for Northwest Territories Exploration (a subsidiary of the Mining Corporation) and Thompson-Lundmark. These contracts covered the whole of Canada and indirectly increased the company's business in other districts. Its position in British Columbia improved when it obtained the Vancouver–Victoria contract and the Vancouver–Zeballos contract on the west coast of Vancouver Island. Traffic around the Fort St. James base had also increased considerably. All in all, Canadian Airways was holding its own.

By December 1939 the northern air transport industry in Canada was concentrated in ten companies: Canadian Airways (operating across Canada); Quebec Airways (a Canadian Airways subsidiary operating in Quebec); Mackenzie Air Services (Mackenzie River region); Yukon Southern Air Transport (British Columbia and the Yukon); Prairie Airways (Regina–Prince Albert); Wings Limited (midwest region); Starratt Airways (midwest region); Arrow Airways (owned by the Richardson estate's Airways Limited and operating in northern Manitoba); Dominion Skyways (owned by Airways Limited and operating in northern Quebec), and General Airways (Quebec). Canadian Airways' principal competitors remained Mackenzie Air Services, Wings and Starratt. All these companies were in financial trouble.

Just before Richardson's death, on June 23, Thompson had prepared an abbreviated version of his brief on northern air transportation for submission to the Board of Transport Commissioners. This twenty-two-page document outlined the history and drastic state of affairs of the bush operators. Thompson fervently hoped that the board would take action; otherwise, a decade of pioneering was in danger of being wiped out. Thompson wrote eloquently:

> Northern air transport today is of such vital importance to the continued welfare and development of the dominion of Canada that it is just as much entitled to governmental support . . . Eldorado, God's

Lake and Sachigo are examples of producers which owe their discovery and preliminary development to air transport, and their production figures give us tangible evidence of the contribution of northern mining to the economy of Canada ... Every major nation in the world has found it expedient to its national economy to assist air transport. In Canada, however, no support has been forthcoming, until today the capital invested has been depleted to the vanishing point and the northern air transport industry faces bankruptcy.

Thompson was careful to recognize the value of the 1938 Transport Act but tactfully outlined its flaws. The board did not respond.

On December 11, 1939, Hutchins wrote Muriel Richardson that "I have only this afternoon reached an understanding with Sir Edward Beatty ... He prefers that the position of President be left vacant until later on and that he remain a Vice-President and that I be appointed Executive Vice-President, which, of course, should be satisfactory under the circumstances." He made arrangements for J.O. Apps and L.B. Unwin of the CPR and Tommy Thompson of Canadian Airways to be elected at the directors' meeting the following day, with the understanding that they would resign to make way for someone else if that was desired. The two new members of the executive committee were Hutchins and Unwin.

On March 19, 1940, Hutchins wrote H.P. Robinson of New Brunswick that the time had come to incorporate a new company in the Maritimes—Canadian Airways (Maritimes) Limited. This was to be a wholly owned subsidiary of Canadian Airways and would carry out all Canadian Airways operations in the Maritimes. The new company would have seven directors, three from Canadian Airways (Hutchins, Tackaberry and Thompson) and four from the Maritimes. Hutchins asked Robinson to be one of the directors and the president.

Even with this move, Canadian Airways' position was not secure. C.P. Edwards told Thompson in early October that although DOT considered the Maritimes as Canadian Airways' territory, there were areas in which Canadian Airways' interests might clash with those of TCA. Thompson suggested to Hutchins that "we must make haste slowly and close up the gaps between TCA and various points in the Maritimes before we start stretching out to the United States or Newfoundland." Clearly, Canadian Airways was not intimidated by TCA. It was not only working with the CPR to consolidate all the air operations, it also intended to expand into Newfoundland and the United States before TCA established connections there.

In 1940, war made further readjustments necessary. The three most important occurrences for Canadian Airways that year were the establishment of the training schools under the British Commonwealth Air Training Plan, its involvement with the Atlantic Ferry Organization and the government investigation into the problems of the northern air carriers.

In November 1939, Thompson had met with representatives from the British Air Ministry to discuss the possibility of Canadian Airways providing primary flying training. In a memo dated November 10, 1939, he had advised Tackaberry of the meeting: "I think we are assured of an active part in ab initio training of pilots for the Air Force." He was correct. Peter Troup and "Babe" Woollett of Dominion Skyways and Thompson, Tackaberry and Hutchins of Canadian Airways did the preliminary work in establishing the format for the commercial companies to manage the civilian end of the air force training schools. Dominion Skyways obtained the first contract under the British Commonwealth Air Training Plan, and its subsidiary, Dominion Skyways (Training) Limited, incorporated for the purpose with a capital of fifty thousand dollars, opened No. 1 Air Observers School at Malton, Ontario, on May 27, 1940. As Hutchins explained, "Canadian Airways and Dominion Skyways really set the pattern and led the pace in this work ... We showed the boys how to set up a school and how to run it after it was set up."

There was no question of situating any pilot training programs in Britain; it was far too vulnerable to enemy aggression. Canada, however, would be an ideal training ground for aircrew. The scheme that was developed was known as the British Commonwealth Air Training Plan. The federal government supplied all buildings (hangars, maintenance areas, stores, and so on) and left the responsibility for the provisioning and training of all operating personnel (connected with aircrew training and the running of the training school) to the particular civilian operator. The government asked the major bush operators to submit an estimate to DND. Richardson executives wanted to be involved. Hutchins, Peter Troup and "Babe" Woollett established the template. By this time, most of the companies were operating either under CPR or Canadian Airways, although all retained their identity and it was simply a matter of adding the word "Training" to their original names —for example, Canadian Airways (Training) Limited—for operating under the plan. The parent company borrowed the necessary money from the bank, and tendering was done on a competitive basis. The writer of "LAND HERE YOU BASTARDS," the irreverent "Babe" Woollett, described the difficulties.

> Well, going overnight from living out in the backwoods, only responsible for the profitable operation of a few small aircraft, to having to figure out the projected price of running an Air Force Station with so many, many imponderables, would usually be enough to make any full-blown chartered accountant jump off the top of a ten-story building! As for Peter and me, what did we know about the cost of feeding hundreds of airmen three times a day? (And we couldn't even get an accurate figure on how many hundreds!) Then too, what did we know about how expensive it would be to heat all these various buildings— sleeping quarters, offices, hangars? What about the charges for electricity? What would be the final number of staff we would require for the many different trades involved? What would be the total volume of gas and oil? How many hours would we be expected to fly? I hope the foregoing will give you a rough idea of how difficult it was to try to organize an intelligent bid. There were seemingly thousands of similar questions; and there also seemed to be thousands of possible answers. The only problem lay in finding the right ones ...

In spite of the difficulties, "Babe" Woollett and Peter Troup did an excellent job, and both of them received the Order of the British Empire for their work in the initial organization. (After the war, "Babe" accepted an offer "from that grand chap, 'Punch' Dickins, then [vice-] president and general manager of Canadian Pacific Airlines," to become superintendent of the Eastern Division of Canadian Pacific Airlines.) By October 1941, Canadian Airways was increasingly active in the British Commonwealth Air Training Plan through its subsidiaries, its aircraft and engine overhaul plant at Winnipeg (managed by Albert Hutt) and an aircraft overhaul plant at Cap-de-la-Madeleine.

In April 1940, Sir Edward Beatty consented to take over the presidency of Canadian Airways on a temporary basis and Charles Dunning joined the board of directors. Hutchins wrote C.D. Howe twice, once on March 25 and again on April 2, asking for an interview to discuss the situation in the North. Howe responded on April 13, "I have felt for some time that I should have a talk with you about the future of Canadian Airways and the direction in which privately owned aviation should develop." They met before the month was out.

Unfortunately for Canadian Airways, Howe saw "zoning" as the way to eliminate duplication and to produce more pilots and aircraft for the war effort. Hutchins demurred: "The total elimination of such duplication would at the most result in making available for other work say 15 or 20 pilots." He told Howe that it would be more effective to establish pilot training schools. Howe's response on May 25 was that "civil flying must take a back seat to war needs." Hutchins was annoyed that Howe was ignoring the fact that not all bush pilots would be suitable as air force pilots and that bush aircraft were totally unsuitable for the war effort. On June 1 he wrote Howe a lengthy letter about Canadian Airways' attempts to solve the problems of the northern operators, reiterating that zoning would not magically provide the needed pilots and aircraft, and he enclosed a memo from Thompson on the problems in the North.

Howe listened this time, and in June he asked the Board of Transport Commissioners to investigate the duplication of services among the bush companies. Sixteen air operators and eleven other "interested parties" presented written or oral briefs. Canadian Airways' brief was the most comprehensive. It described the evolution of the problems of the bush companies and made three main recommendations. First, all companies should cooperate in the formation of a central traffic organization so as to make joint use of buildings, docks and fuelling services and to stabilize the rates. Second, all licensed carriers should participate in any air mail service in the district in which they were licensed. Third, the Post Office should not be allowed to annul an air mail contract with only thirty days' notice; all aviation companies were entitled to some security of tenure.

The rest of the companies favoured some form of zoning to control the number of companies in each district. This solution had first been suggested by Leigh Brintnell a year earlier, and his criterion was to license the company that held the air mail contracts for that district. Since Mackenzie Air Services held most of the air mail contracts, zoning was most advantageous to it.

The board submitted its fifty-page report to Howe on August 2. It advised against nationalizing the northern air carriers and made the extreme recommendation to "zone" Canada in order to solve the problems of the bush companies. The board suggested that the territory from Quebec to the Pacific, including the Yukon, be divided into zones; that as a general policy only one carrier be permitted to operate in each zone or over each licensed route; and that the "grandfather rights," secured in the Transport Act of 1938, be abolished.

Like the private companies, the board did not know who to license in each zone. This uncertainty was reflected in the report, for the board did not specify which operator should be licensed for each zone, nor did it clearly define the basis on which such a decision should be made. This vagueness as to how the licensing was to be carried out was probably one of the reasons why the government did not implement any zoning action. The CPR's proposal to buy up the smaller companies and thus eliminate much of the duplication of services and competition also militated against any zoning action. Perhaps the most compelling reason against zoning was that officials saw it as facilitating Canadian Airways and the CPR's attempt to gain control of the northern companies, to link them up and eventually put together an airline better placed than TCA.

Zoning would have had serious effects on Canadian Airways. The company was in a different position from the others because it operated in practically all areas of Canada, and its investment in each district was equal to or greater than that of any of the other companies. Hutchins told Beatty that Canadian Airways would lose almost 70 percent of its licensed routes.

The board's proposed action would have involved considerable amendment to the Transport Act. Because the board did not have the authority to carry out the amendments, it also recommended that the necessary additional powers to do so be given to it. Despite arguments from Thompson, Hutchins, Beatty and Dunning, Howe approved the board's recommendations and its request that they be implemented under the War Measures Act. Howe privately sent a copy to Beatty for his comments. Beatty sent it to Hutchins, who responded to Beatty on October 25, 1940, with a lengthy memorandum regarding the whole report. Hutchins noted the importance Howe and the board attached to zoning as a way of providing pilots and aircraft for the war effort. He asked Beatty to make it clear to Howe that only specially established pilot training schools would produce the necessary pilots.

Beatty wrote confidentially to Howe and asked for an opportunity to speak with him before any action was taken by the government. Howe agreed and saw Beatty on November 5, at which time Beatty explained the CPR and Canadian Airways' plans to amalgamate the bush companies. Howe said he was in favour of amalgamation and was prepared to give Beatty reasonable time to bring this about. Howe told J.A. Cross, chief commissioner of the Board of Transport Commissioners, that Beatty was now handling the Richardson interests in Canadian Airways. He suggested that Cross check with Beatty before taking any action on zoning, because the position of the bush companies was likely to change.

With the axe of government intervention hanging over their heads, Beatty pushed Brintnell to start cooperating and on November 12 was successful in making arrangements to purchase a controlling interest in Mackenzie Air Services. As Hutchins said in a memo to Mrs. Richardson on November 13, "This is the first purchase in the plan which we have been working on for over a year, and as we looked upon Brintnell as being the 'hardest nut to crack' I am naturally very pleased with this definite forward step ... I hope to conclude all these negotiations so that there will be no change in my original plans, as previously discussed with you, whereby the money to purchase these companies, or a controlling interest in them, will be subscribed by the CPR who will control Airways Limited while the Richardson interests will control Canadian Airways Limited."

By January 1941 matters seemed to be progressing as planned, and Hutchins wrote, "I hope that we will finally be able to knit the whole into a profitable operation." He outlined his plan of action, the bottom line being an amalgamation of all Canadian air transport companies either into one or two companies, "which would be controlled by friendly interests." There was no indication that Muriel Richardson was considering selling the Richardson estate's interests in aviation. If there had been, Hutchins would certainly not have been doing all of the CPR's negotiations. Cooperation between the two companies was the operative word.

In December 1940, on behalf of the CPR, Hutchins had conducted negotiations to buy out Ginger Coote Airways. The sale was finalized on February 1, 1941, and cost the CPR $42,943. Hutchins made arrangements for Canadian Airways, Yukon Southern Air Transport and Ginger Coote Airways to pool their operations, with Canadian Airways in control. By February all operations on the Pacific coast were pooled under Canadian Airways management. The result, as Thompson stated at Canadian Airways' annual meeting in April, was a substantial increase in revenue per mile flown because there were fewer aircraft and reduced overhead.

In April, Hutchins acquired control, on behalf of the CPR, of Yukon Southern. Brintnell had agreed to pooling, under a committee called United Air Services Ltd., which was made up of Brintnell as manager, along with Thompson, Hutchins, MacDougall and W.M. Neal of the CPR. Hutchins arranged pooling with Mackenzie Air Services in May and with Starratt and Wings in December 1941.

While the Richardson interests and the CPR were happy, the Post Office was not. Officials realized that with the CPR and Canadian Airways together controlling outright all northern air transport, the Post Office could no longer play off one against the other in driving down mail rates. They also believed that Canadian Airways and the CPR would establish a competing airway against TCA. "I think," said Thompson to Hutchins in early April, "this is possibly in the back of their minds in trying to sabotage our combined efforts in bringing order out of chaos in the aviation industry."

The problem of transporting the necessary military aircraft from Canadian and American factories to Britain became even more urgent once Germany overran Belgium and France. The usual method, by ship, was too slow, and besides, there was a shortage of cargo space. Flying the aircraft to Britain was the obvious answer. A Canadian, Maxwell

Aitken, now Lord Beaverbrook and minister of aircraft production under Prime Minister Winston Churchill since May 1940, suggested an Atlantic air ferry service. Characteristically, he did not bother to go through the usual government channels but simply contacted his good friend Sir Edward Beatty and asked him if he were interested. Beatty, who had earlier offered the services of the CPR and Canadian Airways to the government, was happy to oblige.

On July 8, 1940, Morris Wilson, representative in Canada and the United States of the British Ministry of Aircraft Production, wrote Beatty, thanking him for his offer to ferry aircraft. On August 16, Beaverbrook and the CPR came to an agreement. The CPR Air Services Department was quickly formed "for the purpose of manning and dispatching aircraft on account of the Minister [of Aircraft Production] from North America to the British Isles and elsewhere as may be agreed upon hereunder." Carl Christie, in his book *Ocean Bridge,* states that there was no formal correspondence between the British and Canadian governments, and the Canadian Airways papers verify this. The service was considered outside of government control. Beatty was chairman of the Air Services Department; George Woods-Humphrey, former general manager of Imperial Airways and long-time friend of Beatty's, was vice-chairman; and Lieutenant Colonel W.B. Burchall of the British air ministry was manager.

Aircraft bought by the British were delivered to St. Hubert airport in Montreal, and the CPR Air Services Department supplied the pilots to fly the bombers across the Atlantic. The first flight took place on November 11, 1940, when seven bombers took off from Gander airport and arrived in England some ten hours later.

A variety of problems, however, plagued the novel Atlantic ferrying service, and Burchall and Woods-Humphrey resigned before the year was out. Beatty needed a transportation executive and asked Hutchins of Canadian Airways for Tommy Thompson. Hutchins would not release Thompson but offered "Punch" Dickins, general superintendent of Canadian Airways, a man of outstanding ability and excellent management skills. He was one of Canada's best-known pilots and was a pioneer in many areas. Dickins had been awarded the Order of the British Empire in 1936 for his service to Canada and was the logical choice to carry out a pioneering air service across the Atlantic. The CPR appointed Dickins operations manager of the fabled wartime Atlantic ferry service.

Unfortunately, Beatty was forced to resign as chairman of the ferry service after becoming seriously ill and was replaced by Morris Wilson. The ferry service, while delivering necessary aircraft, was having growing pains. Totally unrelated to the task at hand was government's worry of the increasing control that the CPR and Canadian Airways were gaining by flying the Atlantic and the northwest. The Alaska Highway, the Northwest Staging Route (the joint defence air route), oil wells, pipeline projects, and radium and mercury mines were all developed by pilots flying under the banner of either Canadian Airways or the CPR.

Government correspondence in this period indicates its concern. On January 17, 1941, E.E. Fairweather, chief counsel for TCA, wrote C.P. Edwards, director of air services, DOT, that he was worried about the CPR's expansion in air services. Edwards replied on January 20 saying that the situation was "well under control" and "there [was] no occasion for alarm but rather gratification that at last a strong stabilizing influence has been brought into the Northern operations." Edwards reminded Fairweather that control of all licences and routes remained with the Board of Transport Commissioners and DOT, that questions of policy remained with the government and "as no company can operate without a license, no competitor with Trans-Canada Air Lines need be feared without government sanction."

Fairweather had cause for worry. If the CPR gained control of most of the private lines in Canada, with a few extensions and connections it would have a transcontinental route in competition with TCA and would be in a better position to take advantage of future developments in international air routes. In TCA's files there is correspondence among TCA officials about "Punch" Dickins and the Atlantic ferry service and its possible impact on TCA. A worried Ted Larson, general superintendent of TCA, wrote to TCA's president on August 19, 1941, "There are dangers of TCA's retrenchment and outside airlines stepping in." On December 31, he wrote Herb Symington, "You will recall that the Vancouver–Victoria service was originally considered as being a portion of the overall TCA set-up. The service has never been performed by TCA but was sublet by them to Canadian Airways, payment being made to the Trans-Canada Air Lines who in turn made the necessary financial adjustments with Canadian Airways. At a later date the arrangements were changed so that financial handlings were effected directly between the Post Office and Canadian Airways ... Canadian Airways now being secured by the CPR."

At first the ferry service was called the Canadian Pacific Air Services Department because the CPR supplied all the facilities. This name proved to be a thorn to government officials, and the group soon called itself Atlantic Ferry Organization (ATFERO). The necessity for prompt delivery of aircraft, which were being turned out faster and faster as factories perfected their techniques, took the service out of the hands of civilians and handed it over to the military. Undoubtedly TCA feared that it might lose out to the CPR as the trans-Atlantic operator after the war and was pleased when the RAF took over the service.

ATFERO became Ferry Command on July 20, 1941, and transferred over about one thousand personnel. A number of Canadian Airways people remained on loan to the new military organization, mainly in administrative positions. "Punch" Dickins survived the transition from civilian to military control. The immediate outcome of the creation of Ferry Command was, of course, an increase in the number of the aircrew and, in time, a remarkably efficient ferrying organization.

In that year the unexpected happened. In March 1941, the government reneged on the Maritimes air mail contract. It was 1932 all over again. Apparently Halifax's pride had been hurt by the fact that TCA operated into Moncton and not Halifax, and in April 1940 Halifax began exerting pressure on the government to have TCA extend its services to Halifax. Worried, Tommy Thompson contacted C.P. Edwards of DOT, who told him not to be concerned because DOT considered the Maritimes as Canadian Airways' territory. The Post Office may have been aware of Halifax's discontent, for it did not sign the air mail contract with Canadian Airways until August 1940. But the writing was on the wall. In January 1941, Herring informed Thompson that Canadian Airways would lose the Moncton–Halifax service because TCA intended to fly into Halifax. Thompson wrote Hutchins on January 8: "Canadian Airways should not consider any extension in the Maritimes as long as the future of the operations is dependent on the whims of Ottawa people who are so amenable to political pressure."

The axe fell on March 14. With three years remaining on the contract, the acting postmaster general officially told Hutchins that he was cancelling Canadian Airways' Moncton–Halifax contract. Hutchins replied immediately. "The cancellation covers that part of the service between Moncton and Halifax, which represents about 35 percent of the flying of the contract. You state your action has been taken by virtue of a clause in the contract which provides that the Postmaster General reserves the right to annul the agreement on 30 days written notice to the contractor if in his opinion the public interest shall require it. We have understood our service has been satisfactory. We are therefore at a loss to understand that public interest requires cancellation."

Because the cancellation involved such a large percentage of Canadian Airways' revenue, Hutchins told the Post Office that the airline was no longer willing to continue the remainder of the service provided for in the contract and wished to be relieved of the entire contract. He also asked to be relieved of the Charlottetown–Magdalen Islands contract. As in the 1932 cancellation, Canadian Airways found itself up against political pressure. Once again the arbitrary action of the Post Office, no doubt pressured by the government, had undermined Canadian Airways' finances. As well as losing a third of its revenue, it was also out approximately $200,000 on its purchase of two twin-engine Beechcraft to provide the service.

P.T. Coolican said he could not understand why Canadian Airways was upset. Now the acting deputy postmaster general, he took the offensive in his letter to Hutchins on March 18, 1941. "I regret the attitude taken in your letter of the 15th notifying the Post Office of your intention to discontinue the service of Moncton to Charlottetown and Moncton to St. John. I do not know what is meant by compensation because of the Trans-Canada Air Lines taking over the section Moncton to Halifax."

Hutchins responded on March 20 that it was only fair for the Post Office to increase the rate of compensation on what was left of the contract or to make some arrangement on another part of the service to help cover Canadian Airways' loss of revenue. "With the cancellation of the Moncton to Halifax run the potential possibility of building up traffic has been reduced to an absurdity." Coolican disagreed and told Hutchins on March 22 that Canadian Airways was relieved of the entire contract as of April 15. By this action, any chance of international connections in the Maritimes was gone. The government had once again clipped Canadian Airways' wings.

Unlike Richardson, Hutchins went on the offensive. On March 28, he demanded to know why Canadian Airways' service had been cancelled. "I want you to clarify why our service was terminated, why 'public interest' demanded the transfer to TCA. We feel the Company's name has been jeopardized." Coolican replied on April 1, "The question of efficient operation of service was not a determining factor." Canadian Airways' assessment of Coolican's explanation was that the government found it politically expedient to bow to Halifax and run a service that it could afford neither in terms of cost nor in availability of aircraft and personnel. The result was that Canadian Airways, which had prior rights and a four-year contract, was forced out of the Maritimes by TCA.

George Walker, of the CPR's legal department, advised Hutchins that TCA had no licence between Moncton and Halifax and that it intended to exempt itself from the necessity of securing a licence by order in council. "This was an unconscionable thing for the government to do," he said. He thought that the Board of Transport Commissioners might be induced to protest, but he was wrong. The board turned its collective head away.

This event may have been the turning point for Muriel Richardson and her executive officials. They saw TCA's actions as precedent-setting —no contract was safe from the government's or TCA's desires. Canadian Airways viewed the whole affair as further proof of the "arbitrary and unfair" actions of the Post Office. "Curiously enough, [a member] of the Transport Board said almost jokingly that one way to stir up trouble would be to prosecute TCA for operating without a licence," revealed lawyer H.A. Aylen. But the board did not have the nerve to take the appropriate action. Hutchins, now resigned to fate, replied that Canadian Airways would not do anything against TCA unless the CPR advised it otherwise. A few days later, Aylen told Hutchins that Kirk had told him that DOT "seems to consider that TCA can be permitted to do anything." With that piece of information, Aylen and Hutchins agreed that the only effective protest would be one from Sir Edward Beatty directly to Howe.

"Canadian Airways End Maritime Service with Splendid Record," the *Moncton Daily Times* announced on April 12, 1941. "Canadian Airways, which pioneered air mail and passenger transportation service, first of its kind in the Maritimes, ended 13 years of unbroken service in the Maritimes ..." The *Financial Post* added, on April 19, "Canadian Airways served fine but Halifax had protested long and loudly because TCA terminated at Moncton. Its prestige was involved! Seemingly it was politically expedient to meet this demand and the air mail contract was transferred to TCA. The economics of the move do not seem to have influenced the Postmaster General's decision ... The circumstances forcing Canadian Airways out merit consideration."

As soon as TCA had secured the Maritimes, it immediately began a service from Moncton to Newfoundland—effectively cutting off Canadian Airways' plans of initiating the service. Most newspapers across Canada were quick to notice the significance of TCA's move. The *Vancouver Sun*, on June 13, noted that "TCA's venture into the New-foundland service comes as a surprise especially since the CPR, now extensively interested in commercial air transport, has under contract numerous pilots flying bombers across the Atlantic with which to share in the trans-Atlantic air business as part of an all-red route around the world, after the war. While TCA's action will not force CPR completely out of the picture, it does not help its position."

Ironically, Halifax was unhappy with TCA's service and wanted Canadian Airways back. However, this involved too much political manoeuvring for Thompson's liking. Coolican now approached H.S. Jones, a long-time Canadian Airways pilot in the area, and said that if Canadian Airways would hook up with Maritime Airways and "stay in the background, because we are not in favour with the Post Office in Ottawa, then we could get everything we wanted; also we could have a water-tight contract. What are your thoughts on that?" Jones asked of Thompson on August 7, 1941.

Hutchins and Thompson and Unwin of the CPR mulled the request over. The situation was complex. It was not just the Maritimes contract that was at stake; the whole Atlantic flying operation and the route to the Orient hung in the balance. Thompson had already anticipated that the CPR would lose the Atlantic ferry service, and he saw the strong arm of Howe in other places as well, doing his best to curtail the CPR.

Hutchins and Tackaberry were prepared to re-enter the Maritimes, but Thompson was not. His main objection was that Canadian Airways would never receive a guaranteed air mail contract; it was too easy for the government to step in and cancel "in the public's interest." Further proof that the government could run roughshod over the private operators and do what it wished came when TCA did what the CPR had predicted: it began operating between Moncton and Halifax without a licence. Thompson felt they should not risk Canadian Airways' re-entry into the Maritimes until the government provided better security for private companies. Indeed, it appeared that all of Canadian Airways' future operations would be in jeopardy until the government settled on a policy of development for TCA. Thompson's opinion prevailed.

TCA was not the only company watching the action between itself and Canadian Airways. In the West, Northwest Airlines, Mid-Continental Airlines and Western Air Express were all waiting on the sidelines to leap into action on the route through Canada to Alaska. Croil Hunter of Northwest Airlines wrote to Hutchins in late August, "We have been watching with considerable interest the CPR developments and would not be a bit surprised if they have a route to the Orient in mind."

It is difficult to judge when and why there was a change of attitude on the part of the Richardson executives regarding their continued participation in airway affairs. The Maritimes incident and the CPR's loss of the Atlantic ferry service may have influenced Muriel Richardson's decision to sell. Canadian Airways' future was too closely tied to that of TCA's to suit the Richardson people; they preferred to control their own destiny. Despite the creation of TCA, DOT and the Board of Transport Commissioners, the government still had no domestic air services policy. Political expediency, rather than a set of guidelines, was allowed to define its actions. By October 1941, it was clear that Canadian Airways and the Richardson executives would have to do some serious thinking about the company's future. Little did anyone know that the aviation picture was in for a major shakeup.

CHAPTER FOURTEEN

An Era Ended

I N OCTOBER 1941, Muriel Richardson gave the signal to sell the Richardson estate's interests in the airways holdings. Undoubtedly it was a difficult decision for her to make, knowing she was abandoning her husband's plan to build an airline that would ultimately span the globe. Muriel Richardson believed in her husband's aims for airway development, but the continual frustration of political interference meant that Canadian Airways had become an albatross around her neck. She was tired of fighting the whole aviation question. Muriel Richardson had other responsibilities to consider. There was a war on; she had a family to raise and James Richardson & Sons, Limited, to run. And sitting in the wings was (she presumed) a friendly and compatible buyer, which she assumed would carry out her husband's goals. After all, Sir Edward Beatty and the CPR had been with Canadian Airways from the start.

An unsigned three-page memo, written by G.W. Hutchins and dated October 14, 1941, laid out the estimated value of the Richardson airways companies. It was on these evaluations that Hutchins quietly initiated sale discussions with the CPR. There was no fanfare. The estimated value of the Richardson shares in all three companies was pegged at $813,000, although the book value plus 30 percent was shown as $619,000. Hutchins believed other considerations needed to be factored in. He wrote:

> The CPR paid a premium of 20% to Starratt and if we added the same rate the Richardson shares would be worth approximately one million dollars (actually $975,600.00). We would certainly expect more favourable treatment from the CPR than others in view of the fact that
>
> 1) The late Mr. James A. Richardson was a pioneer and in reality built the present picture up and protected it during his lifetime.
> 2) The Richardsons have over two million dollars in cash in airways already. [The amount was in fact closer to three million dollars.]
>   The price of $1¼ million asked is only 62% of the original cash invested.
>
> Mrs. Richardson had $1½ million in mind as a fair price and I had difficulty in getting her to come down to $1¼ million.

Hutchins handled the negotiations with L.B. Unwin, CPR's treasurer. Hutchins's memos, the first written on October 22 in Montreal, give an inside account of these transactions.

> I could see from the outset that the asking price of $1¼ million rather took Mr. Unwin's breath away and he immediately compared it to the book value of Canadian Airways shares at $3.45 per share, and also to the price of $4.00 per share which was the price at which the CPR and the Richardson interests took shares when the company was partially re-organized in 1939 . . .
>
> It was quite apparent to me that Mr. Unwin was not prepared even to submit the price of $1¼ million and he said that before he could go to those who would finally decide on the matter he would have to have some figure which he could properly recommend, and he thought that if the figure I mentioned was so far in excess of what he could recommend he was at a loss to know just how to pursue the matter further . . .
>
> After lunch I left Mr. Unwin and his last remark was that he

would call me on the telephone in the morning and probably have another chat.

Muriel Richardson arrived in Montreal on the evening of October 22, and she and Hutchins discussed the situation. Hutchins then met again with Unwin, who stated that he was prepared to recommend $600,000 for the Richardson stock in Canadian Airways, Dominion Skyways and Arrow Airways, and that was as high as he would go. Hutchins and Mrs. Richardson decided that they would only accept $900,000 and "that we should stand on that price and not do any more trading either up or down." Hutchins reminded Mrs. Richardson that Unwin had not offered $600,000 but had said only that he would recommend it to his people.

Muriel Richardson proved to be a shrewd negotiator. She told Hutchins not to discuss the matter with Unwin the next day but to give the excuse that she wanted time to think the matter over. She realized that they were at a disadvantage in dealing with the CPR's treasurer, not someone that she or her husband had known personally. Regretfully, Sir Edward Beatty, who had suffered a massive stroke while still president, was not active in the discussions. Mrs. Richardson believed they would get further if they met with D'Alton Coleman, vice-president of the CPR, because he would take a broader view of the whole aviation picture than would an accountant, who would be looking only at the bottom line.

Nevertheless, Hutchins had another talk with Unwin on October 23. "He said that all he would be prepared to recommend to his principals would be $600,000 for 'the works' . . . I told him that if I were in his shoes I'd have no hesitation in recommending it either, but that as far as I was concerned I thought it was ridiculous, and would not consider going back to Mrs. Richardson with it."

Gordon Lawson contacted Hutchins on October 25 to say that he had received a call from Muriel Richardson that morning. "We all agreed that his [Unwin's] offer is ridiculous. At the same time I hardly think we could have expected him to take the broad view which must be taken if a price approximating our asking price, or even around $1,000,000, can be recommended."

Indignant at the low offer, on October 25 Muriel Richardson told

Hutchins to tell Unwin that "if that was all they had to offer, the figure was so low and ridiculous there was no use discussing it any further, and that we had better turn our attention to working out our problems with regard to operating." She was prepared to see both Unwin and Coleman and tell them that she was quite willing to accept any reasonable offer for the Richardson interest in the airways. However, she would also tell them that their offer was so low that it was ridiculous, and she would not consider it; and as she still intended to dispose of her interests in Canadian Airways, she would look elsewhere for a buyer.

Hutchins and Lawson discussed the matter and felt that if a figure could not be agreed upon, the discussion should turn to pooling of services and other agreements for handling the various interests. Lawson recognized only too well that "Canadian Airways was in fact a sitting duck for the CPR. After CPR bought up all the other northern companies, there was nowhere where Canadian Airways could sell to and Canadian Airways was forced to negotiate and sell to the CPR."

Obviously concerned that the CPR might call Muriel Richardson's bluff, the diplomatic Lawson suggested to her on October 25 that perhaps they should not consider Unwin's views as representing the official CPR attitude. "If his training has been in the Treasury Department of the CPR he is doubtless trying to make as good a deal as he can on a cold-blooded dollar and cent basis." Hutchins suggested that they try to see Coleman and, if possible, Sir Edward Beatty in order to obtain an idea of their assumptions before looking for another purchaser.

Hutchins wrote, "My whole idea is that I do not think we should let Mr. Unwin put us off our stride this early in negotiations, because, after all, we never did count on his being a card in our hands." Lawson felt it would be best to get the Richardson viewpoint across to senior CPR executives and to keep Muriel Richardson as a trump card. Clearly he wanted to reserve her influence until she could discuss the matter with either Coleman or Beatty.

Hutchins's memo, dated October 27 and written in Montreal, revealed that the Richardson team was attempting to take the upper hand in negotiations. In no uncertain terms, Hutchins told Unwin that morning that it would be better to discuss ways of putting their services together in a way that would be mutually beneficial. He also told Unwin that both he and Mrs. Richardson thought it was unfortunate that they had not been able to discuss matters with either Beatty or Coleman. Unwin replied that he had already discussed the matter with Beatty, who felt that the price of $600,000 "was actually in excess of what Sir Edward had felt was equitable under the circumstances." Hutchins noted, "I told him that I scarcely credited this and that in any event I would like to have a chat with him or with Mr. Coleman, if Sir Edward was not available." Unwin backed down and said that he would take back the figure of $1¼ million. Hutchins then stated that he was prepared to return to Mrs. Richardson with a figure halfway between $600,000 and the $1¼ million. Their discussion then moved to operations, specifically the Mackenzie River situation, and Hutchins told Unwin that Brintnell was not capable of managing United Air Services but would be better at handling the overhaul depot.

Hutchins phoned Muriel Richardson in Kingston to brief her. He reminded her that there was likely no one in Canada who would be prepared to take over Canadian Airways as a whole, that only American companies were interested. "Mrs. Richardson said that of course the last thing she wanted to do was to sell out to any Americans." Hutchins, feeling a little more optimistic, said that he would not be surprised if Unwin called him back. He was correct. Unwin contacted him on October 28 and told him that he thought amalgamation was the most suitable. Hutchins was not happy, believing this was only an extension of the agreement they already had in the Mackenzie River district, but he was prepared to work out the details.

In an effort to sway Unwin's thinking, Hutchins observed that the CPR should not let a matter of a couple of hundred thousand dollars stand in the way of the CPR's having control of all of the northern air operations. "I have had a long talk with Neal and Unwin regarding unification of services and found them both not receptive to the idea of a complete unification. The upshot of these talks is that when we return to Winnipeg Neal is going to talk to Wings and Starratt and that we are to come in and see if we can reach some working agreement in the Mid-West."

Hutchins phoned Muriel Richardson on October 29. "Negotiations are off but the door is open. Unwin still thinks the offer he has made is liberal and I told him I disagreed with him but was prepared to go back to you with a figure of 900M." On November 21 Lawson suggested that they stay in the ground transportation business and strengthen their position by taking over the Starratt ground organization and combining it with Patricia Transportation (acquired by the Richardson interests in 1936). This would give them a monopoly of the ground transportation in the Patricia area. With this in mind, Hutchins and Lawson recommended a counter-offer of $750,000 and Starratt's ground and water equipment, which they thought would be worth $150,000.

Although Sir Edward Beatty was disabled by a stroke, Hutchins wrote a letter to him on November 19, telling him that he did not believe the Richardson interests were being fairly dealt with. "I would like to see you personally." Disturbed by CPR's attitude, Muriel Richardson also contacted Beatty suggesting a way out of the impasse— she would take $750,000 cash, plus Starratt's ground and water equipment, which her people thought was worth $150,000. Sir Edward Beatty responded to her on November 24, "In view of your letter I think we should make another attempt to find a place at which we may reach an agreement."

On November 27, Muriel Richardson saw Sir Edward at his office and outlined in detail the plan she had in mind: that the CPR take over the Richardson interest in the four air transportation companies— Canadian Airways, Arrow Airways, Dominion Skyways and Quebec Airways—and pay for it by turning over to her all the Starratt ground and water assets, together with $750,000 in cash. Beatty was receptive to the proposal, even going so far as to ask her, "Is this going to be alright for you?" When assured by her that it was satisfactory, Beatty said he would be glad to recommend the proposal at the next board meeting on December 9. Muriel Richardson also wanted protection for the staff in all the companies, which Beatty agreed to. He asked her to see Mr. Unwin the next day.

When Muriel Richardson spoke with Unwin he, characteristically, said that the value of the Starratt equipment (the CPR's valuation of $188,000) should be deducted from the $900,000 and the cash consideration set at $712,000, not $750,0000. She replied in no uncertain terms that this was not what she and Sir Edward had agreed to the previous day and that the cash consideration must be $750,000. Realizing that Muriel Richardson was no pushover, Unwin agreed.

Muriel Richardson called Hutchins on November 28 and told him that the deal had gone through on the basis of $750,000 cash, plus all Starratt ground and water equipment and assets, which were finally valued at $188,063, for a total of $938,063. She asked him to advise Neal but to otherwise keep the deal quiet, as it was subject to ratification by the CPR directors on December 9. On that day, Beatty wrote Muriel Richardson, confirming the acceptance by the directors of the CPR of her offer to turn over her holdings in the four air transportation companies "for the sum of $750,000 and the water and ground transport of Starratt Airways and Transportation Limited." She acknowledged his letter on December 10 and said she had asked Hutchins to confer with Unwin regarding the transfer of her interests, as requested by Sir Edward.

The physical assets covered in the agreement were turned over by both parties within a few weeks after December 9, 1941, but the Richardson estate did not receive the bill of sale for Starratt's ground and water assets. The stumbling block was the $188,000 figure. After a number of phone calls, Muriel Richardson again used her personal influence and friendship to close the deal. This time, she wrote to D'Alton Coleman, now president of CPR, on August 26, 1942. (Beatty never regained his strength from his stroke and died in 1943.) Her letter combined friendliness with steely resolution:

> Dear D'Alton:
> I regret the necessity of writing you on a contentious matter but there seems to be no alternative course . . . This refusal to give us an acceptable Bill of Sale is more than I can bear in silence.
>
> I am sorry to write you personally but I do resent such treatment and feel it is imperative to take the matter to the highest court, which is yourself . . . The matter has dragged on so long now that an earlier settlement would be much more acceptable.
> With warm personal regards,
> Yours sincerely,
> *M. S. Richardson*

Her letter succeeded. A Mr. Flintoft, writing on behalf of Coleman, replied on September 9 on the "desirability of maintaining the most harmonious relations between you and the Company." Hutchins saw the problem as a tax matter; the CPR would pay a large tax if the value were $188,000. Muriel Richardson, however, was not concerned with the CPR's tax problems. To Hutchins she wrote:

> The only "chip on my shoulder" is placed there for Mr. Unwin's benefit. As far as Mr. Coleman, Mr. Neal, the CPR generally and, of course, Sir Edward are concerned, I have nothing but the friendliest feelings. I do not propose to have any conversation with Mr. Unwin. If it is suggested, I shall refuse.
>
> I know that if he [Sir Edward Beatty] had been in full mental vigor, we would have received more than we did for Canadian Airways, and finally, I believe, my interview with Sir Edward was just a "plant" arranged by Mr. Unwin to get me to Montreal because he thought, once there, I could be chiselled down by him to his price. When the interview turned out to be different than he expected and the chiselling failed, he made a show of acceptance and then stooped to trickery on the Bill of Sale.
>
> I see no reason whatever for compromise and am not, at present, in the mood to forfeit one dollar of what is rightfully ours. If you know any formidable reasons why we should accept anything less than $188,000, I will be glad to have them. Otherwise, I shall certainly stand out for all—according to the agreement.

Muriel Richardson was one determined woman. Hutchins also was prepared to play hardball. He replied to Mrs. Richardson on September 16, "Our thoughts were that in the event the CPR refuse to show the $188,000 in the Bill of Sale, we would take a Bill of Sale for the nominal sum of $1.00 and exhibit to the Tax Department our files showing that the CPR represented these assets to be worth $188,000 and this could be supported by your representations concerning the deal."

The CPR and the Richardson interests agreed that "it would be as well not to mention from whom they had acquired control of these air companies, and not to mention the amount ... He [Unwin] said we could be assured that whatever was given out would be in keeping with the spirit of the arrangement." The CPR asked Hutchins to continue as an executive officer of Canadian Airways, Quebec Airways, Arrow Airways, Dominion Skyways and their various subsidiaries until they picked up the threads of executive control, and it named "Punch"

Dickins assistant to the president and Grant McConachie assistant to the vice-president.

Hutchins was pleased with the deal and said so to Mrs. Richardson on November 29. "The more I consider the deal, the better I am satisfied that it is a good one for you, and I am very glad that you have been able to conclude it so well. I hope the CPR Board agree." On December 17, 1941, Muriel Richardson confirmed the sale to Tommy Thompson. Like her husband, she ensured that Canadian Airways' personnel were looked after. It was one of the conditions she negotiated. Her letter to Thompson set the tone of the news announcements and outlined the rationale of the sale.

> The advantages of this arrangement [the CPR purchases of the Richardson estate interests in aviation] are so obvious and are such a fulfilment of all that my husband aimed to accomplish that I felt I had no alternative but to accept their offer. My action also implements an understanding entered upon many years ago between my husband and Sir Edward Beatty, when they agreed that whenever the Canadian Pacific Railway Company decided to enter extensively into the field of air transport, Canadian Airways would be available as one medium whereby this entry might be made.
>
> That, briefly, is my reason for selling; I believe my action follows along logical, preconceived lines and assures the continuance of strong and capable ownership for commercial aviation in Canada.
>
> Notwithstanding all this, the decision has caused me real regret. I shall never forget my husband's interest in the opening up of Canada's northland by the pioneer flights of Western Canada Airways' pilots nor later his pride in the achievements of the personnel of Canadian Airways, Arrow Airways and Dominion Skyways. His disappointments were many—as you know—but they were never caused by the failure of anyone within the organization . . .
>
> The Canadian Pacific Railway Company has given me assurance that our entire staff will be taken over by them and assimilated as rapidly as possible with due regard to their various capabilities and length of service. In any amalgamation of this nature there is almost certain to be a period of transition when patience, loyalty and willingness on the part of the staff will have a considerable effect on

future success or failure. Knowing the splendid record of your staff in the past, I have been able to assure the Canadian Pacific Railway Company of the fullest co-operation of every member.

Taking her letter as his cue, Thompson sent a two-page memo with the letter attached to all staff regarding the change in control of Canadian Airways.

I will not attempt to hide my personal regret at the severance of our close association with the Richardson organization, of which we have been a member for so long ...

We are indeed fortunate, and I feel it is very fitting, that the control of Canadian Airways Limited should have passed to that great pioneer of ground transport in Canada, the Canadian Pacific Railway, thereby ensuring the continued welfare of the Air Transport Industry which we have been privileged to help in developing, and in which Mr. Richardson was so closely interested.

With any such change of control there are, of necessity, many rumours and counter-rumours which cannot help but be disconcerting. I would, however, ask you to pay no attention to any such rumours, and to rest assured that your individual interests will not be jeopardized through this change in control.

In conclusion, I would like to thank you all very sincerely for your splendid loyalty to Canadian Airways Limited, and, if I may say so, to me personally, as General Manager. Without your individual efforts and loyalty which have always been given so freely and willingly, the enviable reputation enjoyed by Canadian Airways Limited would not have been possible. I feel sure that the new owners can count on your continued loyal support, thereby ensuring its success.

All of the CPR's newly acquired companies continued to operate under their own names and were controlled by a department of the CPR called Canadian Pacific Air Services. The practice of taking over the smaller companies, begun by Canadian Airways, was concluded by the CPR, and the pattern of amalgamation that had begun in 1939 was now complete. The sale brought to a close more than a decade of pioneering by Canadian Airways. An era had ended.

The CPR bought more than the physical assets of Canadian Airways, Quebec Airways, Dominion Skyways and Arrow Airways. It acquired control of the northern operations in Canada and the possibility of tying the separate routes of all its component companies into an integrated whole. If this were accomplished, the CPR would have a monopoly of the privately owned air services and a transcontinental line in competition with TCA. In many respects, it would be a more profitable line, because (as TCA had realized a year earlier) it would link with the feeders from the North and the all-important route to the Orient.

On January 18, 1941, a very worried member of Parliament, W.P. Mulock, had written the prime minister, enclosing a letter from the postmaster general that pointed out that nearly all the private airlines in Canada "are being absorbed or controlled by Canadian Airways which in turn is controlled by CPR. A map shows that with a few extensions ... the effect of such a development would be to squeeze TCA out of profitable through traffic and demonstrate that public ownership is a failure. This would discredit the present government."

Mulock also wrote to C.D. Howe, on January 29, expressing the same fear of the CPR overtaking TCA. Howe arrogantly replied on January 31, "I see nothing dangerous. TCA will oppose any move by the CPR to link the routes." He carried out his threat; the CPR's hopes of transcontinental and international expansion were dashed when, in 1943, Prime Minister Mackenzie King reiterated that TCA would continue to be Canada's only transcontinental and international operator.

Thus, in the midst of Canada's war effort in aviation, a part of the pattern of its peacetime aviation makeup began to emerge. It included the possibility of establishing an overland air route by way of Alaska and Siberia to Asia, in addition to the American trans-Pacific route to the Orient. The CPR's Air Services inherited the war contracts of its member companies, which meant that it ran training schools and overhaul plants under the British Commonwealth Air Training Plan, flew in men and material for a major hydroelectric plant on the Saguenay River (Canadian Airways) and had the task of building the Alaska Highway and pipeline from Norman Wells to Whitehorse. Since much of its work also involved American defence, it obtained aircraft on top priority from the United States.

In May 1942, the CPR received its charter allowing it to conduct air services under the name of Canadian Pacific Airlines (CPA), and "Punch" Dickins was appointed vice-president and general manager. His task was to amalgamate Canadian Airways with the eight smaller companies (Mackenzie Air Services, Yukon Southern Air Transport, Ginger Coote Airways, Wings Limited, Arrow Airways, Dominion Skyways, Prairie Airways and Quebec Airways) into one cohesive transportation network. He also oversaw the management of six British Commonwealth Air Training Plan schools, which turned out some twelve thousand personnel.

CPA watched its operating expenses closely and stabilized rates. By 1944 it had planned about twenty new routes in Canada, and with the large financial resources of the CPR behind it, CPA planned to purchase new equipment when the war was over. Meanwhile, the government kept a wary eye on CPA. Hastily and without much thought, it introduced a bill in 1944 to make the railways divest themselves of their airlines within one year of war's end. Then, realizing that this would pull the rug out from under TCA, the government rescinded the bill in 1946. However, it was evident that C.D. Howe was worried. He talked about dividing up CPA and giving portions of it to returning airmen.

Howe, of course, was dreaming of the thousands of trips Canadians would make after the war—on TCA. There were, however, two problems with this dream. One was the 1936–37 agreement between Canada, Great Britain and the Irish Free State to develop a trans-Atlantic service with Imperial Airways as the carrier. Howe had already taken the precaution of amending the TCA Act in 1938 so that TCA could undertake international flying, so he was not too concerned about the agreement. It had, after all, been made in the days when Canada had little to offer; now Canada was one of the four major air powers. Howe believed that the 1936–37 agreement would die a natural death.

The second problem was the upstart Canadian Pacific Airlines, whose presidents ignored Howe's and King's declarations in 1943 and 1944 that TCA would be Canada's national and international airline. Howe wanted to see CPA shunted back to the bush. He realized, as he said to W.P. Mulock, that "the development of two transcontinental routes across Canada would, of course, be fatal to the success of Trans-Canada." Mulock's response to Howe was: "I understood yesterday that Trans-Canada Airways [sic] and your Department would immediately take steps to acquire control of Prairie Airways Limited, and this extension from North Battleford to Edmonton would not be granted; that Trans-Canada Airways and the Department will acquire the McConachie Route from Edmonton to Whitehorse to safe-guard the Round-the-World Route, and also that Trans-Canada Airways would extend their services from Moncton to Halifax. I must say I was delighted to hear that this action would be taken, and that you will not agree to any competitive system being set up."

In 1945, W.M. Neal, now president of CPA and senior vice-president of the CPR, was very interested in developing an airline. After all, the CPR had pioneered a rail service across Canada and operated a fleet of passenger and cargo ships on the Atlantic and the Pacific to Australia and the Orient. It was time now to expand its transportation network into the skies. When "Punch" Dickins left CPA, Neal appointed Grant McConachie assistant to the president. CPA's headquarters remained in Winnipeg, as did TCA's. In 1947, Neal appointed McConachie president of CPA.

A thorn in Richardson's side, McConachie would also prove to be a thorn in TCA's side. However, he was just the man to head CPA in its challenge to TCA's monopoly of Canadian airspace and lucrative overseas routes. He never lost an opportunity to speak out against the plush, protected position held by TCA, and agitated throughout the 1940s and 1950s for a change in federal airline policy. CPA's advertisements, echoing Richardson's words of a decade earlier, spoke of the airline running to the top of the world and beyond, in direct defiance of government policy assigning international routes to TCA.

The sale of the Richardson interests in aviation marked the end of one man's dream. It also marked the birth of another airline, one that would become a major Canadian and international carrier. The Canada goose, the familiar symbol of Western Canada Airways and Canadian Airways, would fly again as the emblem of Canadian Pacific Airlines.

The Father of Canadian Aviation

I T IS CUSTOMARY TO SAY that no man is indispensable. This does not apply to James A. Richardson. He was "the Father of Canadian Aviation"—the single most important figure in Canada's developing air transport industry. He was the moving spirit behind what, in its time, was the biggest flying organization in Canada. Richardson was key to Canadian Airways' success, the steadying influence through all the company's financial and political storms.

Canadian Airways supplied the bulk of the pilots, mechanics and management to Trans-Canada Air Lines and Canadian Pacific Airlines. It also provided the blueprint and manpower for many of the British Commonwealth Air Training Plan schools and assisted in the early stages of the trans-Atlantic ferry service. But the memory of the public is short. Today few know of Richardson's achievements in the world of aviation or of the betrayal he suffered at the hands of government officials whom the public fondly remembers.

The years 1919–39 were the pioneer years for civil aviation in Canada, whose development took place in the shadow of a war just finished and another soon to come. Perhaps that explains why civil aviation fought a losing battle with military priorities. Almost no one conceived of commercial aviation's coming importance. Government did not lift a finger. In Canada, "civil aviation flew by itself."

The man at the forefront of the pioneering years was Richardson, a grain merchant. He had a clear vision of what aviation could do to assist in the development of the natural resources of the North. He established Western Canada Airways in 1926 without government subsidy. It was an outstanding success. His introduction of regular, scheduled flying marked the dawn of a new era of travel in the North. Next came his innovative day–night air mail service. Unfortunately, it was short-lived, but it was not duplicated until the government-owned Trans-Canada Air Lines was formed almost a decade later.

A passionate patriot, he formed Canadian Airways in 1930 to prevent the Americans from gaining control of Canada's airways. The sheer size of this undertaking was stupendous. To begin a national airline during a worldwide depression showed Richardson's faith in his vision of the importance of this new mode of transportation. A sense of purpose drove him.

Richardson dreamed first of providing coast-to-coast connections and then of developing routes "to hop over the top of the world" into Europe, Asia and the Orient. He kept pushing at the frontiers. On a practical level he knew that in the depths of the depression the budding aviation industry offered the hope of dramatic future growth and of filling the empty government purse. Unfortunately, the government —shortsighted and foolish—reneged on its legal obligations and cancelled its air mail contracts with Canadian Airways. With his financial security wiped out, Richardson turned back to the bush. "I have been the chief loser through the operations of Canadian Airways," he admitted to Noah Timmins in 1936.

The federal government's negative policy jeopardized its future. Canada stood to profit to a much greater extent than any other country because of its geographic location. Richardson had recognized early on that the trans-Canada airway should not be considered solely as a domestic route but as an integral part of a worldwide system. The shortest routes from North America to Europe and Asia lay through Canadian territory. The North Atlantic trade route in the 1930s was the most important in the world. Richardson perceived the trans-Atlantic, the trans-Canada, the trans-Pacific and the overland routes to Asia and the Orient as the greatest links still to be developed. So too did the United States. He recognized that Juan Trippe of Pan American Airways was doing his best to be there first.

Richardson was prepared to take the risks to place Canadian Airways and Canada at the forefront of airways development. Unfortunately, politicking and indecision among General Andrew McNaughton, the chief of the general staff, DND; John A. Wilson, the controller of civil aviation, DND; and P.T. Coolican, the assistant postmaster general, resulted in both Canadian Airways and Canada being the losers in this high-stakes game. It is possible that Richardson would have put Canadian Airways and Canada in the lead in airways development if the government had not clipped Canadian Airways' wings. As it was, Juan Trippe of Pan American went on to carve up the world, and Richardson and Canada were relegated to the hinterlands. Through governmental procrastination, Canada lost the chance to become a leader in aviation.

Richardson marked time but kept his dream of a national and international airline alive. "The frustrations, the hours of dedication and the financial costs were all secondary to the achievement of his vision," explained his son George Richardson. The darker side of the issue was that after more than a decade of no government policy, Canada found itself with a practically bankrupt aviation industry and an air force that was neither competent to carry on commercial operations nor carry out its original purpose—air defence. Canada's politicians and government officials had failed to comprehend aviation's importance.

Hope for a definite government policy regarding aviation came with the election of the Liberals in 1935. Along with hope came the promise from C.D. Howe that Canadian Airways, in conjunction with the CPR and the CNR, would become the trans-Canada airline company. "There was no doubt in my father's mind that he had C.D.'s assurance that Canadian Airways would be the company chosen," George Richardson recalled. It was not to be. Howe refused R.B. Bennett's requests for parliamentary committee hearings on the proposed national airline and deliberately did not inform members of Parliament that Canadian Airways, the CNR and the CPR had submitted a comprehensive airline blueprint, a proposal that would relieve the beleaguered government purse.

In fact, within a week of emphatically stating that he had no intention of creating a government-owned airline, that was exactly what he did.

Undercut by government in 1932, betrayed by the chief of the general staff in 1933 and double-crossed by the minister of transport in 1937, James Richardson struggled against a policy that was shaped to the advantage of Trans-Canada Air Lines rather than to that of the airline industry as a whole. The government spent lavishly on TCA and only belatedly realized that it had to boost its spending on the air force, but it spent nothing on the northern air transport system and the feeder lines that contributed traffic to TCA and indirect profits to government. By 1939, not only Canadian Airways but the whole Canadian aviation industry was practically bankrupt except for the protected government airline.

The government hit Canadian Airways again when, in 1941, it once more reneged on its air mail contracts to Canadian Airways, taking away more than one-third of the airline's business in the Maritimes. The contract went to TCA. A highly incensed Howie P. Robinson of the New Brunswick Telephone Company likened the Liberal government's action to the earlier Bennett government's "violation of all the common laws of business etiquette, honesty and business integrity" when that government cancelled Canadian Airways' contracts in 1932. Enough was enough.

Richardson's death had left Canadian Airways without its guiding spirit. Business arrangements were made with the CPR, which profited mightily. It acquired more than the physical assets of Canadian Airways and its allied companies. It assumed control of the northern operations in Canada and the possibility of tying the separate routes of all its component companies into an integrated whole. Canadian Pacific Airlines (CPA) proved to be a profitable line, as it was linked with feeders from the North and the all-important route to the Orient. However, C.D. Howe's duplicity eventually resulted in Canada having two major competing airlines. CPA, now Canadian Airlines, struggled throughout the rest of the century against TCA, now Air Canada. It remains to be seen whether the twenty-first century will bear out Richardson's prediction of 1928, that Canada could support only one major airline.

Canada's early aviation history had many glorious moments, but they do not hide the two overriding themes of the period. First, the

Canadian government was blind to the lead that Canada held in aviation after World War I and to the opportunities this lead presented. It was slow in formulating an aviation policy for both national and international airways development. It overlooked the fact that the economics of both were related and that they demanded integrated government control. The result? In the mid-1930s, Canada was the only major country that had not established an integrated system serving its main cities. That Canada ranked first in the world in 1935 in the carriage of freight and express was due entirely to private initiative and enterprise rather than government leadership. The expansion of the Canadian mining industry, which helped to tide Canada over the Great Depression, was hugely assisted by aviation.

Second, the air transport industry was pioneered, financed and developed largely by private enterprise. The main figure was James A. Richardson; by 1934 he had sunk $3 million of his personal fortune into an enterprise against which the cards were stacked. He financed the airways until the end. The company that bore the brunt of the pioneering, laid the basis for the vast network of airways across Canada and provided the blueprint and personnel for TCA and CPA was Canadian Airways.

However, Richardson was a political neophyte. He never understood the real power of lobbying—a fatal mistake. He was entirely without sham and acted with utter integrity, and he expected the same of others. His handshake and his word were as good as a signed contract. When he discovered that the word of key government officials swayed in the wind, he retreated. He should have challenged their lack of integrity, but he did not want to embarrass them. He was a gentleman to the end—another major mistake.

In more than a decade of flying, Canadian Airways made a significant and lasting impact by making the airplane an integral part of the transportation system. Canadian Airways left a legacy of strong foundations. Canadian Pacific Airlines would benefit, but that is another story.

In October 1943, Muriel Richardson wrote to "Punch" Dickins, general manager and vice-president of Canadian Pacific Airlines, to thank him for his tribute to her husband in his Canadian Club speech. She added:

I have watched the splendid development of Canadian Pacific Airlines with proud interest, not only because it is the fulfilment of my husband's idea of what civil aviation in Canada should become but because your direction of CPA links past and present and makes me feel that the story of Canadian Airways will not be lost.

The part that you and Canadian Pacific Airlines will play in post-war aviation may be clouded at present by the possibility of governmental interference but you have the advantage of knowing that "it was ever thus"—and will fight on, not only to ensure your future rights but also, I hope, to avenge past wrongs. Many Canadians, like myself, are watching the lining-up for battle with great interest, and are on your side ...

Canadian Airways' legacy to CPA was not difficult to notice. Richardson's dream of flying "over the top of the world" was echoed in CPA's 1944 ads of "running to the top of the world." CPA also adopted Canadian Airways' logo; the Canada goose continued to fly in Canadian and international skies. In the 1960s, the familiar Canada goose was stylized, but still it flew. Present-day Canadian Airlines traces many of its roots to Canadian Airways, and its logo—a stylized Canada goose—forges a symbolic link between one man's dream in 1926 and the dream of a new millennium.

Appendix

Canadian Airways Limited Board of Directors, 1930

PRESIDENT
James A. Richardson

VICE-PRESIDENTS
Sir Edward Beatty, president of the Canadian Pacific Railway
Sir Henry Thornton, president of Canadian National Railways

DIRECTORS
Selwyn G. Blaylock (Conservative), mining engineer, vice-president and director of
    Consolidated Mining & Smelting Co. of Canada Ltd., British Columbia
Victor Drury (Conservative), financier, industrialist, president and director of E.B.
    Eddy Co. Ltd.; president of Drury & Co. (investment), Montreal; vice-president
    and director of Canadian Vickers Ltd.; chairman and director of Canadian Car
    & Foundry Co. Ltd.
Gordon Edwards, industrialist, president of W.C. Edwards & Co. Ltd., Ottawa;
    director of the Canadian Bank of Commerce, Canadian International Papers Co.
    and Canada Cement Co. Ltd.
Sir Herbert S. Holt (Conservative), past president and current chairman of the board
    of the Royal Bank of Canada; president of the Montreal Trust Co.; vice-president
    of Dominion Textile Co.; director of the Canadian Pacific Railway, Canadian
    General Electric and Sun Life Assurance Co.
F.I. Ker, journalist and professional engineer, editor and managing director of the
    Hamilton Spectator; director of Southam Publications
Beaudry Leman, banker, president and managing director of La Banque Canadienne
    Nationale; vice-president of General Trust; director of Consolidated Paper Co.;
    former member of the Royal Commission on Railways and Transportation
C.E. Neill, vice-president and managing director of the Royal Bank of Canada
J.H. Price, president of Price Bros. & Co., Quebec
Howard P. Robinson, president of the New Brunswick Telephone Co.
T.A. Russell, president of Willy Overland Ltd., Toronto; director of International
    Power Co.
Victor N. Spencer, director of David Spencer Ltd., British Columbia
W.J. Blake Wilson, vice-president and director of Burns & Co. Ltd., British Columbia

Sources

THE MOST USEFUL SOURCE of information was the Western Canada Airways/Canadian Airways Limited Papers (MG 11 A34), which were deposited by the Richardson family with the Provincial Archives of Manitoba in Winnipeg. The sixty-nine archival boxes are a researcher's dream because they provide a detailed picture of James A. Richardson's two airways companies.

The federal government version of how and why aviation in Canada developed as it did was provided by the records found at the National Archives of Canada in Ottawa and those in cold storage in Hull, Quebec. The John A. Wilson Papers and the General Andrew McNaughton Papers were the most useful. The R.B. Bennett Papers (now at the University of New Brunswick, Harriet Irving Library, Archives and Special Collections) filled in some of the gaps, but the Mackenzie King Papers were not as useful as I had anticipated. C.D. Howe's papers were all but missing for the crucial period of late 1936 to the creation of Trans-Canada Air Lines in April 1937.

I believe that Howe destroyed the correspondence between himself and James A. Richardson and Sir Edward Beatty so that there would be little, if any, paper trail documenting why Howe abandoned the plan as proposed by Richardson, Beatty (president of the CPR) and S. J. Hungerford (president of the CNR). C.D. Howe's grandson, Bill Dodge, also believes that certain records were destroyed.

I had the privilege of talking at length with George T. Richardson, James Richardson's son, about his father's love affair with the airways. Please see this book's Acknowledgements for information on the assistance I received from the Richardson family.

Personal interviews with some of the pioneers of the day, former executives with James Richardson & Sons, Limited, and C.D. Howe's grandson, Bill Dodge, added valuable insight to the personalities of some of the key figures.

John Swettenham's *McNaughton,* Jack Granatstein's *The Generals* and Alec Douglas's *The Creation of a National Air Force* provided insight into General McNaughton's personality and the military context. Philip Smith's book on Trans-Canada Air Lines/Air Canada was another useful source, particularly on C.D. Howe. Ken Molson's *Pioneering in Canadian Air Transport* was invaluable for providing technical "nuts and bolts" information on Western Canada Airways/Canadian Airways Limited.

The Bibliography contains a complete listing of all sources, including interviews and letters.

A word on source notes: In my original manuscript I footnoted every quotation and anything that might raise an eyebrow, with the result that many chapters had well over forty exhaustive source notes. If I had followed that format, the reader would have become bogged down. However, I did want to ensure that those who wished to pursue more detail knew where to look for the information and therefore have identified the main sources of information for each chapter. My thanks to Wayne Ralph and his book *Barker VC* for providing a good example.

The sources most frequently used at the National Archives of Canada were:

1. A.G.L. McNaughton Papers: MG 30, E 133, Series 11, Volume 101, File: Committee on Trans-Atlantic Services; Volume 102, File: 4, Interdepartmental Committee; Volume 103, File: Civil Aviation; Volume 104, File: 4; 58, Volume 11, HQ C5936, File: Civil Aviation Policy; 62, Volume 101, File: Civil Aviation Policy Report
2. John A. Wilson Papers: MG 26, J 4, Volume 149: 1242; MG 30, E 243, Volume 2, 1932–37; C10779, Volume 1, 1915–31; T-51 C.O.P.S.
3. Mackenzie King Papers: MG 26, J 4 Memoranda and Notes; MG 26, J 13 Diaries
4. Transport Records: RG 12, Volume 2373, File: 5256, v. 1; RG 12, Volume 2253, File 5258, v. 1, v. 2; RG 12, Volume 1378, File: 5258-118; RG 12, Volume 2117

Abbreviations
Canadian Airways Limited (CAL)
National Archives of Canada/Archives nationales du Canada (NA–AN)
Public Archives of Manitoba (PAM)
University of New Brunswick, Harriet Irving Library, Archives and Special
   Collections (UNB)

INTRODUCTION
Archives: PAM, CAL Box 6, 54 RCAF No. 112 Squadron, 1935–39
Pamphlet: "James Richardson & Sons, Limited and Affiliated Companies"
Newspapers: Financial Post, December 4, 1976; *Winnipeg Free Press,* June 27, 1939,
   reproduced with permission
Interviews: G.T. Richardson, Lawson

CHAPTER ONE
Archives: PAM, CAL Box 9; NA–AN, Wilson, McNaughton; UNB, Bennett.
Statutes: Air Board Act, 1919; Department of National Defence Act, 1922.
Books: Main, Swettenham, Currie

CHAPTER TWO
Archives: PAM, CAL Box 1, 8, 26, 28, 65; NA–AN, Oaks
Books: Molson (Balchen quote), Godsell
Newspapers: Mining and Industrial News, March 25, 1927
Interviews: McMillan, Keith, Lawson, G.T. Richardson, Woollett, Nichols, Dickins,
   Whellams, St. John

CHAPTER THREE
Archives: PAM, CAL Box 1, 2, 6, 8, 14, 24, 26, 43; NA–AN, McNaughton, Wilson,
   Transport Records RG 12 Canadian Colonial Airways; UNB, Bennett
Unpublished material: Mattson
Books: Miller-Barstow
Newspapers: Winnipeg Free Press, Calgary Daily Herald, March 3, 1930

CHAPTER FOUR
Archives: PAM, CAL Box 2, 6, 14, 23, 24, 43, 65; NA–AN, Bennett, Wilson, Transport
   Records RG 12 Mulock, Pan American Airways, Air Services (External Affairs);
   Royal Commission to Inquire into Railways and Transportation in Canada,
   1931–32; UNB, Bennett

Books: Miller-Barstow, Neatby (*The Politics of Chaos*), Bliss, Granatstein (*The Ottawa Men*)
Newspapers: Financial Post, October 7, 1927
Unpublished material: Whitton
Interviews: Lawson

CHAPTER FIVE
Archives: PAM, CAL Box 5, 6, 7, 8, 9, 26, 65; NA–AN, McNaughton, King Transport Records RG 12 Conference of Aircraft Operators, Canadian Colonial Airways; UNB, Bennett
Books: Douglas, Bliss

CHAPTER SIX
Archives: PAM, CAL Box 6, 24; NA–AN, McNaughton, Bennett, Wilson, Transport Records RG 12 Pan American Airways, Skelton; UNB, Bennett
Hansard: Senate Debates
Books: Swettenham
Unpublished material: Whitton
Interviews: G.T. Richardson, Lawson

CHAPTER SEVEN
Archives: PAM, CAL Box 6, 7, 24, 54; NA–AN, McNaughton, RG 30 Fullerton; UNB, Bennett
Books: Swettenham, Douglas, Miller-Barstow
Unpublished material: Whitton

CHAPTER EIGHT
Archives: PAM, CAL Box 6, 7, 14, 24, 66; NA–AN, McNaughton, Wilson; Dominion Bureau of Statistics, Canada 1931; Manitoba Public Accounts for 1933–34
Books: Swettenham, Granatstein (*The Generals*)

CHAPTER NINE
Archives: PAM, CAL Box 7, 8, 24, 66; NA–AN, McNaughton, King
Interviews: Lawson
Newspapers: Financial Post, January 11, February 22, 1936; *Winnipeg Free Press,* January 23, 1936.

CHAPTER TEN
Archives: PAM, CAL Box 7, 8, 24, 66; NA–AN, McNaughton, King, Howe; RG 12 Smart
Hansard: House of Commons Debates
Books: Bothwell and Kilbourn, Norman Lambert diary reference from Philip Smith, *It Seems Like Only Yesterday.* Used by permission, McClelland & Stewart, Inc. The Canadian Publishers
Newspapers: Prince Albert Daily Herald, February 15, 1937
Interviews: Dodge

CHAPTER ELEVEN
Archives: PAM, CAL Box 8, 10, 24
Books: Bothwell and Kilbourn, Bliss
Interviews: Dodge, Bothwell, G.T. Richardson

CHAPTER TWELVE

Archives: PAM, CAL Box 8, 9, 10, 23, 24, 28, 38; NA–AN, Howe, RG 70 Symington, Trans-Canada Air Lines Minute Book, RG 12 Transport Commissioners Inquiry, Sheldon Luck

CHAPTER THIRTEEN

Archives: PAM, CAL Box 9, 10, 54; NA–AN, RG 12 Transport Commissioners Inquiry, Fairweather, MG 27 Brintnell, RG 70 Symington
Books: Woollett, Christie, Miller-Barstow
Interviews: Kathleen Richardson, G.T. Richardson, Woollett

CHAPTER FOURTEEN

Archives: PAM, CAL, Box 10, 54; NA–AN, King Diary, MG 27 Mulock
Hansard: House of Commons Debates
Books: Canada's Aviation Hall of Fame booklet
Interviews: Lawson

CHAPTER FIFTEEN

Archives: PAM, CAL, Box 7, 8, 58
Interviews: G.T. Richardson and Dedication Ceremony of the Richardson Hall of Flight at the Western Canada Aviation Museum

Bibliography

PRIMARY SOURCES

MANUSCRIPTS

National Archives of Canada/Archives nationales du Canada
Prime Minister R.B. Bennett; Les Edwards; Hon. C.D. Howe; Prime Minister
William Lyon Mackenzie King; Sheldon Luck; General Andrew G.L. McNaughton;
H.A. Oaks; V.I. Smart; John A. Wilson

Provincial Archives of Manitoba
Western Canada Airways/Canadian Airways Limited

*University of New Brunswick, Harriet Irving Library, Archives and
Special Collections*
Prime Minister R.B. Bennett

GOVERNMENT RECORDS

National Archives of Canada/Archives nationales du Canada
National Defence; Trans-Canada Air Lines; Transport

GOVERNMENT PUBLICATIONS
Canada, *House of Commons Debates*

OTHER SOURCES

Interviews
Abbreviations:
CAL Canadian Airways Limited
CPA Canadian Pacific Airlines
DND Department of National Defence
JR & Sons James Richardson & Sons, Limited
PWA Pacific Western Airlines
RCAF Royal Canadian Air Force
TCA Trans-Canada Air Lines
WCA Western Canada Airways

Baldwin, John (chairman, Air Transport Board; former president, Air Canada),
    telephone, November 11, 1998
Ballentine, Gordon (WCA–CAL), telephone, November 2, 1983
Benedickson, Agnes Richardson (daughter of James A.), telephone, December 13, 1998
Best, Frederick (World War I pilot), personal, Edmonton, May 19, 1983

Bliss, Michael (historian), telephone, April 27, 1998

Bothwell, Robert (historian), telephone, April 29, 1998

DelBegio, Bill (owner of early airways company in Manitoba), personal, February 15, 1984

Dickins, C.H. "Punch" (WCA–CAL), personal, Victoria, 1981–94

Dodge, Bill (grandson of C.D. Howe), telephone, April 24, May 3, 1998

Douglas, W.A.B. (DND historian), telephone, November 11, 18, 23, 1998

Dunlap, Larry (Air Marshall, RCAF), telephone, April 21, 1998

Farrington, Harold (WCA–CAL), personal, Red Lake, Ont., May 11, 1982

Fletcher, Mary Lizette (personal, secretary to Mrs. Muriel Richardson), telephone, June 3, 1983; April 24, 1998

Fowler, Walter (CAL), personal, Moncton, October 16, 1984

Graham, Robert (son of Stuart Graham, Canada's first bush pilot), personal, Ottawa, January 23, 1984

Granatstein, Jack L. (historian), telephone, November 18, December 22, 1998

Grattan, Rod (CAL), personal, Winnipeg, June 25, 1990

Hadfield, Rube (WCA–CAL, TCA), personal, Winnipeg, November 26, 1993

Hunter, John (JR & Sons executive), telephone, December 16, 1981

Hunter, Rod (former JR & Sons executive), telephone, December 28, 1998

Keith, Ron (aviation historian), telephone, November 2, 1983

Kitching, George, Major-General, telephone, April 21, 1998

Lawson, Gordon (former JR & Sons executive), personal, Winnipeg, December 8, 1982; telephone, May 31, 1983

Leigh, Z. Lewis (air vice-marshal, CAL, TCA), personal, Grimsby, Ont., November 22, 1983

McBurney, Ralph (air vice-marshal, RCAF), personal, Winnipeg, April 12, 1996

McGuire, Frank (historian), telephone, April 20, 1998

MacLaren, Donald (WCA–CAL, TCA), telephone, November 2, 1983

McMillan, Stan (CAL, Mackenzie Air Services), personal, Edmonton, May 17, 1985

Mauro, Arthur (former chairman and CEO, Investors Group; former director, PWA and Canadian Airlines International), telephone, November 14, 1998

Molson, Ken (aviation historian), personal, Kenora, July 3, 1985

Nichols, Reg (CAL), personal, Winnipeg, June 25, 1990

Ralph, Wayne (aviation historian), personal, Winnipeg, October 31, 1997; April 18, 1998

Richardson, George T. (son of James A.), personal, Winnipeg, March 17, 1984; July 18, October 7, 1997

Richardson, The Honourable James (son of James A.), personal, Lake of the Woods, July 6, 1996

Richardson, Kathleen Margaret (daughter of James A.), personal, Winnipeg, October 7, 1997

Roy, Reg (historian), telephone, April 20, 1998

Ryan, Dick (Prairie Airways, CPA), telephone, 1984

St. John, Branson (CAL), telephone, April 30, 1998

Sammons, Bert (CAL), telephone, May 1, 1998

Tackaberry, J.W. (comptroller, CAL), personal, Winnipeg, November 26, 1981; telephone, June 2, 1983

Taylor, Claude (former president, Air Canada), telephone, June 13, November 10, 1998
Wagner, Stan U. (CAL, Trans-Air), personal, Winnipeg, November 19, 1986
Ward, Max (Wardair), personal, Winnipeg, April 24, 1998; telephone, April 25, 1998
Watson, Don (CAL, PWA), personal, Winnipeg, April 24, 1998
Whellams, Don (CAL), personal, Winnipeg, June 25, 1990; telephone, April 30, 1998
Woollett, "Babe" (CAL), personal, Southport, Man., June 1995; telephone, January 25, February 19, March 1, 1997

Audiotape Recordings
Western Canada Aviation Museum ("Punch" Dickins)

Letters (to author)
Baldwin, John R. (chairman, Air Transport Board; deputy minister, Transport), November 24, December 12, 1998
Bisson, Captain Louis (early Arctic pilot), April 8, May 1, 1984
Dickins, C.H. "Punch" (WCA–CAL), November 21, 1981–January 24, 1994
Douglas, W.A.B. (military historian), November 18, 1998
Graham, Robert (son of Stuart Graham), 1983–85
Luck, Sheldon (Yukon Southern Air Transport), 1984–86
McBurney, Ralph (air vice-marshal, RCAF), 1993–97
Terpening, Rex (CAL, CPA), 1988–97, re: "The Way It Was"
Vachon, Georgette (wife of Romeo Vachon, CAL), 1983

Newspapers
Calgary Daily Herald; Canadian Mining Journal; Edmonton Journal; Financial Post; Globe and Mail (Toronto); Mining and Industrial News; Moncton Daily Times; Northern Miner; Ottawa Journal; Prince Albert Daily Herald; Toronto Evening Telegram; Winnipeg Free Press; Winnipeg Tribune; Vancouver Province; Vancouver Sun.

SECONDARY SOURCES

UNPUBLISHED MATERIAL
Catomore, Russell H. "The Civil Aviation Movement in Canada 1919–1939." M.A. thesis, Carleton University, Ottawa 1970
Gosse, Fred P. "The Air Transport Board and Regulation of Commercial Air Services." M.A. thesis, Carleton College, Ottawa, 1955
Mattson, Margaret. "The Growth and Protection of Canadian Civil and Commercial Aviation 1918–1930." Ph.D. thesis, University of Western Ontario, London, 1978
Whitton, C. Draft manuscript on James A. Richardson, circa 1944

PERIODICALS
Aviation Review of the Western Canada Aviation Museum, 1979–96
Canadian Aviation
Canadian Forum 24(228) (January 1945): 227–29. "The Chicago Air Conference"
International History Review 2(4) (October 1980): 585–601. Bothwell, Robert, and J.L. Granatstein. "Canada and the Wartime Negotiations over Civil Aviation: The Functional Principle in Operation"

The Legionary (December 1967). Dodds, Ron. "Canadian Air Giant: Red Mulock's Incredible but Little-Known Career"
Maclean's 57(21) (November 1, 1944): 14–15, 44–45. "Backstage at Ottawa"

BOOKS

Ashley, C.A. *A Study of Trans-Canada Air Lines.* Toronto: Macmillan of Canada, 1963

Bliss, Michael. *Northern Enterprise: Five Centuries of Canadian Business.* Toronto: McClelland & Stewart, 1987

Bothwell, Robert, Ian Drummond, and John English. *Canada 1900–1945.* Toronto: University of Toronto Press, 1987

Bothwell, Robert, and William Kilbourn, *C.D. Howe: A Biography.* Toronto: McClelland & Stewart, 1979

Christie, Carl A. *Ocean Bridge: The History of Ferry Command.* Toronto: University of Toronto Press, 1995

Currie, A.W. *Canadian Transportation Economics.* Toronto: University of Toronto Press, 1967

Daly, Robert. *An American Saga: Juan Trippe and His Pan Am Empire.* New York: Random House, 1980

Dexter, Grant. *Canada and the Building of Peace.* Toronto: Canadian Institute of International Affairs, 1944

Douglas, W.A.B. *The Creation of a National Air Force: The Official History of the Royal Canadian Air Force.* Vol. 2. Ottawa: Minister of Supply and Services, 1986

Ellis, Frank. *Canada's Flying Heritage.* Toronto: University of Toronto Press, 1961

Godsell, Philip. *Pilots of the Purple Twilight.* Toronto: Ryerson Press, 1955

Granatstein, J.L. *The Generals: The Canadian Army's Senior Commanders in the Second World War.* Toronto: Stoddart, 1993

____. *The Ottawa Men: The Civil Service Mandarins 1935–1957.* Toronto: Oxford University Press, 1982

Harbron, John D. *C.D. Howe.* Don Mills: Fitzhenry & Whiteside, 1980

Hyde, H. Montgomery. *The Quiet Canadian: The Secret Service Story of Sir William Stephenson.* London: Hamish Hamilton, 1962

Keith, Ronald A. *Bush Pilot with a Briefcase.* Toronto: Doubleday Canada, 1972

Le Pan, Douglas. *Bright Glass of Memory: A Set of Four Memoirs.* Toronto: McGraw-Hill Ryerson, 1979

Main, J.R.K. *Voyageurs of the Air: A History of Civil Aviation in Canada 1958–1967.* Ottawa: Queen's Printer, 1967

Miller-Barstow, D.H. *Beatty of the C.P.R.: A Biography.* Toronto: McClelland & Stewart, 1951

Molson, Ken. *Pioneering in Canadian Air Transport.* Altona, Man.: D.W. Friesen & Sons, 1974

Neatby, H. Blair. *William Lyon Mackenzie King.* Vol. 3. *The Prism of Unity, 1932–39.* Toronto: University of Toronto Press, 1976

____. *The Politics of Chaos: Canada in the Thirties.* Toronto: Macmillan of Canada, 1972

Pigott, Peter. *Flying Colours: A History of Commercial Aviation in Canada.* Vancouver: Douglas & McIntyre, 1997

___. *Wingwalkers: A History of Canadian Airlines International.* Madeira Park, B.C.: Harbour Publishing, 1998

Ralph, Wayne. *Barker VC: The Life, Death and Legend of Canada's Most Decorated War Hero.* London: Grub Street, 1997

Shackleton, Kathleen. *Arctic Pilot: The Experiences of Walter E. Gilbert.* Toronto: Thomas Nelson & Sons, 1974

Smith, Philip. *It Seems Like Only Yesterday: Air Canada, The First 50 Years.* Toronto: McClelland & Stewart, 1986

Stacey, C.P. *Canada and the Age of Conflict: A History of Canadian External Policy.* Vol. 2. *The Mackenzie King Era, 1921–1948.* Toronto: Macmillan of Canada, 1977.

___. *Arms, Men and Governments: The War Policies of Canada 1939–1945.* Ottawa: Queen's Printer, 1970

Stevenson, William. *A Man Called Intrepid: The Secret War.* New York and London: Harcourt Brace Jovanovich, 1976

Sutherland, Alice Gibson. *Canada's Aviation Pioneers.* Toronto: McGraw-Hill Ryerson, 1978

Swettenham, John. *McNaughton.* Vols. 1 and 3. Toronto: Ryerson Press, 1968

Wise, S.F. *Canadian Airmen and the First World War: The Official History of the Royal Canadian Air Force.* Vol. 1. Toronto: University of Toronto Press, 1980

Woollett, W. ("Babe"). *Have a Banana.* n.p.: Turner-Warwick Publications, 1989

Index